THEORIES OF THE POLICY PROCESS

FOURTH EDITION

THEORIES
OF THE
POLICY
PROCESS

edited by

CHRISTOPHER M. WEIBLE
University of Colorado, Denver

PAUL A. SABATIER
late of University of California, Davis

Routledge
Taylor & Francis Group
New York London

First published 2018 by Westview Press

Fourth Edition: July 2017

Published 2018 by Routledge
711 Third Avenue, New York, NY 10017, USA
2 Park Square, Milton Park, Abingdon, Oxon OX14 4RN

Routledge is an imprint of the Taylor & Francis Group, an informa business

Copyright © 2018 Taylor & Francis

Library of Congress Cataloging-in-Publication Data

Names: Weible, Christopher M. | Sabatier, Paul A.
Title: Theories of the policy process / edited by Christopher M. Weible, University of Colorado, Denver   Paul A. Sabatier, late of University of California, Davis.
Description: Fourth edition. | Boulder, CO : Westview Press, 2017.
Identifiers: LCCN 2017009463| ISBN 9780813350523 (paperback) | ISBN 9780813350783 (ebook)
Subjects: LCSH: Policy sciences. | Political planning. | BISAC: POLITICAL SCIENCE / Public Policy / General.
Classification: LCC H97 .T475 2017 | DDC 320.6—dc23
LC record available at https://lccn.loc.gov/2017009463

ISBN 13: 978-0-8133-5052-3 (pbk)

LSC-C

Print book interior design by Trish Wilkinson

Contents

Preface to the Fourth Edition

Policy process research has never reached as many parts of the globe as it does today. The result of this burgeoning network of scholars has been a rapid upsurge of ideas. It has also generated research that implicitly or explicitly exhibits a comparative research approach. The potential benefits of this changing landscape are fantastic. Only through comparative research can we distinguish knowledge that is localized to a particular context or generalized across contexts. Hence, opportunities abound to overcome some of the past obstacles to advance the field to higher plateaus of knowledge. To realize these opportunities, the fourth edition of *Theories of the Policy Process* reflects this increasing globalization of the field of policy processes.

To underscore the role of these theories in a globalized field, two important changes have been made to this volume. The first is a new chapter on strategies for conducting comparative research authored by Jale Tosun and Samuel Workman. The goal of this new chapter is to offer readers a firm foundation for applying these theories in a global and comparative research environment. The second is that authors of each of the theory-based chapters have been instructed to revise their chapters to describe how their theory fits in this global comparative approach to policy process research. The purpose behind these changes is simple: as the theories of the policy processes become applied in various parts of the world, we must be deliberate in thinking about how our research fits together and how our knowledge could accumulate.

Another change in the fourth edition is a major revision to the introductory chapter that better presents the topic of policy process research and the goals of this volume. To summarize, the goal of this volume is to advance the scholarship of policy process research among a global community of scholars. Obviously, new and experienced scholars can read the original articles or books on these theories and skip this volume. Lost, however, would be the opportunity to compare and contrast the collection of seven of the most established and utilized theories of the policy processes. *Theories of the Policy Process* remains indispensable in offering readers the chance to discover and learn about them as an anthology.

The opening chapter also updates and clarifies the criteria for continuing to include the theories in this volume. On the basis of these criteria, the chapter on the Social Construction Framework by Anne Schneider, Helen Ingram, and Peter deLeon has been removed from this edition. This decision has nothing to do with the quality of the insights from this theory, which remains invaluable in highlighting the distributions of benefits and burdens of public policies based on the power and constructions of target populations. It also has nothing to do with what some might call this framework's postpositivism orientation. Instead, in consideration of the criteria outlined in the Introduction, this particular theory is supported by a less vibrant and active research community without much advancement in knowledge beyond the ideas in its original publication (Schneider and Ingram 1993, 1997). Moreover, Policy Feedback Theory in this volume captures a part of the Social Construction Framework, with its focus on how policies shape politics. For those who want to keep the Social Construction Framework in their course readers, the chapter from the third edition is available online, along with other links and resources to supplement the chapters in this volume (www.westviewpress.com/weible4e).

In preparing this volume, I want to express my gratitude to Ada Fung of Westview Press. Without Ada's support, feedback, and encouragement, the third and fourth editions of *Theories of the Policy Process* would not exist. I also want to thank the referees who commented on the strengths and weaknesses of each chapter from the third edition, including Stephen Ceccoli (Rhodes College); Casey LaFrance (Western Illinois University); Chandra Commuri (California State University, Bakersfield); Sarah Michaels (University of Nebraska); Xufeng Zhu (Tsinghua University); Saba Siddiki (Syracuse University); Stephen Stehr (Washington State University); Claire Dunlop (Exeter University); and others who wished to remain anonymous. Their feedback helped improve many chapters in this volume and definitely motivated the need for a fourth edition. I also want to express my sincerest appreciation to the contributing authors for their efforts in revising their chapters. Their commitment to writing their chapters with the highest standards of quality continues to make this a premier outlet for the most established policy process theories. A special note of gratefulness to Jennifer Armstrong for her excellent comments and feedback on the opening and closing chapters of this volume.

Finally, a great deal of respect must be given to the legacy of Paul Sabatier for leading the efforts in the first two editions of this volume. Following Ted Lowi, Paul used to preach: "Clarity begets clarity, mush begets mush." The point is simple: if we conduct our research with clear theoretical orientations, our results will more likely be clear, both in their mistakes and in their accuracies. The converse is also true: if we conduct our research with mushy theoretical orientations, we will more likely get mushy results. Given the finite number of research projects any of us might undertake, we must heed this advice and strive to make our thoughts and actions as clear of mush as possible. The best way to do this is together, through thoughtful and constructive feedback. As we continue this journey in advancing our knowledge about policy process on a global frontier, let's be diligent in reducing the mush and increasing the clarity in our work.

Introduction: The Scope and Focus of Policy Process Research and Theory

CHRISTOPHER M. WEIBLE

The goal of this volume is to advance the science of policy process among a global community of scholars. In advancing science, theories simultaneously serve as reservoirs of knowledge gained from past research and platforms for guiding new research into the future. The inevitable challenge for anyone learning about or contributing to the policy process is that any one theory inherently focuses on a limited set of concepts and relationships. Therefore, a single theory provides only a partial depiction of the complexity of the policy process. The best strategy to overcome this challenge is to explore and utilize multiple theories of the policy process.[1]

This volume offers an anthology of seven of the most established theories in the field of policy processes. The latest interpretations of these theories are authored by scholars who are among the most knowledgeable and experienced in working with them, a number of whom are the original creators of the theories. By featuring these theories in a single collection, this volume facilitates efforts to compare and contrast their goals and aims, to identify their relative strengths and weaknesses, to learn about how and when to apply them, and to discover the insights embodied in them.

In this introduction, the term *theory* is used generically to represent a research tool. These tools specify scope of inquiry, assumptions, and concepts in various relational forms, such as principles, hypotheses, and propositions. Based on what we know and envision, these relational forms specify a limited set of associations among concepts, from the much larger and untamable set. These relational forms also postulate explanations of why and how, under what conditions, by and for whom, and when the concepts might relate (Whetten 1989). Although the meaning of *theory* varies across the field of policy process research, this generic description is consistent with other uses of the term (McCool 1995, 11). It also represents a deliberate mix of frameworks and theories, as described by Ostrom (2005, 27–29).

A DEFINITION OF POLICY PROCESS RESEARCH

The policy processes emerged as a field of study in the 1950s as part of an endeavor to develop a science that integrates research on politics and government around a policy orientation. Among its early leaders, Lasswell (1951) urged scholars to focus their research on policy formulation and execution toward the realization of human dignity.[2] Another one of the original exposés on the subject was penned by Shipman, who used the term *policy process* to denote a needed area of study that integrates politics, policy, and administration. As Shipman (1959, 545) notes, "When the policy-process approach is used, institutions and mechanisms of political organization, legislative action, executive administration, adjudication, and the rest merge into an intricately interconnected process for seeking satisfaction of societal values." Following the ideas of Lasswell, Shipman, and many others, the phenomenon of policy processes refers to *the interactions that occur over time between public policies and surrounding actors, events, contexts, and outcomes.*[3]

At the center of policy processes lies the elusive concept of public policy. *Public policy* is defined as the deliberate decisions—actions and nonactions—of a government or an equivalent authority toward specific objectives.[4] Examples of public policies include, but are not limited to, statutes, laws, regulations, executive decisions, and government programs (Birkland 2016, 8). Other examples of public policies are the commonly understood rules-in-use that structure behavioral situations in policy processes, such as the sustained practices of street-level bureaucrats in delivering public services (Lipsky 1980; Schneider and Ingram 1997; Ostrom 2005).[5] Public policies can include both means and goals and can range in form from procedural to substantive and from symbolic to instrumental. Alternatively, a public policy can be understood by identifying the institutions that constitute its design and content. For instance, some institutions prescribe specific authority for a given position, and others require exchanges of information under certain conditions (Ostrom 1980). In studying policy processes, researchers sometimes focus on a single public policy (e.g., a particular welfare law) or on many public policies related to a particular issue (e.g., the many types of public policies affecting the issue of welfare in a locale).

Public policy interactions involve actors—individuals or collectives such as organizations, networks, or coalitions—and their attributes, including their knowledge, values, beliefs, interests, strategies, and resources. Individual actors may be part of the general public who occasionally participate politically in a public policy issue. Alternatively, actors may be affiliated with government or nongovernment organizations that regularly seek to influence public policy on a given issue or control the government venues (e.g., a legislature or an executive administration) wherein policy decisions occur.

The context of a public policy is the setting around which the interactions involving public policy happen. Examples of the contextual categories often studied in policy process research might be socioeconomic conditions, culture, infrastructure, biophysical conditions, and institutions. Sometimes the context lies in the theoretical foreground as the target of public policy, such as economic stimulus programs aimed to stimulate an economy. It can also provide a theoretical background in which actors politically interact to influence public policy. In this regard, context can be relatively stable or susceptible to change over time.

All contexts entail various types of events. Events can be anticipated and unanticipated incidents ranging from elections to scientific discoveries and chronic and acute societal dilemmas and crises. Sometimes actors deliberately create events to affect the policy process, as seen in social movements. Other times, events are unintentional and beyond the control of actors, like an earthquake. Because events can be directly or indirectly related to a given public policy issue, they often provide opportunities for achieving policy objectives. For example, a bureaucracy might release an evaluative report that brings attention to the success or failure of a public policy in addressing an issue. This report, in turn, might shape future legislative agendas. This is but one simple example of the many ways in which the theories in this volume can portray the role of events in shaping policy processes.

The outcomes of policy processes are the short- or long-term consequences or impacts of public policy on a society. These outcomes continue to interact with policy processes over time. Outcomes are essentially changes (or stasis) in the context and actors constituting policy processes. Outcomes are separated as a distinct category because of their importance in assessing the effects on society of the policy processes. Thus, whereas one of the goals of policy process research is the generation of knowledge as embodied in theories, the use of this knowledge must eventually help attain societal values and realize a greater human dignity.

To imagine the policy process as interactions involving public policy over time underscores the permanence of politics and continuity of policy processes where "there is no beginning or end" (Lindblom 1968, 4). Indeed, any given output of the policy process in one study can serve as an input of the policy process in another. The choice of any given output and input in policy process research is not absolute but rather a reflection of the priorities of the researcher, the practicalities of available data, and the foci of a given theory.

These ongoing interactions are also best understood by the various interpretations of the "process" in policy process research. A *process* refers to the continuous points in time (e.g., usually in terms of actors' decisions and actions, events, and outcomes) that constitute policy processes. One of the most common depictions of this process is the *policy cycle*. The policy cycle simplifies the policy process by delineating the stages of decision making through which policy proposals must traverse for their manifestation. These stages typically include agenda setting, policy formulation and adoption, policy implementation, evaluation, and termination.

Many have criticized the policy cycle for its overly simplistic and inaccurate portrayal of the policy process (e.g., Sabatier and Jenkins-Smith 1993). But criticisms aside, it remains a useful heuristic archetype. The policy cycle becomes a hindrance when scholars believe the key interactions in the policy process are strictly the policy cycle, force theories into its stages, and ignore important questions that lie outside its scope. Indeed, the problem with the policy cycle is less its simplistic and inaccurate depiction of policy processes and more its overuse by scholars as the sole lens through which to view and organize the field.

The theories in this volume offer additional portrayals of the interactions in policy processes. These interactions might be enduring periods of political conflict and concord observed in the behavior of coalition members or serendipitous circumstances leading to windows of opportunity in changing agendas and policies. In addition, patterns and speed of policy adoption across different units of government, the continuous tinkering with rules by people self-governing a collective action situation, and the various feedback effects on the general public of adopted public policies represent other interactions. Indeed, the theories in this volume depict interactions that vary in what is emphasized or deemphasized. These interactions can reflect the linearity of the policy cycle stages, yet can also portray a policy process that is far more complicated and messy.

THE CRITERIA FOR INCLUDING THEORIES

This volume features the most established theories of the policy process. Their continued inclusion in the fourth edition of this volume was based on several criteria:

(1) *A focus on developing scientific theory of policy processes.* Each of the approaches in this volume represents efforts toward developing a scientific theory that focuses on a set of interrelated concepts involving actors, events, contexts, and outcomes that surround public policies over time. As scientific theories, the approaches in this volume specify sets of assumptions and conditions under which they apply and posit interactions that come in various relational forms (hypotheses, propositions, principals, or other). Underlying these relationships are causal drivers—usually anchored at the individual level—that explain why a relationship could exist. No matter the name, these relational forms serve to enable falsification and learning, to communicate explicitly the relationships under investigation, and to summarize what we know about a given phenomenon. When the concepts are defined abstractly, the relational forms promote comparative applications of the theories to tease apart local versus generalizable understandings and explanations.

(2) *The presence of an active research community.* Science is a "social enterprise" (King, Keohane, and Verba 1994, 8). All theories in this volume must be supported by a community of scholars advancing the science. Such a community might be motivated by a common set of research questions or objectives, a shared vocabulary of concepts, a balanced research effort that interplays theoretical expositions and empirical applications, and common epistemological and ontological assumptions. The composition of these research programs varies, but most involve active and experienced leadership, a regular influx of graduate students, and an expanding base of interested and experienced scholars applying a theory. These scholars often participate on the same research projects and organize and participate on panels at general conferences. In some cases, these communities organize and participate in small workshops or seminars focused on developing their theory.

(3) *A comparative research approach.* To gain knowledge about the policy process, a theory's research community must apply the theory in a comparative approach.[6] Sometimes this is done implicitly, as when one theory is applied in a single country. In this situation, a follow-up study could aggregate the results in a meta-analysis from a number of similarly executed applications of the theory across many countries. Other times this is done explicitly. For example, some research teams might apply a given theory to answer the same question across countries in a single research design; here, the underlying goal of the research might be to ascertain effects of the contextual setting on the results. The comparative approach need not be restricted to country comparisons but may involve comparisons of a variety of different actors, contexts, events, outcomes, or times. The challenge in comparative research agendas is creating and using a shared research platform to foster generalizable knowledge across policy processes while, at the same time, offering enough flexibility to portray a given policy process in a valid way.

(4) *An effort toward making research as public as possible.* The quality of policy process research is only as good as the transparency of its procedures for collecting and analyzing data. Sabatier (1999, 5) made famous the phrase "be clear enough to be proven wrong." The point is that obscure procedures produce results immune to criticism. There will always be some ambiguous steps in a research project, and pure replication is usually impractical or impossible. However, given human fallibility, there is no better way to learn from our mistakes than to be as clear as we can in all aspects of our science.

(5) *Continual growth in knowledge about policy processes.* Theories offer a number of important academic and practical contributions, from teaching to conducting community-based research. Of all these contributions, probably

the most important is advancing the reservoir of localized and generalized knowledge. Given that some of the theories in this volume have been around for decades, we must eventually ask: What new insights have each of these theories produced since its creation? Our understanding of the policy process is, and always will be, incomplete. Yet, if our theories stagnate, then so does progress in reaching higher plateaus of knowledge.

The extent to which the theories in this volume meet the above criteria varies and, in some situations, is debatable. Of these criteria, the most important is an engaged group of scholars advancing the science under a given approach. Indeed, one of the main lessons from decades of developing theory is that it takes teams of scholars working together over extended periods of time to create shared methods and analytical techniques, to conduct their research comparatively, and to aggregate those results into lessons learned. No theory is perfect, and assessing the accumulation of knowledge for a given theory is exceedingly difficult. Thus, the best short-term indicator of future progress is the presence of a large group of scholars working together to advance a theory toward the enrichment of knowledge.

THEORIES INCLUDED IN THIS VOLUME

This volume offers seven different theories of policy process research that meet, to various extents and ways, the criteria outlined above for their inclusion in the discussion.

The first chapter, coauthored by Nicole Herweg, Nikolaos Zahariadis, and Reimut Zohlnhöfer (2017), covers the Multiple Streams Framework. The Multiple Streams Framework depicts a process that emphasizes timing in the merging of problem, political, and policy streams in the creation of windows of opportunity for both agenda setting and decision making. Among the strengths of the Multiple Streams Framework are its accessibility, vibrant research community, and constant evolution.

Chapter 2, by Frank R. Baumgartner, Bryan D. Jones, and Peter B. Mortensen (2017), is on the Punctuated Equilibrium Theory. Under this theory, scarce attention drives incremental and punctuated patterns of policy change over time. Of all the theories in this volume, the Punctuated Equilibrium Theory offers perhaps the best current example of a coordinated policy community leveraging a comparative approach.

The third chapter on the Policy Feedback Theory, coauthored by Suzanne Mettler and Mallory SoRelle (2017), takes a different perspective. Drawing on the notion that policies shape politics, the Policy Feedback Theory seeks to understanding what happens after a policy is adopted, with an emphasis on resource and interpretive effects on mass publics. Policy Feedback Theory represents another vibrant research community that continues to develop this theory.

The Advocacy Coalition Framework is the fourth theory, coauthored by Hank C. Jenkins-Smith, Daniel Nohrstedt, Christopher M. Weible, and Karin Ingold (2017). The Advocacy Coalition Framework deals with ongoing patterns of conflict and concord as reflections of different beliefs, situations fostering belief change and learning, and rationales for major and minor policy change. The literature under the Advocacy Coalition Framework features a strong comparative agenda with applications spanning the globe.

Elizabeth A. Shanahan, Michael D. Jones, Mark K. McBeth, and Claudio M. Radaelli (2017) coauthored Chapter 5 on the Narrative Policy Framework. This relatively new theory focuses on the politics of storytelling and the impacts on public policy. The Narrative Policy Framework is quickly evolving, with an increasing number of applications, a common methodological approach that spurs applications across contexts, and constant refinement to its concepts and posited interactions.

The sixth chapter, coauthored by Edella Schlager and Michael Cox (2017), summarizes the Institutional Analysis and Development framework and its offspring, the Social-Ecological Systems framework. Both frameworks are extremely versatile, with an exceptionally large number of applications in a variety of contexts. Based, in part, on the idea of self-governance and the constant tinkering with institutional rules, these frameworks continue to flourish in describing and explaining a variety of collective action situations.

Chapter 7, the last theoretical chapter, directs scholars to approach policy change by looking at the reasons, speed, and patterns of adoption or rejection of policy proposals across government units, as found in Berry and Berry's (2017) summary of innovation and diffusion models. This chapter provides the latest summary of this long-standing research area in the study of policy processes.

STRATEGIES FOR USING THIS VOLUME

The chapters are organized in a way that facilitates reading the volume from beginning to end, though some instructors and readers will prefer a different order of the theories.[7] Part I encompasses the theory chapters, beginning with the Multiple Streams Framework and Punctuated Equilibrium Theory, given their traditional emphases on agenda setting and policy change. Policy Feedback Theory comes next, with its focus on the impacts of policy design on society. Encompassing a range of phenomena, the next three chapters include the Advocacy Coalition Framework, Narrative Policy Framework, and the Institutional Analysis and Development framework. The last of the theory-based chapters is on innovation and diffusion models, with its emphasis on the adoption and rejection of policy output across space and time.

Part II of this volume includes three summary chapters. The first (Chapter 8), by Tanya Heikkila and Paul Cairney (2017), provides a comparison and critique of the theories in this anthology. Given the importance of the comparative approach in advancing policy process theory, in Chapter 9 Jale Tosun and Samuel Workman (2017) provide tips and strategies for using the theories to conduct comparative research. The final chapter, by Christopher M. Weible (2017), offers an overview of the status of the field and general strategies for moving forward and climbing upward.

Each of the theory chapters should be considered a thorough yet brief summary of a theory. To develop a deeper understanding of any of these theories, readers are encouraged to read the chapter in this volume along with some combination of the foundational pieces of a given theory, previous theoretical depictions of the theory, and empirical applications. For example, advanced graduate students exploring the Multiple Streams Framework could read Cohen, March, and Olsen's (1972) "A Garbage Can Model of Organizational Choice," Kingdon's (1984) *Agendas, Alternatives, and Public Policies*, Chapter 1 by Herweg and colleagues in this volume, and one or two empirical applications. For intermediate graduate or undergraduate students, the theoretical chapters in this volume could be combined with one or two empirical applications.

Theories of the Policy Process is not intended to provide comprehensive coverage of policy process research. Readers are encouraged to supplement this volume with articles or books that cover other topics or theories. Among those deserving attention are the policy cycle (deLeon 1999), policy success and failure (McConnell, 2010), policy styles (Richardson 1982), power (Bachrach and Baratz 1963; Lukes 1974), policy instruments and design (Howlett 2011), policy entrepreneurs (Mintrom and Norman 2009), social capital (Putnam, Leonardi, and Nanetti 1994), implementation (Pressman and Wildavsky 1973; Moulton and Sandfort, 2016), causal stories (Stone 1989), the postpositivist literature (Fischer and Forester 1993; Fischer 2003), and the social construction framework (Schneider and Ingram, 1993; Schneider, Ingram, and deLeon, 2014). Additionally, there has been another burst of innovation in the formation of new and emerging theories of the policy process. In 2013, *Policy Studies Journal* published a collection of these new theories, including the Ecology of Games (Lubell 2013), the Policy Regime Perspective (May and Jochim 2013), the Institutional Collective Action Framework (Feiock 2013), and the Collective Learning Framework (Heikkila and Gerlak 2013).

As mentioned earlier, readers should avoid forcing the theories into a stage of the policy cycle—the result would be an incomplete, and quite possibly an inaccurate, portrayal of them. Although some theories may fit into one or more of the stages, most incorporate the entire policy cycle in one way or another or depict the policy process in an entirely different way.[8] The best strategy is to interpret how the different theories provide insight into policy process rather than to impose an artificial categorization on them.

Readers should also adopt a broad definition of public policy, as previously described, that includes both formal elements of public policy, such as laws and regulations, and public policies as rules-in-use that govern, for example, traditional venues of government, from city councils to legislatures, as well as various associations charged with the provision and production of public goods and services. This strategy is most useful for relating the Institutional Analysis and Development framework to the other theories covered in this volume. The point is that the interactions involving public policies encompass not just the formal structures of government as written down and adopted by officials and other authorities but also the actual rules-in-use that structure the day-to-day behaviors of actors engaged in policy process situations. Any definition of public policy must include both because so much of government activities is informed by what is written down and by the informal rules of a given situation. Arguably, such a broad definition of public policy may inhibit comparison if we do not take into account the type of public policy under study.

The goal of this volume is to provide in a single outlet the latest versions of the major theories of the policy process, to compare and contrast these theories, to offer strategies for strengthening the international community engaged in comparative policy process research, and to help propel policy process research to higher levels of excellence. Whether this book serves as an introduction to the field or as a sturdy reference guide, the hope is that readers will test and develop policy process theories to provide for a better understanding and explanation of policy processes.

NOTES

1. The complexity of the policy process emerges from interactions among a large number of diverse people seeking political influence, periodic as well as unexpected events, a complicated mix of policies that span levels of government, and contextual settings characterized by a range of conditions from geographical to socioeconomic. In studying such complexity, people are innately restrained by cognitive presuppositions that cause them to recognize some aspects of the process and ignore others. Using one or more theories is one strategy to help mitigate the effects of such presuppositions by highlighting the most important items for study and specifying relationships between them. By requiring conscientious rigor in choosing what to study in analyzing the policy process, theories increase the likelihood that errors will be recognized and, thus, they facilitate lesson learning over time. Such benefits are magnified when theories are applied with transparent data collection and analysis methods, especially when compared to research based on unspecified and implicit observations. Ideally, scholars become versed in the use of more than one theory, which is one of the best ways to guard against both theory tenacity and confirmation bias. Theory tenacity is the tendency to maintain commitment to a theoretical argument even in response to disconfirming evidence. Confirmation bias is the tendency to seek out evidence that confirms a theoretical argument. See Loehle (1987) for discussion of both theory tenacity and confirmation bias.

2. For Lasswell (1951), the policy process was a key intellectual pillar of the "policy science." The field of policy analysis and evaluation encapsulates the other key pillar.

3. This definition matches that found in Weible and Carter (2016).

4. The definition of public policy offered in the text seeks to capture common elements found across the literature, most notably in Weible and Carter (2016, 3), Birkland (2016, 8), McCool (1995, 8–9), Parson (1995, 2–16), Cairney (2012, 23–26), Howlett (2011, 15–17), Heclo (1972, 84–88), and Ranney (1968, 6–7).

5. *Rules-in-use* refers to the definitions and logic of the Institutional Analysis and Design Framework (Ostrom 2005, 2010). Ostrom (2010, 647) defines the rules-in-use as rules that "specify common understandings of those involved related to who must, must not, or may take which actions affecting others subject to sanctions." The point is that the content of public policy as formally written may or may not reflect the in-use rules structuring the regular practices and behaviors of government officials or the equivalent. The inclusion of in-use rules as part of the definition of public policies is somewhat atypical compared to most definitions, but it is consistent with a few others (Schneider and Ingram 1997, 2) and necessary in understanding and explaining policy processes, especially when considering the roles of street-level bureaucrats (Lipsky 1980).

6. See the excellent book by Dodds (2013) for some of the inspiration of the ideas underlying this criterion.

7. Of course, some instructors and readers might want to adopt a "machete order" by rearranging the sequence in which the chapters are read. Some instructors, for example, start with the introduction and concluding chapters and then read the theory chapters in a different order than presented.

8. For example, the Advocacy Coalition Framework and Institutional Analysis and Development Framework could be applied to any of the stages of the policy cycle. Consider policy change: (1) analysts could use the Advocacy Coalition Framework to discover how policy change is the result of conflict between adversarial coalitions conditioned by events, learning, and negotiations; (2) analysts could use the Institutional Analysis and Development Framework to understand an instance of policy change as institutional adaptation among actors continuously tinkering with the rules governing a particular situation. Consider implementation: (1) analysts could use the Advocacy Coalition Framework to study implementation and find a continuation of coalition conflict and the absence of learning in rulemaking in yet another political game; (2) analysts could use the Institutional Analysis and Development Framework to study implementation as the behaviors associated with the patterns of enforcement and monitoring of rules governing a particular resource.

REFERENCES

Bachrach, Peter, and Morton S. Baratz. 1963. "Decisions and Nondecisions: An Analytical Framework." *American Political Science Review* 57 (3): 632–642.

Baumgartner, Frank R., Bryan D. Jones, and Peter B. Mortensen. 2017. "Punctuated Equilibrium Theory: Explaining Stability and Change in Public Policymaking." In *Theories of the Policy Process,* 4th ed., edited by Christopher M. Weible and Paul A. Sabatier, 55–101. Boulder, CO: Westview Press.

Berry, Frances Stokes, and William D. Berry. 2017. "Innovation and Diffusion Models in Policy Research." In *Theories of the Policy Process,* 4th ed., edited by Christopher M. Weible and Paul A. Sabatier, 253–297. Boulder, CO: Westview Press.

Birkland, Thomas A. 2016. *An Introduction to the Policy Process.* 4th ed. New York: Routledge.

Cairney, Paul. 2012. *Understanding Public Policy: Theories and Issues.* New York: Palgrave Macmillan.

Cohen, Michael D., James G. March, and Johan P. Olsen. 1972. "A Garbage Can Model of Organizational Choice." *Administrative Science Quarterly* 17 (1): 1–25.

deLeon, Peter. 1999. "The Stages Approach to the Policy Process: What Has It Done? Where Is It Going?" In *Theories of the Policy Process,* edited by Paul A. Sabatier, 19–34. Boulder, CO: Westview Press.

Dodds, Anneliese. 2013. *Comparative Public Policy.* New York: Palgrave Macmillan.

Feiock, Richard C. 2013. "The Institutional Collective Action Framework." *Policy Studies Journal* 41 (3): 397–425.

Fischer, Frank. 2003. *Reframing Policy Analysis.* Oxford: Oxford University Press.

Fischer, Frank, and John Forester, eds. 1993. *The Argumentative Turn in Policy Analysis and Planning.* Durham, NC: Duke University Press.

Heclo, Hugh. 1972. "Policy Analysis." *British Journal of Political Science* 2 (1): 83–108.

Heikkila, Tanya, and Paul Cairney. 2017. "Comparison of Theories of the Policy Process." In *Theories of the Policy Process,* 4th ed., edited by Christopher M. Weible and Paul A. Sabatier, 301–327. Boulder, CO: Westview Press.

Heikkila, Tanya, and Andrea K. Gerlak. 2013. "Building a Conceptual Approach to Collective Learning: Lessons for Public Policy Scholars." *Policy Studies Journal* 41 (3): 484–512.

Herweg, Nicole, Nikolaos Zahariadis, and Reimut Zohlnhöfer. 2017. "The Multiple Streams Framework: Foundations, Refinements, and Empirical Applications." In *Theories of the Policy Process,* 4th ed., edited by Christopher M. Weible and Paul A. Sabatier, 17–53. Boulder, CO: Westview Press.

Howlett, Michael. 2011. *Designing Public Policies: Principles and Instruments.* New York: Routledge.

Jenkins-Smith, Hank C., Daniel Nohrstedt, Christopher M. Weible, and Karin Ingold. 2017. "The Advocacy Coalition Framework: An Overview of the Research Program." In *Theories of the Policy Process,* 4th ed., edited by Christopher M. Weible and Paul A. Sabatier, 135–171. Boulder, CO: Westview Press.

Kingdon, John. 1984. *Agendas, Alternatives, and Public Policies.* New York: Addison Wesley Longman.

King, Gary, Robert O. Keohane, and Sidney Verba. 1994. *Designing Social Inquiry.* Princeton, NJ: Princeton University Press.

Lasswell, Hardold D. 1951. "The Policy Orientation." In *The Policy Sciences,* edited by Daniel Lerner and Harold D. Lasswell, chap. 1. Palo Alto, CA: Stanford University Press.

Lindblom, Charles E. 1968. *The Policy-Making Process.* Englewood Cliffs, NJ: Prentice Hall.

Lipsky, Michael. 1980. *Street-Level Bureaucracy: The Dilemmas of the Individuals in Public Service*. New York: Russell Sage Foundation.

Loehle, Craig. 1987. "Hypothesis Testing in Ecology: Psychological Aspects and the Importance of Theory Maturation." *Quarterly Review of Biology* 62 (4): 397–409.

Lubell, Mark. 2013. "Governing Institutional Complexity: The Ecology of Games Framework." *Policy Studies Journal* 41 (3): 537–559.

Lukes, Steven. 1974. *Power: A Radical View*. London: Macmillan.

May, Peter J., and Ashley E. Jochim. 2013. "Policy Regime Perspective: Policies, Politics, and Governing." *Policy Studies Journal* 41 (3): 426–452.

McConnell, Allan. 2010. *Understanding Policy Success: Rethinking Public Policy*. New York: Palgrave Macmillan.

McCool, Daniel. 1995. *Public Policy Theories, Models, and Concepts: An Anthology*. Englewood Cliffs, NJ: Prentice Hall.

Mettler, Suzanne, and Mallory SoRelle. 2017. "Policy Feedback Theory." In *Theories of the Policy Process*, 4th ed., edited by Christopher M. and Weible Paul A. Sabatier, 103–134. Boulder, CO: Westview Press.

Mintrom, Michael, and Phillipa Norman. 2009. "Policy Entrepreneurship and Policy Change." *Policy Studies Journal* 37 (4): 649–667.

Moulton, Stephanie, and Jodi R. Sandfort. 2016. "The Strategic Action Field Framework for Policy Implementation Research." *Policy Studies Journal*. Published electronically January 29, 2016. doi:10.1111/psj.12147.

Ostrom, Elinor. 1980. "Is It B or Not-B? That Is the Question." *Social Science Quarterly* 61 (2): 198–202.

———. 2005. *Understanding Institutional Diversity*. Princeton, NJ: Princeton University Press.

———. 2010. "Beyond Markets and States: Polycentric Governance of Complex Economic Systems." *American Economic Review* 100 (3): 641–672.

Parson, Wayne. 1995. *Public Policy: An Introduction to the Theory and Practice of Policy Analysis*. Cheltenham, UK: Edward Elgar Publishing.

Pressman, Jeffrey L., and Aaron Wildavsky. 1973. *Implementation*. Berkeley: University of California Press.

Putnam, Robert D., Robert Leonardi, and Raffaella Y. Nanetti. 1994. *Making Democracy Work: Civic Traditions in Modern Italy*. Princeton, NJ: Princeton University Press.

Ranney, Austin, ed. 1968. "The Study of Policy Content: A Framework for Choice." In *Political Science and Public Policy*, edited by Austin Ranney, 3–21. Chicago: Markham Publishers.

Richardson, Jeremy John, ed. 1982. *Policy Styles in Western Europe*. New York: George Allen and Unwin.

Sabatier, Paul A. 1999. *Theories of the Policy Process*. Boulder, CO: Westview Press.

Sabatier, Paul A., and Hank C. Jenkins-Smith. 1993. *Policy Change and Learning: An Advocacy Coalition Approach*. Boulder, CO: Westview Press.

Schlager, Edella, and Michael Cox. 2017. "The IAD Framework and the SES Framework: An Introduction and Assessment of the Ostrom Workshop Frameworks." In

Theories of the Policy Process, 4th ed., edited by Christopher M. Weible and Paul A. Sabatier, 215–252. Boulder, CO: Westview Press.

Schneider, Anne, and Helen Ingram. 1993. "Social Construction of Target Populations: Implications for Politics and Policy." *American Political Science Review* 87 (2): 334–347.

———. 1997. *Policy Design for Democracy.* Lawrence: University Press of Kansas.

Schneider, Anne, Helen Ingram, and Peter deLeon. 2014. "Democratic Policy Design: Social Construction of Target Populations." In *Theories of the Policy Process,* 3rd ed., edited by Paul A. Sabatier and Christopher M. Weible, 105–150. Boulder, CO: Westview Press.

Shanahan, Elizabeth A., Michael D. Jones, Mark K. McBeth, and Claudio M. Radaelli. 2017. "The Narrative Policy Framework." In *Theories of the Policy Process,* 4th ed., edited by Christopher M. Weible and Paul A. Sabatier, 173–213. Boulder, CO: Westview Press.

Shipman, George A. 1959. "The Policy Process: An Emerging Perspective." *Western Political Quarterly* 12 (2): 535–547.

Stone, Deborah A. 1989. "Causal Stories and the Formation of Policy Agendas." *Political Science Quarterly* 104 (2): 281–300.

Tosun, Jale, and Samuel Workman. 2017. "Struggle and Triumph in Fusing Policy Process and Comparative Research." In *Theories of the Policy Process,* 4th ed., edited by Christopher M. Weible and Paul A. Sabatier, 329–362. Boulder, CO: Westview Press.

Weible, Christopher M. 2017. "Moving Forward and Climbing Upward: Advancing Policy Process Research." In *Theories of the Policy Process,* 4th ed., edited by Christopher M. Weible and Paul A. Sabatier, 363–378. Boulder, CO: Westview Press.

Weible, Christopher M., and David P. Carter. 2016. "Advancing Policy Process Research at Its Overlap with Public Management Scholarship and Nonprofit and Voluntary Action Studies." *Policy Studies Journal.* Published electronically December 22, 2016. doi:10.1111/psj.12194.

Whetten, David A. 1989. "What Constitutes a Theoretical Contribution?" *Academy of Management Review* 14 (4): 490–495.

PART I

Theoretical Approaches to Policy Process Research

The Multiple Streams Framework: Foundations, Refinements, and Empirical Applications

NICOLE HERWEG, NIKOLAOS ZAHARIADIS,
AND REIMUT ZOHLNHÖFER

With rising ambiguity and turbulence in global affairs, the Multiple Streams Framework (MSF) is fast becoming a major tool with which to analyze the policy process. In their recent literature review, Jones et al. (2016) report that no fewer than 311 English-language peer-reviewed journal articles published between 2000 and 2013 have empirically applied the framework—with an increasing trend over time. Moreover, in these articles, the MSF is applied to a wide variety of issue areas, countries, and levels of government. In addition, the academic debate of MSF's theoretical refinement has recently broadened, signified by recent special issues of the *European Journal of Political Research* (issue 3/2015), the *Policy Studies Journal* (issue 1/2016), *Policy Sciences* (issue 1/2016), and the *Journal of Comparative Policy Analysis* (issue 3/2016) as well as an edited volume on the framework (Zohlnhöfer and Rüb 2016a).

One of the reasons for the high number of MSF applications could be that the conditions under which policies are made increasingly resemble the framework's assumptions—particularly in contexts for which the MSF originally had not been developed. Problems, from global warming and nuclear energy to migration and trade agreements, have become ever more contested, and even experts disagree fundamentally. Ambiguity has increasingly become (or has come to be realized as) a fact of political life. The same could be said about what the MSF conceptualizes as the political stream. Particularly in the parliamentary systems of Western Europe, things have become much less orderly, with more fragmented party systems, a decreasing relevance of party ideologies, and voting behavior growing ever more volatile. Nonetheless, MSF's success comes at a price. As Jones et al. (2016) as well as Cairney and Jones (2016) show, many of the empirical applications remain superficial; theoretical innovations in the literature are often ignored, and key concepts more often than not lack clear specification.

In this chapter, we present the current state of MSF thinking, including many innovations that have been suggested in the recent surge of MSF literature. We aim to provide an up-to-date presentation and discussion of the framework from which scholars may begin MSF empirical applications or theoretical refinements. We begin by outlining the main assumptions of the MSF before presenting the five structural elements of the framework. Because the MSF was originally developed for the analysis of agenda setting processes, we discuss how it is, or can be, applied to other stages of the policy process (decision making, implementation, etc.) next. We then turn to the question of how the framework is applied empirically in different contexts and how it has to be adapted accordingly. Finally, we deal with the (alleged and real) limitations of the framework and its future prospects.

ASSUMPTIONS

Kingdon (2011), who originally put forth the MSF, was inspired by Cohen, March, and Olsen's (1972) garbage can model of organizational choice. Consequently, the MSF's basic assumptions deal with ambiguity, time constraints, problematic preferences, unclear technology, fluid participation, and stream independence. These terms characterize what Cohen et al. have called organized anarchies, such as universities, national governments, and international organizations. In the following sections, we summarize the meaning of each of these basic assumptions.

Ambiguity

Instead of assuming that policymaking is an exercise in rational problem solving, the MSF negates the existence of a rational solution to a given problem. In contrast, the MSF assumes that because of ambiguity, a multitude of solutions to a given problem exists. Ambiguity refers to "a state of having many ways of thinking about the same circumstances or phenomena" (Feldman 1989, 5). In contrast with uncertainty, which may be reduced by collecting more information (Wilson 1989), more information does not reduce ambiguity. For instance, more information can tell us how AIDS is spread, but it will not tell us whether AIDS is a health, educational, political, or moral issue. Therefore, we often do not know what the problem is. Because problem definition is vague and shifting, in principle, many solutions for the same circumstance are possible.

Time Constraints

Policymakers operate under significant time constraints and often do not have the luxury of taking their time to make a decision. Basically, time constraints arise because attending to or processing events and circumstances in political systems can occur in parallel, whereas individuals' ability to give attention to or to process information is serial. Owing to biological and cognitive limitations, individuals can attend to only one issue at a time. In contrast, organizations and governments can attend to many (though not infinite) issues simultaneously (March and Simon 1958; Jones 2001) thanks to division of labor. Policymakers, for instance, can actively consider only a relatively small number of issues, whereas the US government can simultaneously put out fires in California, conduct trade negotiations with the European Union (EU), investigate mail fraud, and mourn the loss of soldiers killed in action. Thus, because many issues vie for attention, policymakers sense an urgency to address them and to "strike while the iron is hot." Consequently, time constraints limit the range and number of alternatives to which attention is given.

Problematic Policy Preferences

Problematic policy preferences emerge in the presence of ambiguity and time constraints. How actors think about an issue depends on its overarching label (like health, education, politics, or morality) and on the information that has been taken into account. Consequently, actors' policy preferences are not fixed and exogenously given but emerge during (inter)action. To use economic terms, ambiguity and time constraints result in intransitive and incomplete policy preferences.

The assumption of problematic policy preferences only means, however, that policymakers do not have clear preferences with regard to specific policies. It does not imply that they have no preferences at all. With regard to the outcome of the next election or the question of who will be the next president, they take an unequivocal stand: policymakers want to win elections, and they want their candidate to get elected as the next president.

Unclear Technology

In organizational theory, technology refers to work processes that turn inputs into products. If members of an organized anarchy are aware of only their individual responsibilities and exhibit only rudimentary knowledge of how their job fits into the overall mission of the organization, we speak of unclear technology. In political systems, for instance, jurisdictional boundaries are unclear, and turf battles between different departments or agencies are common.

Members of the legislature often complain of unaccountable officials, who, in turn, frequently express their frustration with overburdening reporting rules and independent-minded public managers.

Fluid Participation

Unclear technology is complicated by fluid participation. Fluid participation means that the composition of decision making bodies is subject to constant change—either because it varies with the concrete decision to be made or because turnover is high. Legislators come and go, and bureaucrats, especially high-level civil servants, often move from public service to private practice. In addition, the time and effort that participants are willing and able to devote to any one decision vary considerably.

Stream Independence

In line with the garbage can model, the MSF assumes that independent processes or streams flow through the political system. In a nutshell, the MSF assumes that political problems, policy solutions, and politics—referred to as problem stream, policy stream, and political stream—develop mostly independently of each other. Problems, most obviously in the case of unpredictable problems like those caused by natural disasters, occur regardless of political developments or available policy solutions. Because consensus building in the political stream and in the policy stream takes different forms, these streams also have their own dynamic (Kingdon 2011). In the political stream, the mode of interaction is bargaining; in the policy stream, it is persuasion. More precisely, actors in the policy stream aim to gain acceptance for a policy solution, whereas participants in the political stream build on lobbying and group mobilization.

STRUCTURAL ELEMENTS

The MSF's starting point is the notion of stream independence. Nonetheless, if an issue is to gain agenda prominence, and is ultimately to be decided on, these independent streams need to come together at some point. The opportunity to bring these streams together arises if a "policy window" (sometimes called "window of opportunity") opens. Moreover, because there is no natural or inevitable connection between a problem and a solution, according to MSF thinking, the two often have to be coupled together by a policy entrepreneur and presented to receptive policymakers. We discuss the five structural elements of the MSF in turn—the three streams, the policy or, as we will call it, agenda window, and the policy entrepreneur.

Problem Stream

Policymakers will almost always argue that a policy responds to some problem. But what is a problem? According to the MSF, problems are conditions that deviate from policymakers' or citizens' ideal states and that "are seen as public in the sense that government action is needed to resolve them" (Béland and Howlett 2016, 222). Thus, problems contain a "perceptual, interpretive element" (Kingdon 2011, 110) because people's ideals and reality vary significantly. Moreover, we might come to see a condition that we previously perceived as acceptable as a problem once we learn that other countries are doing better in this regard. Or we start seeing a condition in a different context that turns the condition into a problem. Take the level of unemployment benefits as an example. From a social policy perspective, the relevant problem could be whether the benefits are high enough to provide an acceptable standard of living for recipients. In contrast, from an economic policy perspective, the problem could be that benefits are so high that recipients do not have incentives to look for a new job. As we switch from one perspective to the other, an acceptable condition (benefits are high enough for a decent standard of living) can become a problem (benefits are so high that recipients have no incentives to look for a job).

Nonetheless, many conditions deviate from citizens' or policymakers' ideal states, and not all of them receive political attention. Rather, indicators, focusing events, and feedback bring specific conditions to policymakers' attention. Numerous *indicators* are in principle relevant for policymakers or the public, for instance, unemployment figures, budget balances, and crime statistics. Some of these indicators are published regularly, and in other cases they are collected for a specific occasion. It is important to keep in mind, however, that all of these indicators only inform about conditions until an actor defines them as problems. It will be easier to do so if an indicator changes for the worse because, if people did not worry about a condition previously and the condition has not changed, it is very difficult to frame the condition as a problem now.

According to Tom Birkland's (1997) definition, *focusing events* are sudden and relatively rare, are at least potentially harmful, and are known to policymakers and the public at the same time. Although it is far from certain whether events like natural disasters (earthquakes, hurricanes), severe technical accidents (airplane crashes, nuclear accidents), and particularly serious forms of violent crimes (terrorist attacks, school shootings) will lead to agenda change, they at least increase the probability of agenda change. Moreover, there are different forms of focusing events. Whereas some are so grave that they "simply bowl over everything standing in the way of prominence on the agenda" (Kingdon 2011, 96), others are more subtle, including powerful symbols or personal experiences of policymakers (for an overview, see Birkland and Warnement

2016). Finally, *feedback* about existing programs may direct attention to specific conditions. If it becomes known to policymakers or the public that a program does not attain its goals, that costs are skyrocketing, or that unwanted side effects occurred, this might also be framed as a problem.

Nevertheless, policymakers are made aware of numerous problems on a daily basis, and it is impossible to pay attention to all of them because policymakers can attend to only a limited number of issues at any given time (Kingdon 2011, 184–186; Herweg, Huß, and Zohlnhöfer 2015). Thus, whether a problem receives policymakers' attention also depends upon which other problems are currently discussed. In the aftermath of terrorist attacks or in a deep recession, other problems have a difficult time receiving attention. More generally, the more politically relevant a condition becomes, the more likely it is that it will be dealt with. However, what exactly political relevance means is not entirely clear. Herweg, Huß, and Zohlnhöfer (2015) suggest that political relevance is strongly related to the electoral relevance of a condition: if a problem jeopardizes a policymaker's reelection, it will probably be defined as a relevant problem the policymaker needs to attend to.

Thus, MSF does not see problems (and their severity) as objective facts but rather as social constructs. That implies that agency becomes relevant in the problem stream because someone then has to frame a problem in a specific way if it is to receive policymakers' attention. Moreover, the framing of a problem is of utter importance because how a problem is defined substantially affects the solutions that can be coupled to it.

Recent research suggests different ways of introducing agency into the problem stream (cf. Mukherjee and Howlett 2015; Knaggård 2015, 2016). Knaggård (2015, 452), for example, argues that problem brokers are actors who "frame conditions as public problems and work to make policymakers accept these frames. Problem brokers thus define conditions as problems." Problem brokers can also be the policy entrepreneurs, but not necessarily. The key analytical difference between the two roles is that the problem broker only argues that something must be done about a specific condition, whereas the policy entrepreneur suggests solutions to the problem. For empirical applications, it is necessary to define when the streams are ready for coupling. The problem stream should not pose difficulties in this regard because policy entrepreneurs are always able to frame a condition as a problem that can be coupled with their favored policy proposal.

Policy Stream

In the policy stream, policy alternatives are generated in policy communities. A policy community "is mainly a loose connection of civil servants, interest-groups, academics, researchers and consultants (the so-called hidden participants), who engage in working out alternatives to the policy problems of a specific policy field" (Herweg 2016a, 132). The overwhelming majority of members of a policy community are policy experts who advocate and discuss policy ideas. Thus, various ideas float around in what Kingdon (2011, 116) called a policy "primeval soup." During the process known as "softening up" (Kingdon 2011, 127), members of the policy community discuss, modify, and recombine these ideas. This process is very much characterized by arguing. Although the number of ideas floating around in the primeval soup originally is quite large, the process of softening up filters out many of them until a limited number of viable policy alternatives emerges, each backed by a substantial part of the policy community. Only these alternatives will receive serious consideration.

This process is heavily influenced by the structure of the policy community. Where policymakers search for solutions and how ideas germinate in the primeval soup depend on the degree of integration of the policy community—that is, the linkages among its members. The gestation period of ideas in the policy stream varies from rapid to gradual. The content ranges from totally new to a minor extension of the old. The typology that emerges from these criteria yields four categories: quantum (rapid propulsion of new ideas); emergent (gradual gestation of new ideas); convergent (rapid gestation of old ideas); and gradualist (slow gestation of marginal extensions of existing policies) (Durant and Diehl, 1989). Integration encourages one type of evolution rather than another. Less integrated policy communities, those that are larger in size and interact in a competitive mode, are more likely to facilitate a quantum to gradualist evolution of ideas. More integrated, that is, smaller and consensual policy communities, are likely to follow an emergent to convergent pattern. This is not to say that other combinations are not possible but rather that integration renders such evolutionary trajectories more likely. The hypothesis helps explain the ease with which ideas such as privatization have been gaining prominence among specialists in the United Kingdom but have had relative difficulty doing the same in Germany (Zahariadis 2003).

External influences on the policy stream should also be considered. For example, Lovell (2016) finds that MSF must be supplemented with theoretical insights from policy mobility as ideas move across national boundaries. This point makes policy communities more porous than previously conceived because ideas may not take time to soften up domestically because they acquire "legitimacy" through success in other countries. Whereas originally Zahariadis (1995) conceptualized this phenomenon as part of externally imposed spillover across sectors, in technical policy sectors where innovation is highly prized Lovell (2016) finds external nonstate actors may actually be thought of as regular members of an international network in a more broadly conceived domestic policy community.

Regardless of the structure of the policy community, it is by no means random which proposals survive in the primeval soup. To the extent that proposals fulfill certain criteria, they are more likely to become viable policy alternatives. Kingdon (2011, 131–139) discussed various "criteria for survival": technical feasibility, value acceptability, public acquiescence, and financial viability. Thus, when policy experts doubt an idea can be implemented smoothly, when a proposal contradicts the values of many members of the policy community, when it is perceived as unlikely that an idea can find a majority in the political stream, or when costs are high, it is unlikely that the idea will survive the softening-up process. More recently, other criteria of survival have been suggested (Zohlnhöfer and Huß 2016). In EU member states, for example, ideas that do not conform to EU law have a smaller chance of surviving in the primeval soup. Similarly, if an idea's conformity with constitutional regulations is doubted, the likelihood that this idea is pursued further decreases, particularly in countries with strong judicial review. Finally, path dependence can be incorporated in the selection criteria. If an idea strongly deviates from a previous policy path that is characterized by increasing returns, its chances of becoming a viable alternative are very low—consider the idea to turn a pay-as-you-go pension system into a funded system. Although path dependence could be subsumed under the criterion of technical feasibility, it is important to remind scholars that path dependence can be modeled within the MSF (see also Spohr 2016).

The policy stream can be defined as ready for coupling when at least one viable policy alternative exists that meets the criteria of survival. If no such alternative is available, the MSF leads us to expect that coupling is unlikely.

Political Stream

The policy stream is located at the level of the policy subsystem, and the political stream is located at the level of the political system. Whereas arguing is the dominant mode of interaction in the policy stream, bargaining and powering dominate in the political, as majorities for proposals are sought here. Kingdon identified three core elements in the political stream: the national mood, interest groups, and government.

The *national mood* is certainly the most empirically elusive of these elements. This elusiveness has led some researchers to dismiss it as an analytical category (Zahariadis 1995). The national mood refers to the notion that a fairly large number of individuals in a given country tend to think along common lines and that the mood swings from time to time. Kingdon suggested that government officials sense changes in this mood and act to promote certain items on the agenda according to the national mood. Thus, the national mood is characterized by a strong element of perception on the part of policymakers. Accordingly, Kingdon advises not to confound the national mood with the results of opinion polls because the latter lack the perceptual element. Nonetheless, given the immense professionalization of politics, which includes a proliferation of opinion polls many of which are actually commissioned by policymakers themselves, it seems plausible to follow more recent research (e.g.,

Zahariadis 2015) and rely on opinion poll results for the operationalization of the national mood—preferably in addition to more direct sources of policy-makers' perceptions.

Interest group campaigns are the second element of the political stream. Quite evidently, the more interest groups are opposed to an idea and the more powerful these interest groups are, the less likely it is that that idea will make it on the agenda. It is important to keep in mind, however, that there is more to the activities of interest groups than just campaigns—and that the MSF is able to accommodate this fact. As discussed earlier, interest group representatives can be members of the policy community and thus propose ideas and participate in the softening-up process. But these activities take place in the policy stream and need to be kept distinct from the campaigns interest groups might launch against proposals.

Governments and legislatures, in particular, changes in their composition, constitute the third element of the political stream. For example, some ministers or members of parliament might be more open-minded with regard to some policy proposals, or certain ideas match better with the ideology of one party than with that of another one, and therefore turnover may make a difference for which items enter the agenda. But this element of the political stream is not entirely about elected officials and political parties. Bureaucratic turf battles and important administrators are also highly relevant here.

When is the political stream ready for coupling? For two reasons it is slightly more difficult to answer this question regarding the political stream than for the problem and policy streams—at least as far as agenda setting is concerned. First, the three elements of the political stream do not need to point in the same direction for a given policy proposal. For example, although the government might be receptive to a proposal and policymakers might sense a supportive national mood, interest groups could at the same time be rather negative. How does this constellation affect the possibility of agenda change? Though it is clear from Kingdon's work and other applications that it is not necessary that all elements of the political stream are favorable to a proposal, the MSF literature has not been very explicit about the conditions under which individual elements of the political stream take precedence over others. Building on the work of Zahariadis (1995, 2003), who suggested collapsing all three elements of the political stream (government, national mood, and interest group campaigns) into the variable "party politics," Herweg, Huß, and Zohlnhöfer (2015) argue that government and legislatures are the most relevant actors in the political stream—because ultimately these are the actors who have to adopt a policy change. At the same time, their position may well be influenced, but not determined, by the national mood and interest group campaigns. Thus, it is possible under certain conditions that a government is willing to ignore interest group campaigns and even a reluctant national mood.

Second, it is not yet necessary at the agenda setting stage to build political majorities that may eventually be needed to adopt legislation. Indeed, in many cases legislative majorities are only gathered after an issue is on the agenda. Nonetheless, the political stream is certainly also important during agenda setting. The minimum that is needed to make the political stream ready for coupling is for a key policymaker, such as the relevant minister or an influential member of legislature, to actively support the idea in question and be willing to stitch together a majority for it (Zohlnhöfer 2016). Following Roberts and King (1991, 152), Herweg Huß, and Zohlnhöfer (2015, 446) have suggested calling these actors "political entrepreneurs." In contrast to policy entrepreneurs, political entrepreneurs are neither necessarily members of the policy community nor do they have to be involved in the development of the policy proposal at an early stage. Rather, once a policy entrepreneur has convinced a political entrepreneur of the project, the political entrepreneur, because of the individual's formal leadership position, can further the idea from inside the formal governmental system and work for its adoption.

Agenda (Policy) Window

Even when all three streams are ready for coupling agenda change may not come about automatically. Rather, a coupling of the three streams, and eventually agenda change, becomes much more likely at specific points in time, which Kingdon has called policy windows. A policy window is defined as a fleeting "opportunity for advocates of proposals to push their pet solutions, or to push attention to their special problems" (Kingdon 2011, 165). Although policy window is a generic term widely used in the literature, it has been proposed recently to refine this term to capture important nuances. To distinguish opportunities to get an issue on the agenda from opportunities to get policies adopted, Herweg, Huß, and Zohlnhöfer (2015) have suggested calling the former "agenda window" and the latter "decision window." We follow this suggestion but keep the term policy window for more generic use.

Agenda windows are rare (at least with regard to a particular policy proposal) and ephemeral; they can be predictable (elections, budgets) or unpredictable (disasters). They can open in two of the three streams: the problem or the political stream. A window in the political stream opens if the partisan composition of government changes or new members enter legislature. The incoming actors are interested in new ideas and are therefore open to novel policy proposals. Similarly, a significant shift in the national mood can open an agenda window. In contrast, an agenda window opens in the problem stream when indicators deteriorate dramatically—for example, unemployment or the budget deficit skyrockets in a very brief period. Alternatively, focusing events like natural disasters or terrorist attacks can open an agenda window.

Depending on the stream in which the window opens, coupling differs. In the case of a window that opens in the political stream, we should expect "doctrinal coupling" (Zahariadis 2003, 72) or "problem-focused advocacy" (Boscarino 2009, 429). The main task is finding a problem to a given solution. Take a change of government, for example. The new government is likely to argue that it was elected to adopt new policies and will be eager to prove that it delivers. Thus, although the solution is already in the manifesto, the government looks for problems that these solutions can solve. Because many conditions could be framed as problems, it should not be difficult to find a problem that suits the solution.

Coupling in response to windows opening in the problem stream is called "consequential coupling" (Zahariadis 2003, 72) or "problem surfing" (Boscarino 2009, 429). It differs from coupling in windows that open in the political stream in at least two ways. First, the duration during which the window is open is shorter in the former than in the latter case because response to a problem must be more or less immediate (Keeler 1993). Second, in the case of a window that opens in the problem stream, a solution needs to be found that fits the problem that is on the agenda. Remember, however, that the window is open only for a limited period of time, which in most instances is insufficient to work out a solution after the problem has risen to prominence. Rather, even in the case of consequential coupling the problem will be coupled to a preexisting solution that is somehow linked to the problem. Thus, in both cases, under doctrinal and consequential coupling, the relationship between problem and solution is not particularly tight.

Ackrill and Kay (2011) introduce a third coupling mechanism: commissioning. In contrast to doctrinal and consequential coupling, where policy entrepreneurs sell their pet proposals to policymakers, commissioning captures policymakers' active reaction to the opening of a policy window. The opening of a policy window signals to policymakers that an issue needs to be addressed. Instead of waiting for a policy entrepreneur to sell a solution, policymakers actively select the solution they deem appropriate (and thus the policy entrepreneur who advocates it) as a reaction to changes in the problem or political streams.

The main analytical problem with the concept of the agenda window in empirical applications is that it is usually only identified ex post. Certainly, some agenda windows are predictable, such as elections or budget negotiations. When the three streams are ready for coupling and issue competition is low, the likelihood is high that these kinds of windows can be used for coupling. Many other windows are less predictable, however—think of accidents, high school shootings, and a swing in the national mood. The main problem is not only that these events are very difficult (if not impossible) to predict. Rather, the issue is that it is often hard to decide ex ante whether these events constitute an agenda window for a given policy at all (cf. Béland 2016, 234). Certainly, agenda windows are to an extent construed by problem brokers and are a function of how crowded the agenda is. Nonetheless, according to Herweg, Huß, and Zohlnhöfer (2015), the chances that an event can be utilized as an agenda window increase as the electoral relevance of an issue increases. Take labor market policy under the social democratic chancellor Schröder in Germany as an example (Zohlnhöfer 2016). Although the unemployment rate had more or less stagnated at a high level for almost the entire term of office, the government had failed to do anything about it for three and a half years because it believed that unemployment figures would go down as a result of demographic change. When this hope evaporated and high unemployment rates endangered the government's reelection, even a minor scandal regarding placement statistics by the Federal Labor Office sufficed to initiate the largest labor market reform in living memory. As the government's struggle for reelection critically depended on employment policy, Schröder used the scandal to prove his willingness and ability to introduce a major reform. Thus, less dramatic events can open agenda windows in electorally salient issue areas. Conversely, severe focusing events are indispensable conditions that may open windows in the problem stream in electorally less salient fields.

Policy Entrepreneur

Policy entrepreneurs, that is, "advocates who are willing to invest their resources—time, energy, reputation, money—to promote a position in return for anticipated future gain in the form of material, purposive, or solidary benefits" (Kingdon 2011, 179), are key actors in the MSF. They can be individuals or corporate actors and are not defined by a specific formal position. Essentially, any policy-relevant actor—policymaker, bureaucrat, academic, journalist, representative of an interest group, or member of parliament—can become a policy entrepreneur. Policy entrepreneurs push their proposals ("pet projects," in MSF parlance) in the policy stream and adapt them in order to find broad support among the members of the policy community and make them viable alternatives.

Once that has been achieved, they attempt to couple their pet project with the other two streams. When agenda windows open, policy entrepreneurs must immediately seize the opportunity to initiate action. Otherwise, the opportunity is lost and the policy entrepreneurs must wait for the next one to come along. Policy entrepreneurs are thus more than mere advocates of particular solutions; they are also manipulators of problematic preferences and unclear technology (Mintrom and Norman 2009). Entrepreneurs must be not only persistent but also skilled at coupling. They must be able to attach problems to their solutions and find politicians who are receptive to their ideas, that is, political entrepreneurs. An issue's chances of gaining agenda status dramatically increase when all three streams—problems, policies, and politics—are coupled in a single package.

Not all entrepreneurs are successful at all times. More successful entrepreneurs are those who have greater access to policymakers. For example, the Adam Smith Institute had greater access to the government during Margaret Thatcher's tenure in power in Britain because its ideologies matched more closely than those of other groups. Hence, options put forth by individuals associated with the institute had a greater receptivity among policymakers. Entrepreneurs with more resources, that is, the ability to spend more time, money, and energy, to push their proposals have greater rates of success. Entrepreneurs have a variety of instruments at their disposal, including framing of a problem, affect priming, "salami tactics," and the use of symbols (Zahariadis 2003, 14; 2015).

The MSF argues that agenda setting is not primarily an exercise in rational problem solving. Rather, sometimes a problem comes up that is coupled with a preexisting policy that somewhat "fits" it, whereas at other times a political opportunity arises—with the advent of a new government, for instance—to get a policy on the agenda and that policy then needs to be coupled to some problem. Nonetheless, this does not exclude the possibility of formulating hypotheses for each of the MSF's key elements as well as for the framework as a whole. We present a number of testable, probabilistic hypotheses in Table 1.1.

APPLICATIONS AND ADAPTATIONS TO STAGES OF THE POLICY CYCLE

Originally, Kingdon developed his framework to explain agenda setting in health, transport, and fiscal policy at the federal level of the United States. The subsequent literature, however, has also applied the MSF to different policy domains, further stages of the policy cycle, and different political systems. The policy domains covered range from gender equality policy (Béland 2009) to foreign policy (Travis and Zahariadis 2002). In their literature review, Jones et al. (2016) report that twenty-two policy domains were explored using the MSF, with health, environment, governance, education, and welfare covering almost 80 percent of the MSF applications analyzed (see also Rawat and Morris 2016, 614).

Although applying the framework in various policy domains does not automatically require adaptations, such a need arises when the MSF is applied to different policy stages and political systems. The MSF has mostly been applied to the policy stages of agenda setting and decision making. But it has also been applied to policy implementation and policy termination, though only rarely (e.g., Geva-May 2004). We discuss below some of the adaptations that have been suggested in the literature for decision making and implementation.

TABLE 1.1 MSF Hypotheses on Agenda Setting

HYPOTHESIS FOR THE FRAMEWORK AS A WHOLE	
Agenda change becomes more likely if (a) a policy window opens, (b) the streams are ready for coupling, and (c) a policy entrepreneur promotes the agenda change.	
HYPOTHESES FOR THE FRAMEWORK'S KEY ELEMENTS	
Problem stream	• A problem broker is likely to be more successful framing a condition as a problem the more an indicator changes to the negative, the more harmful a focusing event is, and the more definitely a government program does not work as expected.
Political stream	• Policy proposals that fit the general ideology of a government or the majority in a legislature have a better chance of gaining agenda status.
Policy stream	• If a policy proposal does not fulfill the selection criteria, the likelihood of gaining agenda status, and thus being coupled, decreases significantly. • As the integration of policy communities decreases, it becomes more likely that entirely new ideas can become viable policy alternatives.
Policy window	• The policy window opens in the problem stream as a result of at least one of the following changes: change of indicators, focusing events, or feedback. • The more a condition puts a policymaker's reelection at risk, the more likely it is to open a policy window in the problem stream. • The policy window opens in the political stream as a result of at least one of the following changes: changes in legislature, election of a new government, interest group campaigns, or a change in the national mood.
Policy entrepreneur	• Policy entrepreneurs are more likely to couple the streams successfully during an open policy window if (a) they have more access to core policymakers and (b) they are more persistent.

Decision Making

To understand how the MSF needs to be adapted to apply to decision making, it is necessary to explicate the differences between agenda setting and decision making (see, for example, Knill and Tosun 2012). During agenda setting, a large number of actors compete for attention for various proposals, whereas decision making is about obtaining a majority for a specific proposal. Thus, the number of actors tends to decrease during decision making. At the same time, the relevance of the institutional setting increases as we move from agenda setting to decision making (Baumgartner et al. 2009). This implies that the decision making process is more structured and orderly and that institutions need to be taken into account much more thoroughly. Because the original formulation of MSF essentially failed to integrate institutions (see Zohlnhöfer, Herweg, and Huß 2016 for an overview), this fact alone makes adaptation of the framework necessary.

Several authors have suggested how the MSF can be adapted to explain decision making (see Zahariadis 1992, 2003 as classics, and Howlett, McConnell, and Perl 2015 and Herweg, Huß, and Zohlnhöfer 2015 as elaborate recent attempts). We discuss Herweg, Huß, and Zohlnhöfer's (2015) concept because it leaves the operating structure of the MSF untouched and still explains decision making.

Herweg, Huß, and Zohlnhöfer's (2015) main idea is to distinguish two windows, and consequently two coupling processes (see Figure 1.1): one for agenda setting, which they label agenda window, with its associated agenda coupling (see above); and one for decision making, called decision window, with the related decision coupling. We discussed agenda windows and agenda coupling above, so we concentrate here on decision windows and decision coupling. According to Herweg, Huß, and Zohlnhöfer (2015), a decision window opens once agenda coupling succeeds. The result of successful decision coupling is the adoption of a bill.

The main question during decision coupling is how to build the necessary majorities to adopt a proposal that has already been coupled to a specific problem during agenda setting. Political entrepreneurs, that is, those who hold an

FIGURE 1.1 A Modified MSF

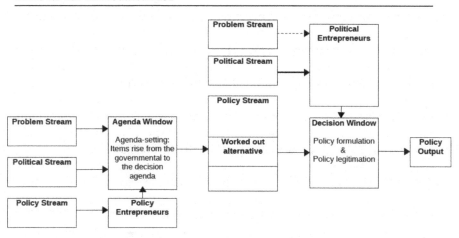

SOURCE: Herweg et al. (2015: 445). Copyright © 2015 European Consortium for Political Research, published by John Wiley & Sons Ltd. Reprinted by permission of John Wiley & Sons Ltd.

elected leadership position and who actively support a proposal (see above), are the key actors in this process. They try to obtain majority support for their projects and bargain over the specific details of the policy.

On the one hand, it is clear that the political stream dominates during decision coupling. As we will see, that is not to say that the problem and policy streams are irrelevant at this stage, but their importance is reduced compared to the agenda setting stage. On the other hand, it should be noted that institutional settings circumscribe whose support is needed. Therefore, there exist differences across countries and sometimes across issue areas and over time. The chances of a political entrepreneur getting a pet proposal adopted once it is on the agenda increase if the entrepreneur is a cabinet member in a Westminster kind of political system. Thus, in systems with few or no veto actors, decision coupling will be smoother in most instances because the adoption of a policy that is supported by the responsible minister is almost certain. The analytical value-added of the concept of decision coupling becomes clearer in situations in which the political entrepreneur does not command a majority for policy adoption—think of divided government, coalition governments, minority governments, or cases in which supermajorities are required. In all these cases, the political entrepreneur must organize the necessary majority during decision coupling; in these cases the concept substantially increases the framework's leverage.

What can a political entrepreneur do to win over enough support to secure a majority for adoption of a proposal? The literature (Herweg, Huß, and Zohlnhöfer 2015; Zohlnhöfer, Herweg, and Huß 2016) suggests three instruments: package deals, concessions, and manipulation.

The basic idea of package deals in an MSF context is that more than one policy proposal can be coupled to any given problem. Therefore, political entrepreneurs may win additional support for their pet proposals if they combine a proposal with another proposal from the policy stream, thus winning the support of those policymakers who prefer the other option. For example, a political entrepreneur who favors a specific spending program in response to a recession could include a tax cut in the proposal to broaden support.

Package deals might not always be feasible, however. To use the above example, budgetary restrictions might prevent the simultaneous adoption of spending programs and tax cuts. Therefore, it might be necessary to make some concessions, that is, to adopt the proposal in a diluted version. Less far-reaching changes are generally easier to adopt for a variety of reasons (see Zohlnhöfer 2009) that may also help political entrepreneurs obtain majorities for their proposals. Strategies for more far-reaching change could be introduced later (known as "salami tactics"; cf. Zahariadis 2003, 14).

Finally, political entrepreneurs could try to manipulate policymakers. There are numerous ways to do so. For example, political entrepreneurs can resort to the problem stream and present the problem that the proposal under discussion is supposed to deal with as growing ever more severe. This way, they can pressure policymakers, particularly if they succeed in presenting the problem as a threat to policymakers' reelection. Another way of manipulating is to centralize policymaking processes. Indeed, case studies (Zohlnhöfer 2016; Herweg 2017) have shown that sometimes policymakers circumvent other relevant actors in the decision making process. For example, German chancellor Gerhard Schröder threatened to resign should his reluctant party not follow his course in labor market policy. The European Commission likewise threatened to take certain member states to court should they not support its liberalization plans. In both (and many other) cases, this allowed political entrepreneurs to get their proposals adopted despite the resistance of veto actors.

The distinction between the two coupling processes thus makes it possible to analyze decision making from an MSF perspective. It allows formulating hypotheses on the likelihood of policy adoption as well as on how much a policy is altered during decision coupling (see Table 1.2). Moreover, by distinguishing agenda coupling and decision coupling we can integrate formal political institutions into the framework. In doing so, MSF sheds a novel light on the well-known effect of political institutions on public policies by bringing back into the debate political entrepreneurs and the possibility that veto actors can be circumvented and majorities built.

Implementation

Clearly, the notion of ambiguity has made its way to implementation studies (e.g., Baier, March, and Sætren 1986). But MSF has not been widely used in

TABLE 1.2 MSF Hypotheses on Decision Making

Policy adoption	• Policy adoption is more likely if the proposal is put forward by political entrepreneurs who hold an elected leadership position in government. • Policy adoption is more likely if the proposal is put forward by a government or majority party that is not constrained by other veto actors. • Policy adoption is more likely if different viable alternatives embraced by different actors can be combined in one package. • Policy adoption is more likely if the problem that the policy is supposed to solve is salient among the voters.
Size of change to the original proposal during decision making	• The policy adopted will likely differ significantly from the original proposal if actors other than the government have veto power (e.g., second chambers). • The more powerful the interest groups' campaign against the original proposal, the more different the adopted policy is likely to be.

implementation research largely because ambiguity raises the specter of purposeless laws and symbolic practices that can be very expensive and conflict prone (Zahariadis 2008b; Matland 1995). Nevertheless, the few implementation studies that have taken MSF seriously agree on the importance of policy entrepreneurs coupling three streams during open policy windows (Sætren 2016). Some (e.g., Zahariadis and Exadaktylos 2016) begin by conceptualizing a nested policy system (Howlett, McConnell, and Perl 2015) and proceed to explain how transitions among phases affect coupling strategies. Others (e.g., Ridde 2009; Boswell and Rodrigues 2016) focus primarily on changes within the stage of implementation. The implication in both cases is that coalitions that support policy during the policy formation phase may be different from the ones that implement it (Aberbach and Christensen 2014, 8). Nevertheless, all view decision outputs as constituting implementation windows (Ridde 2009).

Zahariadis and Exadaktylos (2016) estimate two phases (formation and implementation) with multiple rounds of deliberation. Each phase is marked by continuities with previous actions and by additions of new actors, potentially new resources, or both. They argue the process of reducing ambiguity inherent in many laws involves mechanisms organically linking actors, resources, and strategies in interactive ways. Focusing only on coupling strategies, they maintain that what leads to success in decision making increases the chances of failure in implementation. When policies adversely affect the status quo, successful entrepreneurial strategies of issue linkage and framing, side payments, and institutional rule manipulation are more likely to lead to implementation failure under conditions of crisis, centralized monopoly, and inconsistent political communication. In MSF terms, the mechanisms linking strategy to failure involve decoupling problems from solutions, undermining support in the political stream, and altering estimates of equity and efficiency in the policy stream. Take the example of Greek higher education (Zahariadis and Exadaktylos 2016). The authors argue that the activation of a new set of actors during implementation— university administration, professors, and students (and through them political parties)—likely undermined the successful entrepreneurial coupling strategies of issue linking and framing during policy implementation.

Boswell and Rodrigues (2016) focus on the department or ministry level, arguing that organizations rather than political parties are more important because implementation needs to take into account mainly those who execute policy. They also adapt the dynamics of the political and problem streams to include central commitment to the policy and solution fit to the organization's problem perception. Doing so enables them to construct a two-by-two matrix of likely implementation outcomes and track switches in modes of implementation in the same issue (climate change, defense, and asylum policy) over time.

Ridde (2009) moves in the adaptation direction as well. Although he still finds coupling to be the main ingredient of implementation success, he adds some interesting twists to the MSF logic without adding new concepts. Applying MSF to health policy at the local level in Burkina Faso, he suggests two amendments to the framework. First, following Exworthy and Powell (2004), he differentiates between big and small windows. The former refers to policy windows opening at the federal/national level, and the latter at the local level. Ridde (2009, 948) maintains that the chances of implementation at the local level in a centralized system are higher when solutions are coupled to problems during open big windows, that is, when they originate at the center. Second, international organizations play a big role in two ways. In one way, when agenda setting and decision making are international in origin, international organizations play a critical role in implementation largely through the political stream. In the other way, the more countries rely on external funds for implementation, the greater will be the number of policy windows to facilitate implementation coupling of the streams.

INTERNATIONAL AND COMPARATIVE APPLICATIONS

The MSF has also been employed to explain policy processes in political systems that differ substantially from the original system in which the MSF was devised, namely, the political system of the United States. For instance, MSF has been applied to parliamentary systems, ranging from Australia (Beeson and Stone 2013; Tiernan and Burke 2002; Lovell 2016), Belgium (Vanhercke 2009), Canada (Blankenau 2001), Germany (Storch and Winkel 2013; Zohlnhöfer 2016) and Italy (Natali 2004) to India (Liu and Jayakar 2012; Sharma 2008). We also find a limited number of contributions applying MSF to policymaking processes in autocracies: for instance, Iran (Jafari et al. 2017) and China (Liu and Jayakar 2012; Zhou and Feng 2014; Zhu 2008). But the framework's applicability is not confined to politics at the level of the nation-state. Rather, MSF has proved to be applicable to subnational (Dudley 2013; Lieberman 2002; Liu et al. 2010; Oborn, Barrett, and Exworthy 2011; Ridde 2009; Robinson and Eller 2010) and, increasingly, to international (EU) levels (see Bache 2013; Cairney 2009; Copeland and James 2014; Saurugger and Terpan 2016).

Depending on how much the political system analyzed differs from the US presidential one, it is necessary to adapt the framework to different degrees. Parliamentary systems necessitate fewer adaptations, whereas policymaking in autocracies requires more encompassing modifications. The adaptations necessary to make the MSF applicable to EU policymaking is somewhere in between these extremes. Nonetheless, these adaptation requirements have scarcely been addressed explicitly and systematically. Focusing on the political systems that have gained most scientific attention in non-US MSF applications (i.e., parliamentary systems and the EU), we discuss some promising adaptations that have been suggested.

Parliamentary Systems

Compared to the US presidential system, parliamentary systems have been described as more "orderly" (Zahariadis 2003, 1), and thus less well suited for MSF analysis. In parliamentary democracies, governments depend on the confidence of the majority in parliament to a considerable degree. This implies that party discipline tends to play a much larger role in these systems compared with in the US one. Therefore, parties are the key political actors in most parliamentary systems although they do not figure very prominently in the original formulation of the MSF. Moreover, parties in many parliamentary systems used to be programmatically more coherent than their US counterparts.

Does the assumption that policymakers have unclear policy preferences hold for these actors? Although it cannot be denied that many parties in parliamentary (and many presidential) systems have some basic programmatic positions, these are less and less able to guide concrete policy choices (see Herweg, Huß, and Zohlnhöfer 2015). In other words, although parties might in principle be conservative, liberal, or socialist, it is often very difficult to derive preferences on specific policy proposals from these ideological positions. Therefore, the specific policy preferences of parties in parliamentary systems can be regarded as equally unclear as those of their US counterparts, particularly in recent years.

Nonetheless, the MSF must be adapted to the important role political parties play in parliamentary systems (cf. Zahariadis 2003). The literature on political parties suggests that parties pursue three goals (Strøm 1990): they want to win votes, get into office, and get their preferred policies adopted. Thus, political parties fill different roles at different times and should be included in more than one stream (Herweg, Huß, and Zohlnhöfer 2015; see also Novotný and Polášek 2016).

On the one hand, parties' policy experts are often members of the policy community. They participate in the softening-up process by proposing their ideas, criticizing proposals of other members, and recombining proposals (see the examples in Zohlnhöfer and Huß 2016). Party ideology could play some role here insofar as a party's policy experts will be more likely to support proposals that can be attached to the basic party ideology or that address already well-known core positions of that party (Herweg, Huß, and Zohlnhöfer 2015). Moreover, these policy experts can play an important role in bringing viable policy alternatives to the parties. On the other hand, the party leadership is active in the political stream, where it seeks to organize majorities for policy adoption. In the political stream, party discipline and coalitions, which are typical of many parliamentary systems, are particularly relevant (especially during decision coupling) because political entrepreneurs seeking to obtain majorities will not focus on individual policymakers but rather on party leaders in these systems. In cases in which the political entrepreneur is a member of the governing party or coalition, this is certainly an advantage, while it tends to be a disadvantage for political entrepreneurs from opposition parties.

The fact that parties—and interest groups (Rozbicka and Spohr 2016)—are relevant in two streams does not contradict the assumption of independence of streams as long as the two roles are kept distinct analytically. Moreover, in the case of parties, the different roles are filled by different actors: policy experts in the policy stream and party leadership in the political stream.

European Union

EU policy processes are astonishingly well captured by the features of organized anarchies (Peters 1994; Richardson 2006; Natali 2004; Corbett 2005). Although this similarity qualifies the MSF for being a promising analytical framework to study EU policy processes (see Ackrill, Kay, and Zahariadis 2013), it was only in 2008 that Zahariadis addressed the question of which adaptation requirements arise if the MSF is applied to EU decision making. With regard to the policy areas or issues covered, MSF has since been applied widely (though to different degrees), ranging from economic policy (Borrás and Radaelli 2013; Copeland and James 2014; Huisman and de Jong 2014; Sarmiento-Mirwaldt 2015; Saurugger and Terpan 2016), energy policy (Herweg 2016b; Jegen and Mérand 2013; Maltby 2013), sugar policy (Ackrill and Kay 2011), quality of life (Bache 2013), visa liberalization (Bürgin 2013), and children's rights (Iusmen 2013) to counterterrorism (Kaunert and Giovanna 2010) and defense policy (Jegen and Mérand 2013).

In line with the findings on MSF applications in general (Cairney and Jones 2016; Jones et al. 2016), these contributions do not build on a shared definition of the framework's key concepts. Most obviously, though not exclusively, this applies to the political stream. Nonetheless, in the thirteen EU applications referred to above, we find six articles that do not include a theoretically derived definition of the political stream, and each of the remaining seven articles introduces a different and only partly overlapping definition (Herweg and Zahariadis 2017).

The concept that has gained most attention is the policy window (which refers to both the agenda window and the decision window in our terminology) (cf. Ackrill and Kay 2011; Huisman and de Jong 2014; Saurugger and Terpan 2016). Ackrill and Kay (2011, 75), for instance, introduce the concept of institutional ambiguity in order to address the question why decision windows do not close as quickly as predicted by Kingdon (2011). They define institutional ambiguity as "a policy-making environment of overlapping institutions lacking a clear hierarchy." According to the authors, various policy issues fall in the realm of more than one directorate-general (or policy area) without prioritizing one directorate-general over the other(s). Owing to institutional interconnectedness, a change in the policy issue in one policy area can trigger change in that issue in related policy areas. Ackrill and Kay (2011) refer to this kind of reform pressure as endogenous spillover, whereas exogenous spillover resembles Kingdon's idea that change occurs in institutionally unrelated policy areas.

In terms of theory building, Herweg (2017) presents the most elaborate attempt to transfer the MSF to EU agenda setting and decision making. Building on Zahariadis (2008a), she systematically defines functional equivalents of the MSF's key concepts at the EU level and applies Herweg, Huß, and Zohlnhöfer's (2015) suggestion to differentiate between agenda windows and decision windows. She also explicitly derives and tests hypotheses, using EU natural gas market policy between the mid-1980s and late-2000s as a case study.

Foreign Policy/International Relations

Zahariadis (2005), Mazzar (2007), Travis and Zahariadis (2002), and Durant and Diehl (1989) probe the utility of MSF in foreign policy. They find that MSF is a good candidate to bridge the divide between domestic and foreign policy. The key problem is to link domestic and external variables. Despite differences regarding the ability of interest groups and corporate actors to access the foreign policy establishment of a particular country, particularly those representing or having extensive ties to foreign interests, domestic concerns and actors assess and filter external threats while pursuing their own domestic pet projects. Ultimately, foreign policy outcomes need to be acceptable to domestic audiences who will ratify the solutions. The external environment plays a role, but externally generated problems or solutions still need to be domestically interpreted. Policy entrepreneurs play a major part in coupling, just like in the case of domestic policies (Blavoukos and Bourantonis 2012; Hamson 2014). Having started as an explanation of domestic policy in a "disorderly" presidential democracy, MSF proves to be useful even in small, parliamentary democracies, such as Greece, and in foreign policy where participation is less fluid.

Investigating Greek foreign policy, Zahariadis (2005) probes the utility and explanatory power of three lenses, MSF, rational internationalism, and two-level games, yielding some intriguing findings. Conceptualizing the dependent variable as degree of confrontational or cooperative policy, to avoid idiosyncratic explanations he finds that although MSF provides the better overall fit because it more accurately explains a greater number of occurrences, it systematically underexplains cooperative policy. More recently, Zahariadis (2015) adds the role of emotion as a tool for anchoring foreign policies around specific options, making it exceedingly difficult to take corrective action even when there is widespread agreement that the policy is not producing desirable results.

At the international/systemic level of analysis, Lipson (2007) explains changes in peacekeeping as the result of policy entrepreneurs' linking of a solution (peacekeeping) to a problem (intrastate conflicts) in the context of a policy window created by the ending of the Cold War. More recently, Lipson (2012) looks at administrative reforms in UN peacekeeping. He outlines how lenses of rational design, principal-agent relations, sociological institutionalism, and garbage can processes provide divergent explanations. Examining in depth the case of matrix management operations, he argues that the creation of Integrated Operational Teams in the UN Secretariat is consistent with garbage can expectations. Bossong (2013) focuses on the utility of policy windows and the ensuing narratives and finds MSF to be a useful tool to analyze patterns of agenda setting (as opposed to particular events) and nonincremental policy change in the fields of international security and European counterterrorism.

LIMITATIONS

Despite its wide appeal among policy analysts, MSF has also generated substantial criticism. We discuss the most relevant points in the following (cf. also Zohlnhöfer and Rüb 2016b, 6–10).

Are the Streams Really Independent?

MSF argues that although the streams are not completely independent of one another, they can be viewed as each having a life of its own. Participants drift in and out of decisions, making some choices more likely than others. Problems rise and fall on the government's agenda regardless of whether they are solvable or have been solved. Similarly, people generate solutions, not necessarily because they have identified a particular problem, but because the solution happens to answer a problem that fits their values, beliefs, or material well-being. Changes in the political stream take place whether or not problems facing the nation have changed. Thus, each stream seems to obey its own rules and flows largely independently of the others (Sager and Rielle, 2013).

Critics, including Mucciaroni (1992, 2013) and Robinson and Eller (2010), disagree, questioning the appropriateness of conceptualizing independent streams. The streams can be more fruitfully viewed as interdependent, Mucciaroni maintains, and changes in one stream can trigger or reinforce changes in another. For example, a focusing event, like the public's response to a terrorist attack, may well have an impact on the national mood.

Stream independence is a conceptual device. It has the advantage of enabling researchers to uncover rather than assume rationality. Not all solutions are developed in response to clearly defined problems; rather, sometimes policies are in search of a rationale or they solve no problems (Stone, 2011;

Zahariadis, 2003). Edelman (1988) goes as far as to argue that solutions create problems. Consider, for example, the decision by the Bush administration in 2003 to go to war in Iraq. Whereas the initial rationale had to do with what was claimed to be the clear and imminent danger posed by Saddam Hussein's possession of weapons of mass destruction, subsequent rationalizations emphasized connections to terrorists, the liberation of Iraq, and democratization and nation building. The solution remained the same—depose Saddam—while the problem constantly drifted in search of an anchor. As insiders, such as Richard Clarke (2004), the former counterterrorism "czar," pointed out later, the administration was fixated on Saddam long before the attack. The question was not whether but when and how to do it.

It is impossible to make the preceding argument in the absence of stream independence. The key is to specify when policy may be in search of rationale, but we cannot logically make this statement or explain why unless we differentiate between the development of problems and their solutions. Besides, assumptions are simplifications of reality. If policy analysts readily accept the assumption that people do not have to be rational, that they only need to act *as if* they are rational, analysts can also accept the assumption that streams don't have to be independent, they only need to flow *as if* they are independent.

Is MSF Clear Enough to Be Proven Wrong?

The question of whether MSF is clear enough to be proven wrong, put forward by Kuhlmann (2016) among others, points to two related criticisms. Critics claim that MSF's core concepts lack clear definitions and they do not generate falsifiable hypotheses (for example, Sabatier 2007). Regarding the latter criticism, it is true that Kingdon in his original formulation of the framework did not derive hypotheses. This does not mean, however, that it is impossible to derive hypotheses. In subsequent work, at least some researchers have put forward hypotheses, although many of these were rather case specific (e.g., Blankenau 2001; Boscarino 2009; Saurugger and Terpan 2016). More recently, more general MSF hypotheses have been made explicit, and we present some of these hypotheses in this chapter. We hope that these hypotheses will guide future MSF applications.

The metaphorical language of the approach (Béland and Howlett 2016, 223) poses more intricate problems. Streams and windows, primeval soups and criteria of survival, national mood and focusing events are all somewhat difficult to measure and seem to invite storytelling rather than rigorous empirical analysis. And although it cannot be denied that a significant part of MSF-related research has indeed been plagued by this problem (see the overview in Jones et al. 2016), this does not have to be the case. Rather, as Herweg's (2016a) discussion of policy communities shows, MSF's concepts can be defined with substantial precision. We have tried to move forward in the same direction in this chapter by providing additional conceptual groundwork that, for example, permits more precise analysis of when the individual streams are ready for coupling.

Are Policy Entrepreneurs More Rational Than Policymakers?

Some critics argue that the assumptions about policymakers and policy entrepreneurs do not easily fit together. Policymakers are assumed to have unclear preferences, which means that they do not really know which policies they favor; policy entrepreneurs are expected to know exactly what they want—namely, to get their pet proposals adopted. So it might seem that according to the MSF some people have policy preferences while others do not. That would indeed be a problematic inconsistency.

However, this apparent contradiction can be resolved (Zohlnhöfer and Rüb 2016b, 7). Policy entrepreneurs should not be considered as acting more rationally than average policymakers. Kingdon (2011, 183) already warned us not to "paint these entrepreneurs as superhumanly clever." Rather, on the one hand, MSF presumes that *all* actors, policymakers and policy entrepreneurs, have unclear preferences concerning the vast majority of policies. On the other hand, any policymaker can become a policy entrepreneur for a specific proposal. The exact reasons why a policymaker catches fire for a particular issue can vary: personal reasons, party ideology, or advancing a political career. Whatever the reason, it is unlikely that there is a great amount of rationality involved when it comes to explaining who pushes for the adoption of a particular policy project and not for another one. Most importantly, however, while policy entrepreneurs (sometimes even irrationally) pursue pet projects, they are likely to have entirely unclear preferences with regard to all other issue areas that are under discussion in parallel.

Are Elements Lacking from MSF?

Another important criticism of MSF is that it lacks some elements. Of particular relevance seem to be political institutions and path dependence (for example, Mucciaroni 2013; Rüb 2014). Although until recently it has been tried only rarely (see Béland 2005; Ness and Mistretta 2009; and Blankenau 2001), nothing in the MSF per se precludes the integration of these elements into the framework—as we have shown in this chapter. Institutions affect the integration of policy communities and define whose agreement a political entrepreneur must obtain during decision coupling. Similarly, path dependence can be understood as one of the criteria of survival that affect a proposal's chances of becoming a viable policy alternative. Alternatively, Spohr (2016) suggests a way to combine MSF with Historical Institutionalism.

Another relevant factor that is missing from MSF—and many other policy process theories—is the mass media (Rüb 2014). The way the media report on certain issues, which issues they take up, and which they neglect are likely to have an important impact on the political agenda. The media's role is indeed a topic that has not yet been theorized from an MSF perspective. But it is a matter of lack of empirical application and not theoretical omission.

Can Hypotheses Generated by the MSF Be Tested in Medium- to Large-*N* Studies?

Methodological pluralism may be a virtue, but medium- to large-*n* analyses add weight to a lens's explanatory power in ways that case studies do not. It is noteworthy in this context that the vast majority of MSF studies are case studies (Jones et al. 2016; Rawat and Morris 2016), whereas the number of MSF-guided medium- to large-*n* applications is in the low-single-digit percentage range (Engler and Herweg 2016). Notwithstanding this disparity between case studies and medium- to large-*n* applications, there seems to be broad agreement in the literature that it would be useful to test MSF in a larger sample size (cf. Jones et al. 2016; Zohlnhöfer 2016). How could this be done?

Because quantitative applications are the exception, not the rule, we highlight conceptual considerations exclusively faced by quantitative applications (for the following, see Engler and Herweg 2016). More specifically, we focus on the choice of method. To date, the methods applied in quantitative and medium- to large-*n* MSF applications are regression analysis (for examples, see Liu et al. 2011; Travis and Zahariadis 2002) and qualitative comparative analysis (QCA) (for examples, see Sager and Rielle 2013; Sager and Thomann 2016). Both methods have different advantages and drawbacks in terms of accurately modeling the framework.

Compared to QCA, logistic regression analysis and event history analysis adequately capture hypotheses on individual elements of the MSF. Mirroring the framework's probabilistic logic, the MSF, for instance, hypothesizes "If a policy window opens, agenda change becomes more likely." Building on linear algebra, regression analysis allows for testing "The wider a policy window is open, the more the agenda changes," or with regard to logistic (or event history) analysis, "If a policy window opens, agenda change becomes more likely (the time until agenda change decreases)." Instead, QCA builds on Boolean algebra (and thus on a deterministic logic) and tests "If a policy window opens, the agenda changes." Furthermore, logistic regression analysis and event history analysis manage to capture the MSF's idea that temporality matters by pooling time series and cross-section data and (in case of event history analysis) by modeling an element's duration effect (the time until agenda change occurs).

However, assessing the combined effect of the framework's five key concepts on agenda change is next to impossible in a regression setting because this leaves researchers with the task of interpreting a specification of thirty-one independent variables, including a fivefold and various four-, three-, and twofold interaction terms. A solution might be to test the MSF only partially. Liu et al. (2011), for instance, test whether the opening of a window in the problem stream (indicated by a change in indicators and the occurrence of focusing events and feedback dealing with climate change) is correlated with change in the agenda of the US Congress (measured by congressional hearings dealing with climate change).

In terms of testing how the interplay of different MSF concepts affects agenda change, QCA is the method of choice because it allows for testing which (combinations of) factors are necessary/sufficient for agenda change. Consequently, given their different strengths and weaknesses, regression analysis and QCA should not be treated as substitutes but as complements (Thiem, Baumgartner, and Bol 2016). Regardless of the choice of method, MSF applications must explicitly define the units of analysis, their dependent and independent variables, and the causal mechanisms they expect because they vary with the policy stage analyzed.

PROSPECTS

The MSF has gained a lot of momentum recently. Not only is the number of empirical applications high and rising but also there have been numerous attempts to refine the framework theoretically. Nonetheless, more work is needed. Four issues deserve particular attention in future MSF-related research: (1) further theoretical and definitional refinement; (2) more systematic empirical applications; (3) an adaptation and empirical application of the framework to autocratic regimes; and (4) more MSF-inspired research on global policy.

Refine Hypotheses and More Clearly Operationalize Concepts

The operational definitions of when the streams are ready for coupling need to be further refined. This is particularly true with regard to the political stream. As we argue above, the political stream is ready for (agenda) coupling when a relevant actor is receptive to a proposal and is willing to act as political entrepreneur. The necessary (parliamentary) majorities can be stitched together after the item has been placed high on the government's agenda. But what exactly does it mean to be receptive to a proposal? Similarly, we argue that the policy stream is ready for coupling when a viable policy alternative is available. But how exactly do we know when a policy alternative is viable? Similar efforts could be directed at other core concepts of the framework, like policy windows, policy or political entrepreneurs, and so forth. It may not always be possible to come to definitions that leave no room for interpretation—precisely because of the ambiguity of political life that is the framework's starting point. But we can certainly try to develop more precise definitions and measurements.

Moreover, the recent theoretical advances have hardly been tested empirically and are likely to need further elaboration. In particular, we probably need more well-defined hypotheses derived from the framework. What is more, the policy stages after decision making have rarely been theorized from an MSF perspective (but see Howlett, McConnell, and Perl 2015; Zahariadis and Exadaktylos 2016). More work in this direction would also be extremely helpful to advance the MSF to a framework capable of explaining the complete policy process.

Conduct More Systematic Empirical Analysis

Analysis is viewed here in terms of both method and context. The recent literature reviews (Jones et al. 2016; Cairney and Jones 2016; Rawat and Morris 2016; see also Weible and Schlager 2016) amply demonstrate the point that the overwhelming majority of empirical applications are case studies, and most of them do not speak to each other. Thus, MSF scholars need to find ways to test the framework more systematically. Despite a number of obstacles, researchers should aim at quantitatively testing empirical implications of MSF thinking (see Engler and Herweg 2016). More hypotheses make it easier to collect or find data and thus facilitate a wider range of analytical techniques to probe them. In this regard, the recent surge in hypotheses generated by the MSF is very helpful.

Systematic testing is not necessarily limited to the application of quantitative techniques, however. We should also find ways to use the large number of existing case studies and even more importantly produce case studies that are suitable for knowledge accumulation. Thus, on the one hand, literature reviews that provide more detailed assessments of the cumulative results of existing case studies would be helpful. On the other hand, we should develop criteria that MSF-inspired case studies need to fulfill to ensure their results can be compared with others. Moreover, hypotheses should be tested not only in cases where a change occurred but also in cases characterized by continuity (as an example, see Clark 2004).

In terms of context, scholarship can more sharply differentiate between issues and levels of governance. MSF is theorized to be applicable in particular contexts—national policymaking, for instance—but is it equally applicable to certain types of issues regardless of level? If MSF can explain agenda items across issues within the same level (national context), can it explain with similar ease the same issue across (national, subnational, and international) levels? Surely, the same fundamental assumptions about preferences, participation, and technology apply to some issues (e.g., structural reforms) across national, international, and subnational levels. Zahariadis (2016) mentions this intriguing possibility and constructs a matrix to classify the different types of theorizing. Future research may systematically elaborate on the logic and adaptations needed to accomplish this task.

Apply MSF to Nondemocratic Political Systems

As we have seen, MSF has rarely been applied to agenda setting and policymaking in nondemocratic regimes. In general, the framework should be applicable in these settings, too. Autocratic regimes need to couple problems to solutions and need to decide on which problems or policy projects they want to invest their time and resources—which might be even more limited as the centralization of an autocratic regime increases. In the absence of, or under conditions of limited, political freedom, the processes in the three streams are likely to differ from the processes we observe in democratic systems (see, for example, Liu and Jayakar 2012; Zhu 2008). Policy communities might be smaller, and the most important criterion of survival is probably acquiescence of the dictator. Problem brokers might need to find different ways to convince policymakers of their problem definition, and the national mood and changes in government are unlikely to play an equally important role in autocracies. But the central idea that policies need to be coupled to some kind of problem in certain political contexts can be easily applied in nondemocratic settings. Thus, future research should discuss which characteristics of autocratic regimes require adaptations of the MSF and suggest relevant modifications that would then need to be systematically tested.

Theorize and Apply MSF in Global Contexts

Policymaking beyond the nation-state is a particularly suitable field for the application of the MSF because of fluid conditions (in terms of issues and institutions). If we accept the premise that international organizations are semiautonomous bureaucracies (Barnett and Finnemore 2004), MSF can provide interesting explanations about why and how they make the decisions they do. For example, agenda setting or decision making in global institutions, such as the Security Council, is extremely fluid not only because of (mostly) rotating participation but also because of significant variability in problem definitions and focusing events. Famines as focusing events can sway the global community into action when no such appetite existed before, for example, Ethiopia in the mid-1980s. MSF could also provide fertile theoretical ground for international relations theorists who view transnational activism as external leverage over domestic opponents (e.g., Keck and Sikkink 1998). Activism may be conceptualized as an entrepreneurial activity seeking to couple problems and solutions to receptive political audiences. Transnational activists act as policy entrepreneurs—they reframe issues, build coalitions, lobby, protest, and link internal contention to international conflict (Tarrow 2005). Their strategies could enrich MSF not only by pointing out the obvious venue-shopping implications but also by illuminating the benefits and drawbacks of national policymaking.

CONCLUSION

The academic debate on the MSF is currently more lively and exciting than it has ever been before. A remarkable number of suggestions for the theoretical advancement of the MSF has been published, many of which we have presented in this chapter. Nonetheless, more steps need to be taken in the coming years, including the further refinement of operational definitions of the framework's key terms, the empirical application of the various theoretical innovations that have been suggested, as well as adaptation of the MSF to more contexts such as authoritarian regimes and international relations. The surge in the literature of the last few years makes it clear that there is a lot to be learned about agenda setting and policymaking in various contexts by adapting and applying the MSF.

REFERENCES

Aberbach, Joel D., and Tom Christensen. 2014. "Why Reforms So Often Disappoint." *American Journal of Public Administration* 44:3–16.

Ackrill, Robert, and Adrian Kay. 2011. "Multiple Streams in EU Policymaking: The Case of the 2005 Sugar Reform." *Journal of European Public Policy* 18:72–89.

Ackrill, Robert, Adrian Kay, and Nikolaos Zahariadis. 2013. "Ambiguity, Multiple Streams, and EU Policy." *Journal of European Public Policy* 20:871–887.

Bache, Ian. 2013. "Measuring Quality of Life for Public Policy: An Idea Whose Time Has Come? Agenda-Setting Dynamics in the European Union." *Journal of European Public Policy* 20:21–38.

Baier, Vicki E., James G. March, and Harald Sætren. 1986. "Implementation and Ambiguity." *Scandinavian Journal of Management Studies* 2:197–212.

Barnett, Michael, and Martha Finnemore. 2004. *Rules for the World: International Organizations in Global Politics*. Ithaca, NY: Cornell University Press.

Baumgartner, Frank R., Christian Breunig, Christoffer Green-Pedersen, Bryan D. Jones, Peter B. Mortensen, Michiel Nuytemans, and Stefaan Walgrave. 2009. "Punctuated Equilibrium in Comparative Perspective." *American Journal of Political Science* 53:603–620.

Beeson, Mark, and Diane Stone. 2013. "The Changing Fortunes of a Policy Entrepreneur: The Case of Ross Garnaut." *Australian Journal of Political Science* 48:1–14.

Béland, Daniel. 2005. "Ideas and Social Policy: An Institutionalist Perspective." *Social Policy & Administration* 39:1–18.

———. 2009. "Gender, Ideational Analysis, and Social Policy." *Social Politics* 16:558–581.

———. 2016. "Kingdon Reconsidered: Ideas, Interests and Institutions in Comparative Policy Analysis." *Journal of Comparative Policy Analysis* 18:228–242.

Béland, Daniel, and Michael Howlett. 2016. "The Role and Impact of the Multiple-Streams Approach in Comparative Policy Analysis." *Journal of Comparative Policy Analysis* 18:221–227.

Birkland, Thomas A. 1997. *After Disaster: Agenda-Setting, Public Policy and Focusing Events.* Washington, DC: Georgetown University Press.

Birkland, Thomas A., and Megan K. Warnement. 2016. "Refining the Idea of Focusing Events in the Multiple-Streams Framework." In *Decision-Making under Ambiguity and Time Constraints: Assessing the Multiple-Streams Framework,* edited by Reimut Zohlnhöfer and Friedbert W. Rüb, 91–107. Colchester, UK: ECPR Press.

Blankenau, Joe. 2001. "The Fate of National Health Insurance in Canada and the United States: A Multiple Streams Explanation." *Policy Studies Journal* 29:38–55.

Blavoukos, Spyros, and Dimitris Bourantonis, 2012. "Policy Entrepreneurs and Foreign Policy Change: The Greek–Turkish Rapprochement in the 1990s." *Government and Opposition* 47:597–617.

Borrás, Susana, and Claudio Radaelli. 2011. "The Politics of Governance Architectures: Creation, Change and Effects of the EU Lisbon Strategy." *Journal of European Public Policy* 18:463–484.

Boscarino, Jessica E. 2009. "Surfing for Problems: Advocacy Group Strategy in US Forestry Policy." *Policy Studies Journal* 37:415–434.

Bossong, Raphael. 2013. *The Evolution of EU Counter-Terrorism: European Security Policy after 9/11.* London: Routledge.

Boswell, Christina, and Eugénia Rodrigues. 2016. "Policies, Politics and Organisational Problems: Multiple Streams and the Implementation of Targets in UK Government." *Policy & Politics* 44:507–524.

Bürgin, Alexander. 2013. "Salience, Path Dependency and the Coalition between the European Commission and the Danish Council Presidency: Why the EU Opened a Visa Liberalisation Process with Turkey." *European Integration Online Papers* 17:1–19.

Cairney, Paul. 2009. "The Role of Ideas in Policy Transfer: The Case of UK Smoking Bans since Devolution." *Journal of European Public Policy* 16:471–488.

Cairney, Paul, and Michael D. Jones. 2016. "Kingdon's Multiple Streams Approach: What Is the Empirical Impact of This Universal Theory?" *Policy Studies Journal* 44:37–58.

Clark, Brad T. 2004. "Agenda-Setting and Issue Dynamics: Dam Breaching on the Lower Snake River." *Society & Natural Resources* 17:599–609.

Clarke, Richard A. 2004. *Against All Enemies.* New York: Free Press.

Cohen, Michael D., James G. March, and Johan P. Olsen. 1972. "A Garbage Can Model of Organizational Choice." *Administrative Science Quarterly* 17:1–25.

Copeland, Paul, and Scott James. 2014. "Policy Windows, Ambiguity and Commission Entrepreneurship: Explaining the Relaunch of the European Union's Economic Agenda." *Journal of European Public Policy* 21:1–19.

Corbett, Anne. 2005. *Universities and the Europe of Knowledge.* New York: Palgrave.

Dudley, Geoff. 2013. "Why Do Ideas Succeed and Fail over Time? The Role of Narratives in Policy Windows and the Case of the London Congestion Charge." *Journal of European Public Policy* 20:1139–1156.

Durant, Robert F., and Paul F. Diehl. 1989. "Agendas, Alternatives, and Public Policy: Lessons from the US Foreign Policy Arena." *Journal of Public Policy* 9:179–205.

Edelman, Murray. 1988. *Constructing the Political Spectacle.* Chicago: University of Chicago Press.

Engler, Fabian, and Nicole Herweg. 2016. "Of Barriers to Entry for Quantitative Multiple Streams Applications: Methodologic and Conceptual Considerations." Paper presented at the 2016 ECPR General Conference, Prague, Czech Republic, September 7–10, 2016.

Exworthy, Mark, and Martin Powell. 2004. "Big Windows and Little Windows: Implementation in the 'Congested State.'" *Public Administration* 84:263–281.

Feldman, Martha S. 1989. *Order without Design: Information Production and Policymaking.* Stanford, CA: Stanford University Press.

Geva-May, Iris. 2004. "Riding the Wave of Opportunity: Termination in Public Policy." *Journal of Public Administration Research and Theory* 14:309–333.

Hamson, Fen Osler. 2014. "The Importance of Coupling: The Limited Test Ban Negotiations." In *Banning the Bang or the Bomb? Negotiating the Nuclear Test Ban Regime,* edited by I. William Zartman, Paul Meertz, and Mordechai Melamud, 75–95. Cambridge: Cambridge University Press.

Herweg, Nicole. 2016a. "Clarifying the Concept of Policy-Communities in the Multiple-Streams Framework." In *Decision-Making under Ambiguity and Time Constraints: Assessing the Multiple-Streams Framework,* edited by Reimut Zohlnhöfer and Friedbert W. Rüb, 125–145. Colchester, UK: ECPR Press.

———. 2016b. "Explaining European Agenda-Setting Using the Multiple Streams Framework: The Case of European Natural Gas Regulation." *Policy Sciences* 49:13–33.

———. 2017. *European Union Policy-Making: The Regulatory Shift in Natural Gas Market Policy.* Bastingstoke, UK: Palgrave Macmillan.

Herweg, Nicole, Christian Huß, and Reimut Zohlnhöfer. 2015. "Straightening the Three Streams: Theorizing Extensions of the Multiple Streams Framework." *European Journal of Political Research* 54:435–449.

Herweg, Nicole, and Nikolaos Zahariadis. 2017. "Multiple Streams." In *The Routledge Handbook of European Public Policy,* edited by Nikolaos Zahariadis and Laurie A. Buonanno. New York: Routledge.

Howlett, Michael, Allan McConnell, and Anthony Perl. 2015. "Streams and Stages: Reconciling Kingdon and Policy Process Theory." *European Journal of Political Research* 54:419–434.

Huisman, Jeroen, and Dorrit de Jong. 2014. "The Construction of the European Institute of Innovation and Technology: The Realisation of an Ambiguous Policy Idea." *Journal of European Integration* 36:357–374.

Iusmen, Ingi. 2013. "Policy Entrepreneurship and Eastern Enlargement: The Case of EU Children's Rights Policy." *Comparative European Politics* 11:511–529.

Jafari, Hasan, Abolghasem Pourreza, AbouAli Vedadhir, and Ebrahim Jaafaripooyan. 2016. "Application of the Multiple Streams Model in Analysing the New Population Policies Agenda-Setting in Iran." *Quality and Quantity.*

Jegen, Maya, and Frédéric Mérand. 2013. "Constructive Ambiguity: Comparing the EU's Energy and Defence Policies." *West European Politics* 37:182–203.

Jones, Bryan D. 2001. *Politics and the Architecture of Choice: Bounded Rationality and Governance.* Chicago: University of Chicago Press.

Jones, Michael D., Holly L. Peterson, Jonathan J. Pierce, Nicole Herweg, Amiel Bernal, Holly Lamberta, and Nikolaos Zahariadis. 2016. "A River Runs through It: A Multiple Streams Meta Review." *Policy Studies Journal* 44:13–36.

Kaunert, Christian, and Marina Della Giovanna. 2010. "Post-9/11 EU Counter-Terrorist Financing Cooperation: Differentiating Supranational Policy Entrepreneurship by the Commission and the Council Secretariat." *European Security* 19:275–295.

Keck, Margaret, and Kathryn Sikkink. 1998. *Activists Beyond Borders: Advocacy Networks in International Politics.* Ithaca, NY: Cornell University Press.

Keeler, John T. S. 1993. "Opening the Window for Reform. Mandates, Crises, and Extraordinary Policymaking." *Comparative Political Studies* 25:433–486.

Kingdon, John W. 2011. *Agendas, Alternatives, and Public Policy.* New York: Longman.

Knaggård, Åsa. 2015. "The Multiple Streams Framework and the Problem Broker." *European Journal of Political Research* 54:450–465.

———. 2016. "Framing the Problem: Knowledge-Brokers in the Multiple-Streams Framework." In *Decision-Making under Ambiguity and Time Constraints. Assessing the Multiple-Streams Framework,* edited by Reimut Zohlnhöfer and Friedbert W. Rüb, 109–123. Colchester, UK: ECPR Press.

Knill, Christoph, and Jale Tosun. 2012. *Public Policy: A New Introduction.* Basingstoke, UK: Palgrave Macmillan.

Kuhlmann, Johanna. 2016. "Clear Enough to Be Proven Wrong? Assessing the Influence of the Concept of Bounded Rationality within the Multiple Streams Framework." In *Decision-Making under Ambiguity and Time Constraints: Assessing the Multiple Streams Framework,* edited by Reimut Zohlnhöfer and Friedbert W. Rüb, 35–50. Colchester, UK: ECPR Press.

Lieberman, Joyce M. 2002. "Three Streams and Four Policy Entrepreneurs Converge: A Policy Window Opens." *Education and Urban Society* 34:438–450.

Lipson, Michael. 2007. "A 'Garbage Can Model' of UN Peacekeeping." *Global Governance* 13:79–97.

———. 2012. "Peacekeeping Reform: Managing Change in an Organized Anarchy." *Journal of Intervention and Statebuilding* 6:279–298.

Liu, Chun, and Krishna Jayakar. 2012. "The Evolution of Telecommunications Policy-Making: Comparative Analysis of China and India." *Telecommunications Policy* 36:13–28.

Liu, Xinsheng, Eric Lindquist, Arnold Vedelitz, and Kenneth Vincent. 2010. "Understanding Local Policymaking: Policy Elites' Perceptions of Local Agenda Setting and Alternative Policy Selection." *Policy Studies Journal* 38:69–91.

———. 2011. "Explaining Media and Congressional Attention to Global Climate Change, 1969–2005: An Empirical Test of Agenda-Setting Theory." *Political Research Quarterly* 64:405–419.

Lovell, Heather. 2016. "The Role of International Policy Transfer within the Multiple Streams Approach: The Case of Smart Electricity Metering in Australia." *Public Administration* 94:754–768.

Maltby, Tomas. 2013. "European Union Energy Policy Integration: A Case of European Commission Policy Entrepreneurship and Increasing Supranationalism." *Energy Policy* 55:435–444.

March, James G., and Herbert A. Simon. 1958. *Organizations.* New York: Wiley.

Matland, Richard E. 1995. "Synthesizing the Implementation Literature: The Ambiguity-Conflict Model of Policy Implementation." *Journal of Public Administration Research and Theory* 5:145–174.

Mazzar, Michael J. 2007. "The Iraq War and Agenda-Setting." *Foreign Policy Analysis* 3:1–24.

Mintrom, Michael, and Philippa Norman. 2009. "Policy Entrepreneurship and Policy Change." *Policy Studies Journal* 37:649–667.

Mucciaroni, Gary. 1992. "The Garbage Can Model and the Study of Policymaking: A Critique." *Polity* 24:459–482.

———. 2013. "The Garbage Can Model and the Study of the Policymaking Process." In *The Routledge Handbook of Public Policy,* edited by Eduardo Araral, Scott Fritzen, and Michael Howlett, 320–327. London: Routledge.

Mukherjee, Ishani, and Michael Howlett. 2015. "Who Is a Stream? Epistemic Communities, Instrument Constituencies and Advocacy Coalitions in Public Policymaking." *Politics and Governance* 3:65–75.

Natali, David. 2004. "Europeanization, Policy Areas, and Creative Opportunism: The Politics of Welfare State Reforms in Italy." *Journal of European Public Policy* 11:1077–1095.

Ness, Eric C., and Molly A. Mistretta. 2009. "Policy Adoption in North Carolina and Tennessee: A Comparative Case Study of Lottery Beneficiaries." *Review of Higher Education* 32:489–514.

Novotný, Vilém, and Martin Polášek. 2016. "Multiple Streams Approach and Political Parties: Modernization of Czech Social Democracy." *Policy Sciences* 49:89–105.

Oborn, Eivor, Michael Barrett, and Mark Exworthy. 2011. "Policy Entrepreneurship in the Development of Public Sector Strategy: The Case of London Health Reform." *Public Administration* 89:325–344.

Peters, B. Guy. 1994. "Agenda-Setting in the European Community." *Journal of European Public Policy* 1:9–26.

Rawat, Pragati, and John Charles Morris. 2016. "Kingdon's 'Streams' Model at Thirty: Still Relevant in the 21st Century?" *Politics & Policy* 44:608–638.

Richardson, Jeremy. 2006. "Policymaking in the EU: Interests, Ideas and Garbage Cans of Primeval Soup." In *European Union: Power and Policymaking*, edited by Jeremy Richardson, 3–30. London: Routledge.

Ridde, Valéry. 2009. "Policy Implementation in an African State: An Extension of Kingdon's Multiple Streams Approach." *Public Administration* 87:938–954.

Roberts, Nancy C., and Paula J. King. 1991. "Policy Entrepreneurs: Their Activity Structure and Function in the Policy Process." *Journal of Public Administration Research and Theory* 1:147–175.

Robinson, Scott E., and Warren S. Eller. 2010. "Testing the Separation of Problems and Solutions in Subnational Policy Systems." *Policy Studies Journal* 38:199–216.

Rozbicka, Patrycja, and Florian Spohr. 2016. "Interest Groups in Multiple Streams: Specifying Their Involvement in the Framework." *Policy Sciences* 49:55–69.

Rüb, Friedbert W. 2014. "Multiple-Streams-Ansatz: Grundlagen, Probleme und Kritik." In *Lehrbuch der Politikfeldanalyse*, edited by Klaus Schubert and Nils C. Bandelow, 373–406. München: Oldenbourg.

Sabatier, Paul A. 2007. "Fostering the Development of Policy Theory." In *Theories of the Policy Process*, edited by Paul A. Sabatier, 321–336. Boulder: Westview Press.

Sætren, Harald. 2016. "From Controversial Policy Idea to Successful Program Implementation: The Role of the Policy Entrepreneur, Manipulation Strategy, Program Design, Institutions and Open Policy Windows in Relocating Norwegian Central Agencies." *Policy Sciences* 49:71–88.

Sager, Fritz, and Yvan Rielle. 2013. "Sorting through the Garbage Can: Under What Conditions Do Governments Adopt Policy Programs?" *Policy Sciences* 46:1–21.

Sager, Fritz, and Eva Thomann. 2016. "Multiple Streams in Member State Implementation: Politics, Problem Construction and Policy Paths in Swiss Asylum Policy." *Journal of Public Policy*. 1–28. Published electronically July 12, 2016. doi:https://doi .org/10.1017/S0143814X1600009X.

Sarmiento-Mirwaldt, Katja. 2015. "Can Multiple Streams Predict the Territorial Cohesion Debate in the EU?" *European Urban and Regional Studies* 22:431–445.

Saurugger, Sabine, and Fabien Terpan. 2016. "Do Crises Lead to Policy Change? The Multiple Streams Framework and the European Union's Economic Governance Instruments." *Policy Sciences* 49:33–53.

Sharma, Alankaar. 2008. "Decriminalising Queer Sexualities in India: A Multiple Streams Analysis." *Social Policy and Society* 7:419–431.

Spohr, Florian. 2016. "Explaining Path Dependency and Deviation by Combining Multiple Streams Framework and Historical Institutionalism: A Comparative Analysis of German and Swedish Labor Market Policies." *Journal of Comparative Policy Analysis* 18:257–272.

Stone, Deborah. 2011. *Policy Paradox: The Art of Political Decision-Making.* New York: W. W. Norton.

Storch, Sabine, and Georg Winkel. 2013. "Coupling Climate Change and Forest Policy. A Multiple Streams Analysis of Two German Case Studies." *Forest Policy and Economics* 36:14–26.

Strøm, Kaare. 1990. "A Behavioral Theory of Competitive Political Parties." *American Journal of Political Science* 34:565–598.

Tarrow, Sydney. 2005. *The New Transnational Activism.* Cambridge: Cambridge University Press.

Thiem, Alrik, Michael Baumgartner, and Damien Bol. 2016. "Still Lost in Translation! A Correction of Three Misunderstandings between Configurational Comparativists and Regressional Analysts." *Comparative Political Studies* 49:742–774.

Tiernan, Anne, and Terry Burke. 2002. "A Load of Old Garbage: Applying Garbage-Can Theory to Contemporary Housing Policy." *Australian Journal of Public Administration* 61:86–97.

Travis, Rick, and Nikolaos Zahariadis. 2002. "A Multiple Streams Model of US Foreign Aid Policy." *Policy Studies Journal* 30:495–514.

Vanhercke, Bart. 2009. "The Open Method of Coordination as a Selective Amplifier for Reforming Belgian Pension Policies." In *What We Have Learnt: Advances, Pitfalls and Remaining Questions in OMC Research,* edited by Sandra Kröger. *European Integration Online Papers* 13 (special issue 1): Art. 16. http://eiop.or.at/eiop/texte/2009-016a.htm.

Weible, Christopher M., and Edella Schlager. 2016. "The Multiple Streams Approach at the Theoretical and Empirical Crossroads: An Introduction to a Special Issue." *Policy Studies Journal* 44:5–12.

Wilson, James Q. 1989. *Bureaucracy.* New York: Basic Books.

Zahariadis, Nikolaos. 1992. "To Sell or Not to Sell? Telecommunications Policy in Britain and France." *Journal of Public Policy* 12:355–376.

———. 1995. *Markets, States, and Public Policies: Privatization in Britain and France.* Ann Arbor: University of Michigan Press.

———. 2003. *Ambiguity and Choice in Public Policy: Political Manipulation in Democratic Societies.* Washington, DC: Georgetown University Press.

———. 2005. *Essence of Political Manipulation: Emotion, Institutions, and Greek Foreign Policy.* New York: Peter Lang.

———. 2008a. "Ambiguity and Choice in European Public Policy." *Journal of European Public Policy* 15:514–530.

———. 2008b. "Europeanization as Program Implementation: Effective and Democratic?" *Journal of Comparative Policy Analysis* 10:221–238.

———. 2015. "The Shield of Heracles: Multiple Streams and the Emotional Endowment Effect." *European Journal of Political Research* 54:466–481.

———. 2016. "Bounded Rationality and Garbage Can Models of the Policy Process." In *Contemporary Policy Approaches: Theories, Controversies and Perspectives,* edited by Philippe Zittoun and B. Guy Peters, 155–174. New York: Palgrave Macmillan.

Zahariadis, Nikolaos, and Theofanis Exadaktylos. 2016. "Policies That Succeed and Programs that Fail? Ambiguity, Conflict, and Crisis in Greek Higher Education." *Policy Studies Journal* 44:59–82.

Zhou, Nan, and Feng Feng. 2014. "Applying Multiple Streams Theoretical Framework to College Matriculation Policy Reform for Children of Migrant Workers in China." *Public Policy and Administration Research* 4:1–11.

Zhu, Xufeng. 2008. "Strategy of Chinese Policy Entrepreneurs in the Third Sector: Challenges of 'Technical Infeasibility.'" *Policy Sciences* 41:315–334.

Zohlnhöfer, Reimut. 2009. "How Politics Matter When Policies Change: Understanding Policy Change as a Political Problem." *Journal of Comparative Policy Analysis* 11:97–115.

———. 2016. "Putting Together the Pieces of the Puzzle: Explaining German Labor Market Reforms with a Modified Multiple-Streams Approach." *Policy Studies Journal* 44:83–107.

Zohlnhöfer, Reimut, Nicole Herweg, and Christian Huß. 2016. "Bringing Formal Political Institutions into the Multiple Streams Framework: An Analytical Proposal for Comparative Policy Analysis." *Journal of Comparative Policy Analysis* 18:243–256.

Zohlnhöfer, Reimut, and Christian Huß. 2016. "How Well Does the Multiple-Streams Framework Travel? Evidence from German Case Studies." In *Decision-Making under Ambiguity and Time Constraints: Assessing the Multiple-Streams Framework,* edited by Reimut Zohlnhöfer and Friedbert W. Rüb, 169–188. Colchester, UK: ECPR Press.

Zohlnhöfer, Reimut, and Friedbert W. Rüb, eds. 2016a. *Decision-Making under Ambiguity and Time Constraints: Assessing the Multiple-Streams Framework.* Colchester, UK: ECPR Press.

———. 2016b. "Introduction: Policymaking under Ambiguity and Time Constraints." In *Decision-Making under Ambiguity and Time Constraints: Assessing the Multiple-Streams Framework,* edited by Reimut Zohlnhöfer and Friedbert W. Rüb, 1–17. Colchester, UK: ECPR Press.

2

Punctuated Equilibrium Theory: Explaining Stability and Change in Public Policymaking

FRANK R. BAUMGARTNER, BRYAN D. JONES, AND PETER B. MORTENSEN

Punctuated Equilibrium Theory (PET) seeks to explain a simple observation: although generally marked by stability and incrementalism, political processes occasionally produce large-scale departures from the past. Stasis, rather than crisis, typically characterizes most policy areas, but crises do occur. Large-scale changes in public policies are constantly occurring in one area or another of American politics and policymaking as public understandings of existing problems evolve. Important governmental programs are sometimes altered dramatically, even if most of the time they continue as they have in previous years. Although both stability and change are important elements of the policy process, most policy models have been designed to explain either the stability or the change. Punctuated Equilibrium Theory encompasses both.

In recent years, it has become clear that the general approach, developed in the early 1990s to explain US policymaking, applies to a broader set of governments than just the peculiar American system in which the theory was developed. Scholars around the world have confirmed aspects of the theory in a number of advanced democracies. In this chapter, we review Punctuated Equilibrium Theory, discuss new empirical studies in the United States and elsewhere, and interpret new theoretical developments. These developments have broadened PET to incorporate a general theory of information processing in the policy process, which fails to deal smoothly and seamlessly with new information but rather falls prey to sporadic punctuations. Over time, PET has changed not in the nature of its expectations but in the richness of its empirical support, especially cross-nationally, and in the development of more powerful foundations for its cognitive and institutional drivers.

How are we to explain punctuations and stasis in a single theory? Several loosely related approaches in political science had previously noted that, although policymaking often proceeds smoothly, with marginal or incremental accommodations, it also is regularly torn by lurches and significant departures from the incremental past (Kingdon 1984; Baumgartner and Jones 1991, 1993; Dodd 1994; Kelly 1994). A unifying theme of these approaches is that the same institutional system of government organizations and rules produces both a plethora of small accommodations and a significant number of radical departures from the past. Punctuated Equilibrium Theory extends these observations by placing the policy process on a dual foundation of political institutions and boundedly rational decision making. It emphasizes two related elements of the policy process: issue definition and agenda setting. As issues are defined in public discourse in different ways and rise and fall in the public agenda, existing policies can be either reinforced or questioned. Reinforcement creates great obstacles to anything but modest change, whereas questioning policies at the most fundamental levels creates opportunities for major reversals.

Bounded rationality, which stresses that decision makers are subject to cognitive limitations in making choices, was the major foundation of theories of incremental decision making in the budget process (Wildavsky 1964). Neither incrementalism nor globally rational theories of preference maximization fit well with the joint observations of stasis and dramatic change that are the dual foci of the PET approach. However, if we add the observation that attention spans are limited in governments, just as they are in people, then we have a theory of decision making that is consistent with Punctuated Equilibrium Theory and with what is actually observed. As agenda setting theory has always rested on such a decision making foundation, PET simply extends current agenda setting theories to deal with both policy stasis, or incrementalism, and policy punctuations.

In this chapter, we examine Punctuated Equilibrium Theory and its foundations in the longitudinal study of political institutions and in political decision making (for other reviews, see John 2006b; Robinson 2005, 2006; Jones and Baumgartner 2012; and McFarland 2004, which contextualizes the theory in terms of the development of pluralism).[1] The theory has links to evolutionary biology,[2] though its application in the governmental context differs in important ways from its use in biology. Indeed, its intellectual roots are much closer to the study of complex systems (Érdi 2008), which investigates complex interactions among component parts of a system, including political systems, that can generate considerable unpredictability. Complexity in political systems implies that destabilizing events, the accumulation of unaddressed grievances, or other political processes can change the "normal" process of equilibrium and status quo on the basis of negative feedback (which dampens down activities) into those rare periods when positive feedback (which reinforces activities) leads to explosive change for a short while and the establishment of a new policy equilibrium.

We begin by discussing punctuated equilibrium in the context of the agenda setting literature, extend the theory to national budgeting, and provide some recent evidence of punctuations and equilibria in US national government spending since World War II. Then we turn to how the theory has been generalized, including extensions to policymaking in US state and local governments as well as European national governments. These generalizations have been geographical (testing the ideas in new political systems), methodological (developing new statistical and qualitative means of testing the ideas), and substantive (expanding from only agenda setting and budgeting to a theory of institutional change). Next, we discuss in more detail how research on PET has developed since the first edition of this book. The chapter concludes with an assessment of the strengths and weaknesses of the PET approach to understanding public policymaking and notes the close linkage between the creation of a data infrastructure and the theoretical approach of analyzing policy dynamics.

Punctuated Equilibria in Public Policymaking

Since the pathbreaking work of E. E. Schattschneider (1960), theories of conflict expansion and agenda setting have stressed the difficulty disfavored groups and new ideas face in breaking through the established system of policymaking (Cobb and Elder 1983; Cobb and Ross 1997; Bosso 1987). The conservative nature of national political systems favors the status quo; multiple veto points, separation of powers, and other equilibrium-supporting factors have long been recognized. The key insight of PET is that, as a corollary of any system with a status quo bias, policy change will rarely be moderate: inertial forces for change are eliminated or kept to the smallest scale until and unless they are overpowered. The system generates a pattern of change characterized by stability most of the time, with dramatic shifts when the inertial forces are overcome.

When Baumgartner and Jones (1993) analyzed a number of US policymaking cases over time and across a variety of issue areas, they found that (1) policymaking both makes leaps and undergoes periods of near stasis as issues emerge on and recede from the public agenda, (2) American political institutions exacerbate this tendency toward punctuated equilibria, and (3) policy images play a critical role in expanding issues beyond the control of the specialists and special interests that occupy what they termed "policy monopolies."

Baumgartner and Jones (1991, 1993) saw that the separated institutions, overlapping jurisdictions, and relatively open access to mobilizations in the United States combine to create a dynamic between the politics of subsystems and the macro politics of Congress and the presidency—a dynamic that usually works against any impetus for change but occasionally reinforces it. For example, mobilizations are often required to overcome entrenched interests, but once under way they sometimes engender large-scale changes in policy. The reason is that once a mobilization is under way, the diffuse jurisdictional boundaries that separate the various overlapping institutions of government can allow many governmental actors to become involved in a new policy area. Typically, the newcomers are proponents of changes in the status quo, and they often overwhelm the previously controlling powers. Institutional separation often works to reinforce conservatism, but it sometimes works to wash away existing policy subsystems.

In short, American political institutions were conservatively designed to resist many efforts at change and thus to make mobilizations necessary to overcoming established interests. The result has been institutionally reinforced stability interrupted by bursts of change. These bursts have kept the US government from becoming a gridlocked Leviathan despite its growth in size and complexity since World War II. Instead, it has become a complex, interactive system. Redford (1969) differentiated between subsystem politics and macro politics. Baumgartner and Jones extended Redford's insight and combined it with the issue expansion and contraction insights of Schattschneider (1960) and Downs (1972) to form this theory of long-term agenda change and policymaking. Thus, at the core, the literature on agenda setting has always been concerned with the power of specialized communities of experts and the degree to which they operate with relative autonomy from the larger political system or are subject to more intense scrutiny. Because the members of any professional community of experts (say, farmers, nuclear engineers, or members of the military) may prefer more spending on "their" policy, political scientists have long been concerned with tracing the relative power of these shared interest communities; Redford (1969) gives a good summary of these dilemmas.

No political system features continuous discussion on all issues that confront it. Rather, discussions of political issues are usually disaggregated into a number of issue-oriented policy subsystems. These subsystems can be dominated by a single interest, can undergo competition among several interests, can disintegrate over time, or can build up their independence from others (Meier 1985; Sabatier 1987; Browne 1995; Worsham 1998). They may be called "iron triangles," "issue niches," "policy subsystems," or "issue networks," but any such characterization can be considered only a snapshot of a dynamic process (Baumgartner and Jones 1993, 6). Whatever name one gives to these communities of specialists operating out of the political spotlight, most issues, most of the time, are treated within such a community. Nonetheless, within the spotlight of macro politics, some issues catch fire, dominate the agenda, and result in changes in one or more subsystems. The explanation for the same political institutions producing both stasis and punctuations can be found in the processes of agenda setting—especially the dynamics produced by bounded rationality and serial information processing. These affect the interactions between communities of experts and the larger political system.

SERIAL AND PARALLEL PROCESSING

Herbert Simon (1957, 1977, 1983, 1985) developed the notion of bounded rationality to explain how human organizations, including those in business and government, operate. He distinguished between parallel and serial processing. Individuals devote conscious attention to one thing at a time, so decision making must be done in serial fashion, one thing after the other. Organizations are somewhat more flexible. Some decision structures are capable of handling many issues simultaneously, in parallel. Political systems, like humans, cannot simultaneously consider all the issues that face them at the highest level, so policy subsystems can be viewed as mechanisms that allow the political system to engage in parallel processing (Jones 1994). Thousands of issues may be considered simultaneously in parallel within their respective communities of experts.

Sometimes parallel processing within distinct policy communities breaks down, and issues must be handled serially. In the United States, the macropolitical institutions of Congress and the public presidency engage in governmental serial processing, whereby high-profile issues are considered, contested, and decided one—or at most a few—at a time. An issue moves higher on the political agenda usually because new participants have become interested in the debate: "When a policy shifts to the macro-political institutions for serial processing, it generally does so in an environment of changing issue definitions and heightened attentiveness by the media and broader publics" (Jones 1994, 185). Issues cannot forever be considered within the confines of a policy subsystem; occasionally macropolitical forces intervene. The intersection of the parallel-processing capabilities of the policy subsystems and the serial-processing needs of the macropolitical system creates the nonincremental dynamics of lurching that we often observe in many policy areas. Agenda access does not guarantee major change, however, because reform is often blunted in the decision making stage. But this access is a precondition for major policy punctuations. An interesting but largely untested area is the likelihood of substantial policy change in the absence of salience or agenda access. This could come, for example, by shifting norms within a professional community, but without broad social discussion, or by the accumulation of many small changes each moving in the same direction. Although these are of course possible and many have been documented (see, e.g., Jacob 1988 on the issue of US divorce law), we are aware of no systematic test on a large scale that would determine the proportion of big changes due to sudden punctuations as compared to the slow accretion of small changes.

When dominated by a single interest, a subsystem is best thought of as a policy monopoly. A policy monopoly has a definable institutional structure responsible for policymaking in an issue area, and its responsibility is supported by some powerful idea or image. This image is generally connected to core political values and can be communicated simply and directly to the public (Baumgartner and Jones 1993, 5–7). Because a successful policy monopoly systematically dampens pressures for change, we say that it contains a negative feedback process. Yet policy monopolies are not invulnerable forever.

A long-term view of US policymaking reveals that policy monopolies can be constructed and can collapse. Their condition has an important effect on policymaking within their issue areas. If the citizens excluded from a monopoly remain apathetic, the institutional arrangement usually remains constant, and policy is likely to change only slowly (the negative feedback process). As pressure for change builds up, it may be resisted successfully for a time. But if pressures are sufficient, they may lead to a massive intervention by previously uninvolved political actors and governmental institutions. Generally, this requires a substantial change in the supporting policy image. As the issue is redefined or new dimensions of the debate become salient, new actors that had previously stayed away feel qualified to exert their authority. These new actors may insist on rewriting the rules and changing the balance of power, which will be reinforced by new institutional structures as previously dominant agencies and institutions are forced to share their power with groups or agencies that gain new legitimacy.

Thus, the changes that occur as a policy monopoly is broken up may be locked in for the future as institutional reforms are put in place. These new institutions remain in place after public and political involvements recede, often establishing a new equilibrium in the policy area that lasts well after the issue backs off the agenda and into the parallel processing of a (newly altered) policy community. Important elements of this process are the power, prestige, and legitimacy of the previously established policy monopoly. Such "incumbents" seek to maintain their control. Whether they are or are not discredited enough by policy failures to lose their influence depends on both their levels of policy success and prestige and the strength of those who seek to replace them (see Baumgartner 2013).

POSITIVE AND NEGATIVE FEEDBACK

Punctuated Equilibrium Theory includes periods of equilibrium or near stasis, when an issue is captured by a subsystem, and periods of disequilibrium, when an issue is forced onto the macropolitical agenda. When an issue area is on the macropolitical agenda, small changes in objective circumstances can cause large changes in policy, and we say that the system is undergoing a positive feedback process (Baumgartner and Jones 2002). Positive feedback occurs when a change, sometimes a fairly modest one, causes future changes to be amplified. Observers often use terms like "feeding frenzy," "cascade," "tipping point," "momentum," or "bandwagon effect" to characterize such processes. Negative feedback, on the other hand, maintains stability in a system, somewhat like a thermostat maintains constant temperature in a room.

Physical scientists have studied large interactive systems that are characterized by positive feedback. Physical phenomena like earthquakes can result from fairly modest changes. Pressure inside the earth builds up over time and eventually causes the tectonic plates on the planet's surface to shift violently during an earthquake. Similarly, if we drop grains of sand slowly and constantly onto a small pile of sand in a laboratory, most of the time the pile remains in stasis, with occasional landslides, some of which are minor, and others of which are huge (Bak and Chen 1991; Bak 1997). A landslide may not be caused by a large-scale event; it may be caused by the slow and steady buildup of tiny changes. Like earthquakes and landslides, policy punctuations can be precipitated by a mighty blow, an event that simply cannot be ignored, or by relatively minor events that accumulate over longer periods. What determines whether an issue catches fire with positive feedback? The interaction of changing images and venues of public policies.

As an example of positive feedback in policymaking, let us take the case of the involvement of the US national government in criminal justice. Before the late 1960s, federal involvement in crime policy was relatively modest. At the end of that decade, however, the Lyndon B. Johnson administration initiated several new federal grant-in-aid programs to assist state and local governments in crime prevention and control. Congress passed the Omnibus Crime Control and Safe Streets Act in 1968; between 1969 and 1972 federal spending on crime and justice doubled in real dollar terms.

What happened? Crime was rising during this period, but more importantly other trends highlighted the increasing insecurity citizens were feeling, causing people and government officials to direct their attention to the crime problem. Three important measures of attention and agenda access came into focus all at once: press coverage of crime stories, the proportion of Americans saying that crime was the most important problem (MIP) facing the nation, and congressional hearings on crime and justice. All of this happened as major urban disorders swept many American cities. In the words of John Kingdon, a window of opportunity had opened, and federal crime policy changed in a major way. After 1968, the three trends fell out of focus, going their own ways, and crime policy moved back into the subsystem arena. It is not possible to say which of the three variables was primary; all three were intertwined in a complex positive feedback process. In a classic pattern, public attention to crime jumped, press coverage focused on the problem, and Congress scheduled hearings. The issue left its normal subsystem home, with incremental adjustments, and entered the realm of macropolitics. Congress passed a major law, and spending increased in a major punctuation. US crime policy at the federal level is still powerfully affected by decisions that were made during this surge of attention on the "war on crime" and those that later reinforced them.

Recently, Jones, Thomas, and Wolfe (2014) showed how *policy bubbles* can develop from the processes that lead to policy subsystems. They define a policy bubble as sustained overinvestment in a policy solution (or instrument) or set of solutions relative to the efficiency of the policy solution in achieving goals. To illustrate they study three potential policy bubbles: crime control, privatization and contracting, and charter schools and vouchers. They conclude that the first two policies clearly generated overinvestment bubbles, but the third did not, primarily because countermobilization by affected interests limited the positive feedback effects. The formation of most policy subsystems does not result in bubbles because of countermobilization, but some clearly do. One possible reason is an extremely favorable policy image underlying these policy solutions.

POLICY IMAGES

Policy images are a mixture of empirical information and emotive appeals. Such images are, in effect, information—grist for the policymaking process. The factual content of any policy or program can have many different aspects and can affect different people in different ways. When a single image is widely accepted and generally supportive of the policy, it is usually associated with a successful policy monopoly. When there is disagreement over the proper way to describe or understand a policy, proponents may focus on one set of images while their opponents refer to a different set. For example, when the image of civilian nuclear power was associated with economic progress and technical expertise, its policymaking typified a policy monopoly. When opponents raised images of danger and environmental degradation, the nuclear policy monopoly began to collapse (Baumgartner and Jones 1991; 1993, 25–28, 59–82). As the next section shows, Jones (1994) has further emphasized the importance of policy images not only to issue definition and redefinition in policymaking but also to the serial and parallel processes of individual and collective decision making in a democracy.

A new image may attract new participants, and the multiple venues in the American political system constitute multiple opportunities for policy entrepreneurs to advance their cases. Federalism, separation of powers, and jurisdictional overlaps not only inhibit major changes during periods of negative feedback but also mean that a mobilization stymied in one venue may succeed in another. The states can sometimes act on a problem that has not advanced onto the national agenda, and vice versa. The US system of multiple policy venues is an important part of the process of disrupting policy monopolies during periods of positive feedback.

Each institutional venue has its own language, set of participants, and limitations, leading to evolving sets of strategies among those who would try to affect the agenda setting process. In her pathbreaking study of courts, Vanessa Baird (2006) studied the interaction of justices' priorities, litigant strategies, and agenda setting. Baird wanted to know which dynamics underlie the movement of the Supreme Court into areas of policy it had ignored or avoided in the past. The work is exciting because it unifies the strategic concerns of game theory with the dynamics of agenda setting, hence pointing to new possibilities for integration across approaches.

In summary, subsystem politics is the politics of equilibrium—the politics of the policy monopoly, incrementalism, a widely accepted supportive image, and negative feedback. Subsystem decision making is decentralized to the iron triangles and issue networks of specialists in the bureaucracy, legislative subgroups, and interested parties. Established interests tend to dampen departures from inertia until political mobilization, advancement on the governmental agenda, and positive feedback occur. At that point, issues spill over into the macropolitical system, making possible major change.

Macropolitics is the politics of punctuation—the politics of large-scale change, competing policy images, political manipulation, and positive feedback. Positive feedback exacerbates impulses for change; it overcomes inertia and produces explosions or implosions from former states (Baumgartner and Jones 1991, 1993; Jones, Baumgartner, and Talbert 1993; Jones 1994; Talbert, Jones, and Baumgartner 1995).

Punctuated equilibrium seems to be a general characteristic of policymaking in the United States. Rigorous qualitative and quantitative studies again and again find strong evidence of the process, including studies on regulatory drug review (Ceccoli 2003), environmental policy (Repetto 2006; Busenberg 2004; Wood 2006; Salka 2004), education (Manna 2006; McLendon 2003; Mulholland and Shakespeare 2005; Robinson 2004), firearms control (True and Utter 2002), and regulation of state hospital rates (McDonough 1998).

This sweeping depiction of issue dynamics may hide a great deal of variability in the operation of policy subsystems. For example, Worsham (1998) examines three different subsystem types and finds substantial variation in the actors' ability to control attempts to shift conflict from the subsystem level to the macropolitical level by appealing to Congress (see, in addition, McCool 1998). Research using the Advocacy Coalition Framework (see Chapter 4 in this volume: Jenkins-Smith et al. 2017) has shown that opposing groups can modify certain elements of their belief structures through policy learning born of continual interaction within policy subsystems. This interaction can lead to substantial compromise and important changes in public policy. This belief-adjustment process can lead to a dampening of policy punctuations because appeals from the disaffected are involved in the policymaking subsystem. In his study of federal land management, Wood (2006) shows that even conflictual subsystems can sometimes avoid disruption through conflict-management strategies. More generally, this suggests that institutional arrangements can affect the magnitude of punctuations—a point to which we return later in this chapter.

BOUNDEDLY RATIONAL FOUNDATIONS AND THE CENTRALITY OF DECISION MAKING

Embedded in the Punctuated Equilibrium Theory of policy change is an implicit theory of individual and collective decision making. From a decision making perspective, large-scale punctuations in policy spring from a change in either preferences or attentiveness. If we regard preferences as relatively stable, how can we explain nonmarginal changes in government policy? Particularly, how can we explain apparent cases of choice reversal when later studies find no large changes in the external environment?

Baumgartner and Jones (1993) have explained "bursts" of change and policy punctuations as arising from the interactions of images and institutions. When an agreed-on image becomes contested, a policy monopoly is usually under attack, and the likelihood grows of a new mobilization (a wave of either criticism or enthusiasm) advancing the issue onto the macropolitical agenda. How can policy images play such a central role in government agenda setting? Part of the answer is found in Jones's (1994) analysis of serial attention and rational decision making, both individually and collectively, and part is found in Jones and Baumgartner's (2005) analysis of the disproportionate nature of human individual and collective information processing. They expand on these themes in *The Politics of Information* (Baumgartner and Jones 2015).

Jones (1994) has argued that individual and collective decision changes, including choice reversals, do not spring from rapid flip-flops of preferences or from basic irrationality (choosing to go against our own preferences); they spring from shifts in attention. He has called such rapid changes "serial shifts." In individuals, serial attentiveness means that the senses may process information in a parallel way, but attention is given serially to one thing, or at most a few things, at a time (Simon 1977, 1983). Although reality may be complex, changing, and multifaceted, individuals cannot smoothly integrate competing concerns and perspectives. We usually focus on one primary aspect of the choice situation at a time (Simon 1957, 1985; Jones 1994; see also Tversky 1972; Zaller 1992). Collectively, a shift in the object of attention can lead to a disjointed change in preferred alternatives, even when the alternatives are well defined (Jones 1994).

More generally, bounded rationality undergirds all policy change because the mechanisms associated with human cognitive architecture are also characteristic of organizations, including governments (Jones 2001). Bounded rationality is the decision making underpinning of both the punctuated equilibrium and the advocacy coalition approaches, but the theories emphasize different aspects of the process. Punctuated equilibrium is based in serial processing of information and the consequent attention shifts, whereas the advocacy coalition approach traces policy dynamics to the belief systems of coalition participants (Leach and Sabatier 2005).

Bounded rationality was wedded early to incrementalism (Lindblom 1959; Wildavsky 1964); yet incrementalism proved to be, at best, an incomplete explanation of government policymaking and, at worst, a misleading one. The basic problem with incrementalism surfaced when it was tested empirically. For example, when Davis, Dempster, and Wildavsky (1966) made a longitudinal study of bureau-level budget results, they found and reported empirical evidence of both incremental decision rules and two types of nonincremental shifts. The first shift apparently happened when a decision rule was temporarily set aside for a short period (called a deviant case), and the second occurred when a new decision rule was adopted (called a shift point) (Davis, Dempster, and Wildavsky 1966, 537–542). These punctuations aside, the authors found support for a relatively incremental view of the budgetary process. The punctuations themselves were excluded from the model, and the authors' conclusions pointed to the significance of finding equations for the budget process and to the central role that the prior-year "base" played in those equations.

Focusing solely on incremental changes caused early behavioral decision theorists to downplay empirical evidence of large-scale change, and it led boundedly rational decision making into a theoretical cul-de-sac. Incrementalism did seem to explain much of what happened in the budgetary process, but it had nothing to say about major policy changes. Indeed, boundedly rational decision making even had a difficult time determining when changes could no longer be considered incremental (Wanat 1974; Padgett 1980; Berry 1990; Hayes 1992).

With Jones's reconceptualization, however, boundedly rational decision making is a foundation for both major and minor changes—for both punctuations and equilibria. In the case of public policymaking, the twin foundations of conservative and overlapping political institutions and boundedly rational decision making (especially the role of images in dampening or exacerbating mobilizations against entrenched interests) combine to create a system that is both inherently conservative and liable to occasional radical change.

Although bounded rationality dominates the literature in policy processes, that is not true in the study of governing institutions, where rational choice perspectives hold considerable sway. Yet these models do not fare well in either psychological or economic studies of decision making (Kahneman 2011), and in many cases they predict policy outcomes, particularly their distributions, worse than a boundedly rational approach (Jones 2003; Jones and Thomas 2012). As we show later in this chapter, applying the punctuated equilibrium framework to public budgeting demonstrated this clearly.

INFORMATION PROCESSING

With its foundations in both political institutions and boundedly rational decision making, Punctuated Equilibrium Theory is at base a theory of organizational information processing. Governments are complex organizations that act on the flow of information in producing public policies (Jones, Workman, and Jochim 2009). The manner in which public policy adjusts to these information flows determines the extent of bursts of activity in the system. The general punctuation hypothesis suggests that information processing is disproportionate. That is, policymaking alternates between periods of underreaction and overreaction to the flow of information coming into the system from the environment (Jones and Baumgartner 2005; Wood and Peake 1998). This reaction may stem from a vivid event that symbolizes everything that is wrong (Birkland 1997) or from the accumulation of problems over longer periods. In either case, how the policymaking system allocates attention to the problem is a critical component of problem recognition and subsequent policy action, but so are the institutional arrangements responsible for policymaking.

One would expect a policymaking system, then, to be more subject to punctuations when it is less able to adjust to the changing circumstances it faces. Indeed, Jones and Baumgartner (2005) show that a perfect pattern of adjustment to a complex, multifaceted environment in which multiple informational input flows are processed by a political system will yield a normal distribution of output changes. As a consequence, the extent of the adjustment of a policy system may be gauged by a comparison of its distribution of policy outputs with the normal curve. In an important sense, the more normally public policy changes are distributed, the better the policymaking system is performing (in the sense of producing efficient adjustment to environmental demands).

Using this framework, Robinson (2004) finds that more-bureaucratic school systems adjust their expenditures better to fiscal reality than do less-bureaucratic ones—presumably because bureaucracy enhances information acquisition and processing. Breunig and Koski (2006) find that states with stronger chief executives are subject to smaller and fewer budgetary punctuations, and Berkman and Reenock (2004) show that incremental adjustments in state administrative reorganizations can obviate the need for sweeping reorganizations in the future. Chan (2006), however, reports results on administrative changes in Hong Kong that are very much in keeping with punctuated dynamics.

Adler and Wilkerson (2012) have developed what amounts to a new theoretical approach to the study of congressional behavior by adopting an information and problem-solving approach. They note, for example, that much of the US congressional workload is organized around a small number of "must-pass" pieces of legislation and that lawmakers structure things to ensure that bills that "must" be passed will periodically arise. Theirs is based on a sister project to the Policy Agendas Project: the Congressional Bills Project (http://www.congressionalbills.org) makes available hundreds of thousands of bills—all those ever introduced, not just passed—from 1947 through recent times and is organized according to the same categories as the Policy Agendas Project and Comparative Agendas Project (http://www.comparativeagendas.net).

Complex interactions, however, cannot be confined to activity within fixed institutional frameworks. It must be the case that the entire policymaking system can evolve, that the pieces of the system, in effect, can feed back into the whole, actually changing the decision making structures that acted as policy venues in the first place. Richardson (2000) argues that this is happening in European policymaking at present, and Daviter (2013) recently reinforced this point in the EU context as well. The framework we've set forth in this chapter can serve as a starting point for the analyses of such complicated interactions because they allow the policy process to be viewed as a complex, evolving system.

THE POLITICS OF INFORMATION AND THE PATHOLOGY OF PUNCTUATIONS

The concept of punctuated equilibria in policy studies is based in the theory of policy subsystems, in particular in ideas originating with E. E. Schattschneider and Emmette Redford. In the early work on punctuated equilibria, major policy changes were seen as natural outcomes of normal democratic processes. Friction in policymaking systems was a natural outcome of parallel processing in policy subsystems, rules that limit policy action, and the cognitive capacities of human actors that limit information-processing abilities. As a consequence, changes in collective attention were necessary to overcome the bias of the status quo, leading to disjointed large-scale policy changes. As the *Politics of Attention* showed, such changes could happen even in the absence of crises in the policymaking environment.

It has become clear in recent years that this view is incomplete. Political systems may be designed with such a high level of friction that they so strongly resist change, and when major changes come (and they will) they can be highly destructive. The friction dynamic implies that the more centralized and authoritarian the regime, the larger policy punctuations will be because the system is less able to adjust to the flows of information from the environment. Lam and Chan (2014) show that policy changes were greater when Hong Kong was more centralized but abated as the political system democratized. Chan and Zhao (2016) develop what they call the "information disadvantage of authoritarianism" and show first the large policy punctuations that occur in authoritarian China relative to democratic regimes, and second that punctuations are larger in regions of China with less social discontent. Given the lack of other input means, discontent is one of the few mechanisms for stressing problems that exist.

System-destabilizing policy punctuations are a serious danger in nondemocratic systems but can be problematic in democratic ones as well. For example, more centralized agency structures within government may lead to patterns of less stable outputs (May, Workman, and Jones 2008). Epp (2015) shows that firms in decentralized markets are less punctuated than firms in less competitive situations.

Punctuations are inevitable, but their size and distribution are not. How can policymaking systems be designed so that the size of punctuations can be minimized? It is well established in the policy process literature that the dynamics affecting the discovery and interpretation of policy problems are distinct from the search for solutions. In *Human Problem-Solving,* Newell and Simon (1972) found that people solving problems tended to return to prepackaged sets of policy solutions when encountering a superficially similar problem to one they had solved before (see Jones 2001 for a discussion). The garbage can theory of Cohen, March, and Olsen (1972), extended by Kingdon (1984) to what is now called the Multiple Streams Framework (Herweg, Zahariadis, and Zohlnhöfer 2017; see Chapter 1, this volume), treats problem dynamics and solution search as separate processes at the systems level.

Baumgartner and Jones's *Politics of Information* develops the thesis that problem discovery and definition requires a different organizational system than does solution search. They begin with an information-processing perspective from more recent developments in the punctuated equilibrium approach (Baumgartner and Jones 2015). They show that policymaking systems may reach suboptimal equilibria by suppressing attributes in a complex problem space. They develop the thesis that "entropic search," in which multiple potentially competing jurisdictions of government agencies and legislative committees, yields a superior (in the sense of more consistent input streams of information) depiction of the problem space. But often a collaboration among experts is better at designing solutions than a cacophony of competing voices is. One implication is that organizational design may need to differ for detecting and defining problems and designing solutions.

In general, the most recent developments in the study of policy punctuations lead to a conception that, although punctuations are unavoidable, better governance systems tend to minimize the disruption from such punctuations. Crises of course can be unexpected, what Taleb (2007) calls black swans when they are particularly extreme. But many and probably most crises are foreseeable to some extent; open and even confusing policy systems are better equipped to detect such potential crises than are more centralized and less adaptive ones.

THE DUAL ROLE OF FRICTION IN POLICYMAKING

Punctuated equilibrium in policy studies applies to a particular situation: when political conflict is expanded beyond the confines of expert-dominated policy subsystems to other policymaking venues. It relies on the mechanism of policy image—the manner in which a policy is characterized or understood—and a system of partially independent institutional venues within which policy can be made. The general punctuation hypothesis generalizes this basic framework to situations in which information flows into a policymaking system, and the system, acting on these signals from its environment, attends to the problem and acts to alleviate it if necessary (Jones, Sulkin, and Larsen 2003; Jones and Baumgartner 2005).

This translation is not smooth, however, because decision making activities are subject to decision and transaction costs. These are costs that policymakers incur in the very process of making a decision. Participants in a policymaking system must overcome these costs to respond to the signals from the environment, which themselves are uncertain and ambiguous. There are two major sources of costs in translating inputs into policy outputs. The first consists of cognitive costs: political actors must recognize the signal, devote attention to it, frame the problem, and devise solutions for it. The second source consists of institutional costs: the rules for making policy generally act to maintain stability and incrementalism.

In the case of US national institutions, constitutional requirements of supermajorities to pass legislation mean that policy outputs will be more punctuated than the information coming into government. In stochastic process terms, outputs are more leptokurtic than inputs. Because it should be easier for an issue to gain access to the governmental agenda than to stimulate final policy action, agenda setting policy distributions should be less leptokurtic and more similar to a normal distribution than output distributions. Jones, Sulkin, and Larsen (2003; see also Jones and Baumgartner 2005) report that a variety of agenda setting measures, such as congressional hearings, newspaper coverage, and congressional bill introductions, are less leptokurtic than the distributions for any of several outputs, such as public laws and public budgets. Outputs are more punctuated, characterized by stability interspersed with bursts of activity, than agenda setting distributions. Baumgartner, Breunig, et al. (2009) generalized this finding, showing progressively greater friction in distributions drawn from policy inputs, decision making, and budgeting in the United States, Denmark, and Belgium.

Policymaking institutions seem to add friction to the process of translating inputs into policy outputs. This friction acts to delay action on issues until enough pressure develops to overcome this institutional resistance. Then there is a lurch or punctuation in policymaking. Friction, which leads to punctuated dynamics, rather than gridlock characterizes American national political institutions. Furthermore, this framework may prove useful in understanding differences among political systems, which, after all, add friction to the policymaking process in different ways. Some social movement theorists have critiqued policy process approaches as too narrow, but they do stress issue dynamics (Kenny 2003). A more general formulation may lead to grappling with how one might integrate the voluminous work on social movements with punctuated change within institutional frameworks.

PUNCTUATIONS AND STABILITY
IN GOVERNMENT SPENDING

Over the past twenty years, the Punctuated Equilibrium Theory has been extended to produce an agenda-based model of governmental budgeting (Jones, Baumgartner, and True 1998; True 2000; Jones, Sulkin, and Larsen 2003; Jones and Baumgartner 2005; Jones et al. 2009; see also Jensen, Mortensen, and Serritzlew 2016). Its foundation remains the boundedly rational process of human decision making interacting with disaggregated political institutions, specifically serial attentiveness and parallel subsystems. Collectively, government decision makers usually process information in a parallel way through subsystems, policy monopolies, iron triangles, and issue networks. When that happens, budgets change only incrementally. However, sometimes issues move from subsystem politics to macropolitics, and national attention in the Congress and in the presidency is, of necessity, given to one or a few high-profile items at a time. In the attention limelight of the macropolitical institutions, policies and programs can make radical departures from the past, and budgets can lurch toward large changes. The study of budgets grew from a desire to construct a comprehensive test of PET; Jones and Baumgartner (2005) presented data on thousands of budget changes at the federal level, demonstrating a pattern in the overall distribution that was consistent with the theory. Since then, an entire theory of budgeting has developed based on bounded rationality (Jones et al. 2009).

Choice situations are multifaceted; yet decision makers tend to understand choices in terms of a circumscribed set of attributes, and they tend to have considerable difficulty making trade-offs among these attributes. If a given policy promotes economic growth but simultaneously has some negative consequences in terms of human rights, one or the other of those competing values may be at the forefront of decision makers' attention. If attentiveness to these two dimensions was to shift—say, as a result of scandal or changes in the composition of the group of decision makers, as sometimes occurs—then the chosen policy might shift dramatically as well. In general terms, Jones (2001) has noted that decision makers tend to stick with a particular decision design (a term that refers to the attributes used in structuring a choice) until forced to reevaluate it.

Budgets react to both endogenous and exogenous forces. The forces that might cause a change in the decision design may be external to the decision maker. Such influences may include changing levels of public attention, striking and compelling new information, or turnover in the composition of the decision making body (e.g., when an election changes control of Congress and committee leaderships are rotated from one party to the other). When changing external circumstances force us out of an old decision design, the result is often not a modest adjustment but a major change. Yet subsystem politics and the bureaucratic regularity of annual budget submissions constitute endogenous forces that favor continuing with the same decision design. As a consequence, budget decisions tend to be either static, arrived at by applying the current decision design and subsystem institutions to the new choice situation, or disjointed, arrived at by utilizing a different decision design and macropolitical institutions that may incorporate new attributes into the choice structure or shift attention from one dimension to another. Even these explanations do not exhaust the possible interactions among institutions, images, and the environment, for large changes can also arise from endogenous conflicts over the appropriate image and from shifts in attention when the external circumstances have changed little, if at all.

Because political institutions amplify the tendency toward decisional stasis interspersed with abrupt change (as opposed to smooth, moderate adjustments to changing circumstances), the agenda-based model of policymaking and the serial shift model of decision making together produce a pattern of punctuations and equilibria in the budget processes. As attentiveness shifts to the new aspect or attribute, so, too, do outcomes shift, and this process is often not smooth. Occasionally, in almost every issue area, the usual forces of negative feedback and subsystem maintenance will be replaced by deviation-enhancing positive feedback forces. Positive feedback leads to episodic and sporadic change (as institutionally induced stability reasserts itself after the punctuation).

Punctuated equilibrium's attention-driven, agenda-based budget model encompasses periods of both punctuation and stability. This view of the budget process leads us to expect that annual budget changes within a given spending category will not be distributed in the normal, bell-shaped curve. Rather, these changes should reflect the nonnormal distributions found in earthquakes and other large interactive systems (see Mandelbrot 1963; Padgett 1980; Midlarsky 1988; Bak and Chen 1991; Peters 1991). The "earthquake" budget model anticipates many minuscule real changes, few moderate changes, and many large changes (True 2000).

The model implies that punctuations ought to occur at all levels of policymaking and at all levels of the budget and should not be driven simply by external (exogenous) factors in a top-down manner. This is a consequence of two factors. First, budget decisions are hostage to the statics and dynamics of selective attention to the underlying attributes structuring a political situation. Second, the theory of punctuated policy equilibrium is based in part on a bottom-up process in which policy change may occur in isolated subsystems, may spill over into other, related subsystems, or may be affected by exogenous shocks (Jones, Baumgartner, and True 1998). If punctuations did not occur at all levels of scale in the budget, from the program level to the macropolitical level, and if they did not occur during all time periods, then we would have to question the application of this theory to budgeting.

Yet, because national budget decisions take place within political institutions, we expect that hierarchy will produce an inequality in the transmission of punctuations from one level to another. This inequality of transmission is connected to the notion of parallel versus serial processing of issues. Both the president and Congress are capable of transmitting top-down budget changes to many agencies at once, and they do so when an issue affecting many agencies or programs reaches the national agenda and is processed serially. Such top-down punctuations from fiscal stress will be more easily transmitted to departments, agencies, and bureaus than bottom-up punctuations can be transmitted upward. The reason is that the insular nature of parallel processing within subsystems damps out the spillover effects among subsystems. As a result, we expect fewer punctuations at the top than at the bottom levels of governmental organization.

PUNCTUATIONS IN PREVIOUS BUDGET THEORIES

Many different models of the policy process have predicted abrupt change, but they have generally postulated exogenous change. In particular, the empirical and theoretical literature on public budgeting provides ample precedent to expect budget punctuations, beginning as shown above with Davis, Dempster, and Wildavsky (1966). This study focused on the use by decision makers of budget decision rules. These rules, understood by participants and offering a stable organizational environment for decision making, were based on the concepts of base and fair share, which led to incrementalism in both process and output. But Davis, Dempster, and Wildavsky (1974, 427) later added that "although it is basically incremental, the budget process does respond to the needs of the economy and society, but only after sufficient pressure has built up to cause abrupt changes precipitated by these events." Exogenously caused punctuations in budget results are consistent with findings by Ostrom and Marra (1986), Kamlet and Mowery (1987), Kiewiet and McCubbins (1991), and Su, Kamlet, and Mowery (1993).

The earthquake budget model departs from all of the cybernetic, optimizing, and adaptive models in emphasizing stasis or large change, but not moderate change. The policymaking literature is replete with models of exogenously forced policy change. Such models are suggested not only in the research of the authors cited above but also in the work of comparativists (Krasner 1984) and scholars who study public representation. They see changes in public policy as exogenously driven by changes in public opinion (Stimson, MacKuen, and Erikson 1995) and caused through a thermostat-like process (Wlezien 1995; Soroka and Wlezien 2010). These models call for punctuations only if there is a change in macrolevel exogenous forces.

Other authors have allowed for complex interactions between endogenous and exogenous budget changes. Kiel and Elliott (1992, 143) approached budgeting from a perspective of nonlinear dynamics and noted the existence of likely nonlinearities in the budgeting process in which "exogenous and endogenous forces simply have varying impacts on budget outlays over time." Nonlinear, interactive processes imply occasional punctuations. Thurmaier (1995) reported the results of experiments in budget scenarios in which decision makers shift from economic to political rationales for their decisions after being given new information about political calculations. Such shifts in the bases of decisions can lead to punctuations. True (1995) found that domestic political factors had more influence on spending for national defense than did the dissolution of the Soviet Union. The case for both endogenous and exogenous influences on national budgets seems to be a strong one.

Any work in this area must reckon with the seminal work of John Padgett (1980, 1981) on budget decision making. Padgett's (1980, 366) serial judgment model of the budget process implies "the occasional occurrence of very radical changes." Both Padgett's serial judgment model and our agenda-based approach allow for endogenous mobilizations as well as exogenous shocks. Davis, Dempster, and Wildavsky (1966) suggested only exogenous shocks, but they have suggested punctuations in the budget process. The earthquake budget model alone, however, ties budget making to both an embedded cognitive decision theory and an explicit policymaking theory—the Punctuated Equilibrium Theory of governance.

Following Padgett's lead, our agenda-based budget model assumes that budgeting is a stochastic process. It remains extremely difficult (and perhaps impossible) to specify precise causal linkages among all of the variables that interact nonlinearly or interdependently to produce changes in all of the line items of annual national budgets (especially if, like us, one hopes to do so for the entire postwar period). However, it is possible to develop hypotheses about the distribution of budget changes that can be derived from our agenda-based model and that can be distinguished from previous budgeting models. And that is the strategy we have followed (Jones, Baumgartner, and True 1998; Jones and Baumgartner 2005; Jones et al. 2009; Jones Zalyani, and Érdi 2014).

If budgets generally change very little, but occasionally change a great deal, annual budget changes will be distributed leptokurtically. That is, their univariate distribution should have a large, slender central peak (representing a stability logic), weak shoulders (representing difficulty in making moderate changes), and big tails (representing episodic punctuations). Note that a normal, or Gaussian, distribution would be found if continuous dynamic adjustment were the primary decision mechanism (Davis, Dempster, and Wildavsky 1966; Padgett 1980; for a careful examination of univariate distributions, see Johnson, Kotz, and Balakrishnan 1994).

Because we expect the dynamics of budget decision making to occur at all levels, we hypothesize scale invariance. That is, we expect the underlying, nonnormal distribution of annual changes to be evident at all levels of aggregation (program, function, subfunction, and agency). Yet, because we expect changes in budget decisions to be more easily transmitted down the organizational chain than up, we expect that punctuations will be more pronounced at the bottom of the hierarchy than at the top. That is, we expect subfunctions to be more leptokurtic than functions and functions to be more leptokurtic than higher aggregations.

These expectations diverge from the predictions of other budget and decision models. The boundedly rational models of Davis, Dempster, and Wildavsky (1966, 1974) explicitly describe the normality of their residual terms. That is, year-to-year changes are usually normally distributed, and after an exogenous factor has caused a shift in parameters, the series will again be modeled with a normal residual term. The "cybernetic" models of Ostrom and Marra (1986), Kamlet and Mowery (1987), and Blais, Blake, and Dion (1993) depend on the assumption of normality to justify their use of linear regressions and pooled-regression models.

Budget-maximizing models have made few particular predictions in this area (Niskanen 1971), but it is reasonable to expect a normal distribution of first differences from them as well; indeed, most regression analyses and analyses of variance depend on the central limit theorem for their justification. Maximizing models do not predict punctuations unless there is a shift in exogenous factors, but if such a shift occurs, most maximizing models assume that the accumulation of exogenous factors will asymptotically approach normality.

THE DISTRIBUTION OF BUDGET CHANGES

We first presented tests of this hypothesis in the first edition of this book; since then, policy process scholars have produced a virtual explosion of work on the distribution of budget changes. To study nonnormal budgetary changes, we developed a new dataset of US budget authority for Office of Management and Budget (OMB) subfunctions from fiscal year (FY) 1947 to the present. Budget data present special problems of comparability across time (Baumgartner,

Jones, and Wilkerson 2002; Soroka, Wlezien, and McLean 2006), and our dataset was adjusted for these comparability problems. Budget authority, corrected for inflation, is more accurate than appropriations, which can confuse the timing of contract spending and depend on estimates for trust fund spending. And budget authority is closer to the congressional decision making process than outlay data because outlays can be delayed for several years after the decision has been made. We constructed the relevant estimates from original contemporary budgets on the basis of our analysis of current budget categories. We focused primarily on OMB's subfunction level, which divides the twenty core governmental functions into seventy-six groupings based on the national purposes they are supposed to serve. We have focused on the sixty programmatic subfunctions, eliminating sixteen primarily financial subfunctions.

If we take the annual percentage change for each of the sixty programmatic budget subfunctions from FY 1947 through FY 2012, we get the distribution shown in the histogram in Figure 2.1. The distribution is clearly leptokurtic and positively skewed. Note the very strong central peak, indicating the great number of very small changes, the weak shoulders, indicating fewer than normal

FIGURE 2.1 Distribution of Percentage Changes in U.S. Budgeting, 1947–2012

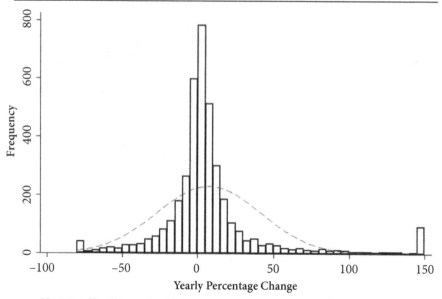

N= 3,944, K= 477.22, LK= 0.620
Note: Extremely high/low values clustered at +150 and –80;
excludes lagged amounts less than $50 million.

NOTE: The figure is based on OMB subfunctions and pools all series from 1947 to 2012, showing the number of each size annual percentage change.

SOURCE: Data from http://www.policyagendas.org.

moderate changes, and the big tails, indicating more than normal radical departures from the previous year's budget. It diverges widely from a normal curve even if we drop the top 5 percent of the outliers when computing the normal curve.[3]

The distribution of annual changes in budget authority is consistent with the earthquake budget model (as called for by the Punctuated Equilibrium Theory), but not with incremental theories. Both rely on bounded rationality, and our approach may be viewed as adding agenda setting and attention allocation to the incrementalist models. That is, the incrementalist models were not far wrong; the central peak of budget change distributions indicates that they are virtually unchanging and hence may be viewed as incremental. But the incremental theories missed the manner in which attention allocation disrupts "normal" budgeting, which PET incorporates.

How general is the finding of punctuated, nonincremental budgeting? So far, every study examining public budgets has found this pattern. Jordan (2003) finds punctuated budget change distributions for US local expenditures; Robinson (2004), for Texas school districts; Breunig and Koski (2006), for state budgets; and Jones and Baumgartner (2005), for US national outlays since 1800. The pattern also emerges in other countries, including the United Kingdom

FIGURE 2.2 Annual Percentage Change in the U.S. Budget Authority for American States, Aggregated across Budget Categories, 1984–2002

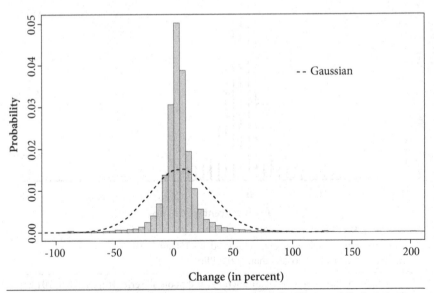

SOURCE: Christian Breunig and Chris Koski, "Punctuated Equilibria and Budgets in the American States," *Policy Studies Journal* 34, no. 3.

(John and Margetts 2003; Soroka, Wlezien, and McLean 2006), Denmark (Breunig 2006; Mortensen 2005), Germany (Breunig 2006), France (Baumgartner, François, and Foucault 2006), Belgium (Jones et al. 2009), Spain (Caamaño-Alegre and Lago-Peñas 2011; Chaqués-Bonafont, Palau, and Baumgartner 2015), and South Africa (Pauw 2007) (see also Jones et al. 2009; Baumgartner, Breunig, et al. 2009; Breunig and Koski 2012; Breunig, Koski, and Mortensen 2010; Breunig and Jones 2011; Soroka, Wlezien, and McLean 2006; Jensen, Mortensen, and Serritzlew 2016). Indeed, the results are so strong and invariant that punctuated equilibrium has been classified as "a general empirical law of public budgets" (see Jones et al. 2009).

Figure 2.2, reproduced from the work of Breunig and Koski (2006), shows the distribution of budgets across the fifty US states; in its basics, it closely resembles Figure 2.1. The pattern persists in centralized democracies as well as in more pluralistic ones such as the United States. Figure 2.3, showing the distribution of annual changes in ministerial funding in France, closely resembles Figure 2.1 as well. This suggests that we need a broader theory of how policy punctuations occur, one that is not so tightly tied to pluralistic forms of government. It is likely that different systems lead to different intensities in punctuations, yet don't escape the process—because it is rooted in the capacities of

FIGURE 2.3 Distribution of Annual Percentage Changes for Ten French Ministerial Budgets, 1868–2002

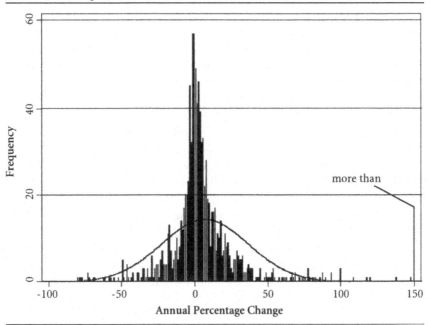

Source: Baumgartner, Foucault, and Francois (2006).

government to process information and allocate attention. We discuss this in more detail below.

Work done by a team of researchers analyzing budget data from seven Western democracies showed that all the national-level frequency distributions not only could be characterized as leptokurtic but also roughly described by a particular probability distribution: the Paretian, or power, function (Jones et al. 2009). Power functions are distinguished by a single parameter, the exponent, which indicates how punctuated the frequency distribution is, and this parameter can be recovered empirically in a straightforward manner. As a consequence, the investigators were able to compare the size of the exponents and relate them to a measure of institutional friction, or stickiness, among the democracies. The higher the levels of friction, the greater the extent of punctuations in the budget data. Although these results are consistent with the Punctuated Equilibrium Theory, it is worth noting that they challenge the standard view in the political economy literature of institutional friction inducing more policy stability (see, e.g., Tsebelis 2002). The stochastic process studies of public budgets indicate that friction does indeed lead to more stability but also to much more dramatic changes when priorities start to change.

Finally, Figure 2.4, showing annual spending in the US federal government adjusted for inflation and divided by population, addresses the issue of macro- and microlevel punctuations. We present the data on a log scale, so a consistent but straight upward slope represents a set percentage growth in the budget. The figure makes clear, however, that per capita spending goes through periods of relative stasis interrupted by major disruptions. At the outset of the series, spending was on the order of $25 per person; it moved temporarily to much higher levels during the War of 1812, was in the range of $30 to $50 until the Civil War, when it spiked dramatically again, then moved to a level of about $100 per person, where it stayed for several decades. This period of stability was interrupted by World War I, which inaugurated a period of steady growth in per capita spending, with huge spikes, of course, while the wars were engaged, but with spending remaining substantially higher after the wars than it was before. Spending in 1927 was just $300 per person, but it had increased by 1939 to $1,060. During World War II, spending reached $9,000 per capita, declined to $2,000 by 1948, and then increased relatively steadily to reach $12,000 in 2010. Of course, incomes rose dramatically during this time, especially during the post-1945 period. As a percentage of gross domestic product, federal spending was no higher in 2008 than it was in 1952 (about 20 percent).

Over the long haul, we can see that punctuations, along with long periods of relative stability, drive changes in the budget. At this level of aggregation, the disruptions associated with major wars seem to be the only catalysts that can shift our expectations of the role of government so completely. But more study is clearly needed to understand the complicated dynamics by which a war

FIGURE 2.4 U.S. Federal Government Outlays per Capita, 1791–2010

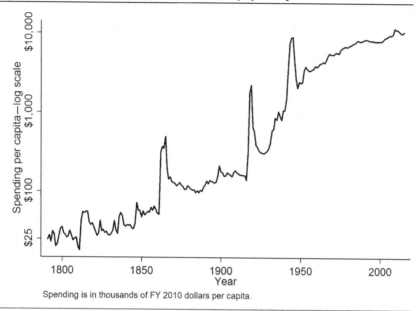

Spending is in thousands of FY 2010 dollars per capita.

NOTES: Spending is in thousands of FY 2010 dollars per capita.
Level in 1791: $25 per person; 2010: $12,040 per person.
SOURCE: Historical Tables of the U.S. Budget, adjusted by the authors with census and CPI data.

creates new taxes and spending capacity; then, after the war is over, government settles into a pattern of spending perhaps twice as much as it did before the war.

PUNCTUATED EQUILIBRIUM THEORY IN COMPARATIVE PERSPECTIVE

The punctuated equilibrium model was originally developed to understand the dynamics of policy change in subsystems, but it has been extended to a more general formulation of punctuated change in policymaking. We have described the first tests of this more general formulation in the study of public budgeting. This testing has resulted in new insights into the process, including (1) an elaboration of an agenda-based, attention-driven budgeting model, (2) the generation of hypotheses concerning the distribution of annual budget changes and the reasons for its shape, and (3) empirical evidence that conforms to the new theory but is antithetical to the normal changes expected from incremental theory or from most other budget theories. Punctuated equilibrium, rather than incrementalism alone, characterizes national budgeting in America and elsewhere, just as punctuated equilibrium, rather than gridlock or marginalism, characterizes overall policymaking in the American political system.

Founded on the bounded rationality of human decision making and on the nature of government institutions, punctuated equilibrium can make a strong claim that its propositions closely accord with what we have observed about US national policymaking. But how general are these dynamics? Do they hold across political systems? The ubiquity of serial attentiveness and organizational routines of operation leads us to expect that stability and punctuations are a feature of policymaking in many governments. At the same time, the institutional aspect of multiple venues interacts with boundedly rational decision making to make Punctuated Equilibrium Theory particularly apt for relatively open democracies. An important component of the initial formulation of the theory includes the multiple policymaking venues of American pluralism. The key questions are whether policy subsystems develop enough autonomy in other political systems to allow for independence from the central government and whether shifts in attention can act to change policymaking in those subsystems. It is likely that the processes of stability enforced by organizational routines interrupted by bursts of activity due to shifts in collective attention are general ones but that these processes are mediated by political institutions.

Where multiple venues occur as a consequence of institutional design, such as in federal systems, one would expect the dynamics of punctuated equilibrium to emerge. In the US Congress, committees are the linchpin of policy subsystems. There, overlapping committee jurisdictions offer opportunities for issue entrepreneurs to change jurisdictions by emphasizing particular issue characterizations (Baumgartner, Jones, and McLeod 2000). To what extent does this kind of dynamic extend beyond US policymaking organizations? Adam Sheingate (2000) has used the basic punctuated equilibrium concepts of policy image and venue shopping to study changes in agriculture policy in the European Union and the United States, and Sarah Pralle (2003) has studied environmental groups' exploitation of policy venues in forest policy in Canada and the United States. These systems have the requisite elements of openness and multiple venues. In the case of the European Union, the emergence of a strong central government from what previously were fully independent governments has offered students of public policy processes the opportunity to observe the effects of new venues in policy change. Princen and Rhinhard (2006, 1) write that "agenda setting in the EU takes place in two ways: 'from above,' through high-level political institutions urging EU action, and 'from below,' through policy experts formulating specific proposals in low-level groups and working parties." That is, the European Union has evolved into a set of policy subsystems that are important in making policy, but macrolevel policymaking forces are also at play. Mark Schrad (2007, 2010) used the idea to explain the global wave of prohibition in Western countries in the early twentieth century. Graeme Boushey (2010, 2012) applies the theory to how policies diffuse across the US states.

These interacting venues operate in many ways similarly to the pluralistic policymaking system in the United States (Guiraudon 2000a, 2003; Wendon 1998; Mazey 1998; Mazey and Richardson 2001). Cichowski (2006) studied how women's groups and environmental groups use EU-level opportunity structures by bringing litigation before the European Court of Justice and engaging in transnational mobilization and organization in Brussels to participate in policymaking. But such venue shopping does not always aid disadvantaged groups. Guiraudon (2000a, 2000b) shows in a study of immigration policy in France, Germany and the Netherlands, and the European Union that simple expansion of the debate—for example, to the electoral arena—does not necessarily benefit the disadvantaged, as Schattschneider originally suggested. Losing in a narrow venue does not mean winning in a broader one; it could instead invite even bigger losses (see also Mortensen 2007, 2009). Moreover, when immigration rights organizations won victories in national courts, conservatives on the issue were able to appeal to the European Union and blunt their victories (see also Givens and Ludke 2004). The whole process of conflict expansion and venue shopping is more dynamic and uncertain than early conflict expansion literature suggested. Losers in one venue may also lose in the next.

If policymaking devolves to experts in all systems, then a key question is, When does the subsystem dominate, and when does the issue spill over into the broader macropolitical arena? Timmermans and Scholten (2006) suggest that, even in the technical arena of science policy in a smaller European parliamentary system—the Netherlands—this does occur, and again the dynamics are roughly similar to those highlighted in the American version of the punctuated equilibrium model. In a study of immigration policy, Scholten and Timmermans (2004) show that immigration policy is punctuated but damped down through the implementation process at the local level.

Punctuated-type dynamics also occur in other European countries. Maesschalck (2002), in a study of a major police failure in Belgium in the Dutroux child abuse scandal, shows that policymaking generated by scandal follows a conflict expansion model consistent with the punctuated equilibrium approach. This finding is no fluke. In a comprehensive study of Belgian public policy processes during the 1990s, Walgrave, Varone, and Dumont (2006) directly compare the party model with the issue expansion model. They note the ability of the Dutroux and other scandals to destabilize the system, basically disrupting the party-dominated policymaking system with highly emotive information that political elites cannot afford to ignore. Similarly, Peter John (2006a) finds that the interaction of media coverage and events is more important in explaining major changes in budget commitment for urban affairs in the United Kingdom than are changes in party control.[4]

Cross-country studies of issue expansion offer the opportunity to examine how different institutional arrangements—that is, variations in the nature of political venues—affect the course of public policy. Timmermans (2001) examined cases of biomedical policy in four countries (Canada, the Netherlands, the United Kingdom, and Switzerland), finding that variation in arenas both at the macropolitical and policy subsystem levels had major effects on the tempo of agenda dynamics. Even where policy dynamics are broadly similar, as they seem to be in European democracies, the specific paths of policy development can be highly varied because of the operation of policy venues, particularly their interconnectedness with each other and with macropolitical forces.

In this enterprise, we need the qualitative studies of Pralle (2003), Princen and Rhinhard (2006), and Timmermans and Scholten (2006), as well as quantitative studies capable of tracing policy changes across longer periods. Such systematic investigations of the dynamics behind change and stability within particular policy domains have continued in recent years (see, e.g., Cashore and Howlett 2007; Busenberg 2011; Daviter 2009). In particular, many of these studies focus on how institutional structures permit change to occur and how the institutional structure influences the speed and magnitude of policy dynamics (e.g., Cashore and Howlett 2007; Mortensen 2005, 2007, 2009; Chaqués and Palau 2009).

THE COMPARATIVE POLICY AGENDAS PROJECT

One of the major outcomes of the policy agenda setting research initiated by Baumgartner and Jones in the early 1990s is the development of an international community of scholars doing policy agendas research. Within this loosely structured Comparative Agendas Project (CAP), some scholars apply and extend PET to countries other than the United States, but many scholars also work with other theories and other research questions. What unites these scholars is the application of the measurement system originally developed to construct the databases of the US-based Policy Agendas Project, as later adjusted for comparative use (Jones 2016). Currently, the CAP project consists of fifteen country projects, with more in the pipeline. Every year in June the group of scholars organizes an annual meeting with around seventy participants on average. Whereas the range of theoretical approaches and research questions is broad, a main advantage from a comparative perspective is the strict enforcement across countries of a common measurement system. This is a necessary requisite for further development of comparative research. Another recent initiative to promote more comparative policy agenda setting research is the setup of a common webpage from which all country datasets can be downloaded and where students and researchers can easily conduct online analyses of the data. CAP's website, www.comparativeagendas.net, is hosted by the University of Texas.

To give an impression of the scope and direction of research inspired by either PET or the methodological approach to agenda setting affiliated with the theory, we performed a set of systematic keyword searches in the major online bibliographic databases Scopus and ProQuest. The search strings were "punctuated equilibrium Jones Baumgartner," "disproportionate information processing Jones Baumgartner," and "agenda setting Jones Baumgartner." Publications just mentioning or briefly referring to the PET or the measurement system of CAP were then excluded. In the second round of searching, we supplemented this list of publications with more ad hoc online searches of relevant websites like the CAP and the European Union Policy Agendas Project (http://www.policyagendas.eu). In the third round, we circulated the list to Comparative Agendas Project scholars and asked them to identify whether some of their relevant publications were missing from the list. As of October 1, 2016, we ended up with a total of 393 relevant publications covering the period from 1991 to the present. For the full list of publications, see the online resources for this chapter at www.westviewpress.com/weible4e.

Figure 2.5 provides a sense of the growth in use of the theory and the measurement system over time. First, the figure inflects sharply upward after 2005,

FIGURE 2.5 Punctuated Equilibrium Articles over Time

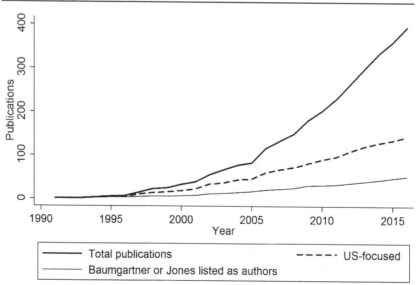

US-focused includes articles focusing exclusively on the US.

SOURCE: Authors' search of the literature.

clearly justifying this update in the assessment of the literature on Punctuated Equilibrium Theory. Second, perhaps the most noteworthy change since the first edition of this book is the marked increase in the number of publications using non-US data. The number of US studies has also increased over the years, but a total of 65 percent of all empirical studies before 2006 were based solely on US data, whereas the equivalent number is reduced to 36 percent for studies published after 2005. The bulk of the studies now focuses on political systems outside the United States. Third, the two most senior authors of this chapter were listed as coauthors for 21 percent of the publications in the early period, but for only 11 percent of those after 2005. Finally, although the figure does not represent this finding, the literature is highly empirical: our review showed just 18 review articles (such as this one), 39 purely theoretical treatments, and 336 empirical works; this last category represents 86 percent of the publications in the field. Table 2.1 shows the journals in which these articles have appeared. This list makes several things clear, particularly the importance of comparative work on the topic. The literature is well established in both US-based and comparative journals. Ninety different journals are represented in the list, including virtually all the major disciplinary journals as well as those focused on public policy, public administration, and US and comparative politics.

The dramatic increase in comparative use of the ideas and policy agenda setting approach associated with the PET is a remarkable development given the initial response to what some perceived as a peculiarly American focus in Baumgartner and Jones's *Agendas and Instability in American Politics*, with its notions of venue shopping in the complicated US system of separation of powers, federalism, and weak political parties. Surely, some surmised, things must be different in more centralized systems with more disciplined political parties. Although many things are indeed different in each political system, the basic limits of human cognition, organizational capacity, and attention at the core of PET give the theory a potential for universal application.

The increase in the number of publications around 2006 coincides with the development of the network of the comparative policy agendas project formed around independent country projects. An overview of the country projects and databases can be found at www.comparativeagendas.net. We've already noted the importance of these databases in the study of public budgeting, but they are critical in tracing changes in policy images and outputs over time.

In Denmark, Christoffer Green-Pedersen and his collaborators have traced the comparative policy dynamics of issues in more than one country, including tobacco policy in Denmark and the United States (Albaek, Green-Pedersen, and Nielsen 2007), euthanasia in Denmark, Belgium, and the Netherlands (Green-Pedersen 2004), and health care in Denmark and the United States (Green-Pedersen and Wilkerson 2006). Green-Pedersen and Mortensen (2010) provided a key insight into the roles of the parliamentary opposition in defining the political agenda in Denmark, discerning both the limits of strategic

TABLE 2.1 Journals in Which Punctuated Equilibrium Articles Have Been Published

Journal	Articles
Policy Studies Journal	59
Journal of European Public Policy	23
Journal of Public Policy	17
American Journal of Political Science	11
West European Politics	11
Policy Sciences	9
Review of Policy Research	9
European Journal of Political Research	8
Governance	8
Political Communication	8
Comparative Political Studies	7
Journal of Public Administration Research and Theory	7
Political Studies	7
Public Administration	7
British Journal of Political Science	6
Canadian Journal of Public Policy	6
Political Research Quarterly	6
Party Politics	5
Journal of Politics	5
Urban Affairs Review	4
American Political Science Review	3
Public Administration Review	3
Scandinavian Political Studies	3
Public Budgeting and Finance	3
Sixty-eight other journals, combined	82
Nonjournal publications	76
Total publications	393

agenda setting available to the government and the power of the opposition to focus attention in those areas the government might prefer to avoid (see also Green-Pedersen and Mortensen 2015).

Similar dynamics are key to Walgrave, Lefevere, and Nuytemans's (2009) discussion of Belgian media coverage of politics. In Canada, Stuart Soroka and

associated researchers have used parliamentary question periods as prime indicators of agenda setting and conflict expansion and have examined in detail
the relative roles of public opinion and the media in the agenda setting process
(Soroka 2002; Penner, Blidock, and Soroka 2006). The mechanisms of issue
expansion and policy development are broadly similar in different democratic
political systems, even though they may play out differently as they are channeled through different decision making institutions.

In an edited book (Engeli, Green-Pedersen, and Larsen 2012), scholars
analyze morality politics through focused case comparisons of the treatment
of such issues as euthanasia, abortion, and in vitro fertilization in the United
States and several Western European countries. Most recently, Green-Pedersen
and Walgrave (2014) have edited a book bringing together more quantitative
findings from the Comparative Agendas Project in Europe to develop a theory
not only of policy agendas and agenda setting but also of the dynamics of institutional evolution more generally. Peter John et al. (2013) have recently developed a similar argument about the development of UK politics from 1945 to
present. John and Jennings's (2010) article had already discussed some of these
findings with reference to punctuated changes in governmental attention, often
unrelated to electoral turnover. Chaqués-Bonafont, Palau, and Baumgartner
(2015) review recent Spanish political history through the lens of the Spanish
agendas project and document a range of new findings.

But there is a further complication. Part of any differences in policies between countries may be attributed to differences in the mobilization of actors and the subsequent timing and sequencing of events. Consequently, even
differences in policies between countries cannot necessarily be attributed to
differences in institutions, as Pralle (2006) has shown in a case study of lawn
pesticide policy in Canada and the United States. Jumping to the conclusion
that Canada provides a more receptive venue for pesticide regulation might not
be warranted without a study of the dynamics of political choice.

The punctuated equilibrium model is also proving useful in understanding
relations among nations, such as in protracted interstate rivalries (Cioffi-Revilla
1998), the role of norms in international politics (Goertz 2003), and agenda setting in global disease control (Shiftman 2003; Shiftman, Beer, and Wu 2002).
The latter study compared three models of policymaking—the incrementalist,
the rationalist, and punctuated equilibrium—and found "a more complex pattern in which interventions are available only to select populations, punctuated
with bursts of attention as these interventions spread across the globe in concentrated periods of time" (Shiftman, Beer, and Wu 2002, 225).

The Goertz work is particularly important because its analysis is based in
organizational analysis, the general basis for punctuated equilibrium in US domestic policies. Goertz focuses on the development and change of organizational routines as critical in governing relations among nations. As in the case
of comparative politics, it is critical in the future to begin to understand which

aspects of policymaking result from more general dynamics based in human cognition and organizational behavior and which relate to the particulars of the institutions under study. Such considerations move us beyond the confines of theories for institutions and toward a more general theory of the interaction of humans in organizations.

Examinations of the role of political parties with regard to stability and change in agendas and public policy represent another new research area—one that is probably a consequence of the expansion of the Punctuated Equilibrium Theory into non-US countries, where political parties traditionally have played a much more prominent role in the analysis of politics than they have in the United States. Two subthemes can be identified within this research agenda. One track offers a new approach to the classic question about the importance of elections and changes in the partisan composition of governments as drivers of policy and agenda changes. This perspective challenges the "politics matter" perspective, which has generally been restricted to looking for election and partisan effects along the left-right dimension. Approaching the question at the issue level, as is characteristic of PET studies, not only offers a fresh and more detailed look at the election-based explanations of change but also challenges conventional wisdom about the importance of elections and ideology as explanations of change. Thus, Mortensen et al. (2011), for instance, in a study of change and stability in government agendas across three different countries and several decades, conclude that there is no evidence that elections, changes in government colors, or changes of prime minister systematically affect the level of change and stability in government agendas. Furthermore, this finding corresponds with studies of agenda setting in France (Baumgartner, Grossman, et al. 2009), the United States (Jones and Baumgartner 2005, 84–85), and the United Kingdom (John and Jennings 2010). Agendas do change over time, but the timing of such changes is not closely related to elections or shifts of governments. To understand these changes requires more elaborate theoretical models about how governments respond to and process new information about changes in their environment (Jones and Baumgartner 2005; Baumgartner, Jones, and Wilkerson 2011; Mortensen et al. 2011).

The other subtheme within this new research agenda on political parties regards how political parties compete with each other when trying to set the political agenda. Though most scholars acknowledge that parties do respond to their competitors' attention to issues, the dominant theoretical accounts (e.g., Budge and Hofferbert 1990; Budge and Farlie 1983; Petrocik 1996; Simon 2002) have had much more to say about ignorance and selective issue emphases than about issue overlap and responsiveness. Inspired by agenda setting research and utilizing the systematic topics coding of political attention developed in the Comparative Agendas Project, recent agenda setting studies have started to challenge the conventional understanding of selective issue emphasis and show how political parties to a large extent do respond to each other instead of simply talking past each other on different issues (Vliegenthart and Wal-grave 2011). Furthermore, the literature has started to investigate the unequal agenda setting power of different political parties to improve the understand-ing of how and why political agendas change (Vliegenthart, Walgrave, and Meppelink 2011; Green-Pedersen and Mortensen 2010, 2015; Mortensen and Green-Pedersen 2015).

Finally, the European Union Policy Agendas Project represents an impor-tant development in which a number of researchers have utilized the topics coding system to systematically trace change and stability in attention to policy issues in the European Union and its institutions (see, e.g., Princen 2009, 2013; Alexandrova and Timmermans 2013; Alexandrova 2015, 2016). Central ques-tions within this research agenda regard which issues feature on the EU agenda at specific points, how the definitions of issues change, and which factors drive the formation of EU priorities. In the next years, we have no doubt that many of the most important studies of policy agendas and the further elaborations of PET will come from the EU and related policy agenda projects worldwide. The vast data infrastructure that has been created and that continues to grow pro-vides both the opportunity to test new theoretical questions and the scientific venue for the development of new ideas.

CONCLUSION

The initial theory of punctuated equilibrium in policy processes is applicable to the dynamics of the specialized politics of policy subsystems. It has proved useful enough that scholars have employed it to understand a variety of policy-making situations in the United States and abroad. It has proved robust enough to survive several rigorous quantitative and qualitative tests. It has spawned a new approach to the study of public budgeting based in stochastic processes, and it hence has satisfied the criterion that any theory be not only verifiable but also fruitful in suggesting new lines of inquiry.

It has also led to considerable discussion among policy practitioners. In his call to action on environmental change, *Red Sky at Morning*, Gustave Speth (2004) cites Punctuated Equilibrium Theory as a policy analysis that can lead to rapid, correcting change in the face of accumulating factual evidence. *Theories of the Policy Process* aims to supply better theory in the study of policy pro-cesses, and better applied work on policy change will occur with better theory; indeed, there is no substitute for this.

The formulation of the theory in stochastic process terms has made it pos-sible to compare policy process theories with general formulations of human dynamic processes. Punctuated dynamics, in which any activity consists of long periods of stability interspersed with bursts of frenetic activity, may be the general case in human systems. For example, Barabasi (2005) shows that when humans prioritize incoming information for action, the distribution of waiting times for action on the information is "heavy tailed"—that is, lepto-kurtic. When prioritization is not practiced and inputs are instead subject to random choice for processing, the distribution is not fat tailed.[5] The policy processes we study fundamentally involve prioritization, although they are much more complex than Barabasi's waiting-time studies. Perhaps the key to these distributional similarities is in setting priorities. If so, then punctuated dynamics may be a direct consequence of disproportionate information processing, in which people and the organizations they inhabit struggle to prioritize informational signals from the environment within a particular institutional frame or structure (Jones and Baumgartner 2005).

The utility of Punctuated Equilibrium Theory and its agreement with what is observed come at a price. The complexity and changing interactions of the American policy process mean that accurate policy predictions will be limited to the system level. Specific predictions about policy outcomes are possible only to the extent that we are able to avoid positive feedback and punctuations when we choose areas and periods for study or that we limit our "predictions" to what we can know, after the fact, were successful mobilizations. Nonlinearity, nonnormality, interdependencies, and high levels of aggregation for empirical data mean that clear causal chains and precise predictions work only in some cases and during some times. Because stasis characterizes most of the cases and most of the times, scholars may be convinced that they have a good working model of the process. But a complete model will not be locally predictable because we cannot foresee the timing or the outcomes of the punctuations.

What will cause the next big shift in attention, change in dimension, or new frame of reference? Immersion in a policy or issue area may lead to inferences about pressures for change, but when will the next attention shift occur in a particular policy area? At the systems level, punctuated equilibrium, as a theory, leads us to expect that some policy punctuation is under way almost all of the time. And the theory joins institutional settings and decision making processes to predict that the magnitude of local changes will be related to their systems-level frequency of occurrence. Punctuated Equilibrium Theory predicts a form of systems-level stability, but it will not help us make point-specific predictions for particular policy issues, unless we look only during periods of stability.

We can have a systems-level model of the policy process even without an individual-level model for each policy. Linear predictions about the details of future policies will fail each time they meet an unforeseen punctuation; they will succeed as long as the parameters of the test coincide with periods of equilibrium. This limitation means that it will be tempting to offer models applicable only to the more easily testable and confirmable periods of relative stability. Or investigators will focus on big changes and work backward from them to try to explain the case. This approach is subject to the fallacy of attributing causality to spurious factors. In our view, a clearer, more complete, and more empirically accurate theoretical lens is that of punctuated equilibrium, especially in its more general form, which integrates large policy changes with periods of stability.

NOTES

1. Special issues of the following journals have also appeared: *Policy Studies Journal* 41, no. 1 (2012); *Comparative Political Studies* 44, no. 8 (2011); and *Journal of European Public Policy* 13, no. 7 (2006).

2. Punctuated equilibrium was first advanced as an explanation for the development of differences among species, or speciation (Eldridge and Gould 1972; Raup 1991). Rather than changing smoothly and slowly, as in the later Darwinian models, evolution and speciation were better characterized as a near stasis punctuated by large-scale extinctions and replacements. For example, there was a virtual explosion of diversity of life in the Precambrian period, an explosion that has never been repeated on such an immense scale (Gould 1989). The notion has been vigorously contested by evolutionary biologists, who claim that disconnects in evolution are not possible (although variations in the pace of evolution clearly are) (Dawkins 1996). Interestingly, some of these scholars have argued that consciousness makes possible punctuations in human cultural evolution; what cannot occur via genes can occur via memes (Dawkins's term for the transmitters of cultural adaptive advantage) (Dawkins 1989; see also Boyd and Richerson 1985).

3. Whether we plot percentage changes, first differences, or changes in logged data, the distributions are leptokurtic and not normal. When we compare annual changes in budget authority for functions and subfunctions, the characteristic leptokurtosis remains, although the subfunctions are more leptokurtic than the functions. When we plot the distribution of annual changes by agency, leptokurtosis remains. We examined plots of the following: subfunction budget outlay data, 1962–1994; subfunction budget authority data, 1976–1994; and agency-level budget authority data, 1976–1994. All exhibited leptokurtosis.

4. Punctuated equilibrium has also proved useful in understanding stability and change in British trunk roads policy (Dudley and Richardson 1996).

5. Prioritization results in a Pareto distribution of waiting times, whereas random processing results in an exponential distribution (Barabasi 2005).

REFERENCES

Adler, E. Scott, and John D. Wilkerson. 2012. *Congress and the Politics of Problem Solving*. New York: Cambridge University Press.

Albaek, Eric, Christoffer Green-Pedersen, and Lars Beer Nielsen. 2007. *Making Tobacco Consumption a Political Issue in US and Denmark*. Aarhus, Denmark: Aarhus University.

Alexandrova, P. 2015. "Upsetting the agenda: The clout of external focusing events in the European Council." *Journal of Public Policy* 35 (3): 505–530.

———. 2016. "Explaining Political Attention Allocation with the Help of Issue Character: Evidence from the European Council." *European Political Science Review* 8 (3): 405–425.

Alexandrova, Petya, and Arco Timmermans. 2013. "National Interest versus the Common Good: The Presidency in European Council Agenda Setting." *European Journal of Political Research* 52 (3): 316–338.

Baird, Vanessa. 2006. *Shaping the Judicial Agenda: Justices' Priorities and Litigant Strategies*. Charlottesville: University of Virginia Press.

Bak, Per. 1997. *How Nature Works*. New York: Springer-Verlag.

Bak, Per, and Kan Chen. 1991. "Self-Organized Criticality." *Scientific American* 264:46–53.

Barabasi, Albert-László. 2005. "The Origin of Bursts and Heavy Tails in Human Dynamics." *Nature* 435 (May): 207–211.

Baumgartner, Frank R. 2013. "Discrediting the Status Quo: Ideas, Levels of Policy Change, and Punctuated Equilibrium." *Governance* 26 (2): 239–258.

Baumgartner, Frank R., Christian Breunig, Christoffer Green-Pedersen, Bryan D. Jones, Peter B. Mortensen, Michiel Neytemans, and Stefaan Walgrave. 2009. "Punctuated Equilibrium in Comparative Perspective." *American Journal of Political Science* 53 (3): 602–619.

Baumgartner, Frank R., Abel François, and Martial Foucault. 2006. "Punctuated Equilibrium and French Budgeting Processes." *Journal of European Public Policy* 13:1086–1103.

Baumgartner, Frank R., Emiliano Grossman, and Sylvain Brouard. 2009. "Agenda-Setting Dynamics in France: Revisiting the 'Partisan Hypothesis.'" *French Politics* 7 (2): 57–95.

Baumgartner, Frank R., and Bryan D. Jones. 1991. "Agenda Dynamics and Policy Subsystems." *Journal of Politics* 53:1044–1074.

———. 1993. *Agendas and Instability in American Politics*. Chicago: University of Chicago Press.

———. 2002. "Positive and Negative Feedback in Politics." In *Policy Dynamics*, edited by Frank R. Baumgartner and Bryan D. Jones, 3–28. Chicago: University of Chicago Press.

———. 2014. *The Politics of Information*. Chicago: University of Chicago Press.

———. 2015. *The Politics of Information*. Chicago: University of Chicago Press.

Baumgartner, Frank R., Bryan D. Jones, and Michael McLeod. 2000. "The Evolution of Legislative Jurisdictions." *Journal of Politics* 62:321–349.

Baumgartner, Frank R., Bryan D. Jones, and John Wilkerson. 2002. "Studying Policy Dynamics." In *Policy Dynamics*, edited by Frank R. Baumgartner and Bryan D. Jones, 29–45. Chicago: University of Chicago Press.

———. 2011. "Comparative Studies of Policy Dynamics." *Comparative Political Studies* 44 (8): 947–972.

Berkman, Michael, and Christopher Reenock. 2004. "Incremental Consolidation and Comprehensive Reorganization of American State Executive Branches." *American Journal of Political Science* 48:796–812.

Berry, William D. 1990. "The Confusing Case of Budgetary Incrementalism: Too Many Meanings for a Single Concept." *Journal of Politics* 52:167–196.

Birkland, Thomas. 1997. *After Disaster: Agenda Setting, Public Policy, and Focusing Events*. Washington, DC: Georgetown University Press.

Blais, Andre, Donald Blake, and Stephane Dion. 1993. "Do Parties Make a Difference? Parties and the Size of Government in Liberal Democracies." *American Journal of Political Science* 37:40–62.

Bosso, Christopher J. 1987. *Pesticides and Politics: The Life Cycle of a Public Issue*. Pittsburgh, PA: University of Pittsburgh Press.

Boushey, Graeme. 2010. *Policy Diffusion Dynamics in America*. New York: Cambridge University Press.

———. 2012. "Punctuated Equilibrium Theory and the Diffusion of Innovations." *Policy Studies Journal* 40 (1): 127–146.

Boyd, Robert, and Peter Richerson. 1985. *Culture and the Evolutionary Process*. Chicago: University of Chicago Press.

Breunig, Christian. 2006. "The More Things Change, the More They Stay the Same: A Comparative Analysis of Budget Punctuations." *Journal of European Public Policy* 13:1069–1085.

Breunig, Christian and Bryan D. Jones. 2011. "Stochastic Process Methods with an Application to Budgetary Data." *Political Analysis* 19 (1): 103–117.

Breunig, Christian, and Chris Koski. 2006. "Punctuated Equilibria and Budgets in the American States." *Policy Studies Journal* 34 (3): 363–379.

———. 2012. "The Tortoise or the Hare? Incrementalism, Punctuations, and Their Consequences." *Policy Studies Journal* 40 (1): 45–68.

Breunig, Christian, Chris Koski, and Peter B. Mortensen. 2010. "Stability and Punctuations in Public Spending: A Comparative Study of Budget Functions." *Journal of Public Administration Research and Theory* 20 (3): 703–722.

Browne, William P. 1995. *Cultivating Congress: Constituents, Issues, and Interests in Agricultural Policymaking*. Lawrence: University of Kansas Press.

Budge, Ian, and Dennis Farlie. 1983. *Explaining and Predicting Elections: Issue Effects and Party Strategies in Twenty-Three Democracies*. New York: Allen & Unwin.

Budge, Ian, and Richard I. Hofferbert. 1990. Mandates and Policy Outputs: U.S. Party Platforms and Federal Expenditures. *American Political Science Review* 84:111–132.

Busenberg, George J. 2004. "Wildfire Management in the United States: The Evolution of a Policy Failure." *Review of Policy Research* 21 (2): 145–156.

———. 2011. "The Policy Dynamics of the Trans-Alaska Pipeline System." *Review of Policy Research* 28 (5): 401–422.

Caamaño-Alegre, José, and Santiago Lago-Peñas. 2011. "Combining Incrementalism and Exogenous Factors in Analyzing National Budgeting: An Application to Spain." *Public Finance Review* 39 (5): 712–740.

Cashore, Benjamin, and Michael Howlett. 2007. "Punctuating Which Equilibrium? Understanding Thermostatic Policy Dynamics in Pacific Northwest Forestry." *American Journal of Political Science* 51 (3): 532–551.

Ceccoli, Stephen J. 2003. "Policy Punctuations and Regulatory Drug Review." *Journal of Policy History* 15:158–191.

Chan, Kwan Nok, and Shuang Zhao. 2016. "Punctuated Equilibrium and the Information Disadvantage of Authoritarianism: Evidence from the People's Republic of China." *Policy Studies Journal* 44:134–155.

Chan, Nikketer. 2006. *An Application of Punctuated-Equilibrium Theory to the Study of Administrative Restructuring Policy in Post-War Hong Kong.* Hong Kong: Department of Politics and Public Administration, Hong Kong University.

Chaqués-Bonafont, Laura, and Anna M. Palau. 2009. "Comparing the Dynamics of Change in Food Safety and Pharmaceutical Policy in Spain." *Journal of Public Policy* 29 (1): 103–126.

Chaqués-Bonafont, Laura, Anna M. Palau, and Frank R. Baumgartner. 2015. *Agenda Dynamics in Spain.* Houndsmills, UK: Palgrave Macmillan.

Cichowski, Rachel. 2006. *The European Court and Civil Society: Litigation, Mobilization and Governance.* Cambridge: Cambridge University Press.

Cioffi-Revilla, Claudio. 1998. "The Political Uncertainty of Interstate Rivalries: A Punctuated Equilibrium Model." In *The Dynamics of Enduring Rivalries,* edited by Paul F. Diehl, 64–97. Urbana: University of Illinois Press.

Cobb, Roger W., and Charles D. Elder. 1983. *Participation in American Politics: The Dynamics of Agenda-Building.* Baltimore: Johns Hopkins University Press.

Cobb, Roger W., and Marc Howard Ross, eds. 1997. *Cultural Strategies of Agenda Denial.* Lawrence: University of Kansas Press.

Davis, Otto A., M. A. H. Dempster, and Aaron Wildavsky. 1966. "A Theory of the Budget Process." *American Political Science Review* 60:529–547.

———. 1974. "Towards a Predictive Theory of Government Expenditure: U.S. Domestic Appropriations." *British Journal of Political Science* 4:419–452.

Daviter, Falk. 2009. "Schattschneider in Brussels: How Policy Conflict Reshaped the Biotechnology Agenda in the European Union." *West European Politics* 32 (6): 1118–1139.

———. 2013. "An Information Processing Perspective on Decision Making in the European Union." *Public Administration* 92 (2). doi:10.1111/padm.12071.

Dawkins, Richard. 1989. *The Selfish Gene.* 2nd ed. Oxford: Oxford University Press.

———. 1996. *Climbing Mount Improbable.* New York: W. W. Norton.

Dodd, Lawrence C. 1994. "Political Learning and Political Change: Understanding Development Across Time." In *The Dynamics of American Politics,* edited by Lawrence C. Dodd and Calvin Jillson, 331–364. Boulder, CO: Westview Press.

Downs, Anthony. 1972. "Up and Down with Ecology: The Issue-Attention Cycle." *Public Interest* 28:38–50.

Dudley, Geoffrey, and Jeremy Richardson. 1996. "Why Does Policy Change over Time? Adversarial Policy Communities, Alternative Policy Arenas, and British Trunk Roads Policy, 1945–95." *Journal of European Public Policy* 3:63–83.

Eldridge, Niles, and Stephen J. Gould. 1972. "Punctuated Equilibria: An Alternative to Phyletic Gradualism." In *Models in Paleobiology,* edited by Thomas J. M. Schopf. San Francisco: Freeman Cooper.

Engeli, Isabelle, Christoffer Green-Pedersen, and Lars Thorup Larsen, eds. 2012. *Morality Politics in Western Europe: Parties, Agendas and Policy Choices.* Basingstoke, UK: Palgrave Macmillan.

Epp, Derek. 2015. "Punctuated Equilibria in the Private System and the Stability of Market Systems." *Policy Studies Journal* 43:417–436.

Érdi, Peter. 2008. *Complexity Explained.* Berlin: Springer.

Givens, Terri, and Adam Ludke. 2004. "The Politics of European Immigration Policy." *Policy Studies Journal* 32:145–165.

Goertz, Gary. 2003. *International Norms and Decision Making: A Punctuated Equilibrium Model.* Lanham, MD: Rowman & Littlefield.

Gould, Stephen Jay. 1989. *Wonderful Life: The Burgess Shale and the Nature of History.* New York: W. W. Norton.

Green-Pedersen, Christoffer. 2004. *The Conflict of Conflicts: Euthanasia in Denmark, Belgium, and the Netherlands.* Aarhus, Denmark: Aarhus University.

Green-Pedersen, Christoffer, and Peter B. Mortensen. 2010. "Who Sets the Agenda and Who Responds to It in the Danish Parliament? A New Model of Issue Competition and Agenda-Setting." *European Journal of Political Research* 49 (2): 257–281.

———. 2015. "Avoidance and Engagement: Issue Competition in Multiparty Systems." *Political Studies* 63 (4): 747–764.

Green-Pedersen, Christoffer, and Stefaan Walgrave, eds. 2014. *Agenda Setting, Policies, and Political Systems: A Comparative Approach.* Chicago: University of Chicago Press.

Green-Pedersen, Christoffer, and John Wilkerson. 2006. "How Agenda Attributes Shape Politics." *Journal of European Public Policy* 13:1039–1052.

Guiraudon, Virginie. 2000a. "European Integration and Migration Policy: Vertical Policy-Making as Venue Shopping." *Journal of Common Market Studies* 38 (2): 251–271.

———. 2000b. *Les politiques d'immigration en Europe: Allemagne, France, Pays-Bas.* Paris: L'Harmattan.

———. 2003. "The Constitution of a European Immigration Policy Domain." *Journal of European Public Policy* 10:263–282.

Hayes, Michael T. 1992. *Incrementalism and Public Policy.* New York: Longman.

Herweg, Nicole, Nikolaos Zahariadis, and Reimut Zohlnhöfer. 2017. "The Multiple Streams Framework: Foundations, Refinements, and Empirical Applications." In *Theories of the Policy Process,* 4th ed., edited by Christopher M. Weible and Paul A. Sabatier, 17–53. Boulder, CO: Westview Press.

Jacob, Herbert. 1988. *Silent Revolution: The Transformation of Divorce Law in the United States.* Chicago: University of Chicago Press.

Jenkins-Smith, Hank C., Daniel Nohrstedt, Christopher M. Weible, and Karin Ingold. 2017. "The Advocacy Coalition Framework: An Overview of the Research Program." In *Theories of the Policy Process,* 4th ed., edited by Christopher M. Weible and Paul A. Sabatier, 135–171. Boulder, CO: Westview Press.

Jensen, J. L., P. B. Mortensen, and S. Serritzlew. 2016. "The Dynamic Model of Choice for Public Policy Reconsidered: A Formal Analysis with an Application to US Budget Data." *Journal of Public Administration Research and Theory* 26 (2): 226–238.

John, Peter. 2006a. "Explaining Policy Change: The Impact of the Media, Public Opinion, and Political Violence on Urban Budgets in England." *Journal of European Public Policy* 13:1053–1068.

———. 2006b. "The Policy Agendas Project: A Review." *Journal of European Public Policy* 13:975–986.

John, Peter, Antony Bertelli, Will Jennings, and Shaun Bevan. 2013. *Policy Agendas in British Politics*. Basingstoke, UK: Palgrave Macmillan.

John, Peter, and Will Jennings. 2010. "Punctuations and Turning Points in British Politics: The Policy Agenda of the Queen's Speech, 1940–2005." *British Journal of Political Science* 40:561–586.

John, Peter, and Helen Margetts. 2003. "Policy Punctuations in the UK." *Public Administration* 81:411–432.

Johnson, Norman L., Samuel Kotz, and N. Balakrishnan. 1994. *Continuous Univariate Distributions*. New York: Wiley.

Jones, Bryan D. 1994. *Reconceiving Decision-Making in Democratic Politics: Attention, Choice, and Public Policy*. Chicago: University of Chicago Press.

———. 2001. *Politics and the Architecture of Choice*. Chicago: University of Chicago Press.

———. 2003. "Bounded Rationality and Political Science: Lessons for Public Administration and Public Policy." *Journal of Public Administration Research and Theory* 13:395–412.

———. 2016. "The Comparative Policy Agendas Projects as Measurement Systems: Response to Dowding, Hindmoor and Martin." *Journal of Public Policy* 36 (1): 31.

Jones, Bryan D., and Frank R. Baumgartner. 2005. *The Politics of Attention*. Chicago: University of Chicago Press.

———. 2012. "From There to Here: Punctuated Equilibrium to the General Punctuation Thesis to a Theory of Government Information Processing." *Policy Studies Journal* 40 (1): 1–19.

Jones, Bryan D., Frank R. Baumgartner, Christian Breunig, Christoffer Wlezien, Stuart Soroka, Martial Foucault, Abel François, Christoffer Green-Pederson, Chris Koski, Peter John, Peter B. Mortensen, Frédéric Varone, and Stefaan Walgrave. 2009. "A General Empirical Law of Public Budgets: A Comparative Analysis." *American Journal of Political Science* 53:855–873.

Jones, Bryan D., Frank Baumgartner, and Jeffrey Talbert. 1993. "The Destruction of Issue Monopolies in Congress." *American Political Science Review* 87:657–671.

Jones, Bryan D., Frank Baumgartner, and James B. True. 1998. "Policy Punctuations: U.S. Budget Authority, 1947–1995." *Journal of Politics* 60:1–33.

Jones, Bryan D., Tracy Sulkin, and Heather Larsen. 2003. "Policy Punctuations in American Political Institutions." *American Political Science Review* 97:151–170.

Jones, Bryan D., and Herschel Thomas III. 2012. "Bounded Rationality and Public Policy Decision-Making." In *The Routledge Handbook of Public Policy*, edited by Eduardo

Araral Jr., Scott Fritzen, Michael Howlett, M. Ramesh, and Xun Wu, 273–286. Oxford: Routledge.

Jones, Bryan D., Herschel Thomas III, and Michelle Wolfe. 2014. "Policy Bubbles." *Policy Studies Journal* 42:146–171. doi:10.1111/psj.12046.

Jones, Bryan D., Samuel Workman, and Ashley Jochim. 2009. "Information Processing and Policy Dynamics." *Policy Studies Journal* 37:75–92.

Jones, Bryan D., László Zalányi, and Péter Érdi. 2014. "An Integrated Theory of Budgetary Politics and Some Empirical Tests: The US National Budget, 1791–2010." *American Journal of Political Science* 58:561–578. doi:10.1111/ajps.12088.

Jordan, Meagan. 2003. "Punctuations and Agendas." *Journal of Policy Analysis and Management* 22:345–360.

Kahneman, Daniel. 2011. *Thinking, Fast and Slow*. New York: Farrar, Straus, and Giroux.

Kamlet, Mark S., and David C. Mowery. 1987. "Influences on Executive and Congressional Budgetary Priorities, 1955–1981." *American Political Science Review* 81:155–178.

Kelly, Sean. 1994. "Punctuated Change and the Era of Divided Government." In *New Perspectives on American Politics*, edited by Lawrence C. Dodd and Calvin Jillson, 162–190. Washington, DC: Congressional Quarterly Press.

Kenny, Sally. 2003. "Where Is Gender in Agenda-Setting?" *Women and Politics* 25: 179–204.

Kiel, Douglas, and Euel Elliott. 1992. "Budgets as Dynamic Systems: Change, Variation, Time, and Budgetary Heuristics." *Journal of Public Administration Theory* 2:139–156.

Kiewiet, Roderick, and Matthew McCubbins. 1991. *The Logic of Delegation: Congressional Parties and the Appropriations Process*. Chicago: University of Chicago Press.

Kingdon, John. 1984. *Agendas, Alternatives, and Public Policies*. 2nd ed. Boston: Little, Brown.

Krasner, Stephen. 1984. "Approaches to the State: Alternative Conceptions and Historical Dynamics." *Comparative Politics* 16:223–246.

Lam, Wai Fung, and Kwan Nok Chan. 2014. "How Authoritarianism Intensifies Punctuated Equilibrium: The Dynamics of Policy Attention in Hong Kong." *Governance* 28:549–570.

Leach, William D., and Paul A. Sabatier. 2005. "To Trust an Adversary: Integrating Rational and Psychological Models of Collaborative Policymaking." *American Political Science Review* 99:491–503.

Lindblom, Charles. 1959. "The Science of Muddling Through." *Public Administration Review* 19:79–88.

Maesschalck, Jeroen. 2002. "When Do Scandals Have an Impact on Policymaking?" *International Public Management Journal* 5:169–193.

Mandelbrot, Benoit. 1963. "New Methods in Statistical Economics." *Journal of Political Economy* 71:421–440.

Manna, Paul. 2006. *School's In: Federalism and the National Education Agenda*. Washington, DC: Georgetown University Press.

May, Peter, Samuel Workman, and Bryan D. Jones. 2008. "Organizing Attention: Responses of the Bureaucracy to Agenda Disruption." *Public Administration Theory and Research* 18:517–541.

Mazey, Sonia. 1998. "The European Union and Women's Rights: From the Europeanization of National Agendas to the Nationalization of a European Agenda?" *Journal of European Public Policy* 5 (1): 131–152.

Mazey, Sonia, and Jeremy Richardson. 2001. "Interest Groups and EU Policy-Making: Organisational Logic and Venue Shopping." In *European Union: Power and Policy-Making,* edited by Jeremy Richardson, 217–237. 2nd ed. London: Routledge.

McCool, Daniel. 1998. "The Subsystem Family of Concepts." *Political Research Quarterly* 51:551–570.

McDonough, John. 1998. *Interests, Ideas, and Deregulation.* Ann Arbor: University of Michigan Press.

McFarland, Andrew W. 2004. *Neopluralism.* Lawrence: University of Kansas Press.

McLendon, M. K. 2003. "The Politics of Higher Education: Toward an Expanded Research Agenda." *Educational Policy* 17 (1): 165–191.

Meier, Kenneth. 1985. *Regulation: Politics, Bureaucracy, and Economics.* New York: St. Martin's Press.

Midlarsky, Manus I. 1988. "Rulers and the Ruled: Patterned Inequality and the Onset of Mass Political Violence." *American Political Science Review* 82:491–509.

Mortensen, Peter B. 2005. "Policy Punctuations in Danish Local Budgeting." *Public Administration* 83:931–950.

———. 2007. "Stability and Change in Public Policy: A Longitudinal Study of Comparative Subsystem Dynamics." *Policy Studies Journal* 35 (3): 373–394.

———. 2009. "Political Attention and Public Spending in the U.S." *Policy Studies Journal* 37 (3): 435–455.

Mortensen, Peter B., and Christoffer Green-Pedersen. 2015. "Institutional Effects of Changes in Political Attention: Explaining Organizational Changes in the Top Bureaucracy." *Journal of Public Administration Research and Theory* 25 (1): 165–189.

Mortensen, Peter B., Christoffer Green-Pedersen, Gerard Breeman, Will Jennings, Peter John, Arco Timmermans, Laura Chaqués, and Anna Palau. 2011. "Comparing Government Agendas: Executive Speeches in the Netherlands, United Kingdom and Denmark." *Comparative Political Studies* 44 (8): 973–1000.

Mulholland, Shaila, and Christine Shakespeare. 2005. *Policy Frameworks for Higher Education Studies.* New York: Alliance for International Higher Education Policy Studies.

Newell, Allen, and Herbert A. Simon. 1972. *Human Problem Solving.* Englewood Cliffs, NJ: Prentice Hall.

Niskanen, William A. 1971. *Bureaucracy and Representative Government.* Chicago: Aldine.

Ostrom, Charles W., Jr., and Robin F. Marra. 1986. "A Reactive Linkage Model of the U.S. Defense Expenditure Policymaking Process." *American Political Science Review* 72:941–957.

Padgett, John F. 1980. "Bounded Rationality in Budgetary Research." *American Political Science Review* 74:354–372.

———. 1981. "Hierarchy and Ecological Control in Federal Budgetary Decision Making." *American Journal of Sociology* 87:75–128.

Pauw, J. C. 2007. "A Measurement of Year-on-Year Variation in the Allocations to National Departments in South Africa (2003/4–2007/8) from a Public Management Point of View." *Politeia* 26 (3): 252–272.

Penner, Erin, Kelly Blidock, and Stuart Soroka. 2006. "Legislative Priorities and Public Opinion: Representation of Partisan Agendas in the Canadian House of Commons." *Journal of European Public Policy* 13:1006–1020.

Peters, Edgar E. 1991. *Chaos and Order in the Capital Markets.* New York: Wiley.

Petrocik, John R. 1996. "Issue Ownership in Presidential Elections, with a 1980 Case Study." *American Journal of Political Science* 40:825–850.

Pralle, Sarah. 2003. "Venue Shopping, Political Strategy, and Policy Change: A Case Study of Canadian Forest Advocacy." *Journal of Public Policy* 23:233–260.

———. 2006. "Timing and Sequence in Agenda Setting and Policy Change: A Comparative Study of Lawn Pesticide Policy in the US and Canada." *Journal of European Public Policy* 13:987–1005.

Princen, Sebastiaan. 2009. *Agenda-Setting in the European Union.* Basingstoke, UK: Palgrave Macmillan.

———. 2013. "Punctuated Equilibrium Theory and the European Union." *Journal of European Public Policy* 20 (6): 854–870.

Princen, Sebastiaan, and Mark Rhinard. 2006. "Crashing and Creeping: Agenda Setting Dynamics in the European Union." *Journal of European Public Policy* 13:1119–1132.

Raup, David M. 1991. *Extinction: Bad Genes or Bad Luck?* New York: W. W. Norton.

Redford, Emmette S. 1969. *Democracy in the Administrative State.* New York: Oxford University Press.

Repetto, Robert, ed. 2006. *By Fits and Starts: Punctuated Equilibrium and the Dynamics of US Environmental Policy.* New Haven, CT: Yale University Press.

Richardson, Jeremy. 2000. "Government, Interest Groups, and Policy Change." *Political Studies* 48:1006–1025.

Robinson, Scott. 2004. "Punctuated Equilibrium, Bureaucratization, and Budgetary Changes in Schools." *Policy Studies Journal* 24:25–40.

———. 2005. "Punctuated Equilibrium." In *Encyclopedia of Public Administration and Public Policy,* edited by Jack Rabin, 1674–1678. New York: Taylor and Francis.

———. 2006. "Punctuated Equilibrium Models in Organizational Decision-Making." In *Handbook on Organizational Decision-Making,* edited by Goktug Morcal, 134–149. New York: Marcel Dekker.

Sabatier, Paul A. 1987. "Knowledge, Policy-Oriented Learning, and Policy Change." *Knowledge: Creation, Diffusion, Utilization* 8:649–692.

Salka, William. 2004. "Mission Evolution: The United States Forest Service Response to Crisis." *Review of Policy Research* 21:221–232.

Schattschneider, E. E. 1960. *The Semi-Sovereign People.* New York: Holt, Rinehart and Winston.

Scholten, Peter, and Arco Timmermans. 2004. "Doorbraken en zacht landingen in het Nederlandse immigrantenbeleid. Een theoretische analyse van beleidsdynamiek." *Beleidswetenschap* 18:3–30.

Schrad, Mark Lawrence. 2007. "Constitutional Blemishes: American Alcohol Prohibition and Repeal as Policy Punctuation." *Policy Studies Journal* 35 (3): 437–463.

———. 2010. *The Political Power of Bad Ideas: Networks, Institutions, and the Global Prohibition Wave.* New York: Oxford University Press.

Sheingate, Adam. 2000. "Agricultural Retrenchment Revisited." *Governance* 23:335–353.

Shiftman, Jeremy. 2003. "Generating Political Will for Safe Motherhood in Indonesia." *Social Science and Medicine* 56:1197–1207.

Shiftman, Jeremy, Tanya Beer, and Yonghong Wu. 2002. "The Emergence of Global Disease Priorities." *Health Politics and Planning* 17:225–234.

Simon, Adam F. 2002. *The Winning Message: Candidate Behavior, Campaign Discourse, and Democracy.* New York: Cambridge University Press.

Simon, Herbert A. 1957. *Models of Man.* New York: Wiley.

———. 1977. "The Logic of Heuristic Decision-Making." In *Models of Discovery,* edited by R. S. Cohen and M. W. Wartofsky. Boston: D. Reidel.

———. 1983. *Reason in Human Affairs.* Stanford, CA: Stanford University Press.

———. 1985. "Human Nature in Politics: The Dialogue of Psychology with Political Science." *American Political Science Review* 79:293–304.

Soroka, Stuart. 2002. *Agenda-Setting Dynamics in Canada.* Vancouver: University of British Columbia Press.

Soroka, Stuart N., and Christopher Wlezien. 2010. *Degrees of Democracy: Politics, Public Opinion, and Policy.* New York: Cambridge University Press.

Soroka, Stuart, Christopher Wlezien, and Iain McLean. 2006. "Public Expenditure in the UK: How Measures Matter." *Journal of the Royal Statistical Society Series A* 169 (Part 2): 255–271.

Speth, Gustave. 2004. *Red Sky at Morning.* New Haven, CT: Yale University Press.

Stimson, James A., Michael B. MacKuen, and Robert S. Erikson. 1995. "Dynamic Representation." *American Political Science Review* 89:543–565.

Su, Tsai-Tsu, Mark S. Kamlet, and David Mowery. 1993. "Modeling U.S. Budgetary and Fiscal Outcomes: A Disaggregated, Systemwide Perspective." *American Journal of Political Science* 37:213–245.

Talbert, Jeffrey, Bryan Jones, and Frank Baumgartner. 1995. "Nonlegislative Hearings and Policy Change in Congress." *American Journal of Political Science* 39:383–406.

Taleb, Nissam N. 2007. *The Black Swan: The Impact of the Highly Improbable.* New York: Random House.

Thurmaier, Kurt. 1995. "Decisive Decision-Making in the Executive Budget Process: Analyzing the Political and Economic Propensities of Central Budget Bureau Analysts." *Public Administration Review* 55:448–460.

Timmermans, Arco. 2001. "Arenas as Institutional Sites for Policymaking: Patterns and Effects in Comparative Perspective." *Journal of Comparative Policy Analysis* 3:311–337.

Timmermans, Arco, and Peter Scholten. 2006. "The Political Flow of Wisdom: Science Institutions as Policy Venues in the Netherlands." *Journal of European Public Policy* 13:1104–1118.

True, James L. 1995. "Is the National Budget Controllable?" *Public Budgeting and Finance* 15:18–32.

———. 2000. "Avalanches and Incrementalism." *American Review of Public Administration* 30:3–18.

True, James L., and Glenn Utter. 2002. "Saying 'Yes,' 'No,' and 'Load Me Up' to Guns in America." *American Journal of Public Administration* 32:216–241.

Tsebelis, George. 2002. *Veto Players: How Political Institutions Work.* New York: Russell Sage Foundation.

Tversky, Amos. 1972. "Elimination by Aspects: A Theory of Choice." *Psychological Review* 79:281–299.

US Department of Commerce. 1990. *National Income and Product Accounts of the United States.* Washington, DC: US Department of Commerce.

———. *Survey of Current Business* [serial]. Washington, DC: US Department of Commerce.

US Office of Management and Budget. *Budget of the United States Government* [serial, fiscal years 1948 through 1996]. Washington, DC: Government Printing Office.

Vliegenthart, Rens, and Stefaan Walgrave. 2011. "Content Matters. The Dynamics of Parliamentary Questioning in Belgium and Denmark." *Comparative Political Studies* 44 (8): 1031–1059.

Vliegenthart, Rens, Stefaan Walgrave, and Connie Meppelink. 2011. "Inter-party Agenda-Setting in Belgian Parliament. The Role of Party Characteristics and Competition." *Political Studies* 59 (2): 368–388.

Walgrave, Stefaan, Jonas Lefevere, and Michiel Nuytemans. 2009. "Issue Ownership Stability and Change: How Political Parties Claim and Maintain Issues through Media Appearances." *Political Communication* 26 (2): 153–172.

Walgrave, Stefaan, Frédéric Varone, and Patrick Dumont. 2006. "Policy with or without Parties? A Comparative Analysis of Policy Priorities and Policy Change in Belgium (1991–2000)." *Journal of European Public Policy* 13:1021–1038.

Wanat, John. 1974. "Bases of Budgetary Incrementalism." *American Political Science Review* 68:1221–1228.

Wendon, Bryan. 1998. "The Commission as Image-Venue Entrepreneur in EU Social Policy." *European Journal of Public Policy* 5:339–353.

Wildavsky, Aaron. 1964. *The Politics of the Budgetary Process.* Boston: Little, Brown.

Wlezien, Christopher. 1995. "The Public as Thermostat: Dynamics of Preferences for Spending." *American Journal of Political Science* 39:981–1000.

Wood, B. Dan, and Jeffrey S. Peake. 1998. "The Dynamics of Foreign Policy Agenda Setting." *American Political Science Review* 92:173–184.

Wood, Robert. 2006. "The Dynamics of Incrementalism." *Policy Studies Journal* 34:1–16.

Worsham, Jeff. 1998. "Wavering Equilibriums: Subsystem Dynamics and Agenda Control." *American Politics Quarterly* 26:485–512.

Zaller, John R. 1992. *The Nature and Origins of Mass Opinion.* New York: Cambridge University Press.

3

Policy Feedback Theory

SUZANNE METTLER AND MALLORY SORELLE

Most theories of the policy process analyze, in one way or another, how policies come into being, and to explain that, they focus on factors that are seemingly exogenous to public policy itself. In contemporary political life, however, policy creation typically occurs in a context that is deeply influenced by existing policies. Perhaps the most obvious and well-documented example of this involves the processes of policy diffusion in which policymakers in one location learn from the experiences of those in another and may be pressured by the same interest groups and associations pushing for change elsewhere. But policies enacted previously reconfigure the political landscape in myriad other ways as well, and these transformed circumstances affect whether and how policymaking occurs in the future.

How do policies, once created, reshape politics, and how might such transformations in turn affect subsequent policymaking? Today we dwell in what might be called a "policyscape," a political landscape densely laden with existing policies that were created at earlier points in time and that structure multiple dimensions of contemporary politics (Mettler 2016). Policies influence the political agenda by shaping the realm of "old business" that requires attention and by offering frames for interpreting new issues and policy alternatives (Adler and Wilkerson 2012). They also affect governing operations through multiple mechanisms, such as by imposing resource commitments and constraints and configuring governing capacity and standard operating procedures.

In addition, policies—for example, by providing social benefits to particular groups of citizens—shape political behavior by influencing the extent to which affected individuals take part in politics and the goals they pursue. They may create incentives for interest groups to form in the first place or, once established, shape their level of activity around or commitment of resources to a particular political agenda. Policies may foster partisan identities associated with the protection of specific public programs and, in the process, enable parties to mobilize voters who rely on them, thus turning those parties into devoted defenders. The possibilities abound.

Over the past quarter century, a growing number of scholars have begun to explore the ways in which "policy, once enacted, restructures subsequent political processes" (Skocpol 1992, 58). This developing literature on the aptly named "feedback effects" of public policies provides insight into the ability of policies—through their design, resources, and implementation—to shape the attitudes and behaviors of political elites and mass publics as well as to affect the evolution of policymaking institutions and interest groups, and through any of these dynamics potentially to affect subsequent policymaking processes (Pierson 1993; Mettler and Soss 2004).

The policy feedback approach not only adds a new dimension to the study of the policy process but also positions scholars to engage in a novel form of policy analysis that has been neglected by the dominant approaches to that task. The field of policy analysis, which aims to predict the most valuable approaches to solving social problems or to evaluate the ability of existing policies to do so, typically focuses exclusively on matters of economic efficiency or social well-being. Analysts assess policy alternatives on the basis of the cost savings they will promote and the social good they will foster, such as higher college graduation rates, lower teenage pregnancy rates, or lower incarceration rates. Meanwhile, scholars of the policy process have helped to illuminate, among other things, whether the adoption of such alternatives is politically feasible and, if not, the circumstances under which it might be. Policy Feedback Theory sits at the intersection of these two approaches: it brings political considerations to bear on policy analysis, assessing how policies affect crucial aspects of governance, such as whether they promote civic engagement or deter it, whether they foster the development of powerful interest groups, and how they affect institutional governing capacity. Such analysis can illuminate the impact of policies on democracy and help reveal what might otherwise become "unintended consequences" of policies, such as the development of vested interests that reconfigure arrangements of power in society. It can also enrich studies of the policy process by highlighting how policies created previously affect the likelihood and form of future policy creation. This approach is still early in its development but possesses a high level of potential value for scholars, policymakers, and the public.

INTELLECTUAL DEVELOPMENT OF POLICY FEEDBACK THEORY

Although scholarship on policy feedback effects constitutes a relatively recent addition to political science literature, the idea that public policies have the capacity to shape the political behavior of a range of actors has a long lineage in the discipline. E. E. Schattschneider (1935) famously argued that "new policies create new politics"; Theodore Lowi (1972) echoed the sentiment several decades later. In the comparative context, Gøsta Esping-Anderson (1990) employed a similar logic in his historical institutional analysis of welfare states, arguing that political behavior is shaped by the content and structure of policies.

Historical institutionalists took these general ideas and began to fashion from them an analytical approach to studying public policy. Putting public policy front and center in the analysis fits neatly with institutionalists' interests in how the state itself affects political and social life. They view public policies, at least when they acquire durability, as possessing the attributes of formal institutions, such as government agencies and governing bodies: policies bestow resources, impose coercive rules, and convey norms and messages. Public policy embodies the "state in action" (Lowi 1985), and therefore it seemed a natural progression for historical institutionalists to turn their attention to it. Historical institutionalists also attempt to explain change over time, including when and how it occurs and, alternatively, the conditions under which political circumstances become "locked-in" and resistant to change (Pierson 1993). Explaining how policies shape politics, with subsequent effects on public policy, necessarily requires analysis that is sensitive to historical developments transpiring over time.

The articulation of policy feedback emerged in the late 1980s and early 1990s in the writings of several historical institutionalist scholars (Hall 1986; Steinmo, Thelen, and Longstreth 1992; Skocpol 1992; Pierson 1993). The term was coined and received prominent attention in Theda Skocpol's (1992) *Protecting Soldiers and Mothers: The Political Origins of Social Policy in the United States*, in which she advanced it as part of a "structured polity" approach to studying political change. Skocpol explained that polices created at "Time 1" could reshape both state capacities and social groups and their political goals and capabilities, in turn affecting policies created at "Time 2." She demonstrated, for example, that Civil War veterans' pensions prompted their recipients to organize in order to protect and expand them, an example of positive feedback. The pensions, which grew to be quite generous and widespread in the late nineteenth century, promulgated negative feedback as well, as policymakers came to associate them with corruption in patronage politics, which dampened policymakers' willingness to embrace other types of social provision in the early twentieth century (Skocpol 1992, 57–60).

These early articulations of the concept of policy feedback primarily summoned scholars to be attentive to how policies shape politics, and they exemplified such an approach in historical case studies. Paul Pierson's (1993) "When Effect Becomes Cause" took the emergent theory to its next stage of development by setting forth a conceptual framework, one that could enable scholars to advance hypotheses. For Pierson, public policies, like other institutional innovations, have the potential to instigate a path-dependent process, whereby each step along a policy pathway makes it increasingly difficult to reverse course. In this seminal work Pierson explained that enacted policies have the ability to shape the political behaviors of government elites, organized interests, and mass publics through two primary pathways: interpretive effects, as policies serve as sources of information and meaning, thus affecting political learning and attitudes; and resource effects, providing means and incentives for political activity. These ideas prompted a turn to in-depth empirical research that aimed to test for these two fundamental effects and, where they were found, to identify the mechanisms at work.

The initial impetus for studies of policy feedback emerged from the historical institutionalist tradition, and Pierson's theory provided an intellectual bridge linking the logic of institutional development and path dependence to the study of individual political behavior. As a result, to date the most productive direction in research to emerge in response to this scholarship has investigated policy feedback effects among mass publics. Political behavior scholars were poised to incorporate new ideas about policy feedback into well-developed approaches to understanding citizen engagement and participation and to test them empirically. Pierson's ideas helped promote such efforts, enabling more precise identification of the mechanisms at work as well as the circumstances under which feedback might be expected to occur and with what effects.

Scholars who pursued such empirical research situated policy feedback inquiry as part of a longer tradition in political behavior scholarship, and they pointed toward a multipronged agenda for further inquiry. Suzanne Mettler and Joe Soss argued that to engage in such research required "bridging policy studies and mass politics," an approach with antecedents in scholarship that shows that political attitudes and behavior are not only produced through psychological processes or social group membership but are often also politically constructed outcomes. They called for multiple forms of inquiry encompassing attention to several major dynamics and engagement among diverse approaches to political science research.

Over the past decade, studies of policy feedback have proliferated. They have become far more varied and wide-ranging in subject matter and methodological approach. For example, scholars have moved from investigating primarily social welfare policies to exploring other policy areas, such as criminal justice (e.g., Weaver and Lerman 2010); from a focus on direct visible policies to a consideration of hidden ones, those in which government support is channeled through private organizations or the tax code (e.g., Mettler 2011; Morgan and Campbell 2011); and from analyzing only Western nations to including non-Western countries as well (e.g., MacLean 2011; Hern 2016a, 2016b). Studies have shifted from focusing on case studies to utilizing large datasets (e.g., Bruch, Ferree, and Soss 2010) and experimental research (Mettler 2011; Lerman 2013). They have grown from a focus on actual effects to a consideration also of noneffects (e.g., Soss and Schram 2007; Hochschild and Weaver 2010).

Some recent assessments of the state of the discipline summarize these developments and offer comprehensive reviews of the literature (Béland 2010; Campbell 2012). In this chapter, we do not intend to repeat this task. Instead, our goal is to introduce readers more generally to the kinds of questions that policy feedback scholars pursue, the types of concepts they explore, and some of the obstacles and possibilities that have become evident in this area of research. In the next section we summarize the major streams of policy feedback research, some of which have attracted more followers to date than others, but each of which possesses considerable potential for future work. Then we delve more deeply into the recent advances in policy feedback scholarship that extend Pierson's work on path dependence to the investigation of the specific mechanisms and pathways through which policies affect political attitudes and behaviors among mass publics. Finally, we provide an overview of the challenges faced by policy feedback scholars and illuminate future directions for inquiry.

MAJOR STREAMS OF POLICY FEEDBACK INQUIRY

The analytical purview of policy feedback is poised to address a wide array of political dynamics. To date, scholars have focused their efforts on examining four major streams of inquiry, each composed of several tributaries (see Figure 3.1). The first two streams of inquiry stem directly from the historical institutionalist tradition, frequently employing the logic of path dependence to demonstrate how past policies constrain future policymaking. First, policies affect *political agendas* and *the definition of policy problems*, with consequences

FIGURE 3.1 Streams of Policy Feedback Inquiry

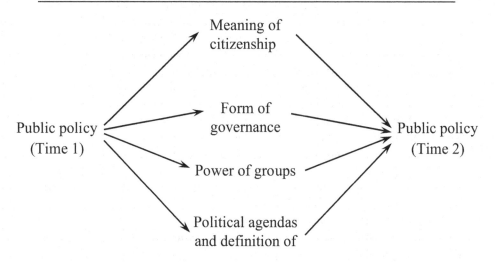

for how issues are understood and which ones receive attention from policy-makers. Second, policies affect *governance* through their impact on the capacity of government and political learning by public officials. The third stream applies the logic of policy feedback to the study of organized interests, arguing that policies influence the *power of groups*. Policies affect what types of interest groups and membership associations emerge and when they do so, whether they expand or deteriorate over time, and how they define their goals. Finally, the fourth stream extends the logic of policy feedback to the study of individual political behavior by examining how policies shape the *meaning of citizenship*, which we define broadly as the reciprocal relationship between government and ordinary people under its domain.

Policy Agendas and Problem Definition

Policies created at earlier points affect, going forward, how social problems are understood, whether they are defined as matters worthy of public attention and government action, and whether they find a place on the political agenda. Once policies are created, they themselves populate the political agenda because they require maintenance and oversight if they are to continue to function as lawmakers intended. Policies may require regular reauthorization or, less formally, reforms from time to time as a means of upkeep. Existing policies may also shape how lawmakers view new policy issues. How issues are framed through policies influences their likelihood of engendering broader, enduring effects and the type of influence they bear on subsequent policy debates.

In the United States, for example, proponents of child care provisions have had little success in defining such issues as a matter of public concern and getting them on the policy agenda (Morgan 2006). The idea that child care is a matter to be handled in the private realm is likely reinforced by the legacy of other employee-related benefits, which have been channeled through the workplace in policies that obscure government's role, paired with the equal rights frame of laws such as the Equal Pay Act, both described below. In recent years, lawmakers have increasingly put pre-K education on the policy agenda; for many working parents, the services it involves may, like child care, help them to manage work and family responsibilities, but achieving it through the education policy frame has been far more effective, likely because it builds on the long tradition of government's role in public education.

Similarly, the existing system of employee health benefits presented an obstacle to health reform in the United States because it became easy for opponents to engender concern among those with such coverage that they would be worse off if policies changed (Hacker 2002, 122). President Bill Clinton's health reform plans in 1994 easily stimulated such fears (Skocpol 1996). President Barack Obama learned from Clinton's failure and instead advanced plans that built on existing policies, enjoyed the support of insurance companies and other major stakeholders, and made the preservation of existing policies more apparent (Blumenthal and Morone 2009).

In addition, public policies can shape the future conflicts that emerge over them, including which groups are mobilized and whether coalitions or cleavages form within groups. Policies forged by a particular political party often become viewed as "owned" by that party, and subsequent action over such laws or related issues is likely to mobilize that party's members as supporters and the other's as opponents (Petrocik 1996). Not all issues become framed in partisan terms, however. Some, because of historical precedents, may mobilize support across partisan divisions.

Immigration policies, for example, have often brought together "strange bedfellows," typically cutting across party lines by uniting some proponents from the business and minority communities and some from the ranks of conservatives and labor supporters (Skrentny 2011; Tichenor 2002). Recently, immigration appears to have served as an important issue in fueling the emergence of the Tea Party; this development has in turn moved the Republican Party to the right and exacerbated partisan polarization in Congress, with implications for a wide array of policy issues (Skocpol and Williamson 2012; Parker and Barreto 2013).

Finally, the construction of target populations, groups at which policies are aimed, often affects the alternatives policymakers consider legitimate in future evaluations of policy programs (Schneider and Ingram 1993). New policies can also create new constituencies and organized interest coalitions that become major players in the policymaking process (Patashnik 2008). Both of these effects of policy design introduce path dependence into the policymaking process (Pierson 1993), and they are likely further reinforced by group dynamics, a subject to which we now turn.

Governance

Some of the foundational literature on policy feedback suggested that policies, once established, may affect future governance: they may shape the policy alternatives that lawmakers select, the type of administrative arrangements assigned to new policies, and even the parameters—and limits—of government action. Such outcomes may emerge if new policies enable government to develop capacities it lacked previously, such as administrative arrangements and standard operating procedures, which can then be deployed for the delivery of policies developed subsequently. Policies may promote political learning by public officials, affecting how they view and respond to future situations (Heclo 1974). Once the Social Security Administration (SSA) gained a reputation for successful administration of retirement benefits, lawmakers created health benefits for beneficiaries and handed that new program, Medicare, to the SSA to run as well (Derthick 1979). This could be considered an example of positive feedback. By contrast, Skocpol (1992, 59–60) shows how the delivery of Civil War veterans' pensions through the patronage system of the era engendered negative feedback effects as many reformers viewed the system as riddled with corruption and on that basis believed that "the United States could not administer any new social spending programs efficiently or honestly."

Existing policies may also shape what both public officials and the general public perceive to be the legitimate domain of government and, conversely, what belongs to the private sector. Jacob Hacker argues that in the United States, the chances for government to extend health benefits to working-age adults became slimmer once benefits that were channeled through the private sector, in the form of employee benefits, became more established. Although the government subsidized such benefits, its role was less than obvious, and therefore Americans became accustomed to thinking of health coverage as belonging to the private sphere (Hacker 1998).

Policies also establish resource commitments and constraints. Today the US federal budget contains vast commitments to existing programs, many of which are "mandatory," given that benefits are owed by law to particular citizens, and numerous others, even if formally regarded as "discretionary," that convey long-term standing commitments by government. Meanwhile, the nation has reduced tax rates for corporations and wealthy households over time. The resulting fiscal constraints present formidable challenges to new policy initiatives.

Power of Groups

Analysts most typically examine how organized groups and associations influence government and shape policy outcomes, but ample evidence shows that the relationship often works in reverse as well. Jack Walker, after investigating the origins and maintenance of 564 organizations existing in 1980, concluded that most groups established in the post–World War II period did not emerge solely from outside the political system but rather benefited from substantial "patronage" from government. Walker (1983, 403) observed that many groups "sprang up *after* the passage of dramatic new legislation that established the major outlines of public policy in their areas," concluding that in such instances, "the formation of new groups was one of the *consequences* of major new legislation, not one of the *causes* of its passage." As an example, Walker noted that out of forty-six organizations that represent senior citizens, more than half of them formed after 1965, when President Lyndon Johnson signed into law both Medicare and the Older Americans Act.

Interest group activity cannot be explained simply as the function of changes in public opinion or entrepreneurial leaders, reasoned Walker; to the contrary, several public policies influenced the likelihood of groups to form. These included "provisions of the tax code governing the ability of business firms to claim deductions for the expenses of lobbying, subsidies in the form of reduced postal rates for not-for-profit groups heavily dependent on direct mail solicitation, the availability of financial support from regulatory agencies for groups that wish to testify at administrative hearings, the rules concerning the registration of lobbyists and the financial disclosures they are required to make, legal restraints on the accessibility of foundations," and so forth (Walker 1983, 404). Public officials routinely seek to mobilize their allies through the policies they promote, as evidenced by numerous policies adopted by the Johnson administration; conversely, they may also try to demobilize those who oppose them, as did the Reagan administration through budget cuts to Great Society programs, increases in postal rates, and challenges to the not-for-profit status of many organizations.

Public policies themselves can also shape which kinds of groups form and grow and which fail to coalesce. In part, this is a function of the types of resources provided by policies, whether directly or through opportunities they may create. Beginning in the mid-twentieth century, many scholars challenged the prevailing pluralist view that individuals with shared interests will necessarily organize, fostering healthy competition between multiple groups. To the contrary, as Mancur Olson explained, public goods present a "free rider" problem because individuals can benefit equally whether or not they take action. By contrast, small groups in which the benefits of resources to each member are significant will be more likely to compel collective action, and thus they offer greater incentives to organize (Olson 1965). Olson's theory, when paired with Walker's observations, helps to explain why, in the wake of policy enactment, trade associations and other industry groups that stand to benefit substantially from the existence of public policies are more likely to mobilize and take political action than are ordinary citizens, whose interest in a given policy is more diffuse.

These dynamics are evidenced in the case of higher education policy, in which those parties that profit from students exhibit much higher levels of political organization than do students and their families. In 1972, lawmakers amended the Higher Education Act of 1965 to incentivize banks to make more loans at better terms to students. In the 1980s, as tuition costs soared ahead of inflation but the value of Pell grants for low-income students fell behind, students borrowed more and more in order to attend college. Profits for lenders soared. In turn, these businesses grew increasingly active in politics to protect the policies that benefited them so lucratively. Several additional organizations formed to represent lenders in the 1990s, and those already in existence channeled greater amounts than ever into lobbying and campaign contributions. Yet only two organizations at the time represented students, the US Student Association and the Public Interest Research Group, and both suffered from flagging membership rolls. This imbalance is not surprising given the likelihood of those with concentrated interests to organize and those with diffuse interests to refrain from doing so. Such dynamics led to policy feedback effects, as bank-based student lending—aided by policies favoring it—prevailed over the costly alternative, direct lending (Mettler 2014, 78–79, 82–83).

In addition to resources, the visibility of the costs and benefits flowing from a public policy can shape the likelihood that groups will coalesce around it. Much of US social welfare policy is channeled through relatively hidden mechanisms that obscure government's role. This includes government regulation and subsidization, through the tax code, of employee benefits for health and retirement and tax savings for homeowners who are paying mortgages. The existence of these policies has not been missed, however, by those industries that stand to make a profit from consumption of the goods and services the policies make more affordable for consumers, such as health care and real estate. Insurance companies and real estate organizations have invested considerable energy and resources in protecting the existing policies (Hacker 2002; Howard 1997). Whenever reformers propose changes that would scale back such benefits, these vested interests mobilize quickly to oppose them. For citizens generally, however, such policies obscure government's role; the benefits appear to emanate from the private sector or individuals' participation in the market, not from their shared participation as members of a political community. The invisibility of these arrangements as public policies makes them unlikely to stimulate organization among ordinary citizens who are or could be affected by them (Mettler 2011, chap. 2).

Public policies may vary in the extent to which they stimulate social movement and associational activity on the part of ordinary citizens and the types of goals that such groups pursue. Kristin Goss explains such feedback dynamics in *The Paradox of Gender Equality: How American Women's Groups Gained and Lost Their Public Voice*. Goss addresses a puzzle: labor, suffrage, and maternal health policies adopted in the early twentieth century were followed by an expansion of women's associational activity and extensive lobbying by such groups on behalf of a wide array of social and educational policies affecting Americans broadly; by contrast, the equal rights laws adopted in the 1960s and early 1970s were followed by a decline in women's presence on Capitol Hill and the narrowing of the issues their organizations addressed to those regarded as "women's issues." To explain this, Goss (2013, 168) argues that policy feedback effects are contingent on not only the sociopolitical context but also the design of particular policies: "Different policies of inclusion can have different effects on participatory citizenship." The Nineteenth Amendment stimulated women's civic engagement in the polity as fully participating citizens, and it did nothing to preclude the involvement of groups that defined gender roles in terms of difference, which many did at the time. By contrast, the equal rights laws adopted in the 1960s and 1970s inadvertently disempowered such associational activity. They did this in part because their liberal feminist underpinnings displaced organizing based on gender differences; they stressed women's economic rights as individuals, not their political inclusion; and they left unfinished business that seemed to pertain primarily to the private realm of marriage and family and therefore did less to promote public mobilization (Goss 2013, chap. 7). As a result, women's organizations rarely testify on Capitol Hill today, and when they do, they tend to address "women's issues" only, not the much wider array of issues that they addressed with far greater frequency in the mid-twentieth century.

Meaning of Citizenship

Citizenship encompasses the rights, duties, and obligations imposed by government as well as citizens' responses to them, including their political attitudes and participation. Political behavior scholarship certainly fits within this stream of research, but it is joined by other types of inquiry as well, including historical analysis.

First and foremost, public policies fundamentally affect *membership in the political community.* Certainly immigration and naturalization policies play a primary and obvious role in defining which individuals are included in the polity and the nature of their rights. This point is exemplified by Aristide Zolberg's comprehensive history of US immigration policy, *Nation by Design,* which indicates that policymakers throughout American history selected the traits of the nation's inhabitants, determining how many of which groups were to be included. As World War I began, for example, Congress overrode a veto by President Woodrow Wilson and made literacy a requirement for new entrants; this stipulation increased immigrant flows from northern and western Europe and limited those from the southern and eastern parts of the continent. Later, in 1965, the Hart-Celler Act, while eliminating the existing national origins quota system established in 1921, placed new quotas on the number of immigrants to be admitted from the Western Hemisphere, an approach that inadvertently led to higher rates of illegal immigration (Zolberg 2006).

Such policies have in turn shaped politics. In *Becoming a Citizen,* Irene Bloemraad (2006) posits a policy feedback explanation for the differential political incorporation of immigrants across contexts. Focusing on a comparative case study of immigrants to Canada and the United States, Bloemraad contends that the context of their reception—specifically, the policies governing settlement and ethnic diversity in a country—can offer symbolic and material resources that incentivize citizenship and participation to varying degrees. She dubs this process "structured mobilization" and argues that Canadian public policy—which has a normative bias toward citizenship, offers greater public assistance to new immigrants, and promotes an official policy of multiculturalism—leads to greater political incorporation of immigrants than does policy in the United States, which largely focuses on border control and offers little settlement assistance to new immigrants.

Beyond affecting membership in a polity, public policies also affect the *status*, or what Judith Shklar (1991) called "standing," of those who are legal citizens of a political community. They can engender social stratification—for example, by extending political and civil rights to members of some groups and denying them to others—and through such means promote feedback effects. Historically, in the United States, some people have enjoyed the right to vote and others have not (Keyssar 2000). The United States granted manhood suffrage to white men, regardless of whether they owned property, by the 1830s; this form of inclusion simultaneously enforced exclusions on the bases of gender and race, and it meant that political cleavages in the United States occurred along those lines in the latter nineteenth and early twentieth centuries, unlike in Britain, where political rights tied to property and class divisions prevailed instead. As a result, according to Theda Skocpol, American women acquired a gender identity as belonging to a separate, domestic sphere, but reformers ingeniously leveraged that identity in a manner that permitted them to be politically effective by claiming a distinct moral authority. On that basis, though women lacked suffrage and other political and civil rights, they nonetheless managed to influence policy developments and to forge the beginnings of a maternalist welfare state, contributing to the passage of protective labor laws, mothers' pensions, and other provisions (Skocpol 1992).

More recently, soaring incarceration rates after 1980 paired with the prevalence of felon disenfranchisement laws meant that a large and growing segment of the population lacked voting rights. Christopher Uggen and Jeff Manza found that these changes, by altering the composition of the electorate through exclusion of disproportionately low-income and minority individuals, effectively altered the outcome of several US Senate races and at least one presidential election. They speculated that such electoral outcomes might in turn shape future policy developments, thereby epitomizing feedback dynamics (Uggen and Manza 2002).

The British sociologist T. H. Marshall ([1950] 1998, 94) drew attention additionally to social rights, meaning everything "from the right to a modicum of economic security and welfare to the right to share to the full in the social heritage and to live the life of a civilized being according to the standards prevailing in the society." Social welfare, education, and other economic policies thus affected what Marshall termed "social citizenship," which he viewed as essential for individuals' free exercise of other rights on terms of equality with each other. A similar idea was articulated by the American political scientist Robert Dahl (2003, 152): "In order to exercise the fundamental rights to which citizens in a democratic order are entitled—to vote, speak, publish, protest, assemble, organize, among others—citizens must also possess the minimal resources that are necessary in order to take advantage of the opportunities and to exercise their rights." These scholars, by arguing that policies guaranteeing social rights affect political participation, implied potential feedback effects.

Several scholars have advanced ideas about how social rights affect citizens' status in society. Gøsta Esping-Anderson argued that different nations structure social citizenship in different ways. He identified conservative, liberal, and social democratic variants, each of which features distinct constellations of public policies. Each of these policy regimes bears particular implications for the stratification of society and the status of distinct groups (Esping-Anderson 1990). A crucial distinction, to Esping-Anderson, involved the presence or absence of public policies that insulated citizens from market forces, for example, in the case of illness or old age. Ann Orloff challenged this framework by taking greater account of gender roles and status; she pointed out that women's status depended not only on being able to leave the labor market to fulfill parenting responsibilities but also on having the social supports—for example, through child care policy—to be able to enter or remain in the workforce (Orloff 1993). Cybelle Fox (2012) shows that New Deal relief policies were administered in a manner that granted generous inclusion to European immigrants, excluded African Americans, and subjected Mexicans seeking assistance to expulsion: they were often deported as a result. In effect, such policies created what she calls "three worlds of relief," each with its distinct form of social citizenship—or lack thereof.

A few scholars have built on these ideas to explore how policies that affect social citizenship in terms of stratification can influence political mobilization, with subsequent effects on public policy. This is demonstrated by Suzanne Mettler's *Dividing Citizens: Gender and Federalism in New Deal Public Policy*. Mettler shows how men, particularly white men, were incorporated into New Deal social and labor policies that were to be administered at the national level. By contrast, most women and minority men were relegated to policies to be administered by the individual states. For example, the workers who gained rights under the National Labor Relations Act and Fair Labor Standards Act were predominantly men, given that the labor unions empowered by the first organized mostly men, and the latter included predominantly occupations employing men. As a result, in the decades following, political action remained highly gendered and distinct, with men across the nation mobilized by unions in pursuit of improved federal policies and women left to fight battles in all fifty individual states in pursuit of improved protective labor laws. Divided citizenship prevented the emergence of a larger, stronger, and more unified labor movement, and it perpetuated a gendered division between men and women as workers and citizens (Mettler 1998).

Public policies can also influence *identity*. Steve Engel (2014, 683) conceptualizes citizenship less as a matter of rights or obligations and more as "a lens through which the regulatory authorities of the state define and see the individual." This is exemplified by public policies that effectively constructed homosexuality. Margot Canaday (2009, 4), in *The Straight State*, argues that "the state's identification of certain sexual behavior, gender traits and emotional ties as ground for exclusion . . . was a catalyst in the formation of homosexual identity." Engel (2014) points out that political development contains multiple strands, some of which coexist simultaneously even if they appear contradictory. Therefore, for example, besides the state constructing homosexuality, several other forms of "state recognition" exist, embodied in regulatory policies: criminalization and exclusion; seeing the gay person as oppressed; decriminalizing homosexuality but privatizing same-sex relationships; and recognizing same-sex relationships.

Such state activity in shaping identity has in turn affected social movement activity and the particular form it takes in a given polity. For example, in her study of the divergence of lesbian, gay, bisexual, and transgender (LGBT) policy trajectories in Canada and the United States, Miriam Smith (2008) argues that the legislative centralization of both political and legal authority for criminal and marriage law in Canada makes it easier for the party in power and its associated organized interests to advance their agenda. By contrast, the federated structure and separation of powers in the United States provide more points of access for both policy supporters and opponents to contest legislative initiatives. These differences result, Smith argues, in a much smoother pathway to passage for LGBT protections in Canada than in the United States. In addition to the different institutional opportunities for contesting legal protections, Smith highlights policy feedback dynamics, explaining that the legacy of equal rights in Canada is much different from its US counterpart. Whereas equal rights in the United States has traditionally been tied to race, thus defining equal rights as a special interest, equal rights policies in Canada are often utilized to limit autonomous regions' ability to make sovereignty claims—a policy legacy that largely unifies the rest of the Canadian populace (Smith 2008).

Public policies can also affect how citizens view themselves and others in the polity. For example, some policies convey messages to beneficiaries that they are deserving of the support they receive, whereas other policies are stigmatizing and imply lack of deservingness or second-class citizenship (Soss 1999). Some have suggested that universal policies may help incorporate less-advantaged individuals as full members of the political community and also prompt others to see them as such, whereas targeted policies may accentuate their marginalized status (Skocpol 1991; Wilson 1991). Studies of European social service provision in particular have found that highly inclusive, or universal, social welfare policies engender mass support for a broader, cross-class definition of social citizenship. By contrast, policies that provide benefits to a select, often means-tested, group of recipients lead to zero-sum debates over the appropriate targets of redistribution (Korpi and Palme 1998; Rothstein 2002; Jordan 2013).

Alternatively, the basis of eligibility for a policy may influence its impact on views of deservingness. Beneficiaries of Social Security may perceive themselves as benefiting from funds they themselves earned through workplace participation, even if they receive far more in benefits than they paid into the system (Harrington Meyer 1996). Conversely, public benefits that are understood to flow directly from taxpayer dollars, such as welfare benefits or Temporary Assistance for Needy Families (TANF), may be more likely to be perceived as handouts (Skocpol and Williamson 2012, 60–61). Yet means testing alone does not make policies stigmatizing; Joe Soss (1999) finds, for example, that Head Start, a program for low-income children that engaged parents in democratic participation, yielded empowering effects.

Public policies are also known to affect what might be considered active citizenship, or people's degree of involvement in politics or other forms of civic engagement. Scholars have found that some policies, namely, Social Security, Medicare, and the GI Bill, promote active participation, making their beneficiaries more involved in public life than they would otherwise have been (Campbell 2003; Mettler 2005). Educational policies, for example, generally build civic capacity by endowing individuals with the skills, resources, and social networks that engender participation (Verba, Schlozman, and Brady 1995). Conversely, other policies—such as those hidden in the tax code or channeled through private organizations, or what has been called the "submerged state"—fail to engender comparable rates of activity (Mettler 2011). Some policies, such as welfare and incarceration, appear to actually depress civic engagement, rendering those who experience them directly less likely to participate than they would have been in the absence of the policy experience (Soss 1999; Weaver and Lerman 2010). We probe the underlying mechanisms explaining these outcomes in the next section.

Our discussion thus far indicates the broad array of ways in which policies can reshape the contours of politics and in time affect the next round of policymaking. To date, scholars have only begun to explore these pathways, some more than others. The next generation of those who make forays into this area will undoubtedly forge new pathways, requiring a new mapping of the field. Now we turn to a subject at the center of recent policy feedback scholarship: the specific mechanisms through which feedback dynamics may occur—particularly in the realm of individual political behavior.

FEEDBACK MECHANISMS AMONG MASS PUBLICS

The final line of inquiry in the previous section—how policies affect the meaning of citizenship—is the central focus of much of the recent policy feedback research. In particular, scholars are delving into the intricacies of the relationship between policies and mass political behavior in an effort to identify and explicate the mechanisms by which policies produce the variety of effects on politics discussed above. Guided by the logic put forth by Pierson in 1993, these studies examine the ways in which policy design, implementation, and resource provision shape the political preferences and behaviors of ordinary citizens.

FIGURE 3.2 **Mechanisms of Policy Feedback for Mass Politics**

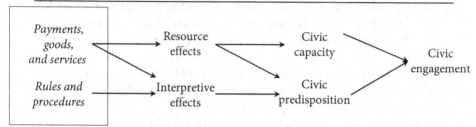

Just as institutionalist scholars have "opened the black box" of governing institutions, policy feedback scholars have delved into what could also be termed the "black box" of public policy to discern how specific components of policies affect the political behavior of ordinary citizens. A model of how such features of policies affect civic engagement among mass publics appears in Figure 3.2 (Mettler 2002). This model builds on Pierson's delineation of resource and interpretive effects.

Many public policies offer citizens payments, goods, or services—or in the case of taxes, they may collect payments from them—and any of these experiences may engender resource effects, shaping participation. This dimension of the model draws on the Civic Voluntarism Model advanced by Sidney Verba, Kay Schlozman, and Henry Brady (1995), which indicates that resources—free time, money, and civic skills—each bear a positive relationship to civic engagement. When a policy provides an individual with benefits that have monetary value, those resources may help overcome the costs of participation. Similarly, when policies provide education benefits—another key predictor of civic and political engagement (Wolfinger and Rosenstone 1980)—participation may increase.

Public policies also impose rules and procedures on citizens, features emanating from policy design and implementation, and these may be the source of interpretive effects, which could also be termed "cognitive" or "learning effects." Interpretive effects refer to the ability of public policies to shape norms, values, and attitudes. This dimension of the policy feedback model draws in part on Anne Schneider and Helen Ingram's theory of social construction and policy design, elaborating how policies shape citizens' subjective experiences of the meaning of citizenship and affect their status, identity, and role in the political community (Schneider and Ingram 1993, 1997, 78–89, 140–45).

In addition, the Civic Voluntarism Model implies that some resources may themselves also foster interpretive effects, for example, by promoting the psychological predisposition to be involved in public affairs. This might occur if resources facilitate enhanced political efficacy, meaning individuals' understanding that government is responsive to people like them (external efficacy) or that they are personally capable of influencing government (internal efficacy). Alternatively, greater engagement might transpire as resources such as education inculcate a sense of civic duty or as policies that join people together by treating or regarding them similarly foster a sense of a fate linked to others (Verba, Schlozman, and Brady 1995).

The interpretive effects of public policies may affect primarily those who experience them directly, such as beneficiaries of social welfare policies, or those bound by regulatory procedures. Alternatively, they may influence the attitudes of other citizens, by shaping their perceptions of members of a particular group in society to which they themselves do not belong. They may make them think of claimants of the home mortgage interest deduction as deserving, for example, and welfare recipients as undeserving. Or a policy may influence citizens' views of their own standing in society, depending on government's responsiveness to them or to people like them. These values are formed and transmitted through both the design of a specific policy and the experiences with its implementation.

The following sections explore each of these dimensions—resource and interpretive effects—in greater depth and highlight related research findings.

Resource Effects

Scholars find that the actual fungible resources provided by social welfare policies have an impact on civic engagement. This was the case, for example, with the GI Bill's education and training benefits, which provided veterans with access to education. Veterans who utilized the GI Bill, compared to veteran nonusers with similar background characteristics, participated in 50 percent more civic membership organizations and 30 percent more political activities in the immediate post–World War II era. This occurred in part because the policy provided them with resources, namely, education, which actively increased participation through the civic skills it gave them, the social networks they developed as students, and the increased income and job prospects they acquired as a result of their degrees. Resource effects were most pronounced among African American veterans, for whom access to the GI Bill provided educational opportunities not otherwise available. The skills, resources, and networks these beneficiaries gained led them to become involved particularly as leaders in the civil rights movement and in formal politics later on (Mettler 2005). Similarly, women who gained access to college in later decades by using federal student aid policies such as student loans and Pell grants became more engaged in politics than similarly situated individuals. In each case, the resources accrued through access to education disposed individuals to participate in public affairs to an extent not possible otherwise (Rose 2012).

Policy benefits can also increase political participation by providing individuals and organizations with incentives to mobilize and advocate in their defense. This effect is most clearly captured by Campbell's (2002) study of Social

Security recipients, which finds that the resources provided by Social Security offer a powerful incentive for individuals to engage in political activity to maintain and strengthen their benefits. The economic self-interest generated by the benefits compels older adults, particularly low- and middle-income older adults, who rely most heavily on their monthly Social Security checks, to engage in a variety of political activities to encourage their representatives to protect those benefits.

Providing resources to beneficiaries may not boost turnout for all who receive benefits. Recent work by Jowei Chen (2013) finds that the distribution of government aid can differentially shape the partisan distribution of turnout. In his study of the policy feedback effects of Federal Emergency Management Agency (FEMA) hurricane disaster aid in Florida, Chen finds that the effect of distributive aid on turnout depends on the partisan affiliation of voters and their relationship to the incumbent party. Specifically, voters receiving FEMA aid who were affiliated with the incumbent party turned out at higher rates in the election following aid distribution. By contrast, voters who received aid but were affiliated with the opposition party exhibited reduced turnout. In both cases, according to Chen, the incumbent party was rewarded for providing distributive aid.

Such results may occur because policy resources create an impetus for political mobilization by political parties and other organizations. Campbell's study of participation patterns among low- and moderate-income Social Security recipients finds that the policy created a brand-new constituency group for political actors to mobilize. Both the Democratic Party and the AARP seized the opportunity (Campbell 2002). Such mobilization is also itself a powerful predictor of political participation (Rosenstone and Hansen 1993).

Political actors are keenly aware of policy benefits' capacity to alter participatory dynamics in such ways. They can leverage this fact to develop or diminish the provision of social benefits to suit their immediate political goals. Political actors have the ability to exacerbate or mitigate existing inequalities by providing resources to some groups rather than to others.

Work on resource effects is still in its infancy. Scholars have yet to specify the variation in impact of resources of different values or sizes or administered over different durations (Campbell 2012). Research to date focuses predominantly on social welfare and education policies; scholars have just begun to examine the impact of extraction of resources through the tax code, for example, and how different policy mechanisms might affect citizens' responses (e.g., Faricy 2011).

Interpretive Effects

Interpretive effects of policies may be fostered through the impact of resources or directly through features of policy design and implementation. Any of these may convey messages to people about government or their relationship to it or the status of other citizens, and the resulting attitudinal responses may shape people's subsequent participation.

Living under a particular policy regime can affect the way people view their identities as citizens (Mettler and Soss 2004; Patashnik 2008). In some instances, this occurs deliberately as policymakers construct target groups to whom policies apply and the associated norms and benefits ascribed to those groups (Schneider and Ingram 1993). The policy spells out who is a member of the identified group, on the basis of some shared characteristics, and who is not. By defining group membership, policymakers essentially offer a government endorsement of those individuals who are worthy of benefits, those who should endure punitive measures, and those whose behavior should change in some specified way (Schneider and Ingram 1993).

In addition to designating recipients for a particular policy, the language and content of the policy can assign a social or political standing to the targeted population, whether intentionally or not (Mettler and Soss 2004). For example, some policies offer a full extension of benefits to those who have "earned" them, whereas others provide "welfare" support to beneficiaries who are forced to consistently prove their need. Constructed identities may be both normative and evaluative in nature, and they can ascribe a group with either positive or negative attributes (Schneider and Ingram 1993). Frequently, these characterizations become imbedded in the public symbology associated with a particular group. As a result, the creation of target populations can influence how members see themselves and the relative value of their participation as well as how society, more broadly, construes a particular group's identity (Schneider and Ingram 1993; Mettler and Soss 2004). Terms like "welfare queen" enter the vernacular, and suddenly entire groups of welfare beneficiaries are viewed through that lens. Once created, these conceptions are perpetuated by media coverage and political discourse.

The perceptions of beneficiaries engendered by certain policy designs have also been found to affect the willingness of businesses to participate in government programs. In her comparative exploration of British and Danish business implementation of labor market programs, Cathie Jo Martin (2004) finds that welfare policy designs can shape employers' attitudes toward program beneficiaries and perceptions about the advantage of participation, thus affecting the willingness of those employers to implement programs.

In addition to Martin, several other comparativists have undertaken studies of policy feedback effects. A significant focus of their scholarship is the degree to which social welfare policy designs affect political attitudes and support for the programs (Andreß and Heien 2001; Edlund 1999; Jakobsen 2011; Larsen 2008; Svallfors 1997). Following a logic similar to Campbell's, these studies typically find that welfare programs that are universal in nature—providing benefits to the majority of citizens—garner greater popular support because they generate larger constituencies and shift "the focus of the welfare state away from redistribution and toward common market insecurities felt by both the middle and working classes" (Jordan 2013). By contrast, welfare programs providing means-tested benefits to the poor create a much smaller constituency and establish contentious relations between beneficiaries and contributors, ultimately generating hostility toward welfare expansion (Korpi and Palme 1998). As noted earlier, however, this distinction between universal and means-tested policies has been called into question in more recent work on the American case.

Although the design of a policy can influence both elite and mass attitudes about the relative value of a particular group of beneficiaries, the implementation of a particular policy can also affect people's attitudes toward both government and their own personal political efficacy. For many beneficiaries of public policy, interactions with various disbursement or oversight agencies provide citizens with their primary, and sometimes their only, direct experience with government. It therefore comes as no surprise that these interactions can serve as a proxy for the whole of government, significantly affecting individual evaluations of government capacity and the efficacy of participating in political activity (Soss 1999; Mettler 2011). The way a policy is implemented is not, of course, wholly unconnected to its design; in fact, legislation and subsequent bureaucratic rules usually determine the manner in which policy benefits are distributed. On some occasions, however, the process of policy disbursement produces distinctive effects, particularly when those engaged in service delivery retain a large measure of discretion or ability to interpret the law differently from how its creators intended or foresaw or when a distinct level of government, court, or nongovernmental agency retains the ability to determine some aspect of how the policy will actually be put into practice.

Joe Soss (1999, 362) explains that "policy designs structure participant program experiences in ways that teach alternative lessons about the nature of government." To test this claim, he conducted surveys of a number of recipients of two distinctive social policy programs: the now defunct Aid to Families with Dependent Children (AFDC) and Social Security Disability Insurance (SSDI). Soss finds that recipients of AFDC, a means-tested program that he claims disempowered beneficiaries through constant casework and the need to prove eligibility, held more negative views of government and felt less participatory efficacy. By contrast, recipients of SSDI, a social insurance program in which recipients tend to initiate government contact and play a more empowered role in the process of obtaining benefits, felt more positively inclined toward government capacity and engagement. Individuals' experiences with agencies functioned like microcosms of government for them, and they extrapolated from these experiences in considering their relationship to government as a whole. As a result, their experiences of policy receipt affected their sense of political efficacy and, in turn, their participation.

Several other studies confirm Soss's conclusion that the nature of individuals' interaction with government agencies, as dictated by a particular policy design, can shape their views about government. A study of TANF, the replacement for AFDC established by welfare reform in 1996, found that variation in the implementation of the same policy program across state and local jurisdictions produced different attitudes toward political efficacy (Soss, Fording, and Schram 2011). Similarly, Weaver and Lerman (2010, 4) write that "criminal justice contact weakens attachment to political process and heightens negative views about government." They found that the more extensive citizens' experience of the criminal justice system, the stronger its negative impact on their likelihood of voting; such experiences created "custodial citizenship." Moynihan and Herd (2010) explain that, as policies are implemented, citizens run up against cumulative red tape—the administrative procedures of implementation that are not directly necessary for the distribution of benefits—generated throughout the various stages of policymaking. Administrative red tape imposes barriers that citizens must overcome to access their political and social rights, and some citizens possess greater capacity to overcome those barriers. As a result, Moynihan and Herd (2010) argue, administrative red tape can have a deleterious effect on the experience of citizenship for already disadvantaged groups.

Of course, not all policy beneficiaries have negative interactions with government programs. Wood and Waterman's (1994) exploration of bureaucratic dynamics reports that a majority of Americans say that their experiences with government agencies are efficient and positive. A number of studies find that those beneficiaries who have primarily positive encounters with policy disbursement agencies report similarly positive attitudes toward government and about their own political efficacy. Besides the resource effects of the GI Bill, veteran beneficiaries also found the provisions of the law to be generous, and they felt themselves treated with dignity and respect throughout the implementation process. As a result, they became incorporated as full social citizens, and their appreciation of and generally positive interactions with governing agencies resulted in a sense of efficacy and civic-mindedness (Mettler 2005). Of course, even positive experiences with government may pose problems for evaluations of political efficacy. Patashnik's (2008) study of policy reform cautions that when positive government reforms unravel, citizens may lose faith in the ability of government to solve problems.

Although both positive and negative experiences with government agencies during policy disbursement have the power to shape people's beliefs about their own political efficacy, scholars have shown that public policies administered without interaction with an obvious government presence can affect views of government capacity as well. A recent study examined citizens' responses to policies administered through the relatively hidden policies of the "submerged state," those that channel benefits to citizens through market institutions and the federal tax system (Mettler 2011, 7). Unlike benefits delivered directly through obvious government organizations, benefits provided by the submerged state are intentionally obscured, so many people only see the free market or private enterprise at work. The hidden nature of these policies not only makes it difficult for citizens to form and express preferences about them but also fosters a sense that the market, not government, is responsible for addressing public needs.

Numerous studies of European—and particularly Scandinavian—social welfare policies have also found that the implementation of government programs can shape political attitudes. For example, Staffan Kumlin's (2004) exploration of social welfare experience in Sweden finds evidence to suggest that personal experiences with welfare provision actually have a greater impact on political trust and ideology than do personal economic experiences. In her study of African state retrenchment and its effect on patterns of citizenship, Lauren MacLean (2011) finds that Africans who experience government social service provision participate in both electoral and nonelectoral political activities at higher rates than do those without similar government interactions. Erin Hern (2016b) finds evidence that in low-capacity African states the absence of government service provision can lead to greater levels of collective action, but whether that action turns political is conditioned by citizens' feelings of political efficacy.

Actual policy decisions themselves can affect citizens' sense of political efficacy, depending on whether or not their preferred policy outcome prevails. Patrick Flavin and John Griffin found evidence of such outcomes, as least among politically knowledgeable citizens. Both policy "winners" and "losers" became more politically active in the wake of decisions about military intervention in Iraq and the Bush tax cuts, but different mechanisms produced each outcome (Flavin and Griffin 2009).

In combination, a specific policy's design and implementation can shape both the way that individuals and groups view the value of their citizenship and how they assess the efficacy of government agencies. These evaluations can in turn affect citizens' decision to participate in politics (Mettler and Soss 2004). If, for example, an individual is part of a target population ascribed with negative characteristics, he may view his citizenship as worth less than that of others and be less likely to participate. Similarly, if an individual has negative experiences with government agencies, she may decide that participation is futile and choose not to engage. As in the case of the submerged state, if individuals have no concept that government is involved with the provision of a particular benefit, they may also be dissuaded from participating in political activity. Because interpretive effects engender political learning for political elites as well as for the mass public, policies have the ability to entrench and exacerbate participatory inequalities as specific designs and implementation schemes become path dependent. Taken together, these two types of interpretative effects can provide individuals with powerful incentives or disincentives for political engagement.

In the past fifteen years, scholars have made perhaps the greatest headway in probing when interpretive effects occur and the mechanisms underlying them. Policies seem to generate distinct attitudinal responses depending on such factors as the terms of eligibility, the degree of visibility of government's role, the means of financing, the scope of coverage, the degree of automaticity of benefit receipt, and the degree of discretion and intervention by government officials. We have yet to reach a comprehensive understanding of these topics, but scholars are building on each other's work to refine our expectations about when and how policy feedback effects may or may not occur.

CHALLENGES TO POLICY FEEDBACK RESEARCH

The recent research conducted by scholars of policy feedback has contributed innovative insight into the workings of the political process across multiple dimensions. As with many research agendas, however, work in the field of policy feedback effects faces a number of challenges. The most significant limitations to research thus far emanate from methodological concerns and data limitations.

As discussed previously, policy feedback work to date consists primarily of single-policy case studies (e.g., Soss 1999; Campbell 2002; Mettler 2005), most of which employ some combination of historical analysis, interviews, and statistical analyses of cross-sectional survey data to test proposed hypotheses. Critics of this scholarship have argued that some of the work in the feedback domain fails to address problems of endogeneity, particularly those introduced by potential self-selection bias between recipients and nonrecipients of government benefits. The concern is that some preexisting characteristics affect which individuals elect to utilize a particular program, and those same factors may determine later participatory or attitudinal differences between beneficiaries and nonbeneficiaries. If analysts lack the appropriate data or statistical tools to control for this possibility, they cannot with confidence specify the existence of policy feedback effects (Mead 2004). Work in the field of policy feedback is sensitive to this charge, and increasingly scholars are leveraging a variety of methodological tools to substantiate their causal claims.

In their study of the effect of contact with the criminal justice system on attitudes toward government and political engagement, Weaver and Lerman (2010, 5–6) contend with the issue of selection bias—specifically that individuals who come into contact with the criminal justice system may be inherently different from those who do not draw the attention of law enforcement. They utilize panel data from both the National Longitudinal Study of Adolescent Health (AdHealth), a nationally representative longitudinal study, and Fragile Families, a panel study of disadvantaged parents and their children. Their analysis employs standard control variables as well as controls for type of government contact and criminal propensity (Weaver and Lerman 2010, 6). Finally, they employ nonparametric estimation through the use of genetic matching to confirm their causal relationship (Weaver and Lerman 2010, 7). Drawing on data from the same two surveys in her analysis of the effect of Medicaid on beneficiaries' political participation, Jamila Michener (2014) employs coarsened exact matching to control for confounding variables in her analysis. She then uses seemingly unrelated regression to further account for selection bias.

Another attempt at solving the puzzle of endogeneity is exemplified by Mettler and Welch's (2004) analysis of the impact of the GI Bill on political participation, in which they employed a two-stage statistical model to control for the determinants of which veterans chose to use the benefits. Their use of an instrumental variable helped to disentangle factors that may have influenced program usage from those affecting political participation. Similarly, Deondra Rose (2012) used a two-stage model to examine how use of student aid policies affected later political participation. Statistical techniques such as these help to provide more robust results and mitigate the problem of selection bias in policy feedback studies.

In addition to statistical techniques, several scholars are also beginning to employ experimental methods to better untangle the relationship between policies and public perceptions. Mettler and Guardino use a Web-based survey experiment to test the effect of policy-related information on citizen attitudes toward government social welfare programs (Mettler 2011, chap. 3). Lerman (2013) leverages both field and quasi-natural experiments in her work on citizen preferences for both public and private service provision. The use of random assignment allows for the direct comparison of average treatment effects between treatment and control groups, helping to account for endogeneity and establish causation (see Druckman 2011).

The increasing methodological rigor of feedback literature, as evidenced by these examples, signals a promising step forward for the field. But the ability to continue to improve will depend on the availability of appropriate data. Studies—particularly those dealing with historic or underexplored cases—face serious data limitations; however, new work in policy feedback has successfully begun using several rich panel surveys that allow scholars to account for variables identified by critics as important confounders that many of the traditional political science datasets lack information for.

Weaver and Lerman (2010), Bruch, Ferree, and Soss (2010), and Michener (2014) all employ panel data from Fragile Families and/or AdHealth in their analyses. Soss, Fording, and Schram (2011) use a variety of sources, including data from the Youth Development Study, a panel survey of Minnesota public school children, in *Disciplining the Poor*. These surveys all provide a wealth of demographic data as well as information on usage of a variety of social welfare programs, allowing scholars interested in the feedback effects of these programs to further reduce the potential for omitted variables and to use the tools discussed above to account for issues of selection.

Of course, existing survey data does not always provide the information necessary to gain leverage over a question of interest, a problem that is compounded for scholars attempting to conduct feedback research in countries with limited survey data available to begin with. A growing number of policy feedback scholars are turning to original data collection to remedy this gap. For example, scholars who are interested in capturing the effects of policy change are designing and implementing their own panel surveys. Morgan and Campbell (2011) wanted to understand how enrollment in certain Medicare programs created by the 2003 Medicare Modernization Act could change attitudes and behavior among older adults. They conducted a panel survey in three waves—2005, 2007, and 2009—allowing them to identify shifts in preferences and behavior that correlated with enrollment in different Medicare plans. Jacobs and Mettler (2011) have undertaken a similar data collection effort to capture changing preferences for the Affordable Care Act as it is implemented.

Scholars of policy feedback are increasingly relying on more advanced methodological techniques and access to an array of rich datasets to gain better leverage over the causal questions of interest to them. Most of these advances in the study of feedback effects, however, have still focused primarily on social welfare provision. Perhaps the next step is to extend these techniques to study how other types of policies shape the attitudes and behavior of beneficiaries as well as the broader impact of policies on the views of citizens generally, not only those affected directly.

RECOMMENDATIONS FOR FUTURE RESEARCH

Policy Feedback Theory is indispensable for scholars trying to understand how policies, once developed, reshape politics. Furthermore, today more than ever, the creation of new policies is deeply influenced by the existence of other policies, many of which reshape the political landscape in multiple and profound ways. The approach is also critical for those who want to understand how we can create better policies or assess existing policies with an eye toward promoting good governance, active civic engagement, and a fair playing field among groups and interests.

For the past fifteen years, scholars have done yeoman's work in developing this area of research. Going forward, they can test hypotheses in more rigorous ways and identify mechanisms with greater specificity. They can also assess the varying strengths of different feedback effects and specify when they may and may not be likely to develop (Patashnik and Zelizer 2013). A critically important avenue for future feedback research is to expand the scope of inquiry to different types of policies and policymaking bodies. Much of the existing scholarship explores redistributive or distributive policies; yet how do regulatory or procedural policies produce feedback effects? What are the effects of experiencing multiple policies in combination with one another? Beyond broadening the scope of policies considered, scholars can go further to examine the effects of policies administered through complex policy arrangements, which so often involve states, nongovernmental actors, and increasingly supranational lawmaking bodies that are common in countries around the world. How do citizens respond to policies and services that are channeled through nongovernmental organizations? Do citizen experiences with policies enacted by international lawmaking bodies produce different feedback effects than those implemented by national governments? How do federal systems of governance complicate policy feedback processes?

Besides taking these directions, policy feedback scholars—who have studied primarily the impact of policy on individual behavior—need to ask, "What impact does policy have on collective action?" Skocpol's (1992) work on the maternalist welfare state explores the potential for policies to shape collective identities, and Mettler, Katzenstein, and Reese each offered considerations of feedback effects and collective action in an edited volume titled *Routing the Opposition* (Meyer, Jenness, and Ingram 2005). The bulk of the work on the subject, however, simply aggregates individual effects for members of certain groups. In light of the research by social movement scholars establishing the importance of political opportunities for successful collective mobilization (e.g., McAdam 1982; Tarrow 1998), it seems prudent to explore further how policies can create openings in the political system that may influence collective action. Scholars should investigate whether feedback effects make collective framing either easier or more difficult to accomplish, affect the organizational resources necessary for collective action, and create or expunge political opportunities for successful mobilization. This is an especially timely question as we witness the rise in global protest.

Another productive line of exploration might consider whether different governmental institutions and arrangements within a state—specifically electoral, legislative, executive, and bureaucratic institutions—produce patterns in the policy designs they favor and the implications of those dynamics. Mettler (2011) and Soss, Fording, and Schram (2011) grapple with larger governmental patterns of the neoliberalization of social welfare policymaking and the political pressures to maintain certain policy designs. But to what extent are pressures such as those the same for all governing institutions and actors? For example, in many countries individual members of the national legislature are driven by the "electoral connection," but in other governing arrangements where legislative seats are assigned proportionally by party these mechanisms may work differently. Do elected officials under these different systems face different incentives when it comes to designing policies that are more favorable to their own constituents? To what extent are bureaucratic arrangements affected by the policy designs enacted by legislators? Does the arrangement of bureaucratic authority in a particular state or policy arena lead to trends in the policies produced by those bureaucratic agencies? Identifying patterns in policy design and their associated impact on the participation of beneficiaries across policymaking institutions may be especially important in countries where executives and executive agencies claim more policymaking responsibility.

The study of policy feedback represents an exciting and still relatively new direction in policy research, one ripe with possibilities for further inquiry. It engages scholars in the study of how policies, once created, reshape the political world in myriad ways. The past two decades have seen innovative new explorations in this domain and growing specification of mechanisms and dynamics. These accomplishments pave the way for future researchers to carry on.

REFERENCES

Adler, E. Scott, and John D. Wilkerson. 2012. *Congress and the Politics of Problem Solving*. New York: Cambridge University Press.

Andreß, H. J., and T. Heien. 2001. "Four Worlds of Welfare State Attitudes? A Comparison of Germany, Norway, and the United States." *European Sociological Review* 17 (4): 337–356.

Béland, Daniel. 2010. "Reconsidering Policy Feedback: How Policies Affect Politics." *Administration and Society* 42 (5): 568–590.

Bloemraad, Irene. 2006. *Becoming a Citizen: Incorporating Immigrants and Refugees in the United States and Canada*. Berkeley: University of California Press.

Blumenthal, David, and James A. Morone. 2009. *The Heart of Power: Health and Politics in the Oval Office*. Berkeley: University of California Press.

Bruch, Sarah K., Myra Marx Ferree, and Joe Soss. 2010. "From Policy to Polity: Democracy, Paternalism, and the Incorporation of Disadvantaged Citizens." *American Sociological Review* 75 (2): 205–226.

Campbell, Andrea Louise. 2002. "Self-Interest, Social Security, and the Distinctive Participation Patterns of Senior Citizens." *American Political Science Review* 96 (3): 565–574.

———. 2003. "Participatory Reactions to Policy Threats: Senior Citizens and the Defense of Social Security and Medicare." *Political Behavior* 25 (March): 29–49.

———. 2012. "Policy Makes Mass Politics." *Annual Review of Political Science* 15: 333–351.

Canaday, Margot. 2009. *The Straight State: Sexuality and Citizenship in Twentieth-Century America*. Princeton, NJ: Princeton University Press.

Chen, Jowei. 2013. "Voter Partisanship and the Effect of Distributive Spending on Political Participation." *American Journal of Political Science* 57 (1): 200–217.

Dahl, Robert A. 2003. *How Democratic Is the American Constitution?* 2nd ed. New Haven, CT: Yale University Press.

Derthick, Martha. 1979. *Policymaking for Social Security*. Washington, DC: Brookings Institution.

Druckman, James N. 2011. *Cambridge Handbook of Experimental Political Science*. Cambridge: Cambridge University Press.

Edlund, Jonas. 1999. "Trust in Government and Welfare Regimes: Attitudes to Redistribution and Financial Cheating in the USA and Norway." *European Journal of Political Research* 35 (3): 341.

Engel, Stephen M. 2014. "Seeing Sexuality: State Development and the Fragmented Status of LGBTQ Citizenship." In *The Oxford Handbook of American Political Development,* edited by Richard Valelly, Suzanne Mettler, and Robert Lieberman. Oxford: Oxford University Press.

Esping-Andersen, Gøsta. 1990. *The Three Worlds of Welfare Capitalism.* Princeton, NJ: Princeton University Press.

Faricy, Christopher. 2011. "The Politics of Social Policy in America: The Causes and Effects of Indirect versus Direct Social Spending." *Journal of Politics* 73:74–83.

Flavin, Patrick, and John D. Griffin. 2009. "Policy, Preferences, and Participation: Government's Impact on Democratic Citizenship." *Journal of Politics* 71 (2): 544–559.

Fox, Cybelle. 2012. *Three Worlds of Relief: Race, Immigration, and the American Welfare State from the Progressive Era to the New Deal.* Princeton, NJ: Princeton University Press.

Goss, Kristin A. 2013. *The Paradox of Gender Equality: How American Women's Groups Gained and Lost Their Public Voice.* Ann Arbor: University of Michigan Press.

Hacker, Jacob S. 1998. "The Historical Logic of National Health Insurance: Structure and Sequence in the Development of British, Canadian, and U.S. Medical Policy." *Studies in American Political Development* 12 (1): 57–130.

———. 2002. *The Divided Welfare State: The Battle over Public and Private Social Benefits in the United States.* New York: Cambridge University Press.

Hall, Peter A. 1986. *Governing the Economy: The Politics of State Intervention in Britain and France.* New York: Oxford University Press.

Harrington Meyer, Madonna. 1996. "Making Claims as Workers or Wives: The Distribution of Social Security Benefits." *American Sociological Review* 61 (June): 449–465.

Heclo, Hugh. 1974. *Modern Social Politics in Britain and Sweden: From Relief to Income Maintenance.* New Haven, CT: Yale University Press.

Hern, Erin A. 2016a. "Better Than Nothing: How Policies Influence Participation in Low-Capacity Democracies." *Governance* (July). doi:10.1111/gove.12228.

———. 2016b. "In the Gap the State Left: Policy Feedback, Collective Behavior, and Political Participation in Zambia." *Studies in Comparative International Development* (August): 1–22. doi:10.1007/s12116-016-9226-6.

Hochschild, Jennifer, and Vesla Mae Weaver. 2010. "'There's No One as Irish as Barack O'Bama': The Policy and Politics of American Multiracialism." *Perspectives on Politics* 8 (3): 737–759.

Howard, Christopher. 1997. *The Hidden Welfare State: Tax Expenditures and Social Policy in the United States.* Princeton, NJ: Princeton University Press.

Jacobs, Lawrence, and Suzanne Mettler. 2011. "Why Public Opinion Changes: The Implications for Health and Health Policy." *Journal of Health Politics, Policy and Law* 36 (6): 917–933.

Jakobsen, Tor Georg. 2011. "Welfare Attitudes and Social Expenditure: Do Regimes Shape Public Opinion?" *Social Indicators Research* 101 (3): 323–340.

Jordan, Jason. 2013. "Policy Feedback and Support for the Welfare State." *Journal of European Social Policy* 23 (2): 134–148.

Keyssar, Alexander. 2000. *The Right to Vote: The Contested History of Democracy in the United States.* New York: Basic Books.

Korpi, Walter, and Joakim Palme. 1998. "The Paradox of Redistribution and Strategies of Equality: Welfare State Institutions, Inequality, and Poverty in the Western Countries." *American Sociological Review* 63 (5): 661.

Kumlin, Staffan. 2004. *The Personal and the Political: How Personal Welfare State Experiences Affect Political Trust and Ideology.* New York: Palgrave Macmillan.

Larsen, Christian. 2008. "The Institutional Logic of Welfare Attitudes." *Comparative Political Studies* 41 (2): 145–168.

Lerman, Amy. 2013. "Public Opinion Towards Privatization." Paper presented at the annual meeting of the American Political Science Association, Chicago, August 29 to September 1.

Lindblom, Charles E. 2010. "The Science of 'Muddling' Through." *Emergence: Complexity and Organization* 12 (1): 70–80.

Lowi, Theodore J. 1972. "Four Systems of Policy, Politics, and Choice." *Public Administration Review* 32 (4): 298–310.

———. 1985. "The State in Politics: The Relation Between Policy and Administration." In *Regulatory Policy and the Social Sciences,* edited by Roger G. Noll, 67–96. Berkeley: University of California Press.

MacLean, Lauren. 2011. "State Retrenchment and the Exercise of Citizenship in Africa." *Comparative Political Studies* 44 (9): 1238–1266.

Marshall, T. H. [1950] 1998. "Citizenship and Social Class." In *Citizenship Debates: A Reader,* edited by Gershon Shafir. Minneapolis: University of Minnesota Press.

Martin, Cathie J. 2004. "Reinventing Welfare Regimes: Employers and the Implementation of Active Social Policy." *World Politics* 57 (1): 39–69.

McAdam, Doug. 1982. *Political Process and the Development of Black Insurgency, 1930–1970.* Chicago: University of Chicago Press.

Mead, Lawrence M. 2004. "The Great Passivity." *Perspectives on Politics* 2 (4): 671–675.

Mettler, Suzanne. 1998. *Dividing Citizens: Gender and Federalism in New Deal Public Policy.* Ithaca, NY: Cornell University Press.

———. 2002. "Bringing the State Back into Civic Engagement: Policy Feedback Effects of the G.I. Bill for World War II Veterans." *American Political Science Review* 96 (2): 353.

———. 2005. *Soldiers to Citizens: The G.I. Bill and the Making of the Greatest Generation.* New York: Oxford University Press.

———. 2011. *The Submerged State: How Invisible Government Policies Undermine American Democracy.* Chicago: University of Chicago Press.

———. 2014. *Degrees of Inequality: How the Politics of Higher Education Sabotaged the American Dream.* New York: Basic Books.

———. 2016. "The Policyscape and the Challenges of Contemporary Politics to Policy Maintenance." *Perspectives on Politics* 14 (2): 369–390.

Mettler, Suzanne, and Joe Soss. 2004. "The Consequences of Public Policy for Democratic Citizenship: Bridging Policy Studies and Mass Politics." *Perspectives on Politics* 2 (1): 55–73.

Mettler, Suzanne, and Eric Welch. 2004. "Civic Generation: Policy Feedback Effects of the GI Bill on Political Involvement over the Life Course." *British Journal of Political Science* 34 (3): 497–518.

Meyer, David S., Valerie Jenness, and Helen M. Ingram. 2005. *Routing the Opposition: Social Movements, Public Policy, and Democracy.* Minneapolis: University of Minnesota Press.

Michener, Jamila D. 2014. "Shaping the Health of the Polity: Medicaid and the Political Inaction of the Poor." Unpublished manuscript, Cornell University.

Morgan, Kimberly J. 2006. *Working Mothers and the Welfare State: Religion and the Politics of Work-Family Policies in Western Europe and the United States.* Stanford, CA: Stanford University Press.

Morgan, Kimberly, and Andrea Louise Campbell. 2011. *The Delegated Welfare State: Medicare, Markets, and the Governance of Social Policy.* New York: Oxford University Press.

Moynihan, Donald, and Pamela Herd. 2010. "Red Tape and Democracy: How Rules Affect Citizenship Rights." *American Review of Public Administration* 40 (6): 654–670.

Olson, Mancur, Jr. 1965. *The Logic of Collective Action: Public Goods and the Theory of Groups.* Cambridge, MA: Harvard University Press.

Orloff, Ann Shola. 1993. *Gender and the Social Rights of Citizenship: The Comparative Analysis of Gender Relations and Welfare States.* Madison: University of Wisconsin.

Parker, Christopher S., and Matt A. Barreto. 2013. *Change They Can't Believe In: The Tea Party and Reactionary Politics in America.* Princeton, NJ: Princeton University Press.

Patashnik, Eric M. 2008. *Reforms at Risk: What Happens After Major Policy Changes Are Enacted.* Princeton, NJ: Princeton University Press.

Patashnik, Eric M., and Julian E. Zelizer. 2013. "The Struggle to Remake Politics: Liberal Reform and the Limits of Policy Feedback in the Contemporary American State." *Perspectives on Politics* 11 (4): 1071–1087.

Petrocik, J. R. 1996. "Issue Ownership in Presidential Elections, with a 1980 Case Study." *American Journal of Political Science* 40 (3): 825–850.

Pierson, Paul. 1993. "When Effect Becomes Cause: Policy Feedback and Political Change." *World Politics* 45 (4): 595–628.

Rose, Deondra Eunique. 2012. "The Development of U.S. Higher Education Policy and Its Impact on the Gender Dynamics of American Citizenship." PhD diss., Cornell University.

Rosenstone, Steven J., and John Mark Hansen. 1993. *Mobilization, Participation, and Democracy in America.* New York: Macmillan.

Rothstein, B. 2002. "The Universal Welfare State as Social Dilemma." In *Restructuring the Welfare State: Political Institutions and Policy Change*, edited by B. Rothstein and S. Steinmo, 206–222. New York: Palgrave Macmillan.

Schattschneider, E. E. 1935. *Politics, Pressure, and the Tariff*. New York: Prentice Hall.

Schneider, Anne, and Helen Ingram. 1993. "Social Construction of Target Populations: Implications for Politics and Policy." *American Political Science Review* 87:334–347.

———. 1997. *Policy Design for Democracy*. Lawrence: University Press of Kansas.

Shklar, Judith N. 1991. *American Citizenship: The Quest for Inclusion*. Cambridge, MA: Harvard University Press.

Skocpol, Theda. 1991. "Targeting within Universalism: Politically Viable Policies to Combat Poverty in the United States." In *The Urban Underclass*, edited by Christopher Jencks and Paul E. Peterson, 411–436. Washington, DC: Brookings Institution.

———. 1992. *Protecting Soldiers and Mothers: The Political Origins of Social Policy in the United States*. Cambridge, MA: Belknap Press of Harvard University Press.

———. 1996. *Boomerang: Clinton's Health Security Effort and the Turn Against Government in U.S. Politics*. New York: W. W. Norton.

Skocpol, Theda, and Vanessa Williamson. 2012. *The Tea Party and the Remaking of Republican Conservatism*. New York: Oxford University Press.

Skrentny, John D. 2011. "Obama's Immigration Reform: A Tough Sell for a Grand Bargain." In *Reaching for a New Deal: Ambitious Governance, Economic Meltdown, and Polarized Politics in Obama's First Two Years*, edited by Theda Skocpol and Lawrence R. Jacobs, 273–320. New York: Russell Sage Foundation.

Smith, Miriam Catherine. 2008. *Political Institutions and Lesbian and Gay Rights in the United States and Canada*. New York: Routledge.

Soss, Joe. 1999. "Lessons of Welfare: Policy Design, Political Learning, and Political Action." *American Political Science Review* 93 (2): 363–380.

Soss, Joe, Richard C. Fording, and Sanford Schram. 2011. *Disciplining the Poor: Neoliberal Paternalism and the Persistent Power of Race*. Chicago: University of Chicago Press.

Soss, Joe, and Sanford Schram. 2007. "A Public Transformed? Welfare Reform as Policy Feedback." In *Remaking America: Democracy and Public Policy in an Age of Inequality*, edited by Joe Soss, Jacob S. Hacker, and Suzanne Mettler, 99–118. New York: Russell Sage Foundation.

Steinmo, Sven, Kathleen Ann Thelen, and Frank Longstreth. 1992. *Structuring Politics: Historical Institutionalism in Comparative Analysis*. Cambridge: Cambridge University Press.

Svallfors, Stefan. 1997. "Worlds of Welfare and Attitudes to Redistribution: A Comparison of Eight Western Nations." *European Sociological Review* 13 (3): 283–304.

Tarrow, Sidney G. 1998. *Power in Movement: Social Movements and Contentious Politics*. Cambridge: Cambridge University Press.

Tichenor, Daniel J. 2002. *Dividing Lines: The Politics of Immigration Control in America*. Princeton, NJ: Princeton University Press.

Uggen, Christopher, and Jeff Manza. 2002. "Democratic Contraction? The Political Consequences of Felon Disenfranchisement in the United States." *American Sociological Review* 67 (6): 777.

Verba, Sidney, Kay Lehman Schlozman, and Henry E. Brady. 1995. *Voice and Equality: Civic Voluntarism in American Politics.* Cambridge, MA: Harvard University Press.

Walker, Jack L. 1983. "The Origins and Maintenance of Interest Groups in America." *American Political Science Review* 77 (2): 390–406.

Weaver, Vesla M., and Amy E. Lerman. 2010. "Political Consequences of the Carceral State." *American Political Science Review* 104 (4): 817–833.

Wilson, William Julius. 1991. "Public Policy Research and the Truly Disadvantaged." In *The Urban Underclass,* edited by Christopher Jencks and Paul E. Peterson, 411–436. Washington, DC: Brookings Institution.

Wolfinger, Raymond E., and Steven J. Rosenstone. 1980. *Who Votes?* New Haven, CT: Yale University Press.

Wood, B. Dan, and Richard W. Waterman. 1994. *Bureaucratic Dynamics: The Role of Bureaucracy in a Democracy.* Boulder, CO: Westview Press.

Zolberg, Aristide R. 2006. *A Nation by Design: Immigration Policy in the Fashioning of America.* New York: Russell Sage Foundation.

4

The Advocacy Coalition Framework: An Overview of the Research Program

HANK C. JENKINS-SMITH, DANIEL NOHRSTEDT,
CHRISTOPHER M. WEIBLE, AND KARIN INGOLD

The study of policy processes brings focus to many questions of both theoretical and practical significance. Some questions concern policy change and stasis over time: What factors explain the likelihood of occurrence of major and minor policy change? To what extent is policy change affecting government agencies and procedures and, through them, broader public opinion? Another set of questions involves learning by actors: To what extent are actors learning from their experiences, from the experiences of others, or from scientific and technical information? What factors facilitate learning among allies and among opponents? Yet another set of questions centers on the behavior of actors who directly or indirectly attempt to influence policy processes by advocating for change or maintenance of the status quo: Under what conditions do actors form and maintain coalitions to achieve their policy objectives in a coordinated fashion? What are the characteristics of the network structures of these coalitions? To what extent, and in what ways, do opposing coalition actors interact?

To answer these questions is to provide insight into some of the fundamental themes of governance and politics that ultimately affect the composition, dynamics, and course of society. The purpose of this chapter is to provide an overview of one framework that can help answer these questions: the Advocacy Coalition Framework (ACF).[1] The chapter begins with a summary of the intellectual foundations of the ACF. It then provides an overview of the framework and its theoretical foci, including assessments of the hypotheses based on extensive empirical applications. The chapter ends by suggesting an ongoing agenda to continue the advancement of the ACF research program.

INTELLECTUAL FOUNDATIONS OF THE ACF

The ACF was created in the early 1980s by Paul Sabatier and Hank Jenkins-Smith. Chief inspirations were drawn from past shortcomings in policy process research, including a need to develop an alternative policy process theory to overcome the limitations of the stages heuristic; a need to provide theoretical insight into the role of scientific and technical information in policy debates; a need to shed light on ideological disagreement and policy conflicts; and a need to provide a comprehensive approach to understanding politics and policy change over time that went beyond traditional emphases in political science on government institutions (e.g., executive, legislative, and judiciary) and a few forms of political behavior (e.g., voting and lobbying) (see the discussion in Sabatier 1991). Establishing the framework took several years of effort that included conference papers written by Sabatier and Jenkins-Smith, ongoing data collection through interviews and surveys, and the creation of code forms for measuring belief systems and coalition stability over time.[2]

The foundations of the ACF were also influenced by debates in the philosophy of sciences that were still prominent in the 1970s and 1980s. Partly in response to Thomas Kuhn's (1962) notion of scientific revolutions and paradigm shifts, Imré Lakatos developed his conception of the evolution of scientific research "programmes" in an effort to rescue the conception of cumulative, falsifiable science and the growth of knowledge (Lakatos 1970). A key contribution from Lakatos was the notion that scientific theories can be described as consisting of a "hard core" of unchanging and largely axiomatic propositions surrounded by a "protective belt" of auxiliary hypotheses that can be adjusted (or rejected) in response to potentially falsifiable evidence. This concept is a recognizable ancestor of the structure of belief systems in the ACF, which are characterized as hierarchically structured with a deep core of ontological and normative beliefs that are extraordinarily difficult to change, and "secondary aspects" of more specific propositions about how to effectively translate core beliefs into policy.[3]

A second important contribution was drawn from Lakatos's related proposition that—given that Popper's ([1935] 2002) ideal of falsifiable theories had proven implausible—theoretical progress was most readily evident in "progressive problem-shift." As noted by Kuhn (1962), counterevidence need not displace a theory; empirical anomalies can persist for hundreds of years while a theory hangs on because (1) ad hoc defense of a theory was too effective to displace a vital theory and (2) a ready replacement theory was not available. Lakatos argued that ad hoc defense of a theory fails if it is persistently *regressive*—meaning ad hoc "adjustments" of theories to accommodate counterevidence do not add new theoretical content that can be (and eventually is) empirically verified. Lakatos also argued that healthy theories experience *progressive* problem-shift, wherein theoretical adjustments (i.e., new concepts and hypotheses added to the theory) not only address counterevidence but also add new empirical content that extends the explanatory reach of the theory. Hence, defense (or expansion) of a theory needs to be progressive to be scientifically legitimate. For Sabatier and Jenkins-Smith, this conception of scientific progress characterized the spirit of the theoretical growth of the ACF. The basic framework of the ACF (e.g., the assumptions and general subsystem dynamics) characterized the hard core while new propositions and theoretical logic (e.g., the addition of the concepts of coalition opportunity structures and endogenous pathways to policy change) occupy the auxiliary belt. Thus, revisions to the auxiliary belt were acceptable as long as they added new substantive theoretical content to the ACF. Indeed, the many additions to, and revisions of, key ACF hypotheses are reflections of this view of theory change and the growth of knowledge. Naturally, the assessment of whether these cumulative changes are truly *progressive* remains an open and important question.

The earliest journal publications of the ACF began with Sabatier (1986), where the ACF was described as a synthesis of top-down and bottom-up approaches to implementation, and continued with Sabatier and Pelkey (1987), where the ACF was described as an approach to understand regulatory policymaking.[4] The first overview of the ACF by Sabatier (1987) was published in *Knowledge*, and a nearly identical publication by Sabatier (1988) led to the symposium on the ACF in *Policy Sciences*.[5] Jenkins-Smith's work on policy analysis within a process characterized by advocacy coalitions was published soon after (Jenkins-Smith, 1990). Applications of the framework slowly accumulated, with a coedited volume by Sabatier and Jenkins-Smith published in 1993.

The ACF has since become one of the most utilized frameworks of the policy process. The ACF has been the topic of five special issues in peer-reviewed journals, including *Policy Sciences* (Sabatier 1988), *PS: Political Science & Politics* (Sabatier 1991), *Policy Studies Journal* (Weible et al. 2011), *Administration & Society* (Scott 2012), and *Journal of Comparative Policy Analysis* (Henry et al. 2014). Weible, Sabatier, and McQueen (2009) and Pierce et al. (2017) conducted comprehensive reviews of over 240 English-language ACF applications from 1987 through 2014 that span the globe.[6] Additionally, Sotirov and Memmler (2012) reviewed ACF applications in the context of environmental and natural resource issues. Country-specific reviews have been conducted for applications of the ACF in South Korea (Jang et al. 2016) and Sweden (Nohrstedt and Olofsson, 2016b). Jang et al. (2016) found 62 ACF applications in Korean, suggesting the ACF is frequently applied in other languages. One edited volume compares and contrasts advocacy coalitions and policy change on the topic of unconventional oil and gas development across seven countries in North America and Western Europe (Weible et al. 2016). In aggregate, these reviews confirm the portability of the ACF to different policy issues and governing systems, but they also expose areas where the ACF's concepts and assumptions appear to be less applicable and problematic. We return to these issues below when discussing a research agenda for the future.

The ACF offers a general foundation for single case studies and for comparative analyses of policy processes across a wide range of policy issues and governing systems. Although a single chapter cannot adequately summarize the development of the ACF over time, present all the intricacies of the framework, list all the hypotheses offered by various analysts, or synthesize the findings from various applications of the framework, we offer here a synthesis of the most recent developments in the ACF and encourage interested readers to explore past theoretical and empirical publications as cited herein.

THE FRAMEWORK AND THEORETICAL EMPHASES

Borrowing from Easton (1965), Laudan (1977, 70–120), Lakatos (1970), and Ostrom (2005, 27–29), the ACF is best thought of as a framework supporting multiple, overlapping theoretical foci.[7] The purpose of a framework is to provide a shared research platform that enables analysts to work together in describing, explaining, and, sometimes, predicting phenomena within and across different contexts. The components of a framework include a statement of the assumptions, description of the scope or type of questions the framework is intended to help answer, and the establishment of concept categories and their general relations. Most importantly, a framework provides a common vocabulary to help analysts communicate across disciplines, from different substantive policy areas, and from different parts of the world. Akin to Lakatos's hard core foundation of a research program, a framework should be fairly stable in its basic premises over time. Additionally, frameworks are not directly testable but provide guidance toward specific areas of descriptive and explanatory inquiry. This is an important reminder, given the misperception among some students and researchers that a comprehensive "test" of the ACF requires empirical assessments of all its components and relationships among them.

Rather, a framework supports multiple theories, which are narrower in scope and emphasize a smaller set of questions, variables, and relationships. Theories provide more precise conceptual and operational definitions of concepts and interrelate concepts in the form of testable and falsifiable hypotheses or propositions. The theories within the framework are where students and researchers should attempt to test and develop descriptions and explanations. Theories are, hence, akin to Lakatos's protective belt that can (and should) be subject to experimentation, adjustment, and modifications over time. Although hypotheses should ideally offer refutable expectations among concepts, a pragmatic reason for using hypotheses is to highlight the most important relationships that describe what, why, and how those concepts relate and when and where those relationships are expected to be evident (Whetten 1987).

A SUMMARY OF THE ACF AS A "FRAMEWORK"

A framework is best described by its assumptions, scope (type of questions), and basic categories of concepts and general relations for answering research questions. This section provides an overview of the framework of the ACF.

Assumptions

The policy subsystem is the primary unit of analysis for understanding policy processes. Policy subsystems are defined by a policy topic, territorial scope, and the actors directly or indirectly influencing policy subsystem affairs. Policy subsystems have several defining properties that help in interpretation and application (Sabatier 1998; Nohrstedt and Weible 2010). First, subsystems contain a large set of components that interact in nontrivial ways to produce outputs and outcomes for a given policy topic. These components range from physical and institutional characteristics to actor attributes, including belief systems and political resources. One of the purposes of a framework and its theories is to specify some of the most important subsystem components to study in attempting to help solve puzzles concerning the policy process. Second, policy subsystems demarcate the integrated and nonintegrated actors on a given policy topic. Policy subsystems do not involve all people interested and affected by the policy decisions. Indeed, given limited time and attention, most people do not engage in any subsystem and, for those who do, the number of policy subsystems where they are active is finite and usually small in number. Third, policy subsystems are semi-independent but overlap with other subsystems and are nested within yet other subsystems. For example, an energy policy subsystem in Colorado overlaps with a food policy subsystem in the same state and nests within a national energy policy subsystem in the United States.[8] Fourth, policy subsystems often provide some authority or potential for authority. Such authority may exist in the enforcement and monitoring of policy, the legislative or legal processes, or the potential for new policies that may alter the status quo. Fifth, policy subsystems undergo periods of stasis, incremental change, and major change.

The set of relevant subsystem actors include *any* person regularly attempting to influence subsystem affairs. Borrowing from Heclo (1978), the depiction of subsystem actors expands beyond traditional interpretations of the policy process that tends to focus narrowly on legislative committees, government agencies, and interest groups. Subsystems are affected by any actor directly or indirectly influencing subsystem affairs and may include officials from any level of government, representatives from the private sector, members from nonprofit organizations, members of the news media, academic scientists and researchers, private consultants, lobbyists, think tanks, and even members of the courts (Hjern and Porter 1981). The extent and consistency of involvement and influence of these actors, of course, varies.

Individuals are boundedly rational, with limited ability to process stimuli, motivated by belief systems, and prone to experience the "devil shift." The ACF conception of individuals is based on a modified version of methodological individualism, that is, change in the world is primarily driven by people and not by organizations (Sabatier 1987, 685). In the terms *coalition beliefs, coalition behavior,* and *coalition learning, coalition* is used metaphorically in reference to the individuals comprising the coalition. Indeed, coalitions do not learn, but rather the actors within coalitions learn. Furthermore, the modified version of methodological individualism in the ACF does not suggest that people's behavior is independent of context. Indeed, the theory within the ACF would expect that people's behavior is shaped by various contextual factors, particularly, the nature of relevant institutions, the intensity of conflict, and the perceived severity of threats posed by opponents.

The ACF's assumption that individuals are boundedly rational means that people are motivated instrumentally by goals but are often unclear how to achieve those goals, and they are limited in their cognitive abilities to process stimuli such as information and experience (Simon 1957, 1985). Additionally, given limited cognitive abilities, individuals simplify the world through their belief systems and are, therefore, prone to biased assimilation of stimuli (Munro and Ditto 1997; Munro et al. 2002).

The ACF assumes that policy actors have a three-tiered belief system structure. *Deep core beliefs* are fundamental normative values and ontological axioms. Deep core beliefs are not policy specific and, thus, can be applicable to multiple policy subsystems. One way to conceptualize and measure deep core beliefs is by incorporating insights from cultural theory (Douglas and Wildavsky 1982; Ripberger et al. 2014; Jenkins-Smith et al. 2014; Trousset et al. 2015). Cultural theory offers four distinct orientations—hierarchs, egalitarians, individualists, and fatalists. Each of these orientations is buttressed by a set of "myths"—about human nature, society, and natural systems—that can serve both to justify the orientation and its values and to imply appropriate forms of social organization (Douglas and Wildavsky 1982; Thompson, Ellis, and Wildavsky 1990). Whereas cultural theory has demonstrated its utility as one way of conceptualizing and measuring deep core beliefs especially for comparative analyses, other ways certainly exist and could be developed.

In contrast to deep core beliefs, *policy core beliefs* are bound by scope and topic to the policy subsystem and thus have territorial and topical components. Policy core beliefs can be normative and empirical. Normatively, policy core beliefs may reflect basic orientation and value priorities for the policy subsystem and may identify whose welfare in the policy subsystem is of greatest concern. Empirically, policy core beliefs include overall assessments of the seriousness of the problem, basic causes of the problem, and preferred solutions for addressing the problem (called policy core policy preferences). *Secondary beliefs* deal with a subset of the policy subsystem or the specific instrumental means for achieving the desired outcomes outlined in the policy core beliefs.[9] Finally, the ACF borrows one of the key findings from prospect theory that people remember losses more readily than gains (Quattrone and Tversky 1988). Remembering losses and the tendency to filter and assimilate stimuli through belief systems result in the "devil shift," where actors exaggerate the power and maliciousness of their opponents (Sabatier, Hunter, and McLaughlin 1987). The expected result is a noncollaborative attitude, growing mistrust, the protraction of conflict, and the obstruction of effective policy solutions (Fischer et al. 2016).

Subsystems are simplified by aggregating actors into one or more coalitions. Depicting policy subsystems as consisting of any actor attempting to directly or indirectly influence subsystems affairs presents a dilemma for analysts: there might be hundreds of actors somehow involved in a policy subsystem. Also, analysts encounter subsystems at different levels of maturity; mature subsystems comprise relatively established and clearly differentiated coalitions, whereas nascent or emergent subsystems are characterized by ambivalence and unclear political positions. Simplifying assumptions must be made to describe and analyze.[10] Analysts could organize subsystems by organizational affiliation, which provides important insight into the resources and strategies of actors in the policy subsystem, but the organizational level of analysis comes at the cost of realizing that the number of organizations involved in the policy subsystem is not many fewer than the number of actors.

A more effective approach is to organize actors into one or more advocacy coalitions on the basis of shared beliefs and coordination strategies. By grouping and analyzing actors by coalitions, the analysts can simplify the hundreds of actors and their organizational affiliations into groupings that may be stable over time (Sabatier and Brasher 1993) and that are instrumental for understanding policy actors' strategies for influence and policy change (Nohrstedt 2010). Aggregating actors into coalitions can follow the rule of first identifying actors sharing similar belief systems, and subsequently searching for a nontrivial degree of coordination among those actors (Henry 2011). It then also raises original questions such as the degree of cross-coalition interactions, intracoalition cohesiveness, and factors contributing to coalition defection (Jenkins-Smith, St. Clair, and Woods 1991).

Policies and programs incorporate implicit theories reflecting the translated beliefs of one or more coalitions. Public policy can be conceptualized and defined in multiple ways (Birkland 2010, 8). Whereas some definitions can be simply stated and communicated, such as defining public policy as any inaction and action by government, other definitions are more nuanced and insightful. Lasswell and Kaplan (1950, 71), for example, describe policy as "a projected program of goal values and practices." Notable from this definition, and from similar ones, is the insight that public policy consists of translations of the belief systems of the designers. In this regard, public policies represent the political maneuvering and negotiations not just among coalitions but also of causal theories (Pressman and Wildavsky 1973, xv; Mazmanian and Sabatier 1983, 5). Causal theory, when used to describe the implicit or explicit content of public policy, refers to the sequence of steps, a linking of anticipated events, or desired procedures that describe the reasoning for achieving outputs and outcomes of a public policy. Analysts applying the ACF should, therefore, interpret policies not just as the actions or inactions of government but also as the translations of belief systems as manifested in goals, rules, incentives, sanctions, subsidies, taxes, and other instruments regulating any given issue (Jenkins-Smith et al. 2014, 486). This interpretation of policy provides insight into why coalition actors advocate so intently over time and how they interpret public policies as bolstering or as being antithetical to their belief systems.

Scientific and technical information is important for understanding subsystem affairs. In the previous assumption, belief systems were described as the mechanism for simplifying and interpreting the world. Belief systems are not, however, simply abstract representations of values and priorities but also encapsulate policy actors' perceived causal patterns and relationships that shape the empirical world. A major source of this causal representation in a given context is scientific and technical information that can point to specific causal relations, problem attributes, and, sometimes, policy alternatives. To better understand policy processes is thus to understand how scientific and technical explanations are integrated into (or deflected from) belief systems, used in political debates and negotiations, and integrated with other forms of knowledge, especially local knowledge.[11]

Researchers should adopt a long-term time perspective (e.g., ten years or more) to understand policy processes and change. Policy processes are ongoing without beginning or end (Lindblom 1968, 4) and, thus, strategic behavior and learning of coalition actors, the reasoning and patterns of policy change, and assessments of the success or failure of public policy should be understood from a long-term perspective. The point has been misinterpreted to mean that a perspective of ten years or more is required to interpret policy processes through the ACF. This is too literal of an interpretation and often prevents interested analysts from applying the ACF even if the framework could help answer their research question. Some questions, for example, require intensive methods of data collection that preclude longitudinal data, such as an understanding of coalition structure using quantitative network analysis approaches (Henry 2011). Other datasets permit long-term perspectives, such as the multidecade perspectives taken by Albright (2011), Andersson (1999), and others to understand patterns of policy change. We also know that coalitions, though existing for decades, often take short-term perspectives as opportunities and constraints alter their immediate strategies (Jenkins-Smith, St. Clair, and Woods 1991). The general meaning behind this assumption is the recognition that understanding public policy requires focusing on temporal processes that characterize public policy over time.

Scope

A framework's scope provides the set of general questions about the policy process that it helps the analyst answer. The traditional scope of the ACF includes questions involving coalitions, learning, and policy change. As suggested by the assumptions above, the framework is most useful for understanding these topics in high-conflict situations at the subsystem level of analysis. However, the framework has been applied in other settings, such as at the organizational level in collaborative settings (Leach and Sabatier 2005; Leach et al. 2013), a form of application to which we return when discussing future research agendas.

General Conceptual Categories and Relations

Flow diagrams are useful for identifying general categories of concepts and how they relate. Figure 4.1 presents a flow diagram depicting the policy process

FIGURE 4.1 Flow Diagram of the Advocacy Coalition Framework

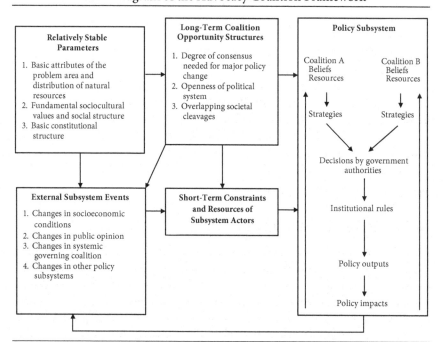

SOURCE: Adapted from Sabatier and Weible (2007).

within the ACF.[12] The policy subsystem is represented by the rectangle on the right illustrating a case with two competing coalitions representing their actors' beliefs and resources. The two coalitions use various strategies to influence decisions by government authorities that affect institutional rules, policy outputs, and, eventually, policy outcomes. These decisions then feed back into the policy subsystem but also can affect external subsystem affairs.

One category of variables that condition subsystem affairs includes relatively stable parameters, which are the basic social, cultural, economic, physical, and institutional structures that embed a policy subsystem (Hofferbert 1974; Heclo 1974). Some concepts within relatively stable parameters are best conceptualized as external to subsystem affairs, such as the basic constitutional structure of the political system, whereas others can be internal to the subsystem, such as physical conditions of the subsystem. A second category of variables consists of dynamic external events, which includes relevant features external to the subsystem and prone to change. Examples include socioeconomic conditions, the state of subsystem-relevant technology, public opinion, the composition of governing coalitions (Burnham 1970), and spillover effects from other policy subsystems. The listings under relatively stable parameters and dynamic external events in Figure 4.1 are illustrative examples and are not exhaustive; clearly, other concepts can be placed in each category, such as crises and disasters under dynamic external events (Nohrstedt 2011; Jenkins-Smith, St. Clair, and Woods 1991). In between relatively stable parameters and a policy subsystem is an intermediary category of concepts concerning the nature of the long-term coalition opportunity structures that establish the degree of consensus needed for major policy change, the openness of the political system, and overlapping societal cleavages.

Essentially, long-term coalition opportunity structures are some of the important by-products of the relatively stable parameters on policy subsystems. Between external events and policy subsystems are the short-term constraints and resources of subsystem actors; this means that changes outside the subsystem provide short-term opportunities for coalitions to exploit.

THEORETICAL EMPHASES

Theoretical Focus on Policy Change

One of the central objectives of the ACF is to contribute to the understanding of policy change and stability, and this has been the subject of considerable empirical investigation. Thanks to these contributions, we now have more detailed knowledge about the nature and causes of policy change within and across policy subsystems than we had just a few decades ago. What has provoked this focus is the recurrent observation that, although many public policies and programs remain stable over long periods of time, others are subject to periods of dramatic and nonincremental change (Sabatier 1988; Baumgartner and Jones 1993).[13] For example, indicators of such policy change may include revisions in policy core components of governmental programs, termination of programs, or launching of new programs.

Similarly to other theoretical perspectives on policy change (Baybrook and Lindblom 1963; Hall 1993; Rose 1993), the ACF focuses on the directionality of policy evolution and makes a clear distinction between minor and major policy change (Capano 2009, 2012; Howlett and Cashore 2009; Nisbet 1972). The level of change in a governmental program is defined according to the extent to which alterations deviate from previous policy. The ACF assumes that public policies and programs are translations of policy-oriented beliefs and can be conceptualized and measured hierarchically, like belief systems. Change in the core aspects, defined as "major policy change," indicates significant shifts in the direction or goals of the subsystem, whereas change in secondary aspects (e.g., change in means for achieving the goals) is evidence for "minor policy change" (Sabatier and Jenkins-Smith 1999, 147–148). Advocacy coalitions often disagree on proposals related to these components, and policy debates therefore often revolve around diverging preferences regarding initiatives to either change or preserve governmental programs (Sabatier and Weible 2007, 195).

Since the belief system categories differ according to their susceptibility to change, minor policy change should be not as difficult to achieve as major policy change (Sabatier 1988). For example, minor changes in administrative rules, budgetary allocations, statutory interpretation, and revision are relatively frequent and do not necessitate as much evidence, agreement among subsystem actors, or redistribution of resources. By contrast, because normative (policy core) beliefs are rigidly held and screen out dissonant information, major policy change is unlikely as long as the advocacy coalition that instituted the program remains in power.

The ACF offers four conceptual pathways to policy change. The first is attributed to some external source (e.g., as might be found in the categories of dynamic external events or even relatively stable parameters from Figure 4.1). External shocks, or perturbations, include events outside the control of subsystem participants (in terms of their ability to influence underlying causes and triggers) and involve change in socioeconomic conditions, regime change, outputs from other subsystems, and extreme events such as some crises and disasters. These events increase the likelihood of major policy change but require one or several enabling factors (causal mechanisms), including heightened public and political attention, agenda change, and most importantly redistribution of coalition resources and opening and closing of policy venues (Sabatier and Weible 2007, 198–199). A key factor in this regard is mobilization by minority coalitions to exploit the event, for instance, by pursuing public narratives to attract attention to favored courses of action and by appealing to new actors (Sabatier and Jenkins-Smith 1999, 148; see also McBeth et al. 2007;

Nohrstedt 2008). Because of the importance of these intervening steps, it has been hypothesized that significant perturbations external to the subsystem are one of the necessary, but not sufficient, paths for changing the policy core attributes of a governmental program (Sabatier 1988).

Major policy change may also result from a second pathway based on *internal events* that (1) occur inside the territorial boundaries and/or the topical area of the policy subsystem and (2) are more likely affected by subsystem actors (Sabatier and Weible 2007, 204–205). Various types of internal events, including crises, policy fiascoes, scandals, and failures, are likely to influence beliefs and heighten attention to certain governmental programs (Birkland 2006; Bovens and 't Hart 1996). Advocacy coalitions can be expected to engage in framing contests over such events and debate the severity of problems, their underlying causes, attribution of responsibility, and policy implications (Boin, 't Hart, and McConnell 2009; Nohrstedt and Weible 2010). Internal events can be expected to confirm the policy core beliefs of minority coalitions and increase doubts about the core beliefs of the dominant coalition and bring into question the effectiveness of their policies. Whether or not internal shocks result in major policy change depends on the same mechanisms that mediate the effect from external shocks.

A third source of minor policy change is policy-oriented learning, but this is likely to happen incrementally over longer periods of time. Following Caplan, Morrison, and Stanbaugh (1975) and Weiss (1977), Sabatier (1988) expects that policy analysis seldom influences specific governmental decisions but often serves an "enlightenment function" by gradually altering the concepts and assumptions of subsystem participants. In addition, learning can also facilitate major policy change, but this is more likely when learning takes place in conjunction with an external or internal shock (Nohrstedt 2005).

A fourth pathway to policy change is through negotiated agreement among previously warring coalitions and may result in substantial change in governmental programs. Negotiated agreements may emerge in a variety of ways but are facilitated by collaborative institutions conducive to negotiation. Specifically, Sabatier and Weible (2007, 205–206) identify nine prescriptions fostering negotiation: a "hurting stalemate," broad representation, leadership, consensus decision rules, funding, commitment by actors, importance of empirical issues, trust, and lack of alternative venues. The most important condition instigating negotiations is a "hurting stalemate," which occurs when warring coalitions perceive the status quo as unacceptable and do not have access to alternative venues for achieving their objectives (Weible and Nohrstedt 2012, 132).

A recent review of ACF case studies shows that among 161 empirical applications from 2007 to 2014, learning is the most frequently cited source of policy change (identified in 29 percent of the applications reviewed), followed by external sources and events (28 percent), negotiated agreements (14 percent), and internal events (6 percent) (Pierce et al. 2017).

In summary, the original version of the ACF offered two hypotheses of policy change, focusing on external perturbations and power shifts. However, Weible and Nohrstedt (2012, 133) merge the four pathways to policy change into a single hypothesis:

Policy Change Hypothesis 1. Significant perturbations external to the subsystem, a significant perturbation internal to the subsystem, policy-oriented learning, negotiated agreement, or some combination thereof is a *necessary, but not sufficient,* source of change in the policy core attributes of a governmental program.

There has been strong support for the first policy change hypothesis. Many find support for at least one of the pathways (Barke 1993; Bischoff 2001; Green and Houlihan 2004; Tewari 2001; Kübler 2001; Dudley and Richardson 1999). One challenge in testing this hypothesis is the occurrence of one of the pathways without a change in policy (Weible, Sabatier, and McQueen 2009; Sotirov and Memmler 2012). Another challenge is explaining minor policy changes after an external shock (Burnett and Davis 2002; Davis and Davis 1988). Critical in testing the first hypothesis about policy change is to understand how a coalition can capitalize on (or exploit) the opportunity, which ultimately involves attempts to either preserve the status quo or seek policy change. This has led some analysts to focus heavily on coalition resources and strategies following various external events and developments (Smith 2000; Ameringer 2002; Albright 2011; Ingold 2011; Nohrstedt 2005, 2008).

The second hypothesis relates coalition influence in the subsystem, major policy change, and nested policy subsystems:

Policy Change Hypothesis 2. The policy core attributes of a government program in a specific jurisdiction will not be significantly revised as long as the subsystem advocacy coalition that instated the program remains in power within that jurisdiction—except when the change is imposed by a hierarchically superior jurisdiction.

There is strong to partial support for Policy Change Hypothesis 2 (Sotirov and Memmler 2012). Studies that confirm the logic of the second policy change hypothesis include Ellison (1998), Olson, Olson, and Gawronski (1999), Elliot and Schlaepfer (2001), and Kübler (2001). However, this second policy change hypothesis has been tested but a few times.

One of the next steps in studying policy change will be to focus on developing best practices for documenting and explaining policy while accounting for context. Too many studies of policy change apply different methods of data collection and analysis, with the result that comparison across cases is difficult. In addition, studies adopt slightly different definitions of *policy,* which complicates the task of comparing drivers of policy change across governing systems.

Advocacy Coalitions

Advocacy coalitions are defined by actors who share policy core beliefs and who coordinate their actions in a nontrivial manner to influence a policy subsystem. In studying coalitions, analysts typically focus on a range of topics, from the structure and stability of coalition actor belief systems to the formation and maintenance of coalitions over time. The traditional hypotheses about advocacy coalition include the following:

> *Coalition Hypothesis 1.* On major controversies within a policy subsystem when policy core beliefs are in dispute, the lineup of allies and opponents tends to be rather stable over periods of a decade or so.
>
> *Coalition Hypothesis 2.* Actors within an advocacy coalition will show substantial consensus on issues pertaining to the policy core, although less so on secondary aspects.
>
> *Coalition Hypothesis 3.* Actors (or coalitions) will give up secondary aspects of their belief systems before acknowledging weaknesses in the policy core.
>
> *Coalition Hypothesis 4.* Within a coalition, administrative agencies will usually advocate more moderate positions than their interest group allies.
>
> *Coalition Hypothesis 5.* Actors within purposive groups are more constrained in their expression of beliefs and policy positions than actors from material groups.

From these hypotheses, evidence to date largely confirms Coalition Hypothesis 1 about the stability of coalitions over time (see Pierce et al. 2017 review paper). To assess the stability of coalitions, most of these studies use coded legislative statements (Jenkins-Smith, St. Clair, and Woods 1991; Jenkins-Smith and St. Clair 1993; Sabatier and Brasher 1993; Zafonte and Sabatier 2004; Pierce 2011; Nohrstedt 2010), with a few studies using survey and interviews (Weible, Sabatier, and McQueen 2009; Ingold 2011) and discourse analysis (Leifeld 2013). Important in these studies is the documentation that although coalitions are generally stable over time defection is not uncommon and membership often changes. Analysts have documented a range of reasons for defection or change in coalition composition, such as extreme coalition actors defecting to prevent the adoption of "balanced" policies (Munro 1993, 126); major internal or external events that switch allegiances, especially elections (Jenkins-Smith, St. Clair, and Woods 1991; Zafonte and Sabatier 2004; Pierce 2011); and strategic decisions by coalition actors to achieve short-term political objectives (Nohrstedt 2005; Larsen, Vrangbaek, and Traulsen 2006). To further develop Coalition Hypothesis 1, the next steps must develop and test a range of theoretical rationales for the stability or instability of coalitions.

The testing of Coalition Hypotheses 2 and 3 has resulted in only a few confirmations (Weyant 1988; Elliot and Schlaepfer 2001; Kim 2003) but many falsifications and, at best, findings of partial support (Barke 1993; Jenkins-Smith and St. Clair 1993; Sabatier and Brasher 1993; Olson, Olson, and Gawronski 1999; Sobeck 2003; Larsen, Vrangbaek, and Traulsen 2006; Ingold 2011; Zafonte and Sabatier 2004). There are at least two interpretations for the mixed support for Coalition Hypotheses 2 and 3. The first interpretation involves variation in conceptualizations and measurement of belief systems in establishing coalitions. If this interpretation is correct, there needs to be a concerted effort to clarify the theoretical distinction between policy core and secondary aspects as well as methodological guidelines for measurement. Olson, Olson, and Gawronski (1999), for example, found it difficult to isolate policy core beliefs from secondary aspects. The second interpretation points to a faulty or imprecise model of the belief system and overall logic of Coalition Hypotheses 2 and 3. To put it simply, even if analysts could adequately measure and distinguish policy core and secondary aspects, perhaps Coalition Hypotheses 2 and 3 are wrong. Although we are not in a position in this chapter to reject both hypotheses, we underscore the mixed support for them and draw attention to a need for better approaches in conceptualizing and measuring belief systems in the ACF.

The fourth and fifth hypotheses are rarely tested in the ACF. Evidence supporting the Coalition Hypothesis 4 remains mixed, with some evidence offering confirmation (Jenkins-Smith, St. Clair, and Woods 1991; Jenkins-Smith and St. Clair 1993) and others providing only partial to no support (Sabatier and Brasher 1993). The most important confirmation for Coalition Hypothesis 5 remains Jenkins-Smith, St. Clair, and Woods (1991) and Jenkins-Smith and St. Clair (1993). The implication from this assessment is clear enough: there is a need for renewed testing and development of Coalition Hypotheses 4 and 5.

Although it is not a traditional hypothesis, a large number of studies have tested the expectation that coalitions form on the basis of shared beliefs, known as the Belief Homophily Hypothesis. Studies confirming this hypothesis can be found in a number of publications, including Weible (2005), Matti and Sandström (2011), Henry (2011), Ingold (2011), and Leifeld (2013). Whereas the results tend to confirm the Belief Homophily Hypothesis, the findings raise two new implications for studying coalitions under the ACF. The first implication is the presence of other factors, outside of beliefs, that affect coalition formation and stability. These other factors include, but are not limited to, perceived influence or resources of others (Weible 2005; Matti and Sandström 2011), interests (Nohrstedt 2010), and trust (Henry, Lubell, and McCoy 2011). The second implication is that coalitions are shaped more by sharing opponents than by sharing beliefs (Henry, Lubell, and McCoy 2011). Research on the Belief Homophily Hypothesis supports the argument that beliefs remain a major factor in forming and maintaining coalitions, but other factors clearly have an effect, and the precise role of beliefs in shaping coalitions needs theoretical refinement.

The traditional hypotheses about coalitions highlight some of the theoretical logic about coalitions and many of the most important concepts. However, the theoretical argument about coalitions is broader than is articulated in the listed hypotheses and sometimes includes additional concepts and their interrelations, some of which are summarized below in four categories.

- *Dominant and minority coalitions.* Although some subsystems exhibit advocacy coalitions steeped in conflict marked by long periods of ongoing one-upmanship, other subsystems exhibit a "dominant" coalition that largely controls (most likely through resource superiority) subsystem politics and policy, and either a "minority" coalition vying for influence or the absence of any coordinated opposition. Even though a number of studies have documented the stability of dominant advocacy coalitions in steering a policy subsystem, the attributes of various coalitions remain underdeveloped, particularly the comparison of beliefs, resources, strategies, and activities.
- *Overcoming threats to collective action.* One of the critical theoretical arguments that has yet to be sufficiently developed involves how coalitions overcome threats to collective action (Schlager 1995). Actors form coalitions and overcome threats to collective action on the basis of three rationales (Zafonte and Sabatier 1998; Sabatier and Weible 2007, 197). First, similar beliefs among allies reduce the transaction costs for coordination. Second, actors are involved in policy subsystems at different levels of intensity and, thus, some engage in weak forms of coordination (sharing information) and others in strong forms of coordination (jointly developing and executing shared plans). Third, actors often experience the devil shift and, therefore, exaggerate the costs of inaction and the need for action (Sabatier, Hunter, and McLaughlin 1987).
- *Principal and auxiliary coalition actors.* Network analysis techniques have shown that some coalition actors are more central to a coalition than others and that sometimes actors rarely interact with their allies. To account for this variation in coalition membership, a distinction is made between actors who are principal and those who are auxiliary to a coalition (Larsen, Vrangbaek, and Traulsen 2006; Silva 2007; Zafonte and Sabatier 2004; Weible 2008). Principal actors are expected to be more central and consistent coalition members, whereas auxiliary actors are expected to be on the periphery, involved intermittently or sometimes only for a short period of time, and therefore not as regularly engaged in coalition-related activities.
- *Resources, strategies, and activities.* Coalitions are marked not only by shared beliefs and coordination patterns but also by their resources. These resources include formal legal authority to make policy decisions,

public opinion, information, mobilizable supporters, financial resources, and skillful leadership (Sabatier and Weible 2007; Weible 2007; Nohrstedt 2011; Ingold 2011; Albright 2011; Elgin and Weible 2013). Resources are an important contribution that provide the theoretical leverage for understanding the capacity of a coalition to make strategic decisions and engage in various activities to influence policy subsystems.

Overall, the support for the study of coalitions is strong for Coalition Hypothesis 1 and for the Belief Homophily Hypothesis, mixed for Coalition Hypotheses 2 and 3 that involve the hierarchical belief systems in the ACF, and mostly untested for Coalition Hypotheses 4 and 5. Several underdeveloped areas within this theoretical emphasis involve the role of coalition resources, strategies, and activities; the role and type of coalition members; the testing of the argument involving the collective action rationale for the formation of coalitions; and the continued development of dominant and minority coalitions.

Policy-Oriented Learning

Policy-oriented learning is one prominent pathway within the ACF for the explanation of policy change and plays a central role in belief change and reinforcement of members of advocacy coalitions. If it has always been of central focus within the ACF, it is possibly still the most intractable concept to study (Bennett and Howlett 1992; Levy 1994). Policy-oriented learning is defined as "enduring alternations of thought or behavioral intentions that result from experience and which are concerned with the attainment or revision of the precepts of the belief system of individuals or of collectives" (Sabatier and Jenkins-Smith 1993, 42). Learning is associated with changes in beliefs systems of coalition members that include not only the understanding of a problem and associated solutions but also the use of political strategies for achieving objectives (see May 1992). Some of the important questions in the study of learning include: What belief system components change or remain the same through learning? What contexts foster learning by coalition members? How does learning diffuse among allies and possibly among opponents? What is the role, if any, of policy brokers in facilitating learning among opponents?

The theory underlying learning in the ACF emphasizes four categories of explanatory factors.

- *Attributes of forums.* Forums are the venues where coalitions interact, debate, and possibly negotiate. Jenkins-Smith (1982, 1990, 99–103) makes the theoretical argument about how the attributes of a forum, essentially the forum's institutional arrangement, affect the extent that learning occurs among allies and opponents. A couple of the most important attributes defining a forum are the degree of openness in participating (open vs. closed forums) and the extent that participating actors share a common analytical training and norms of conduct.

- *Level of conflict between coalitions.* Level of conflict relates to the extent that actors perceive a threat to their policy core beliefs from their opponents' objectives or actions. Jenkins-Smith (1990, 95–97) and Weible (2008) essentially argue for an inverted quadratic relationship between level of conflict and learning between members of opposing coalitions, which has been called "cross-coalition learning." At low levels of conflict, there is little cross-coalition learning because coalition actors attend to other subsystem affairs. At high levels of conflict, there is also little cross-coalition learning because coalition actors defend their positions and reject information that disputes their belief systems. At intermediate levels of conflict, opposing coalitions are threatened just enough to attend to the issue and remain receptive enough to new information to increase the likelihood for cross-coalition learning.
- *Attributes of the stimuli.* Attributes of the stimuli relates to the type of information and experience coalition actors are exposed to. Jenkins-Smith (1990, 97–99) argues that analytically intractable phenomena involve uncertainty, low-quality data, and, hence, variation in interpretation and high levels of disagreement. The more intractable an issue, the lower the level of cross-coalition learning expected.
- *Attributes of actors.* Attributes of the individual actors include their belief system, resources, strategies, and network contacts. Given the importance of belief systems in filtering and interpreting information, for example, the expectation is that coalition actors with extreme beliefs are less likely to learn from opponents than are coalition actors with more moderate beliefs. Additionally, some actors can serve as policy brokers who primarily seek to mitigate the level of conflict and help opponents reach agreements (Sabatier and Jenkins-Smith 1993, 27). There are no predetermined criteria defining who can or cannot be a broker within a subsystem; indeed, a broker could be affiliated with any organization type, from academia to government to the private or nonprofit sector. One important role for brokers is facilitating learning among opponents (Ingold and Varone 2012).

These four attributes can be found in the following five hypotheses on policy-oriented learning within the ACF:

Learning Hypothesis 1. Policy-oriented learning across belief systems is most likely when there is an intermediate level of informed conflict between the two coalitions. This requires that: (1) each has the technical resources to engage in such a debate, and (2) the conflict is between secondary aspects of one belief system and core elements of the other or, alternatively, between important secondary aspects of the two belief systems.

Learning Hypothesis 2. Policy-oriented learning across belief systems is most likely when there exists a forum that is: (1) prestigious enough to force professionals from different coalitions to participate and (2) dominated by professional norms.

Learning Hypothesis 3. Problems for which accepted quantitative data and theory exist are more conducive to policy-oriented learning across belief systems than those in which data and theory are generally qualitative, quite subjective, or altogether lacking.

Learning Hypothesis 4. Problems involving natural systems are more conducive to policy-oriented learning across belief systems than those involving purely social or political systems because in the former many of the critical variables are not themselves active strategists and because controlled experimentation is more feasible.

Learning Hypothesis 5. Even when the accumulation of technical information does not change the views of the opposing coalition, it can have important impacts on policy—at least in the short run—by altering the views of policy brokers.

Studies of policy-oriented learning have not always supported these hypotheses. A good number of studies have documented learning at both secondary (expected) and policy core (not expected) levels of the belief system (Sabatier and Brasher 1993; Eberg 1997; Elliot and Schlaepfer 2001; Larsen, Vrangbaek, and Traulsen 2006). These results echo the mixed support for Coalition Hypotheses 2 and 3. That is, the hierarchical belief system of the ACF—especially the distinction between policy core and secondary aspects—is not finding strong support in many of the hypothesis tests.

In support of Learning Hypothesis 3, Sotirov and Memmler (2012) find in their review of the literature that a handful of studies show that learning was limited when data were lacking or were of qualitative or subjective nature (e.g., Weyant 1988; Elliot and Schlaepfer 2001; Nedergaard 2008), but the findings also show the same for situations for learning using quantitative data (Elliot and Schlaepfer 2001; Kim 2003).

Studies have found that learning is more likely to occur with tractable issues, with intermediate levels of conflict, and with the availability of scientific and technical information (Larsen, Vrangbaek, and Traulsen 2006; Meijerink 2005; Elliott and Schlaepfer 2001). Providing indirect support for learning within the ACF, Leach et al. (2013) find forum structure, attributes of the individual learner, and level of scientific certainty affected belief change and knowledge acquisition. This is an area in need of renewed theoretical and empirical attention.

One promising direction of research involves development of the policy broker concept (Ingold and Varone, 2012). This work finds support for Learning Hypothesis 5 and identifies some systematic evidence that certain actor types are more likely to play the broker role than others. These actors are not acting in an altruistic way: to engage in a brokerage role, they need a certain level of self-interest and an awareness of the potential benefits from policy compromise or the potential losses from the status quo.

Across many of the applications of learning, the most pressing concern is the inconsistency in conceptualization and measurement of the concept. And similarly to the change hypotheses, what also needs to be addressed in this theoretical emphasis is a set of best practices for studying learning within and across advocacy coalitions. There must also be a fresh look at the factors that shape learning, including levels of conflict, attributes of the actor, the role of policy brokers, nature of stimuli, and characteristics of the forum.

A FUTURE RESEARCH AGENDA

The future trajectory of the ACF depends on the innovative and creative efforts of numerous analysts from around the world. Nonetheless, we offer a research agenda for analysts to consider in moving the framework forward.

Reconsider the ACF's belief system. Empirical applications of the ACF suggest that the belief system model needs to be further specified. There are many ways forward, including clarifying the distinction between policy core and secondary beliefs, combining the policy core beliefs and secondary beliefs into a single category under deep core beliefs, and drawing inspiration from other theories, such as the value-belief-norm theory (Stern 2000; Henry and Dietz 2012), cultural theory (Douglas and Wildavsky 1982; Jenkins-Smith et al. 2014), and Narrative Policy Framework (Shanahan, Jones, and McBeth 2011).

Advance the theory and measures of learning. Despite its centrality to the framework, conceptual development of policy-oriented learning—including causes, kinds of learning, and implications—is among the least mature components of the ACF. Analysts are encouraged to undertake reexamination of this concept within the framework as well as the theoretical implications. Research in this domain should emphasize clear conceptualization and measurement of various products of learning and the processes by which it is encouraged and inhibited (Heikkila and Gerlak 2013).

Refine the theory of coalition structures and coordination. The study of coalitions remains a staple of the framework, and significant advances in understanding coalitions have occurred over the past decade, particularly with network analysis techniques (Henry 2011). This effort should continue with special attention to the assumed hierarchy of belief homophily and coordination patterns among coalition members (Calanni et al. 2015; Ingold and Fischer 2014). It also needs to focus on the sources of stability of coalitions, with attention to the likelihood and reasons for defection by coalition members.

Develop a hierarchy for coalition resources. The ACF assumes that access to and exploitation of various political resources are important for advocacy coalitions as they seek to influence public policy. Following Sewell (2005) and Sabatier and Weible (2007, 201–204), we encourage efforts to identify a typology of political resources that includes formal legal authority to make policy decisions, public opinion, information, mobilizable troops, financial resources, and skillful leadership. Although coalition resources were long neglected in empirical research (Sabatier and Weible 2007, 201), recent studies have investigated how coalitions mobilize and exploit resources in the policy process (Albright 2011; Ingold 2011). These studies confirm that redistribution of political resources is an important step in explaining policy change. Meanwhile, as suggested by Nohrstedt (2011, 480), some resources are more important than others for coalitions to achieve influence, which is ultimately given by governing system attributes such as constitutional rules. For example, having coalition actors in positions of legal authority is a major resource because legislators are veto players whose agreement is needed for policy change (Tsebelis 1995; see also Sabatier and Pelkey 1987). Legal authority is also one defining element of a dominant coalition, which has more of its allies in positions of formal authority than do minority coalitions (Sabatier and Weible 2007, 203). Resources could therefore be hierarchically arranged with regard to their perceived usefulness and effectiveness to coalitions, which in turn raises challenges and questions for future research (Weible et al. 2011, 356–357). For example, under what conditions are some resources more important than others for coalitions to gain influence? Which strategies do coalitions utilize to select which resources to exploit? What is the relative importance of specific kinds of resources in different political systems? How does redistribution of resources influence policy change and learning? A related challenge is to advance approaches to operationalize resources by, for example, network analysis (Ingold 2011) and qualitative research (Mintrom and Vergari 1996; Nohrstedt 2011).

Study venues and forums within policy subsystems. The focus of the ACF on policy subsystems has important impacts on conducting research. However, some notable applications of the ACF have focused on organizational-level analysis, especially in the area of collaborative partnerships (Leach and Sabatier 2005; Leach et al. 2013). For example, Leach and Sabatier (2005) applied the ACF in the study of watershed partnerships. These partnerships, however, do not encapsulate the entire policy subsystem but rather involve a single venue within the subsystem. As a result, the study of the partnership represents a selected sample of subsystem actors choosing to participate in the partnership. Such organizational-level applications of the ACF are encouraged because we gain a deeper understanding of how coalition actors learn from each other and negotiate agreements. Additionally, because coalitions seek to affect government decisions through venues, the choice of one venue over another remains an important topic of study.

Use the ACF for comparative public policy research. Most comparative work on the ACF has been based on implicit comparison across political-institutional systems. Few empirical studies based on the ACF systematically compare policy subsystems, coalition behavior, and policy processes across political systems (Gupta 2012). One is an ACF study applied in seven countries (Canada, France, Germany, Sweden, Switzerland, the United Kingdom, and the United States) that compares the policies and regulations related to oil and gas development using hydraulic fracturing (Weible et al. 2016). Using different methods of data collection and analyses, the same research questions about advocacy coalitions and the propensity for policy change were asked and answered. The comparison confirmed the importance of subsystem properties for explaining differences observed across the seven countries (Ingold et al. 2016). Not only do basic institutional and constitutional arrangements of the political system decisively affect coalition formation and the propensity for policy change but also subsystem attributes (such as jurisdictional level, maturity, or autonomy) and issue characteristics (such as salience and potential threat to certain values within the belief system) do as well. We encourage future work in this direction, developing systematic comparisons of policy subsystems across countries to disentangle the factors accounting for advocacy coalitions, policy-oriented learning, and policy change.

The expansion of applications to new countries is a trend that can inspire future comparison across systems. Comparative work obviously brings additional costs in terms of data acquisition and analysis but also important gains in terms of new insights regarding the role of political institutions and cultures in shaping the formation, maintenance, and behavior of advocacy coalitions in the policy process. Here is a gap waiting to be filled. Fruitful avenues for future comparative work involve vicarious policy-oriented learning (how coalitions learn from the experience of others) and policy transfer (how policies diffuse from one political system to another) (Bandura 1962; Dolowitz and Marsh 1996). Following the emphasis on coalition opportunity structures (Kübler 2001; Sabatier 1998; Sabatier and Weible 2007), there is also a need to investigate how specific institutional attributes such as veto players, the required level of consensus, and system openness shape coalition interaction and policy change (Fischer 2015; Gupta 2013). Empirical research in these areas would yield important insights about the policy process and expose questions and areas for future research, including the role and importance of advocacy coalitions as a type of political organization actors exploit to coordinate strategies and gain influence. Although comparative analysis is a long-term challenge and will probably generate limited generalizability in the short term given the complexity of the policy process (Schmitt 2012), the ACF offers concepts and assumptions that should stimulate and facilitate comparative analysis.

Focus on types of actors, including auxiliary and principal coalition actors, policy brokers, and policy entrepreneurs. Exceptional actors often play critical roles in policy subsystems. Some of these actors could be principal coalition actors but possibly auxiliary coalition actors. Other categories are policy brokers (Ingold and Varone 2012) and policy entrepreneurs (Mintrom 2009; Mintrom and Vergari 1996). From its earliest renditions, the ACF has suggested that brokers can play important roles in policy-oriented learning (Sabatier and Jenkins-Smith 1993), and empirical applications have provided some evidence on brokers' impact on policy outputs (Ingold and Varone 2012; Ingold 2011). But further research is needed to theoretically and empirically refine the role of brokers in policy subsystems in general (Christopoulos and Ingold 2015) and in the design of learning mechanisms in particular. Policy entrepreneurs might also be critical players in maintaining coalitions and causal drivers of policy change, but few have analyzed this type of exceptional actor in ACF studies.

Focus on nascent and mature policy subsystems. Most studies of the ACF focus on mature policy subsystems. In mature policy subsystems, policy actors have typically fortified their belief systems about the risks and benefits associated with an issue, they interact in stable advocacy coalitions, and conflicts among opponents have endured over time both within and across decision making venues. Sometimes, mature policy subsystems absorb new issues as they emerge on the political agenda, whereas on other occasions new issues provoke the formation of a new policy subsystem (Nohrstedt and Olofsson 2016a). Unfortunately, few scholars have studied nascent policy subsystems (Ingold, Fischer, and Cairney 2016; Stritch 2015; Beverwijk, Goedegebuure, and Huisman 2008). As a result, theoretical insights about nascent subsystems remain underdeveloped. Speculatively, nascent policy subsystems are likely to feature policy actors with ambiguous perceptions of the risk and benefits of a policy issue, unclear preferences for known policy solutions, and unstable alliances among allies and opponents. Studies on nascent subsystems could yield insights about the initial conditions of policy subsystem characteristics, the process of coalition formation, the establishment of interactions within and across coalitions, and the role of coalitions in agenda setting. A focus on nascent policy subsystems will allow scholars to adopt a prospective approach (e.g., how does the variation in initial conditions in nascent policy subsystems give rise to differences in conditions in mature policy subsystems?), help identify the reasons for nascent subsystem formation (e.g., in response to a crisis, a policy change, or other), and assist in investigating the propensity for future policy change (Weible et al. 2016).

Expand our understanding of science and policy analysis in the policy process. The ACF was originally created to help inform the role of scientists and science in the policy process. Several recent publications address this area. Much of this work began with Jenkins-Smith's (1990) theoretical and empirical efforts in studying the role of policy analysis in the policy process. Since then the effort has shifted mostly to the roles of scientists and technicians and scientific and technical information in the policy process (Jenkins-Smith and Weimer 1985; Weible 2008; Silva and Jenkins-Smith 2007; Silva, Jenkins-Smith, and Barke 2007; Weible, Sabatier, and Pattison 2010; Montpetit 2011; Lundin and Öberg 2014). This research strongly suggests that the use of science and policy analysis is driven by the level of conflict in the policy subsystem (Jenkins-Smith 1990; Weible 2008). The next step is to test these expectations under different conditions and develop a coherent theoretical explanation for the findings.

Establish common methods of data collection and analyses for applying the framework, identify trade-offs in using different methods, and promote contextually based theoretical innovations. The ACF is a tool for comparative analyses of policy processes. To foster comparative work, there is a need to develop common methods of collecting and analyzing data given common research questions. Clearly, some methods of data collection and analysis are more suitable in some contexts than in others (e.g., online surveys vs. interviews). Similarly, other methods of data collection and analysis are feasible when directly comparing policy subsystems over time (e.g., newspaper content analysis). The best strategy is not to promote one method of data collection and analysis over another but rather to utilize the best methods given the research questions, contexts, and resources of the researchers. To support such an effort, researchers must recognize the trade-offs of different approaches and, ideally, combine more than one to capture their respective strengths and compensate for their weaknesses.

Explore the need for theoretical refinement emanating from application in nontraditional settings. Underlying the need for comparative methods is a simultaneous need for contextually based theoretical development. The majority of empirical applications of the ACF involves cases of mature policy subsystems marked by high conflict in heavily democratized political systems (Weible et al. 2016; Pierce et al. 2017). Application of the ACF to nascent subsystems, to policy subsystems marked by low or moderate levels of conflict, or to policy subsystems within different types of political systems is less frequent and might require theoretical innovations and adjustments. Prior comparative work on the ACF outside the United States and Western Europe reports strengths as well as weaknesses; studies confirm the applicability of the ACF's concepts and assumptions, and they identify limitations related to descriptive and explanatory validity (Henry et al. 2014). Although some of these limitations (as discussed above in this chapter) apply more broadly, scholars should also identify limitations that are related to the attributes of policy processes in (for example) hybrid or authoritarian regimes. Ascertaining how the ACF might be adapted to address this expanded array of contexts (without altering the framework's axiomatic propositions) and how the ACF fares compared to alternative frameworks are important questions for the future.[14]

CONCLUSION

Our intent in this chapter is to provide an overview of the ACF research program. The framework has attracted worldwide attention and scholarship over several decades, and we readily acknowledge that in this short chapter we have not been able to adequately incorporate all of the important theoretical and empirical contributions. To supplement this chapter, we highly recommend the excellent theoretical and methodological insights that can be found in Fischer (2015) on the role of institutions on coalition formation, in Sotirov and Memmler (2012) on the ACF in environmental and natural resource contexts, and in Leifeld (2013) on discourse coalitions. In addition, some of the best emerging work can be found in recent PhD dissertations (Gupta 2013; Valman 2014; Donadelli 2016). The continuing growth of ACF scholarship gives us some confidence that—over thirty years after its initial articulation—the framework is still undergoing progressive problem-shift.

We conclude this chapter with a challenge. Although the ACF has spawned a fruitful research program on coalitions, learning, and policy change, we must raise the question: What ends will ACF research serve? Clearly, analysts applying the ACF must continue to use the best science available to improve and develop the framework and to seek answers to some of the most pressing puzzles about policy processes. But some analysts must also work toward developing the framework as a tool for informing and, possibly, improving actual policy processes. To what extent can the framework be used as a policy analysis tool for informing decisions (Nohrstedt 2013; Weible, 2007)? Can the logic of the framework help people strategically influence the policy process (Weible et al. 2012)? And can we eventually draw lessons from the framework to inform what may enhance (or undercut) the capacities of a policy process for the betterment of society? We do not have answers to these questions, but we encourage new and experienced analysts to take them on.

NOTES

1. We must disclose our liability to Paul Sabatier, who permanently influenced how we think as serious social scientists. After years of exposure to Paul, Hank's sense of humor is permanently warped, Daniel remains addicted to clarifying mush, Chris will never overcome his impulsive inclination to code everything (this footnote is already coded), and Karin suffers from chronic periods of transfixion in the absence of theoretical guidance. Given that we cannot escape from the influence of Paul's way of thinking, we have learned to embrace his impact on our lives by drinking a beer or stinger in his name, a habit we trust others will soon adopt. Furthermore, whereas all errors and omissions will forever be wrought by those sinister forces in the world muddying the lucidity of our thoughts and communications, we remain steadfast in achieving greater clarity in our theories and methods and in believing that this effort will eventually beget clarity in our understandings and explanations.

2. Sabatier submitted the initial theoretical manuscript of the ACF, as the lead article in a special issue on the ACF, to *Policy Sciences*. The manuscript was eventually rejected with a scathing blind review in 1984.

This paper has little to recommend it. The conceptual framework is a conceptual mishmash that makes no obvious contributions to our ability to do policy analysis, to design institutions to use policy analysis, or to understand policy processes. The author never explains the potential value of a conceptual framework such as he attempts to develop. The unit of analysis is incoherent. The hypotheses offered are banal and/or nonoperational. There are no data, only allusions, adductions, and sketchy examples. The organization is loose and wandering. There is little to disagree with in this paper; refutation would require more operational concepts, a tighter logic and/or data. . . . The problems with this paper are legion.

Other attempts to publish a theoretical overview of the ACF by Sabatier continued with rejections received from the *Journal of Policy Analysis and Management* (*JPAM*) in 1985 and the *American Journal of Political Science* (*AJPS*) in 1985.

3. The ACF adds a third layer, the policy core, which includes beliefs that are general to, and highly salient for, the concrete policy subsystem.

4. Interested readers will also find one of the first publications of the ACF in Jenkins-Smith's dissertation (1985).

5. A symposium on the ACF was also accepted in *Knowledge: Creation, Diffusion, and Utilization* with a projected publication in 1987 (Sabatier 1987). Early in 1987, however, Sabatier and Jenkins-Smith withdrew the symposium from *Knowledge* and submitted it to *Policy Sciences*, wherein it was published in 1988.

6. Pierce et al. (2016) tabulated the number of applications from 2007 through 2014 by the following topical areas: environmental or energy issues (n = 70), public health (n = 15), education (n = 14), science and technology (n = 12), social welfare (n = 12), foreign and defense (n = 8), economic and finance (n = 7), urban planning and transportation (n = 5), and other (n = 18). Pierce et al. (2016) also found most applications in North America and Western Europe but an increasing number that span the world.

7. In the ACF literature, there have been differences in the interpretation of the terms *framework* and *theory* (see, for example, Sabatier and Jenkins-Smith 1999, 154–155). Despite the different interpretations and uses in the past, we find the clearer and more explicit articulation of the framework-theory distinction is needed because the components of the ACF have become increasingly complex, requiring some attention to the internal organization of the concepts and logic, and because modifications of the ACF over time have clouded the essential and nonessential components of the framework, making it difficult for any reader—and even these authors—to keep track of what has changed and what has remained the same. With the distinction between frameworks and theories, our goal is to convey the more stable components of the ACF at the "framework" level from the theoretical components, which are subject to development through systematic empirical testing and imaginative thinking (Weible and Nohrstedt 2012; Weible et al. 2011).

8. With respect to subsystems being nested and overlapping in the ACF, this property is important to recognize because many theories and perspectives in the field of policy process maintain traditional depictions of policy subsystems as subgovernments with a requirement that a legislative subcommittee dealing primarily with the subsystem topic must be present for a subsystem to exist. This is most evident in the Policy Regime Perspective (May and Jochim 2013) and some applications of Punctuated Equilibrium Theory (Worsham and Stores 2012). The point is not to argue that one definition is better than the other but rather to recognize the subtle differences in the use of the term and to use those subtle differences as leverage in conducting research.

9. A comprehensive listing of the different components of the belief system of the ACF, circa 1999, can be found in Sabatier and Jenkins-Smith (1999, 133).

10. This dilemma in the 1980s was particularly pertinent given that traditional public administration scholarship often focused on a single government agency and the top-down implementation literature focused on a single program. When the unit of analysis was broadened to a policy subsystem characterized by high levels of conflict, the concept of advocacy coalitions emerged as a useful device for simplifying policy actors. In current ACF studies, analysts often focus their attention on organizations rather than on individuals. This is done for a range of reasons, including to maintain confidentiality of the identity of the research subject and because organizations supply the resources and are often the unit that individuals represent in policy subsystem politics (Fischer 2015; Ingold 2011; Knoke et al. 1996).

11. The point of this assumption is not that scientific and technical information is better than other forms of knowledge but rather that scientific and technical information is critically important in understanding policy debates. Indeed, other forms of knowledge can be just as important.

12. Careful observers of the ACF have noted that brokers are no longer listed in the current Figure 4.1, as was also the case in Jenkins-Smith et al. (2014). The reason is not to discount the importance of the concept but to recognize that not all policy subsystems have policy brokers and that other types of exceptional actors might also be present, such as policy entrepreneurs.

13. A public program is the means by which a public service is delivered given a policy directive. In this respect, a public program is concrete in its application, may operate under one or more policies, and may vary across locations.

14. People interested in applying the ACF are welcome to contact the authors for some of the previously used survey, interview, and coding instruments.

REFERENCES

Albright, Elizabeth A. 2011. "Policy Change and Learning in Response to Extreme Flood Events in Hungary: An Advocacy Coalition Approach." *Policy Studies Journal* 39 (3): 484–511.

Ameringer, Carl F. 2002. "Federal Antitrust Policy and Physician Discontent: Defining Moments in the Struggle for Congressional Relief." *Journal of Health Politics, Policy and Law* 27 (4): 543–574.

Andersson, Magnus. 1999. *Change and Continuity in Poland's Environmental Policy.* Dordrecht, the Netherlands: Kluwer Academic.

Bandura, Albert. 1962. "Social Learning through Imitation." In *Nebraska Symposium of Motivation,* edited by M. R. Jones, 211–269. Lincoln: University of Nebraska Press.

Barke, Richard. 1993. "Managing Technological Change in Federal Communications Policy: The Role of Industry Advisory Groups." In *Policy Change and Learning,* edited by Paul Sabatier and Hank Jenkins-Smith, 129–146. Boulder, CO: Westview Press.

Baumgartner, Frank, and Bryan Jones. 1993. *Agendas and Instability in American Politics.* Chicago: Chicago University Press.

Baybrook, David, and Charles E. Lindblom. 1963. *A Strategy of Decision: Policy Evaluation as a Social Process.* New York: Fee Press of Glencoe.

Bennett, Colin, and Michael Howlett. 1992. "The Lessons of Learning: Reconciling Theories of Policy Learning and Policy Change." *Policy Sciences* 25 (3): 275–294.

Beverwijk, Jasmin, Leo Goedegebuure, and Jeroen Huisman. 2008. "Policy Change in Nascent Subsystems: Mozambican Higher Education Policy 1993–2003." *Policy Sciences* 41 (4): 357–377.

Birkland, Thomas A. 2006. *Lessons of Disaster: Policy Change After Catastrophic Events.* Washington, DC: Georgetown University Press.

———. 2010. *An Introduction to the Policy Process.* 3rd ed. Armonk, NY: M. E. Sharpe.

Bischoff, Dale P. 2001. "Extension of Authority to Confer Bachelor of Education Degrees in Alberta." *Alberta Journal of Educational Research* XLVII (i): 40–46.

Boin, Arjen, Paul 't Hart, and Allan McConnell. 2009. "Crisis Exploitation: Political and Policy Impacts of Framing Contests." *Journal of European Public Policy* 16 (1): 81–106.

Bovens, Mark, and Paul 't Hart. 1996. *Understanding Policy Fiascoes.* New Brunswick, NJ: Transaction Publishers.

Burnett, Miles, and Charles Davis. 2002. "Getting Out the Cut: Politics and the National Forest Timber Harvests." *Administration and Society* 34 (2): 202–228.

Burnham, Walter Dean. 1970. *Critical Elections and the Mainsprings of American Politics.* New York: W. W. Norton.

Calanni, John, Saba N. Siddiki, Christopher M. Weible, and William D. Leach. 2015. "Explaining Coordination in Collaborative Partnerships and Clarifying the Scope of the Belief Homophily Hypothesis." *Journal of Public Administration Research and Theory* 25 (3): 901–927.

Capano, Giliberto. 2009. "Understanding Policy Change as an Epistemological and Theoretical Problem." *Journal of Comparative Policy Analysis* 11 (1): 7–31.

———. 2012. "Policy Dynamics and Change: The Never-Ending Puzzle." In *Routledge Handbook of Public Policy*, edited by Eduardo Araral, Scott Fritzen, Michael Howlett, M. Ramesh, and Xun Wu, 451–461. London: Routledge.

Caplan, Nathan, Andrea Morrison, and Russell J. Stanbaugh. 1975. *The Use of Social Knowledge in Public Policy Decisions at the National Level.* Ann Arbor, MI: Institute for Social Research.

Christopoulos, Dimitris, and Karin Ingold. 2015. "Exceptional or Just Well Connected? Political Entrepreneurs and Brokers in Policy Making." *European Political Science Review* 7 (3): 475–498.

Davis, Charles, and Sandra Davis. 1988. "Analyzing Change in Public Lands Policymaking: From Subsystems to Advocacy Coalitions." *Policy Studies Journal* 17 (1): 3–24.

Dolowitz, David, and David Marsh. 1996. "Who Learns What from Whom: A Review of the Policy Transfer Literature." *Political Studies* 44 (2): 343–357.

Donadelli, Flavia M. M. 2016. *Reaping the Seeds of Discord: Advocacy Coalitions and Changes in Brazilian Environmental Regulation.* PhD diss., London School of Economics.

Douglas, Mary, and Aaron Wildavsky. 1982. *Risk and Culture: An Essay on the Selection of Technical and Environmental Dangers.* Berkeley: University of California Press.

Dudley, Geoffrey, and Jeremy Richardson. 1999. "Competing Advocacy Coalitions and the Process of 'Frame Reflection': A Longitudinal Analysis of EU Steel Policy." *Journal of European Public Policy* 6 (2): 225–248.

Easton, David. 1965. *A Framework for Political Analysis.* Chicago: University of Chicago Press.

Eberg, Jan. 1997. *Waste Policy and Learning: Policy Dynamics of Waste Management and Waste Incineration in the Netherlands and Bavaria.* Delft, the Netherlands: Uitgeverij Eburon.

Elgin, Dallas, and Christopher M. Weible. 2013. "Stakeholder Analysis of Colorado Climate and Energy Issues Using Policy Analytical Capacity and the Advocacy Coalition Framework." *Review of Policy Research* 30 (1): 116–134.

Elliot, Chris, and Rudolphe Schlaepfer. 2001. "The Advocacy Coalition Framework: Application to the Policy Process for the Development of Forest Certification in Sweden." *Journal of European Public Policy* 8 (4): 642–661.

Ellison, Brian A. 1998. "The ACF and Implementation of the Endangered Species Act: A Case Study in Western Water Politics." *Policy Studies Journal* 26 (1): 11–29.

Fischer, Manuel. 2015. "Institutions and Power Distribution among Coalitions in Decision-Making Processes." *Journal of Public Policy* 35 (2): 245–268.

Fischer, Manuel, Karin Ingold, Pascal Sciarini, and Frédéric Varone. 2016. "Dealing with Bad Guys: Actor- and Process-Level Determinants of the 'Devil Shift' in Policy Making." *Journal of Public Policy* 36:309–334.

Green, Mick, and Barrie Houlihan. 2004. "Advocacy Coalitions and Elite Sport Policy Change in Canada and the United Kingdom." *International Review for the Sociology of Sport* 39 (4): 387–403.

Gupta, Kuhika. 2012. "Comparative Public Policy: Using the Comparative Method to Advance Our Understanding of the Policy Process." *Policy Studies Journal* 40 (1): 11–26.

———. 2013. *Order in a Chaotic Subsystem: A Comparative Analysis of Nuclear Facility Siting Using Coalition Opportunity Structures and the Advocacy Coalition Framework.* PhD diss., Department of Political Science, University of Oklahoma, Norman.

Hall, Peter. 1993. "Policy Paradigms, Social Learning and the State: The Case of Economic Policy Making in Britain." *Comparative Politics* 35 (3): 275–296.

Heclo, Hugh. 1974. *Social Policy in Britain and Sweden.* New Haven, CT: Yale University Press.

———. 1978. "Issue Networks and the Executive Establishment." In *The New American Political System,* edited by A. King, 87–124. Washington, DC: American Enterprise Institute.

Heikkila, Tanya, and Andrea K. Gerlak. 2013. "Building a Conceptual Approach to Collective Learning: Lessons for Public Policy Scholars." *Policy Studies Journal* 41 (3): 484–512.

Henry, Adam. 2011. "Power, Ideology, and Policy Network Cohesion in Regional Planning." *Policy Studies Journal* 39 (3): 361–383.

Henry, Adam, and Thomas Dietz. 2012. "Understanding Environmental Cognition." *Organization & Environment* 25 (3): 238–258.

Henry, Adam Douglas, Karin Ingold, Daniel Nohrstedt, and Chris Weible. 2014. "Policy Change in Comparative Contexts: Applying the Advocacy Coalition Framework Outside the United States and Western Europe." *Journal of Comparative Policy Analysis* 16 (4): 299–312.

Henry, Adam Douglas, Mark Lubell, and Michael McCoy. 2011. "Belief Systems and Social Capital as Drivers of Policy Network Structure: The Case of California Regional Planning." *Journal of Public Administration Research and Theory* 21 (3): 419–444.

Hjern, Benny, and David Porter. 1981. "Implementation Structures: A New Unit of Administrative Analysis." *Organization Studies* 2:211–227.

Hofferbert, Richard I. 1974. *The Study of Public Policy.* Indianapolis, IN: Bobbs-Merrill.

Howlett, Michael, and Benjamin Cashore. 2009. "The Dependent Variable Problem in the Study of Policy Change: Understanding Policy Change as a Methodological Problem." *Journal of Comparative Policy Analysis* 11 (1): 33–46.

Ingold, Karin. 2011. "Network Structures within Policy Processes: Coalitions, Power, and Brokerage in Swiss Climate Policy." *Policy Studies Journal* 39 (3): 435–459.

Ingold, Karin, and Manuel Fischer. 2014. "Drivers of Collaboration: What Impact Do Joint Preferences and Actors' Power Have? An Illustration of Swiss Climate Policy over 15 Years." *Global Environmental Change* 24:88–98.

Ingold, Karin, Manuel Fischer, and Paul Cairney. 2016. "Drivers for Policy Agreement in Nascent Subsystems: An Application of the Advocacy Coalition Framework to Fracking Policy in Switzerland and the UK." *Policy Studies Journal.* Published electronically August 18, 2016. doi:10.1111/psj.12173.

Ingold, Karin, Manuel Fischer, Tanya Heikkila, and Christopher M. Weible. 2016. "Assessments and Aspirations." In *Comparing Coalition Politics: Policy Debates on Hydraulic Fracturing in North America and Western Europe,* edited by Christopher M. Weible, Tanya Heikkila, Karin Ingold, and Manuel Fischer. Basingstoke, UK: Palgrave Macmillan.

Ingold, Karin, and Frédéric Varone. 2012. "Treating Policy Brokers Seriously: Evidence from the Climate Policy." *Journal of Public Administration Research and Theory* 22 (2): 319–346.

Jang, Sojin, Christopher M. Weible, and Kyudong Park. 2016. "Policy Processes in South Korea through the Lens of the Advocacy Coalition Framework." *Journal of Asian Public Policy,* 1-17. doi:10.1080/17516234.2016.1201877.

Jenkins-Smith, Hank. 1982. "Professional Roles for Policy Analysts: A Critical Assessment." *Journal of Policy Analysis and Management* 2 (1): 88–100.

———. 1985. *The Politics of Policy Analysis.* PhD diss., Department of Political Science, University of Rochester. Rochester, NY.

———. 1990. *Democratic Politics and Policy Analysis.* Pacific Grove, CA: Brooks/Cole.

Jenkins-Smith, Hank, Carol L. Silva, Kuhika Gupta, and Joseph T. Ripberger. 2014. "Belief System Continuity and Change in Policy Advocacy Coalitions: Using Cultural Theory to Specify Belief Systems, Coalitions, and Sources of Change." *Policy Studies Journal* 42 (4): 484–508.

Jenkins-Smith, Hank, and Gilbert St. Clair. 1993. "The Politics of Offshore Energy: Empirically Testing the Advocacy Coalition Framework." In *Policy Change and Learning,* edited by Paul Sabatier and Hank Jenkins-Smith, 149–175. Boulder, CO: Westview Press.

Jenkins-Smith, Hank, Gilbert St. Clair, and Brian Woods. 1991. "Explaining Change in Policy Subsystems: Analysis of Coalition Stability and Defection over Time." *American Journal of Political Science* 35 (November): 851–872.

Jenkins-Smith, Hank, and David Weimer. 1985. "Analysis as Retrograde Action: The Case of Strategic Petroleum Reserves." *Public Administration Review* 45 (4): 485–494.

Kim, Seoyong. 2003. "Irresolvable Cultural Conflicts and Conservation/Development Arguments: Analysis of Korea's Saemangeum Project." *Policy Sciences* 36 (2): 125–149.

Knoke, David, Franz Urban Pappi, Jeffery Broadbent, and Y. Tsujinaka. 1996. *Comparing Policy Networks: Labor Politics in the US, Germany, and Japan.* Cambridge: Cambridge University Press.

Kübler, Daniel. 2001. "Understanding Policy Change with the Advocacy Coalition Framework: An Application to Swiss Drug Policy." *Journal of European Public Policy* 8 (4): 623–641.

Kuhn, Thomas. 1962. *The Structure of Scientific Revolutions.* Chicago: University of Chicago Press.

Lakatos, Imré. 1970. "Falsification and the Methodology of Scientific Research Programmes." In *Criticism and the Growth of Knowledge,* edited by Imré Lakatos and
Alan Musgrave, 170–196. Cambridge: Cambridge University Press.

Larsen, Jakob Bjerg, Karsten Vrangbaek, and Janine M. Traulsen. 2006. "Advocacy
Coalitions and Pharmacy Policy in Denmark." *Social Science and Medicine* 63 (1):
212–224.

Lasswell, Harold, and Abraham Kaplan. 1950. *Power and Society.* New Haven, CT: Yale
University Press.

Laudan, Larry. 1977. *Progress and Its Problems: Towards a Theory of Scientific Growth.*
Berkeley: University of California Press.

Leach, William D., and Paul A. Sabatier. 2005. "To Trust an Adversary: Integrating Rational and Psychological Models of Collaborative Policymaking." *American Political
Science Review* 99 (4): 491–503.

Leach, William D., Christopher M. Weible, Scott R. Vince, Saba N. Siddiki, and John
Calanni. 2013. "Fostering Learning through Collaboration: Knowledge Acquisition
and Belief Change in Marine Aquaculture Partnerships." *Journal of Public Administration Research and Theory.* Advanced online publication. http://www.ucdenver.edu
/academics/colleges/SPA/researchandoutreach/Buechner%20Institute%20for%20
Governance/Centers/WOPPR/Documents/Leach,%20Weible,%20Vince,%20Siddiki
%20and%20Calanni_Fostering%20Learning%20through%20Collaberation.pdf.

Leifeld, Philip. 2013. "Reconceptualizing Major Policy Change in the Advocacy Coalition Framework: A Discourse Network Analysis of German Pension Politics." *Policy
Studies Journal* 41 (1): 169–198.

Levy, Jack. 1994. "Learning and Foreign Policy: Sweeping a Conceptual Minefield." *International Organization* 48 (2): 279–312.

Lindblom, Charles E. 1968. *The Policy-Making Process.* Englewood Cliffs, NJ: Prentice
Hall.

Lundin, Martin, and Perola Öberg. 2014. "Expert Knowledge Use and Deliberation in
Local Policy Making." *Policy Sciences* 47 (1): 25–49.

Matti, Simon, and Annica Sandström. 2011. "The Rationale Determining Advocacy
Coalitions: Examining Coordination Networks and Corresponding Beliefs." *Policy
Studies Journal* 39 (3): 385–410.

May, Peter J. 1992. "Policy Learning and Failure." *Journal of Public Policy* 12 (4):
331–354.

May, Peter J., and Ashley E. Jochim. 2013. "Policy Regime Perspectives: Policies, Politics, and Governing." *Policy Studies Journal* 41 (3): 426–452.

Mazmanian, Daniel, and Paul Sabatier. 1983. *Implementation and Public Policy.* Lanham, MD: University Press of America.

McBeth, Mark, Elizabeth Shanahan, Ruth Arnell, and Paul Hathaway. 2007 "The Intersection of Narrative Policy Analysis and Policy Change Theory." *Policy Studies
Journal* 35 (1): 87–108.

Meijerink, Sander. 2005. "Understanding Policy Stability and Change: The Interplay of
Advocacy Coalitions and Epistemic Communities, Windows of Opportunity, and

Dutch Coastal Flooding Policy 1945–2003." *Journal of European Public Policy* 12 (6): 1060–1077.

Mintrom, Michael. 2009. "Policy Entrepreneurship and Policy Change." *Policy Studies Journal* 37 (4): 649–667.

Mintrom, Michael, and Sandra Vergari. 1996. "Advocacy Coalitions, Policy Entrepreneurs, and Policy Change." *Policy Studies Journal* 24 (Fall): 420–434.

Montpetit, Eric. 2011. "Scientific Credibility, Disagreement, and Error Costs in 17 Biotechnology Policy Subsystems." *Policy Studies Journal* 39 (3): 513–533.

Munro, John. 1993. "California Water Politics: Explaining Change in a Cognitively Polarized Subsystem." In *Policy Change and Learning*, edited by Paul Sabatier and Hank Jenkins-Smith, 105–128. Boulder, CO: Westview Press.

Munro, Geoffrey D., and Peter H. Ditto. 1997. "Biased Assimilation, Attitude Polarization, and Affect in Reactions to Stereotype-Relevant Scientific Information." *Personality and Social Psychology Bulletin* 23 (6): 636–653.

Munro, Geoffrey D., Peter H. Ditto, Lisa K. Lockhart, Angela Fagerlin, Mitchell Gready, and Elizabeth Peterson. 2002. "Biased Assimilation of Sociopolitical Arguments: Evaluating the 1996 U.S. Presidential Debate." *Basic and Applied Social Psychology* 24 (1): 15–26.

Nedergaard, Peter. 2008. "The Reform of the 2004 Common Agricultural Policy: An Advocacy Coalition Explanation." *Policy Studies* 29 (2): 179–195.

Nisbet, Robert. 1972. "Introduction: The Problem of Social Change." In *Social Change*, edited by Robert Nisbet, 1–45. New York: Harper and Row.

Nohrstedt, Daniel. 2005. "External Shocks and Policy Change: Three Mile Island and Swedish Nuclear Energy Policy." *Journal of European Public Policy* 12 (6): 1041–1059.

———. 2008. "The Politics of Crisis Policymaking: Chernobyl and Swedish Nuclear Energy Policy." *Policy Studies Journal* 36 (2): 257–278.

———. 2010. "Do Advocacy Coalitions Matter? Crisis and Change in Swedish Nuclear Energy Policy." *Journal of Public Administration Research and Theory* 20 (2): 309–333.

———. 2011. "Shifting Resources and Venues Producing Policy Change in Contested Subsystems: A Case Study of Swedish Signals Intelligence Policy." *Policy Studies Journal* 39 (3): 461–484.

———. 2013. "Advocacy Coalitions in Crisis Resolution: Understanding Policy Dispute in the European Volcanic Ash Cloud Crisis." *Public Administration* 91 (4): 964–979.

Nohrstedt, Daniel, and Kristin Olofsson. 2016a. "The Politics of Hydraulic Fracturing in Sweden." In *Comparing Coalition Politics: Policy Debates on Hydraulic Fracturing in North America and Western Europe*, edited by Christopher M. Weible, Tanya Heikkila, Karin Ingold, and Manuel Fischer. Basingstoke, UK: Palgrave Macmillan.

———. 2016b. "A Review of Applications of the Advocacy Coalition Framework in Swedish Policy Processes." *European Policy Analysis* 2 (2): 18–42.

Nohrstedt, Daniel, and Christopher M. Weible. 2010. "The Logic of Policy Change After Crisis: Proximity and Subsystem Interaction." *Risks, Hazards, and Crisis in Public Policy* 1 (2): 1–32.

Olson, Richard Stuart, Robert A. Olson, and Vincent T. Gawronski. 1999. *Some Buildings Just Can't Dance: Politics, Life Safety, and Disasters*. Stanford, CT: Jai Press.

Ostrom, Elinor. 2005. *Understanding Institutional Diversity*. Princeton, NJ: Princeton University Press.

Pierce, Jonathan J. 2011. "Coalition Stability and Belief Change: Advocacy Coalitions in U.S. Foreign Policy and the Creation of Israel, 1922–44." *Policy Studies Journal* 39 (3): 411–434.

Pierce, Jonathan, J., Holly L. Peterson, Michael D. Jones, Samantha Garrard, and Theresa Vu. 2017. "There and Back Again: A Tale of the Advocacy Coalition Framework." *Policy Studies Journal*. Published electronically February 15, 2017. doi:10.1111/psj.12197.

Popper, Karl. 2002. *The Logic of Scientific Discovery*. New York: Routledge. First published 1935 by Verlag von Julius Springer.

Pressman, Jeffrey L., and Aaron B. Wildavsky. 1973. *Implementation*. Berkeley: University of California Press.

Quattrone, George A., and Amos Tversky. 1988. "Contrasting Rational and Psychological Analysis of Political Choice." *American Political Science Review* 82:719–736.

Ripberger, Joseph T., Kuhika Gupta, Carol L. Silva, and Hank C. Jenkins-Smith. 2014. "Cultural Theory and the Measurement of Deep Core Beliefs within the Advocacy Coalition Framework." *Policy Studies Journal* 42 (4): 509–527.

Rose, Richard. 1993. *Lesson-Drawing in Public Policy: A Guide to Learning across Time and Space*. Chatham, UK: Chatham House.

Sabatier, Paul A. 1986. "Top-Down and Bottom-Up Models of Policy Implementation: A Critical Analysis and Suggested Synthesis." *Journal of Public Policy* 6 (January): 21–48.

———. 1987. "Knowledge, Policy-Oriented Learning, and Policy Change: An Advocacy Coalition Framework." *Knowledge: Creation, Diffusion, Utilization* 8 (4): 649–692.

———. 1988. "An Advocacy Coalition Model of Policy Change and the Role of Policy-Oriented Learning Therein." *Policy Sciences* 21 (Fall): 129–168.

———. 1991. "Toward Better Theories of the Policy Process." *PS: Political Science & Politics* 24 (2): 147–156.

———. 1998. "The Advocacy Coalition Framework: Revisions and Relevance for Europe." *Journal of European Public Policy* 5 (March): 98–130.

Sabatier, Paul A., and Anne M. Brasher. 1993. "From Vague Consensus to Clearly Differentiated Coalitions: Environmental Policy at Lake Tahoe, 1964–1985." In *Policy Change and Learning*, edited by Paul Sabatier and Hank Jenkins-Smith, 177–208. Boulder, CO: Westview Press.

Sabatier, Paul A., Susan Hunter, and Susan McLaughlin. 1987. "The Devil Shift: Perceptions and Misperceptions of Opponents." *Western Political Quarterly* 40:51–73.

Sabatier, Paul A., and Hank C. Jenkins-Smith. 1993. *Policy Change and Learning: An Advocacy Coalition Approach*. Boulder, CO: Westview Press.

———. 1999. "The Advocacy Coalition Framework: An Assessment." In *Theories of the Policy Process*, edited by Paul Sabatier and Hank Jenkins-Smith, 117–168. Boulder, CO: Westview Press.

Sabatier, Paul A., and Neil Pelkey. 1987. "Incorporating Multiple Actors and Guidance Instruments into Models of Regulatory Policymaking: An Advocacy Coalition Framework." *Administration and Society* 19 (2): 236–263.

Sabatier, Paul A., and Christopher M. Weible. 2007. "The Advocacy Coalition Framework: Innovations and Clarifications." In *Theories of the Policy Process*, 2nd ed., edited by Paul Sabatier, 189–222. Boulder, CO: Westview Press.

Schlager, Edella. 1995. "Policy Making and Collective Action: Defining Coalitions within the Advocacy Coalition Framework." *Policy Sciences* 28:242–270.

Schmitt, Sophie. 2012. "Comparative Approaches to the Study of Public Policy-Making." In *Routledge Handbook of Public Policy*, edited by E. Araral, S. Fritzen, M. Howlett, M. Ramesh, and X. Wu, 29–43. New York: Routledge.

Scott, Ian. 2012. "Analyzing Advocacy Issues in Asia." *Administration & Society* 44 (6): 4–12.

Sewell, Granville C. 2005. "Actors, Coalitions, and the Framework Convention on Climate Change." PhD diss., Department of Urban Studies and Planning, Massachusetts Institute of Technology, Cambridge, MA.

Shanahan, Elizabeth, Michael Jones, and M. K. McBeth. 2011. "Policy Narratives and Policy Processes." *Policy Studies Journal* 39:535–561.

Silva, Carol. 2007. "Scientists and the Policy Process: Research Substance, and Policy Participation." Paper presented at the Midwest Political Science Association Meeting, April 12–14, 2007, Chicago.

Silva, Carol, and Hank Jenkins-Smith. 2007. "Precaution in Context: US and EU Scientists' Prescriptions for Policy in the Face of Uncertainty." *Social Science Quarterly* 88 (3): 640–664.

Silva, Carol, Hank Jenkins-Smith, and Richard Barke. 2007. "From Experts' Beliefs to Safety Standards: Explaining Preferred Radiation Protection Standards in Polarized Technical Communities." *Risk Analysis* 27 (3): 755–773.

Simon, Herbert A. 1957. *Models of Man: Social and Rational.* New York: Wiley.

———. 1985. "Human Nature in Politics: The Dialogue of Psychology with Political Science." *American Political Science Review* 79 (June): 293–304.

Smith, Adrian. 2000. "Policy Networks and Advocacy Coalitions: Explaining Policy Change and Stability in UK Industrial Pollution Policy?" *Environmental Planning C: Government and Policy* 18:95–114.

Sobeck, Joanne. 2003. "Comparing Policy Process Frameworks: What They Tell Us about Group Membership and Participation for Policy Development." *Administration & Society* 35 (3): 350–374.

Sotirov, Metodi, and Michael Memmler. 2012. "The Advocacy Coalition Framework in Natural Resource Policy Studies—Recent Experiences and Further Prospects." *Forest Policy and Economics* 16 (March): 51–64.

Stern, Paul C. 2000. "Towards a Coherent Theory of Environmentally Significant Behavior." *Journal of Social Issues* 56 (3): 407–424.

Stritch, Andrew. 2015. "The Advocacy Coalition Framework and Nascent Subsystems: Trade Union Disclosure Policy in Canada." *Policy Studies Journal* 43 (4): 437–455.

Tewari, Devi Datt. 2001. "Is Commercial Forestry Sustainable in South Africa? The Changing Institutional and Policy Needs." *Forest Policy and Economics* 2:333–353.

Thompson, Michael, Richard J. Ellis, and Aaron Wildavsky. 1990. *Cultural Theory.* Boulder, CO: Westview Press.

Trousset, Sarah, Kuhika Gupta, Hank C. Jenkins-Smith, Carol L. Silva, and Kerry Herron. 2015. "Degrees of Engagement: Using Cultural Worldviews to Explain Variations in Public Preferences for Engagement in the Policy Process." *Policy Studies Journal* 43 (1): 44–69.

Tsebelis, George. 1995. "Decision Making in Political Systems: Veto Players in Presidentialism, Parliamentarism, Multicameralism and Multipartyism." *British Journal of Political Science* 25 (3): 289–325.

Valman, Matilda. 2014. *Three Faces of HELCOM: Institution, Organization, Policy Producer.* PhD diss., Stockholm University, Stockholm.

Weible, Christopher M. 2005. "Beliefs and Policy Influence: An Advocacy Coalition Approach to Policy Networks." *Political Research Quarterly* 58 (3): 461–477.

———. 2007. "An Advocacy Coalition Framework Approach to Stakeholder Analysis: Understanding the Political Context of California Marine Protected Area Policy." *Journal of Public Administration Research and Theory* 17:95–117.

———. 2008. "Expert-Based Information and Policy Subsystems: A Review and Synthesis." *Policy Studies Journal* 36 (4): 615–635.

Weible, Christopher M., Tanya Heikkila, Peter deLeon, and Paul A. Sabatier. 2012. "Understanding and Influencing the Policy Process." *Policy Sciences.* 45:1–21.

Weible, Christopher, Tanya Heikkila, Karin Ingold, and Manuel Fischer. 2016. *Comparing Coalition Politics: Policy Debates on Hydraulic Fracturing in North America and Western Europe.* Basingstoke, UK: Palgrave Macmillan.

Weible, Christopher M., and Daniel Nohrstedt. 2012. "The Advocacy Coalition Framework: Coalitions, Learning, and Policy Change." In *Handbook of Public Policy,* edited by E. Araral, S. Fritzen, M. Howlett, M. Ramesh, and X. Wu, 125–137. New York: Routledge.

Weible, Christopher M., Paul A. Sabatier, Hank C. Jenkins-Smith, Daniel Nohrstedt, and Adam Douglas Henry. 2011. "A Quarter Century of the Advocacy Coalition Framework: An Introduction to the Special Issue." *Policy Studies Journal* 39 (3): 349–360.

Weible, Christopher M., Paul A. Sabatier, and Kelly McQueen. 2009. "Themes and Variations: Taking Stock of the Advocacy Coalition Framework." *Policy Studies Journal* 37 (1): 121–140.

Weible, Christopher M., Paul A. Sabatier, and Andrew Pattison. 2010. "Harnessing Expert-Based Information for Learning and the Sustainable Management of Complex Socio-Ecological Systems." *Environmental Science & Policy* 13:522–534.

Weiss, Carol. 1977. "Research for Policy's Sake: The Enlightenment Function of Social Research." *Policy Analysis* 3 (Fall): 531–545.

Weyant, John P. 1988. "Is There Policy-Oriented Learning in the Analysis of Natural Gas Issues?" *Policy Sciences* 21:239–261.

Whetten, David A. 1987. "What Constitutes a Theoretical Contribution?" *Academy of Management Review* 14 (4): 490–495.

Worsham, Jeff, and Chan Stores. 2012. "Pet Sounds: Subsystems, Regimes, Policy Punctuations, and the Neglect of African American Farmers, 1935–2006." *Policy Studies Journal* 40 (1): 169–190.

Zafonte, Matthew, and Paul A. Sabatier. 1998. "Shared Beliefs and Imposed Interdependencies as Determinants of Ally Networks in Overlapping Subsystems." *Journal of Theoretical Politics* 10 (4): 473–505.

———. 2004. "Short-Term versus Long-Term Coalitions in the Policy Process: Automotive Pollution Control, 1963–1989." *Policy Studies Journal* 32 (1): 75–107.

5

The Narrative Policy Framework

ELIZABETH A. SHANAHAN, MICHAEL D. JONES, MARK K. MCBETH, AND CLAUDIO M. RADAELLI[1]

"Narratives are the lifeblood of politics"—this appears to be our refrain. Politicians, political strategists, and media reporters understand intuitively that how a story is rendered is as important to policy success and political longevity as are which actions are undertaken. For example, the former Italian prime minister Matteo Renzi, in his interview with the *Washington Post,* argued that the European Union should change the narrative from austerity to hope: "The problem is not the immigrants. The problem is the lack of reaction of Europe. The [European Union] is without vision. We need a strategy for the next year and the next decade. I think we have to change the narrative" (Weymouth 2016).[2] Renzi positions narrative construction as a powerful tool that can shape people's realities and emotions. The Narrative Policy Framework (NPF) is a theory of the policy process[3] whose central question turns an empirical eye on the truth claim of the power of narrative: Do narratives play an important role in the policy process?

The NPF starts with the assertion that the power of policy narratives is something worth understanding. The basic reasons for doing so are twofold. First, policy debates are *necessarily* fought on the terrain of narratives, constituted by both formal institutional venues (e.g., floor debates and testimonies in the House or lower chambers) and informal venues (e.g., media, interest group websites, Twitter, YouTube, blogs). Both serve to reflect and shape the contours, elevations, and chasms of the narrative terrain. Second, narratives are often asserted to affect the policy process at different points—policy decisions, implementation, regulation, evaluation, and so forth. Thus, the NPF contends that understanding the role of narratives is critical to understanding the policy process, on various terrains and at multiple junctures within said process.

The NPF is hardly the first to conceptualize the import of narrative. As a close cousin of narrative, rhetoric has long been studied with famous orators like Franklin Roosevelt or Winston Churchill or more infamous ones like Adolf Hitler. In addition, the study of narrative is found in many disciplines, including psychology (e.g., Green and Brock 2005; Brock, Strange, and Green 2002), marketing (e.g., van den Hende et al. 2012; Escalas 2004; Mattila 2000), and health care (e.g., Hinyard and Kreuter 2007). Within public policy, postpositivist scholars (e.g., Fischer 2003; Roe 1994) have also provided important insights into policy narratives. To date, however, systematic approaches to the understanding of the role of policy narratives in the public policy process are limited but emergent. The goal of this chapter is to detail the NPF in an effort to provide a means by which policy researchers in a variety of contexts can advance scientific discoveries surrounding our central research question.

Although the NPF was not named until 2010 (i.e., Jones and McBeth 2010), the work that led to the framework began in the years following the publication of the first edition of this volume in 1999. This collection of policy theories was criticized for its exclusion of postpositivism (see the March 2000 symposium issue in *Journal of European Public Policy*) in favor of more positivist-oriented policy theories such as Advocacy Coalition Framework (Sabatier and Jenkins-Smith 1999, 117–166) and Institutional Analysis and Development (Ostrom 1999, 35–71). By 2000, two camps emerged over what constitutes legitimate public policy theory: postpositivists, who understand policy as contextualized through narratives and social constructions and more positivist-oriented theorists (Sabatier 2000, 137),[4] whose approach is based on clear concepts and propositions, causal drivers, prediction, and falsification. The NPF was developed in response to these debates, ultimately conceiving of the framework as a "bridge" (Shanahan et al. 2013, 455) between divergent policy process approaches by holding that narratives *both* socially construct reality and can be measured empirically.[5] In 2013, Smith and Larimer questioned whether the NPF would be successful with "essentially post-positivist theory and rational methods" (Smith and Larimer 2013, 234). By 2015, they answer their own question with a resounding yes—"This array of estimation techniques and methodologies used by NPF scholars should be commended, not scorned" (Smith and Larimer 2015, 87).

Now the NPF is a framework being widely tested, continually improved, and applied in a growing variety of policy contexts to advance knowledge of the policy process. For example, NPF concepts are becoming more precisely specified (e.g., Merry 2016 on expanding character types; Schlaufer 2016 and Smith-Walter et al. 2016 on use of evidence). Additionally, the validation and use of digital media have revealed massive repositories of narrative data (e.g., Merry 2015 on Twitter; Gupta, Ripberger, and Wehde 2016 on Twitter). Innovative methodologies (e.g., Weible et al. 2016 on the use of social network analysis; O'Bryan, Dunlop, and Radaelli 2014 on the use of comparative methods;

Gray and Jones 2016 on the use of interpretive methods) have also expanded the ways in which the NPF contributes to understanding the policy process.

Application of the NPF outside the United States (e.g., Gupta, Ripberger, and Collins 2014; Jones, Fløttum, and Gjerstad 2017; Lawton and Rudd 2014) reveals the transportability of the NPF to diverse political systems and contextually nuanced policy domains. The NPF is also being applied to understand a greater array of public policies within US and international contexts (e.g., Ertas 2015 on US education policy; Leong 2015 on water policy in Jakarta; Radaelli, Dunlop, and Fritsch 2013 on the European Union; Merry 2015 on US gun policy; Gupta et al. 2016 on US nuclear energy policy; Crow et al. 2016 on US environmental policy). In sum, the latest pulse of NPF scholarship has improved NPF concepts, expanded data sources, employed new methodologies, transported the NPF to non-US contexts, and widened policy issues of interest—all with an eye toward enhancing how the NPF contributes to building knowledge of the role of narratives in the policy process.

In this chapter, we begin by detailing the NPF through a discussion of form and content of policy narratives. The core NPF assumptions are then described. The bulk of the rest of the chapter is devoted to describing NPF concepts, hypotheses, and extant research, demarcated by level of analysis (micro-, meso-, and, to some extent, macro-), with further discussion on the linkages of levels of analysis. We address four new directions in NPF research, which includes comparative public policy approaches, use of evidence, validation of digital media as a source of narrative data, and a new proposition regarding policy narrative learning in the context of policy change.

THE NPF: FORM AND CONTENT OF POLICY NARRATIVES

Narrative scholars frequently describe narratives in terms of their content and form. *Form* refers to the structure of narratives, and *content* refers to the policy context and subject matter. Contrary to postpositivism, where most of narrative public policy scholarship has held that both form and content are unique, the NPF embraces a structuralist[6] interpretation of narrative, asserting that policy narratives have precise narrative elements (form) that can be generalized across space and time to different policy contexts (see Jones and McBeth 2010; Jones, McBeth, and Shanahan 2014). Furthermore, whereas postpositivists assert that all narrative content is unique (e.g., Fischer 2003), the NPF addresses this problem of narrative relativity by empirically studying content in terms of strategy and belief systems. We detail these arguments below.

Form: Defining a Policy Narrative

Narrative elements constitute the structure of a narrative. Informed by narratology, the NPF focuses on four policy narrative core elements:

1. *Setting:* Policy narratives always have something to do with policy problems and are situated in specific policy contexts. As such, the setting of a policy narrative consists of policy phenomena such as legal and constitutional parameters, geography, evidence, economic conditions, norms, or other features that some nontrivial amount of policy actors agree or assert are consequential within a particular policy area. Like a stage setting for a theatrical play, the props (e.g., laws, evidence, geography) are often taken for granted, but—at times—also may become contested or the focal point of the policy narrative.

2. *Characters:* Policy narratives must have at least one character. As with any good story, there may be victims who are harmed, villains who do the harm, and heroes who provide or promise to provide relief from the harm and presume to solve the problem (Ney 2006; Stone 2012; Verweij et al. 2006). Recent NPF studies have explored different and more nuanced character types, such as "beneficiaries" of a policy outcome (Weible et al. 2016), "allies" and "opponents" (Merry 2016), and "entrepreneurs" and "charismatic experts" (Lawton and Rudd 2014).

3. *Plot:* The plot situates the characters and their relationship in time and space. The plot provides the arc of action where events interact with actions of the characters and the setting, sometimes arranged in a beginning, middle, and end sequence (Abell 2004; Roe 1994; Somers 1992). Although the NPF has leaned on operationalizing Stone's (2012) narrative plot lines, we recognize that there are likely other theoretically grounded ways to define plots.

4. *Moral of the story:* In a policy narrative, policy solutions are the moral or normative actions incarnate. The moral of the story gives purpose to the characters' actions and motives. As such, in the NPF, the moral of the story is often equivalent to the policy solution (Stone 2012; Ney and Thompson 2000; Verweij et al. 2006).

To date, NPF scholarship has maintained a definition of a policy narrative as featuring at least one character and containing some public policy referent (Shanahan et al. 2013, 457). We acknowledge that other policy scholars (e.g., Shenhav 2015) define narrative with different parameters. Although we do not prima facie reject alternative definitions, should an alternative definition be invoked, scholars must be clear about which definition they adhere to and why. Additionally, if the definition were to fall under the umbrella of the NPF, it must also provide additional theoretical *and* empirical traction (within the parameters of the NPF assumptions, of course).

Content: Policy Beliefs and Strategies

Policy debates exist in rich and unique policy contexts. For example, the debate over the installation of windmills off the coast of Nantucket is contextually different from the debate over the installation of windmills in Judith Gap, Montana. The stakeholders are different. The landscapes are different. With the NPF, however, the variation in narrative content can be systematically studied through narrative strategies and the belief systems invoked within different policy narratives. For example, *narrative strategies* used in different policy contexts reveal that proponents of the windmills in both Nantucket and Judith Gap are likely to make claims that the costs of the status quo (no windmills) are diffused, whereby all American citizens suffer from a lack of energy independence from foreign energy. Opponents, on the other hand, are likely to make claims that the benefits of the status quo are concentrated on those whose pristine views of the landscape are sullied by the placement of the windmills. Similarly, examining these narratives through *policy beliefs* about federalism may reveal that those opposing the windmills consistently hold that a policy decision to site windmills affects local people and should reside with local officials; conversely, those supporting windmill installation are more likely to hold that the decision affects the nation more generally and thus decision making authority should be more appropriately held at the federal level. Importantly, the NPF's approach to content allows researchers the tools needed to examine unique policy contexts while still aspiring toward generalizable findings.

Policy Narrative Strategies

Narrative strategies are used in an attempt to influence the policy process. Although there may be additional narrative strategies operationalized in the future, current NPF scholarship has focused on the following three strategies: scope of conflict, causal mechanisms, and the devil-angel shift.

1. *Scope of conflict:* Influenced by E. E. Schattschneider (1960) and more recently by Pralle (2006), NPF scholars have studied the strategic construction of policy narratives to either expand or contain policy issues (e.g., Crow and Lawlor 2016; Gupta et al. 2014; McBeth, Shanahan, et al. 2010; Shanahan et al. 2013). In short, when authors portray themselves as losing on an issue, they engage in narrative strategies that aim to expand the scope of conflict (e.g., diffusing costs and concentrating benefits). Conversely, when authors portray themselves as winning, they engage in narrative strategies that contain an issue to the status quo (e.g., concentrating costs and diffusing benefits; see McBeth et al. 2007).

2. *Causal mechanisms*: Causal mechanisms strategically arrange narrative elements to assign responsibility and blame for a policy problem.[7] These responsibility and blame ascriptions can be thought of as explanations of why and how one or more particular factors (e.g., income disparities and lack of education) lead to another (e.g., political unrest) in public policy (see Delahais and Toulemonde 2012 for use of logic models to indicate causal effect). To date, NPF causal mechanisms have been based on Stone (2012), who defines four causal theories: intentional, inadvertent, accidental, and mechanical.

3. *Devil-angel shift*: Weible, Sabatier, and McQueen (2009, 132–133) describe the devil shift in this way: "The devil shift predicts that actors will exaggerate the malicious motives, behaviors, and influence of opponents" (also see Sabatier, Hunter, and McLaughlin 1987). The angel shift, on the other hand, occurs when groups or policy actors emphasize their ability to solve a problem and de-emphasize villains (Shanahan et al. 2013). The NPF measures the devil-angel shift as the extent to which the narrator identifies the opposing narrators as villains in comparison to how much the narrator identifies him- or herself as a hero.

Policy Beliefs

The NPF identifies operational measures of policy beliefs through narrative elements such as characters (e.g., Shanahan, McBeth, and Hathaway 2011; Shanahan et al. 2013) and other symbolic, metaphorical, or contextual means by which collective understandings of the policy subsystem (and the processes and objects therein) are generated. Importantly, the identification of policy beliefs must be theoretically grounded, for example, in cultural theory (Thompson, Ellis, and Wildavsky 1990), human-nature relationship (Muir-Pinchot debate), political ideology (Lakoff 2002), or political identity (Bernstein and Taylor 2013).

CORE NPF ASSUMPTIONS

At the core of every major school of thought, framework, or scientific approach, there is a set of core assumptions. Below are the NPF's core assumptions.

I. *Social constructions matter in public policy*: Although it is true that there is a reality populated by objects and processes independent of human perceptions, it is also true that what those objects and processes mean varies in terms of how humans perceive them. *Social construction* in this context refers to the variable meanings that individuals or groups assign to various objects or processes associated with public policy.

II. *Bounded relativity:* Social constructions of policy-related objects and processes vary to create different policy realities; however, this variation is bounded (e.g., by belief systems, ideologies, norms, normative axioms) and thus is not random.

III. *Policy narratives have generalizable structural elements:* The NPF takes a structuralist stance on narrative, where narratives are defined as having specific generalizable structures such as plots and characters that can be identified in multiple narrative contexts.

IV. *Policy narratives operate simultaneously at three levels:* For purposes of analyses, the NPF divides policy narratives into three interacting categories: microlevel (individual level), mesolevel (group and coalitional level), and macrolevel (cultural and institutional level). Policy narratives are assumed to operate simultaneously at all three levels.

V. *Homo narrans model of the individual:* Narrative is assumed to play a central role in how individuals process information, communicate, and reason.

Three of the NPF's assumptions are derived from longstanding academic approaches (I, II, and III); one is simply assumed for practical reasons (IV); one is rooted in developing empirical research (V); and all of the assumptions combined form the foundation for the NPF's approach to the study of public policy.

THREE LEVELS OF ANALYSIS

The NPF assumes that policy narratives operate simultaneously at three levels of analysis (see assumption IV above). These demarcations are drawn largely for purposes of determining scope and offering direction related to the units of analyses in which the researcher is interested. At the microlevel the researcher is concerned with the individual and how individuals both inform and are informed by policy narratives. At the mesolevel, the researcher is focused on the policy narratives that policy actors who compose groups and advocacy coalitions deploy over time within a policy subsystem. Finally, at the macrolevel the researcher is interested in how policy narratives embedded in cultures and institutions shape public policy. Table 5.1 summarizes the three levels of analysis.

MICROLEVEL NPF: *HOMO NARRANS*

To be classified as a policy framework, the NPF must clearly specify its model of the individual (Schlager 1999, 2007). *Homo narrans,* the model of the

TABLE 5.1 NPF's Three Levels of Analysis

	Micro	Meso	Macro
Unit of Analysis	Individual	Policy actors (e.g., groups, coalitions, organizations) in the policy subsystem	Institutions, culture

Core NPF Variables	Policy narrative
	  Setting
	  Characters
	  Plot
	  Moral
		Policy narrative
		  Setting
		  Characters
		  Plot
		  Moral
			Policy narrative
			  Setting
			  Characters
			  Plot
			  Moral

Imported Theories	Belief Systems Canonicity and Breach (In)congruence Narrative Transportation Narrator trust	Belief systems Devil-angel shift Heresthetics Instrumental learning Scope of conflict	Meta-narrative Institutional theory Cultural theory Social learning
Methods and Analysis	Experiments Interviews Focus groups Survey instruments Participant observation Statistical analyses (cluster analysis, latent trait analysis, etc.)	Content analysis Network analysis Game theory Statistical analyses (cluster analysis, latent trait analysis, etc.)	Historical-institutionalism Process tracing American political development Counterfactual analysis
Potential Data	Survey data Transcripts Observed behavioral data	Written texts Speeches Videos Tweets and other digital media	Archives Secondary sources Original artifacts

individual invoked by the NPF, identifies ten postulates derived from existing and well-established research findings and theories in a host of academic fields. The *homo narrans* model is best understood as an evolving psychological model of the individual that acknowledges and tests the primacy of affect and narration in human decision making and cognitive processes.

Foundation of *Homo Narrans*

Taken in total, these are the ten postulates that form the foundation of *homo narrans* (assumption V identified in the previous section).

1. *Boundedly rational:* Drawing on the classic work of Herbert Simon (e.g., Simon 1947), the NPF understands individuals to make decisions under conditions of limited time and limited information. Under such conditions, individuals satisfice or, more simply, settle for a satisfying alternative.

2. *Heuristics:* Given bounded rationality, individuals rely on information shortcuts to process information and to facilitate decision making. These shortcuts, known as heuristics, are many but are rooted in phenomena such as what information is available at the time, past experience, expertise and training, and biological biases (see Jones 2001, 71–75; Kahneman 2011, 109–255).

3. *Primacy of affect:* As political scientist Bryan Jones (2001, 73–74) observes, emotions play a critical role in focusing attention (see Peterson and Jones 2016) in human cognition by "highlighting what is important and setting priorities." In this context, emotion—termed "affect" in academic parlance—is the positive to negative value that an individual ascribes to stimuli. Recent research supports Jones's observation, finding that this positive to negative value assignment (which can be neutral) takes place some 100–250 milliseconds prior to cognition (Lodge and Taber 2005, 2007, 16; Morris et al. 2003). In short, emotions precede reason and direct attention.

4. *Two kinds of cognition:* According to psychologist Daniel Kahneman (2011), cognition (or, simply, "thinking") can be characterized as operating simultaneously, but not equally, within two systems. The first system, System 1, refers to unconscious, involuntary, and automatic thought processes that we are either born with (e.g., noticing sudden movement in your peripheral vision) or learn through prolonged practice (e.g., 2 + 2; see Kahneman 2011, 20–23). The overwhelming majority of human cognition is handled by System 1, which serves to inform or alert System 2 via affective cues (e.g., fear, anger). Like System 1, System 2 cognition is also always active but has been evolutionarily primed to run in a low-effort mode to conserve energy unless called upon. When engaged, System 2 focuses attention on cognitively cumbersome tasks that are beyond the capacity of System 1. These operations are varied but could include solving a complex math equation, following cooking directions, or attempting to determine whether somebody is telling the truth. Importantly, individuals cannot perform multiple System 2 operations simultaneously; rather, these cognitive tasks must be conducted serially. Although System 2 can recondition System 1 through updating, System 1 is stubbornly resistant to change and also serves as the default mode of human cognition.

5. *Hot cognition:* In public policy, all social and political concepts and objects can be understood as affect laden (Lodge and Taber 2005; Morris et al. 2003) or, at least, potentially so. If a concept or object is unfamiliar, individuals will perform a "search" in order to assign affect to the new concept or object in terms of their existing understanding of the world. When concepts or mental impressions of objects are cognitively activated or situated in the individual's existing understanding of the world, so, too, are their System 1 affective attachments (see Redlawsk 2002, 1023).

6. *Confirmation and disconfirmation bias:* Individuals engage in confirmation bias where they treat congruent evidence that agrees with their priors (beliefs, knowledge, etc.) as stronger than incongruent evidence (Taber and Lodge 2006), and process congruent stimuli more quickly than incongruent stimuli (Lodge and Taber 2005); likewise, individuals also engage in disconfirmation bias, where evidence that is incongruent with an individual's priors is counterargued (Taber and Lodge 2006) and takes longer to process than evidence that is congruent (Lodge and Taber 2005).

7. *Selective exposure:* Individuals select sources and information that are congruent with what they already believe (Kunda 1990, 495; Taber and Lodge 2006). A practical example of this behavior is found in the fact that conservatives in the United States like to watch Fox News while liberals prefer to watch MSNBC (Stroud 2008).

8. *Identity-protective cognition:* Selective exposure, confirmation bias, and disconfirmation bias are conditioned by knowledge and prior beliefs and are used by individuals in a way that protects their prior identity, or who they already understand themselves to be (e.g., Kahan et al. 2007). Those with the strongest prior attitudes, especially those with higher levels of knowledge and political sophistication, employ what they know to protect their priors (Taber and Lodge 2006).

9. *Primacy of groups and networks:* Individuals do not process information in a vacuum; rather, the social, professional, familial, and cultural networks and groups in which they find themselves immersed play a vital role in helping individuals assign affect to social and political concepts and objects (e.g., Kahan and Braman 2006; Kurzban 2010). In short, people look to their trusted relationships and associations to help them make sense of the world.

10. *Narrative cognition:* Psychologist Donald E. Polkinghorne (1988, 11) writes that narrative is the primary means by which human beings make sense of and situate themselves in the world, and in doing so narrative renders human existence meaningful. Exogenous (external) to the individual and in terms of our prior nine postulates, it is posited that narratives are the primary communication device

within and across groups and networks; internal to the individual (endogenous), narratives are also the preferred means for organizing thoughts, memories, affect, and other cognitions (Berinsky and Kinder 2006; Jones and Song 2014). Thus, in academic terms, narrative is the preferred heuristic employed by all for the purposes of making sense of the world because it provides essential linkages between System 1 and System 2 cognition. In plain language, people tell and remember stories.

Proceeding from the *homo narrans* model of the individual, the NPF makes the empirically testable conjecture that narrative likely plays an important role in public policy.

Microlevel NPF Applications

Table 5.2 lists several microlevel NPF hypotheses detailed by Jones and McBeth (2010, 343–344) and Shanahan, McBeth, and Hathaway (2011) related to canonicity and breach, narrative transportation, congruence and incongruence, narrator trust, and the power of characters. Research testing these hypotheses has been primarily concerned with how policy narratives affect individual-level preferences, perceptions of risk, and opinion related to specific public policy areas. The dominant methodologies at this level of analysis have been experimental.

Micro Hypotheses 1 and 3: Narrative breach and congruence and incongruence. Several NPF studies (e.g., Ertas 2015; Shanahan et al. 2014) have leveraged hypotheses 1 and 3 to assess narrative persuasiveness as two countervailing conditions: when the narrative runs counter to (breach or incongruence) or supports (congruence) a person's expectations, preferences, or beliefs. Generally speaking, this body of experimental research finds that breaching narratives move individuals away from priors and toward the preferences and beliefs within the narrative; similarly, congruent narratives intensify an individual's policy stances and beliefs. Shanahan et al. (2014) and Shanahan, McBeth, and Hathaway (2011) found congruent policy narratives to significantly strengthen policy preferences and beliefs; these scholars and Ertas (2015) also found breaching policy narratives to significantly influence opinion.

Many studies have explored congruence specifically. Jones and Song (2014) found that respondents exposed to climate change narratives in experimental treatments were more likely to cognitively mirror the organization of the narrative presented to them if the narrative was culturally congruent with the respondent's prior cultural type. Employing the macrobelief of American individuality, Niederdeppe, Roh, and Shapiro (2015) found increased empathy toward the narrative's character and policy support when individual

TABLE 5.2 Microlevel NPF Hypotheses and Relevant Studies

Hypothesis	Exact Wording and Source	Extant Research
H_1: *Breach*	On the basis of an individual's expectations, *as a narrative's level of breach increases,* the more likely an individual exposed to the narrative will be persuaded (Jones and McBeth 2010).	Ertas 2015 Shanahan et al. 2014 Shanahan, McBeth, and Hathaway 2011
H_2: *Narrative transportation*	As *narrative transportation* increases, the more likely an individual exposed to that narrative is to be persuaded (Jones and McBeth 2010).	Jones 2014a
H_3: *Congruence and incongruence* (of beliefs or worldviews)	As perception of *congruence* (of belief systems) increases, the more likely an individual is to be persuaded by the narrative (Jones and McBeth 2010).	Ertas 2015 Husmann 2015 Niederdeppe, Roh, and Shapiro 2015 Shanahan et al. 2014 Jones and Song 2014 Lybecker, McBeth, and Kusko 2013 McBeth, Lybecker, and Stoutenborough 2016 Shanahan, McBeth, and Hathaway 2011 McBeth, Lybecker, and Garner 2010
H_4: *Narrator trust*	As *narrator trust* increases, the more likely an individual is to be persuaded by the narrative (Jones and McBeth 2010).	Ertas 2015
H_5: *The power of characters*	The portrayal of policy narrative *characters* (heroes, victims, and villains) has higher levels of influence on opinion and preferences of individuals than scientific or technical information (Shanahan et al. 2011b).	Jones 2010 Jones 2014b Jones, Fløttum, and Gjerstad 2017

responsibility (congruent with the macrobelief) was included in the narrative; conversely, when it was not included, the authors found decreased empathy and policy support. Using a survey methodology, McBeth, Lybecker, and Garner (2010) and Lybecker, McBeth, and Kusko (2013) and McBeth, Lybecker, and Husmann (2014) found that individuals and practitioners preferred stories about recycling that were congruent with their beliefs about citizenship. Husmann (2015) found that liberal and Democrat participants (as well as women participants) were more likely to support government intervention benefiting obese children if exposed to ideologically congruent obesity policy narratives (consistent with Lakoff 2002). Similarly, testing Lakoff's (2002) conservative and liberal parenting metaphors, Clemons, McBeth, and Kusko (2012) found that individuals' view of parenting was only partially congruent with their choice of obesity policy stories.

However, recent research (Lybecker, McBeth, and Stoutenborough 2016; McBeth et al. 2016) has found that breaching and congruency are not necessarily mutually exclusive. These NPF scholars found that characters can effectively breach policy preferences by positioning congruent characters—those who align with one's individual identity—with an opposing (breaching) policy preference. For example, consider a person who has a deep philosophical commitment to libertarian notions of freedom. This individual is also a business person and thus has certain expectations about how business is talked about; narrative theory refers to such conventions of thinking as canonicity (Herman 2002, 2003). Canonical language for a business person usually invokes markets, competition, and certain characters where environmentalists are often cast as villains. This person will also have canonical understandings of the narratives espoused by enemies (like the environmentalist) that paint the business community as the villain. Now suppose this same person encounters an environmentalist narrative that casts business as a hero, invokes markets to protect the environment, and paints competition as the social engine that makes all of this happen. Such a narrative would be congruent in a worldview sense for this hypothetical person but breaching in terms of the individual's expectations about the environmentalist narrative.

In all, these studies largely support hypotheses H_1 and H_3. However, given the nuanced differences between congruence and incongruence, canonicity and breach, we have modified H_3 to specifically apply to beliefs and worldviews. Additional research is needed to further understand the conditions under which narrative breach and congruence affect beliefs, preferences, and more.

Micro Hypothesis 2: Narrative transportation. Narrative transportation "is related to a narrative's ability to mentally transport the reader into the world created by the narrative" (Jones 2014a, 648; also see Green and Brock 2005). A book, movie, or even campaign speech is often determined to be good by the extent to which the reader/viewer/listener can imagine him-/herself surrounded by the scene and embroiled in the plot alongside the characters. Jones (2014a) conducted an experiment and found that the more a person is able to picture a story (in this case, about climate change), the more positively that person responds to the hero of the story, which in turn leads to a higher willingness to accept arguments and solutions argued for in the policy narrative.

Micro Hypothesis 4: Narrator trust. Ertas (2015) conducted a microlevel study regarding charter schools and found that narrator trust increased shifts in policy preferences toward the preferred policy presented in the narrative, but that this occurred to a greater extent when there was also congruence.

Micro Hypothesis 5: The power of characters. Characters have been found to play an important role in shaping individual preferences. Jones (2010, 2014b) has found that the hero character is a primary driver of narrative persuasion. Conducting an experimental study examining the role of cultural narratives in shaping policy preferences related to climate change, Jones found that respondents tended to have more positive affect for hero characters than for other characters, regardless of their priors. Moreover, as positive affect for the hero character increased, so, too, did the respondents' willingness to accept the assumptions imbedded in the narrative and the argued-for policy solutions. In this case, this meant that the more respondents liked the hero, the more likely they were to believe climate change was real and that it posed a threat both to them as individuals and to society more generally, the more they were willing to take action to stop climate change, and the more likely they were to support the policy solution within the policy narrative. Similar results were found by Jones, Fløttum, and Gjerstad (2017) when examining the impact of climate change policy narratives on Norwegian citizens.

Some microlevel work deviates from the hypotheses outlined in Table 5.2. For example, Jorgensen, Song, and Jones (2017) use a survey experimental design to test the influence of causal mechanisms within policy narratives addressing US campaign finance reform. Their study found that mechanical causal mechanisms were more persuasive with participants who have high levels of political knowledge. On the other hand, Shanahan et al. (2014) found that intentional causal mechanisms have some short-term effectiveness in influencing public opinion in favor of the narrator. Gray and Jones (2016) step outside of the NPF's hypothesis orientation using qualitative interviews to describe stories of expression and equality told by elites about campaign finance reform policy in the United States. The authors argue that although the study is descriptive it points to the NPF's as of yet untapped ability to empower citizens by describing competing policy narratives in complex policy areas in a way that both is easy for citizens to understand and uses a methodology they themselves could easily employ.

Notably, unlike most policy process frameworks and theories, the NPF is a framework that promotes research intended to refine its model of the individual (like comparative agenda setting [see Jones 2001] and policy learning [see the discussion of microfoundations in Kamkhaji and Radaelli 2016]). Our reasons for doing microfoundational analysis are straightforward. If we are to understand how, when, and why policy narratives shape public policy at the larger meso- and macroscales, we need an accurate and refined understanding of how narrative works at an individual level in order to make valid assumptions at larger scales of analyses.

MESOLEVEL NPF: *AGORA NARRANS*

In ancient Greece, the agora was the physical and public space where citizens took action to achieve, reflect upon, and implement a policy goal, principally through reasoned and impassioned narratives. A plethora of policy process research today focuses on our modern-day agora, known as the policy subsystem. Building from the *homo narrans* foundation, NPF mesolevel research focuses on the role of policy narratives in the agora. Thus, *agora narrans* is NPF's mesolevel examination of the strategic construction and communication of policy narratives by policy actors[8] organized in a variety of ways: charismatic individuals, groups, constellations of actors, coalitions, and so on. The discussion that follows details the mesoconceptual model, defines mesolevel concepts, and concludes with hypotheses and a discussion of extant mesolevel applications.

Conceptual Model of the Mesolevel NPF

Understanding how narratives function in a policy subsystem, we turn to a seminal work regarding how systems work. As described by von Bertalanffy (1968), systems are composed of objects that are organized and related to one another while being shaped or affected by external feedbacks. How do these ideas inspire how NPF conceptualizes mesolevel? First, objects in systems theory are the component parts of a system or the variables of interest. For the NPF, the "objects" of primary interest within subsystems are policy narratives. However, additional objects in policy subsystems are also relevant, including but not limited to standard public policy process variables such as resources, issue saliency, institutions, and the policy actors themselves. Second, objects in systems theory are not haphazardly organized but rather function in some coordinated or strategic fashion; for the NPF, policy narratives are constructed by policy actors, who are organized in any number of ways (e.g., a charismatic individual, a group, a coalition). Third, relationships between objects in a system constitute the dynamic nature of the system; in the study of policy, this is generally referred to as the policy process. We look to existing policy process

FIGURE 5.1 Model of Policy Narratives at the Mesolevel of the Narrative
Policy Framework

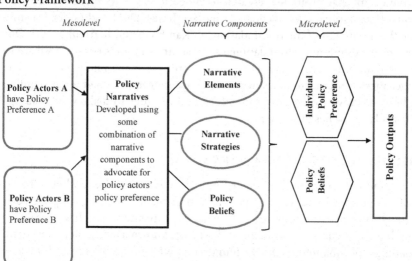

THE EXTERNAL CONTEXT
(e.g., legal constraints; cultural norms; political, social,
and economic contexts; information; public opinion)

theory and findings to shape expectations about how policy subsystem objects
interact; however, the NPF adds to this existing understanding by theorizing
expectations regarding the role of narrative. These theorized expectations are
manifest in the mesolevel NPF hypotheses. Finally, systems have boundaries,
meaning that the system exists in an external environment or context that may
influence the subsystem. Figure 5.1 illustrates the NPF's conceptualization of
how policy narratives function at the mesolevel of analysis and is further explained below.

At the mesolevel, policy actors may derive from institutions or organizations (e.g., a member of the media or the British Parliament), play different
roles (e.g., citizen or political leader), and organize in networks (e.g., advocacy
coalitions, interest groups, organizations). These policy actors, however arranged and derived, develop or adopt policy narratives to reflect their policy
preferences. Competing policy actors have divergent policy preferences, which
are expressed in policy narratives. These competing policy narratives utilize
some combination of narrative components, and the mesolevel NPF contribution comes in the analysis of how the generators of these policy narratives
use these components. For example, whereas both entities employ characters,
Policy Actors A may use the federal government as a hero while Policy Actors
B may use private industry as a hero. Similarly, Policy Actors A may use the
narrative strategy of diffusing costs to consumers and concentrating benefits

to CEOs; Policy Actors B may use the narrative strategy of diffusing costs to taxpayers and concentrating benefits to a federal agency. With regard to policy beliefs, for example, the NPF provides guidance on how to operationalize narrative components to test changes in policy beliefs over time, both within and between policy actors. Taken together, narrative components are the building blocks of policy narratives and are strategically constructed by policy actors in the policy subsystem to affect policy preferences to achieve favorable policy outputs, whether they are decisions, implementation activities, or evaluations.

As indicated in the introduction of the microlevel discussion, the mesolevel of analysis cannot (and should not) be decoupled conceptually from the microlevel of analysis. The *agora narrans* centers on dynamics both within and between policy actors' policy narratives as well as the association with narratives and policy outputs. In sum, the *agora narrans* in the NPF brings to the fore the role of narratives in the subsystem(s) and, hence, the policy process as well. The discussion that follows defines mesolevel concepts and concludes with hypotheses and a discussion of extant mesolevel applications.

Policy subsystems. As with many policy process theories, NPF scholarship studies public policymaking within and across policy subsystems. Public policy issues within policy subsystems are either dominated by one constellation of policy actors or contested by many. Policy subsystems consist of a variety of actors (e.g., elected officials, interest groups, experts, judicial actors, media) who vie to control a policy issue. For example, the NPF has studied contentious policy subsystems of hydraulic fracking in Colorado (Heikkila et al. 2014), drug policies in Australia (Fitzgerald 2013), forest policy in Finland (Peltomaa, Hilden, and Huttunen 2016), Greater Yellowstone wildlife management (e.g., McBeth, Shanahan, et al. 2010), and Massachusetts wind energy policy (Shanahan et al. 2013).

Although a focus on individual policy subsystems is the norm for policy process approaches and current NPF scholarship, evolving research suggests that examining multiple subsystems (Jones and Jenkins-Smith 2009) or policy regimes (May and Jochim 2013) could strengthen our understanding of the policy process. At least two recent NPF studies have moved in this direction. Crow and Berggren (2014) examine policy narratives across four cases of environmental policymaking in Colorado, and O'Bryan et al. (2014) conduct the first NPF comparative public policy study. Given the known linkages between subsystems and the likely case that narratives play a role in such linkages, we suspect future NPF scholarship will similarly trend toward theory and method that make such examinations possible.

The NPF and policy actors in the subsystem. The NPF has historically employed coalitions as the way to understand the organization of policy actors; the NPF now recognizes that not all policy debates emerge from coalitions alone.

Some debates occur between interest groups and organizations (e.g., environmental and energy companies); sometimes an interest group is so powerful (e.g., the National Rifle Association) that it is the dominant voice; some authoritarian political leaders alone control the narrative (e.g., Gaddafi in Libya). Thus, the NPF seeks a more comprehensive view of the generators of narratives in the policy process while maintaining that approaches to understanding coalition formation and behavior remain an important way to understand policy actor behavior.

Jenkins-Smith, St. Clair, and Woods (1991) summarize two of the lines of research on coalition formation and change. The first can be termed the *instrumental* approach, and it focuses on Harold Lasswell's ([1936] 1990) classic instrumental definition of politics: "who gets what, when, and how," and sees policy actor interests as a primary driver of coalitional formation and change (Jenkins-Smith, St. Clair, and Woods 1991, 853n2). The second "line of research holds that members of advocacy coalitions adhere to hierarchically structured 'belief systems,' in which the most basic beliefs (e.g., fundamental ontological and normative axioms) constrain more specific or operational beliefs and policy positions" (852). The Advocacy Coalition Framework (ACF) is the dominant policy process theory that promotes the belief system approach to coalitional formation and change (e.g., Sabatier and Jenkins-Smith 1993; Sabatier and Weible 2007; Weible, Sabatier, and McQueen 2009), but as we have already discussed—and will detail below—beliefs and policy narratives are often intertwined.

The NPF accepts that both understandings of coalition formation and change are likely to play a role in public policy. Regarding belief systems and coalition formation and change, the NPF has expended considerable efforts on this front. Shanahan, Jones, and McBeth (2011, 546–547), for example, focus specifically on synergies between the ACF and NPF, providing policy narrative measurement strategies that operationalize belief stability, strength, and cohesion (but also see Shanahan et al. 2013). Similarly, the media are observed to participate in coalitions, with embedded policy beliefs and preferred policy preferences (Choi 2016; McBeth et al. 2013; Shanahan et al. 2008). Regarding instrumental coalition formation and change, the NPF hypothesizes (Jones and McBeth 2010, 346) that members of coalitions use the perception of costs and benefits to heresthetically (e.g., Riker 1986) expand or contain coalition membership in their favor. The instrumental approach to coalition formation and change, and how it relates to policy narratives, still remains an underexamined aspect of mesolevel NPF.

Mesolevel Applications

Several hypotheses at the mesolevel have been developed to test relationships with key dependent variables. Table 5.3 summarizes previously specified NPF

TABLE 5.3 NPF Mesolevel Hypotheses and Origins

Hypothesis	Exact Wording and Source	Extant Literature
H_1 Narrative Strategy	Policy actors who are portraying themselves as losing on a policy issue will use narrative elements to expand the policy issue to increase the size of their coalition (Jones and McBeth 2010).	McBeth et al. 2007 Shanahan et al. 2013 Gupta, Ripberger, and Collins 2014
H_2 Narrative Strategy	Policy actors who are portraying themselves as winning on a policy issue will use narrative elements to contain the policy issue to maintain the coalitional status quo (Jones and McBeth 2010).	McBeth et al. 2007 Shanahan et al. 2013 Gupta et al. 2014
H_3 Narrative Strategy	Policy actors will heresthetically employ policy narratives to manipulate the composition of political coalitions for their strategic benefit (Jones and McBeth 2010).	None
H_4 Narrative Strategy	The devil shift: higher incidence of the devil shift in policy subsystems is associated with policy intractability (Shanahan et al. 2013).	Shanahan et al. 2013 Crow and Berggren 2014 Heikkila et al. 2014 Leong 2015 Merry 2015
H_5 Policy Beliefs	Coalition glue and policy outcomes: advocacy coalitions with policy narratives that contain higher levels of coalitional glue (coalition stability, strength, and intracoalition cohesion) will more likely influence policy outcomes (Shanahan et al. 2013; Shanahan, Jones, and McBeth 2011).	Kusko 2013 McBeth et al. 2010
H_6 Policy Learning	Variation in policy narrative elements helps explain policy learning (Shanahan, Jones, and McBeth 2011).	None
H_7 Coalition Membership	The media are a contributor (a policy actor) in policy debates (Shanahan et al. 2008).	Shanahan et al. 2008 Peltomaa, Hilden, and Huttunen 2016 Crow and Lawlor 2016

continues

TABLE 5.3 NPF Mesolevel Hypotheses and Origins *continued*

Hypothesis	Exact Wording and Source	Extant Literature
H_8 Role of Media Actors within Subsystems	Media acting as conduits of policy information will show stability of policy narratives across media outlets, whereas media acting as contributors to policy debates will show a greater degree of variation in narrative structure and framing across media outlets (Crow and Lawlor 2016).	None
H_9 Role of Narrative Elements in Policy Communication	Policy actors* using rhetorical narrative strategies (character-driven plots, melodramatic narratives, stories of decline, metaphors, etc.) to a greater degree are more likely to prevail in policy debates than those using technical or scientific communication (Crow and Lawlor 2016).	McBeth et al. 2012 Crow and Berggren 2014
H_{10} Role of Framing	Policy actors using thematic framing of policy problems are more likely to sway public opinion in favor of their articulated problem and solution than policy actors that employ episodic frames or other human interest frames, leading to higher success passing their proposed solutions (Crow and Lawlor 2016).	Shanahan et al. 2008
H_{11} Role of Story Frames	Policy actors using story frames consistent with specific audience beliefs, but varying across media platforms, will influence policy outcomes toward their policy preference (Crow and Lawlor 2016).	None

* The original hypotheses posited by Crow and Lawlor (2016) use the term *coalitions;* we have replaced *coalitions* with *policy actors* to reflect the NPF's accommodation of the variety of ways actors organize (e.g., interest groups, organizations, coalitions).

hypotheses and their origins. The dominant methodology at the mesolevel has been content analysis. Some hypotheses are well-worn (H_1, H_2, H_4, H_5, H_7), some remain untested (H_3, H_6), some dropped (those on endogenous and exogenous public opinion), and some are new propositions (H_8, H_9, H_{10}, H_{11}).

Meso Hypothesis 1: Issue expansion as a narrative strategy. McBeth et al. (2007) used E. E. Schattschneider (1960) to argue that when groups perceive themselves as losing, they construct a policy narrative to expand the issue. Groups do this by diffusing costs and concentrating benefits of the opposing policy. For example, a losing narrative contains many victims who pay the "cost" of the opposing policy, whereas the elite few (typically villains) benefit. McBeth et al. (2007) found that this strategy occurred in their study of interest group conflict in Greater Yellowstone. In a study of wind energy off the coast of Cape Cod, Shanahan et al. (2013) found that the losing coalition (anti-wind coalition) concentrated benefits and diffused costs 88 percent of the time, compared to 46 percent of the time for the winning coalition (pro-wind coalition). Similarly, in the case of siting a nuclear power plant in India, Gupta, Ripberger, and Collins (2014) found the losing coalition attempted to expand the scope of conflict by predominantly focusing on the many who would be affected by the power plant.

Meso Hypothesis 2: Issue containment as a narrative strategy. Again using Schattschneider (1960), McBeth et al. (2007) empirically demonstrate that winning groups construct narratives to contain a policy issue by using political strategies of concentrating costs and diffusing benefits when discussing their policy preference. The idea behind this strategy is that winning groups want to maintain their minimal winning coalition and either maintain the status quo or control the policy outcome within the existing political context. This narrative strategy is empirically tested in McBeth et al. (2007), Shanahan et al. (2013), and Gupta, Ripberger, and Collins (2014).

Meso Hypothesis 4: Devil-angel shift. A few studies have examined the devil and angel shifts. In the study of the installation of windmills off the coast of Cape Cod, Massachusetts (Shanahan et al. 2013), there was a narrative arc in the winning coalition from devil shift to angel shift. Similarly, Schlaufer (2016) found the winning coalition in the Swiss school policy debates to employ the angel shift at statistically higher rates than the losing coalition did. However, some studies (i.e., Heikkila et al. 2014 and Crow and Berggren 2014) found no statistical association between winning and losing groups and the use of this strategy in their policy debates. Merry (2015) found that when averaging individual tweets, overall, both the Brady Campaign and the National Rifle Association (NRA) leaned toward the angel shift; another (Leong 2015) found the winning coalition to use the devil shift. A cousin to the devil-angel shift is found in intentional (where the villain is engaging in willful nefarious action) and inadvertent (no one is at fault) causal mechanisms (McBeth et al. 2012). This narrative strategy remains of interest to NPF scholars because results of this strategy's use and effect are inconsistent.

Meso Hypothesis 5: Coalitional glue and policy beliefs. NPF scholarship has consistently found statistically significant differences between opposing interest groups and coalition use of policy beliefs (e.g., McBeth, Shanahan, and Jones 2005; Shanahan et al. 2013; McBeth, Lybecker, and Garner 2010). These same measures (i.e., coalition stability, strength, and cohesion over time) can also be used to assess intra- and intercoalition behavior and dynamics (Shanahan, Jones, and McBeth 2011, 546–548). For example, Shanahan et al. (2013) found that intracoalition diversity of policy beliefs may be a way to expand coalition membership. Work by Kusko (2013) in her study of 1980s US foreign policy toward El Salvador demonstrated, using content analysis of policy narratives, that the religious right coalition in the United States had greater stability, strength, and cohesion and that this might have accounted for the coalition's greater policy success compared to that of a more progressive religious coalition. Shanahan et al. (2013) content-analyzed policy narratives of policy actors involved in a wind energy controversy in Massachusetts. The research demonstrated the two coalitions had high levels of cohesion on two of three policy beliefs. Finally, McBeth, Shanahan, et al. (2010) showed that the wildlife activist group Buffalo Field Campaign was consistent in two of its three identified policy beliefs over a ten-year period.

Meso Hypothesis 7: Coalition membership. Shanahan et al. (2008) explore the role of the media as conduit of policy stakeholders or as a contributor in policy debates. This study helped determine that media do contribute to policy debates. Given the ability of media to disseminate messages to a wide audience, this finding has been important in identifying an important policy actor and set of policy narrative data in policy subsystems. Subsequent studies have confirmed this hypothesis (Peltomaa, Hilden, and Huttunen 2016; Crow and Lawlor 2016).

Meso Hypothesis 9: Role of narrative elements in policy communication. Crow and Lawlor (2016) have recently added this hypothesis to the set of mesolevel hypotheses. McBeth et al. (2012) previously referred to the collective use of narrative elements as "narrativity." Using more traditional narrative data from public consumption documents, these authors, along with Crow and Berggren (2014), found an association with narrativity and policy success. However, this hypothesis remains untested with digital media such as Twitter.

Meso Hypothesis 10: Role of framing. Iyengar (1990) and Iyengar and Simon (1997) are the originators of the concepts of episodic (specific) and thematic (general) framing in the media. Crow and Lawlor (2016) have articulated a new hypothesis predicting the greater effectiveness of the use of thematic framing in the policy process. Shanahan et al. (2008) are early explorers of the use of these framing techniques in media narratives, finding that both national and local media outlets employed thematic frames in their narrative (as measured by the casting of the victim), but local coverage used thematic framing at a statistically higher rate than the national media did.

MACROLEVEL NPF: GRAND NARRATIVES

Macrolevel narratives are "communal, historical narratives that are expansive enough to explain a variety of human events across time and place" (Danforth 2016, 584). These grand policy narratives create socially constructed realities that manifest as institutions, society, and cultural norms. Macrolevel policy narratives are relatively stable (e.g., "progress is good") when compared to those at the microlevel and mesolevel, with mesolevel policy debates occurring within the larger macrolevel narratives ("let the market dictate progress" vs. "government needs to regulate to ensure progress"). However, macrolevel narratives can, and do, change over time and space, resulting in marked institutional and cultural shifts (e.g., knowledge comes from the divine to knowledge comes from observations). These macrolevel narratives nonetheless are composed of narrative elements, beliefs, and strategies. They may be found in historical events (education policy change post–World War II to open education for all; Veslkova and Beblavy 2014), historic debates (Decision of 1789; Cook 2014), and cultural orientations (cultural frames and institutional spaces; Ney 2014).

As indicated in Table 5.1, as a framework, the NPF conceptualizes macrolevel analyses through imported theories. For example, Lyotard's (1984) meta-narrative is a story that functions to explain events, constructing meaning of events or ideas through shared cultural knowledge. Scott's (1995, 2008) institutional theory identifies means by which institutional structures (e.g., rules, procedures) provide the sideboards for accepted social norms and behaviors. Cultural theory (Thompson, Ellis, and Wildavsky 1990) identifies four distinctive ways of life that can be leveraged to understand and research the relationship between macrolevel cultural and policy narratives (Ney 2014). Finally, analyzing a "relevant counterfactual" (Lukes 1974, 2005, 44–48) policy narrative allows researchers to hone in on what policy narratives *did not* develop. Such research has the benefits of both revealing minority macropolicy narratives and illuminating preferences, values, and policy outputs that are simply not on the agenda (see Peterson and Jones 2016). Though we are not at all suggesting that researchers should limit macrolevel approaches to the theories we list here, these theoretical perspectives may serve as initial grounding that can facilitate macrolevel research addressing questions such as how such narratives are created, diffused, accepted, changed, and debunked over time and space.

LINKING MICRO-, MESO-, AND MACROLEVELS

Although each level of analysis provides rich areas for NPF research, there is a growing interest in understanding the connectedness between the macro-meso-micro levels. Interestingly, a road map as to how this might be accomplished can be found in one of the narrative studies that provided the impetus for the NPF. Published in *Policy Sciences* in 2004, "Public Opinion for Sale" (McBeth and Shanahan 2004) addresses the development of "wicked problems" in environmental policy subsystems where groups are unable to reframe disputes to work toward resolution.[9] Whereas the 2004 article invokes the term *frames,* the NPF now tells us that what the authors really spoke to were the active policy narratives at all three levels of analysis. To avoid confusion, we use the term *policy narrative* in our discussion below, but, to be clear, the original 2004 article does not.

McBeth and Shanahan (2004, 319–320) argue that with intractable policy issues, "there is a general lack of theory addressing macro-level driving forces in the political system that influence how [policy narratives] develop among policy actors and the public at large." If viewed retroactively through the NPF's lens on the policy process, McBeth and Shanahan were attempting to identify the macrolevel narrative driving mesolevel coalitional politics. The macrolevel condition identified in their study as driving the policy process was consumerism. The authors argue that consumerism permeates not only American economic habits but also political habits as well. Potentially linking this consumerist macrolevel with mesolevel actors and coalitions, the authors tap the notion of "backwards loops" (Clemons and McBeth 2001) in political systems, where policy marketers (interest groups, the media, and elected officials) actively construct policy narratives and market them to the public. Providing a road map for how the macrolevel interacts with the mesolevel and how the mesolevel, in turn, interacts with the microlevel, the article goes on to demonstrate how policy marketers "sell public opinion" and how this marketing contributes to intractability. The authors conclude "public policy problems are defined by policy marketers not citizens" and "the ensuing policy solutions are related more to ephemeral lifestyle choices than they are to rational debate and political interests" (McBeth and Shanahan 2004, 328).

Exemplifying all three levels of analysis, the 2004 McBeth and Shanahan article provides a way to link the three levels of analysis in the NPF. Importantly, it also draws our attention to the central role of the policy marketer in shaping that opinion. As such, the policy marketer is potentially a critical link between micro- and mesolevel research. The 2010 variant of the NPF theorizes that the microlevel model of the individual is most relevant in terms of how policy narratives shape public opinion. However, Jones and McBeth (2010, 345) also note public opinion is likely to have limited and conditional effects on public policy.

Given that the majority of microlevel NPF scholarship has focused on the effect of policy narratives on public opinion (see Table 5.2), the NPF may be expending considerable energy to explain a relatively small slice of the variation in public policy processes, designs, and outcomes. Crow (2012) and Gray and Jones (2016), however, offer a potential link between the microlevel and mesolevel that may allow NPF researchers to extract more out of the microlevel than just studies of public opinion.

Crow (2012) suggests researchers examine how elite actors process and convey policy narratives. Such approaches could tap the NPF's *homo narrans* model of the individual to better understand mesolevel phenomena such as the behavior of policy marketers and other elites. In theory, a microlevel analysis is only required to focus on the individual as the unit of analysis and could rightfully pursue questions related to other actors in the policy process, not just the public. Correspondingly, the NPF at the mesolevel is concerned not only with group narratives but also with the use and interpretation of policy narratives by key *individual* elite players within a particular coalition and, more specifically, with how that use shapes coalition composition. This is an intriguing underdeveloped facet of NPF mesolevel research that presents opportunities to link microlevel findings related to narrative persuasion and cognition with mesolevel coalitional politics.

At least one study has already moved along this arc. Using qualitative semistructured interviews, Gray and Jones (2016) examine the policy narratives disseminated by elite actors in the campaign finance policy subsystem. Although mostly a descriptive study, this analysis of elite actors reveals several NPF-relevant concepts, including belief systems and narrative elements. Importantly, it also reminds us that although the NPF is empirical it is not necessarily quantitative. In fact, in some cases—maybe even the most important cases—the NPF needs to be qualitative and rely on traditional qualitative tools such as the interview, focus groups, and participant observation.

Finally, the NPF has also made some minor inroads in terms of validating findings from the microlevel at the mesolevel, albeit indirectly. Jones's work (2010, 2014a, 2014b) at the microlevel reveals that heroes were the driving force behind preferences and perceptions of risk related to climate change. The more individuals liked a hero in a story about climate change, the more likely they were to believe climate change was real, a threat, and the more willing they were to take action (Jones 2010, 2014b; Jones et al. 2017). Similarly, Shanahan et al. (2013), conducting a mesolevel content analysis of wind farm policy in Massachusetts, find that the winning coalition focused on hero-based stories and less on villains.

Finding the interconnections between the three levels of NPF analysis and working out contradictions are ongoing processes, ones that will benefit the NPF's attempt to scientifically study the role of policy narratives in the public policy process.

NEW DIRECTIONS IN THE NPF

Four substantive new directions have opened up for the NPF. The first is the prospect of NPF comparative analyses, with policy issue and theoretical concept comparisons across countries becoming a rich new direction of research. A second avenue is recent work that focuses on a deeper exploration of the use of evidence in NPF analyses. A third path follows the emergence of digital media as valid narrative data. Finally, we posit a new NPF hypothesis on policy change grounded in policy narrative learning. We discuss these in detail below.

Comparative Analysis

Comparative approaches tend to fall into two categories: country comparisons (e.g., case study comparing countries) and concept comparisons (e.g., comparison of policy process theory constructs in different contexts) (Orvis and Drogus 2014). Application of comparative public policy is nascent in NPF scholarship, but the central research question of NPF remains relevant when applied to a comparative context: What is the role of narratives in the policy process in different regime contexts? Whether scholarly pursuits focus on a country comparison of policies with policy narratives as the data for analysis or a comparison of the use of narrative elements and strategies in different policy contexts (such as comparing narratives across sectors in a single country or across levels of governance), NPF is a viable framework for comparative analysis.

Cross-country comparisons focus on understanding differences and similarities across regimes (Orvis and Drogus 2014). This comparative NPF approach is a growing field (Exadaklyos and Radaelli [2012] suggest it to researchers working on the politics of the European Union) and relevant for both diffusion-oriented research (e.g., how different countries respond to policy narrative inspired by the Organisation for Economic Co-operation and Development, European Union, or World Bank) and policy area research (e.g., how two structurally similar political systems differ in their narratives of a similar policy problem). At least one NPF study has conducted systematic cross-country comparison. O'Bryan, Dunlop, and Radaelli (2014) compare narratives on the Arab Spring of 2011–2012 as found in the hearings of the UK House of Commons Select Committee on Foreign Affairs and the US House of Representatives Committee on Foreign Affairs. They deploy qualitative methodology to compare narrative structure, narrative learning, and narrative strategies in the two institutions across the Atlantic.

Given that the NPF is a relatively new and developing theory of the policy process, a proliferation of internationally situated scholarly studies focus on the development and refinement of NPF concepts (narrative elements and strategies), with insights into the case itself being secondary to the theoretical advancement. As such, concept comparisons focused on understanding diversity in the policy process (Gupta 2012; e.g., what is the role of policy narratives in the policy process in different countries?) are a ripe but unchartered area of research. For example, with the policy setting being India, Weible et al. (2016) suggest a set of minimal conditions to unambiguously determine the presence of a narrative, adding to the NPF concepts from network analysis (the ego-alter dyad) and identifying "beneficiaries" as a distinct type of actor. Turning to within-country comparisons, Schlaufer (2016) examines policy debates at the level of the Swiss cantons, advancing NPF's previous use of evidence in narratives by discovering how evidence is refracted and manipulated in narratives of different coalitions.

This leads to empirically testable hypotheses on coalitions and evidence utilization in public controversies. In the United Kingdom, Lawton and Rudd (2014) identified an additional set of characters (entrepreneurs and charismatic experts) at the connection between the production of scientific evidence and policy decisions. Their work (and Schlaufer 2016) opens the door to a more intense dialogue between the NPF and the field of knowledge utilization. The case of nuclear power plant siting choices in India (Gupta, Ripberger, and Collins 2014) illuminates how narratives expand or contain the scope of conflict, thus providing NPF authors with propositions that can be tested again in other settings. In the case of the European Commission, the bureaucratic arm of the European Union, evidence and expertise are discursively portrayed in regulatory impact assessments, with the aim of defining roles, identity, and ultimately legitimacy of a bureaucracy in crisis. This points to connections with the wider field of bureaucratic behavior and the construction of reputation (Radaelli, Dunlop, and Fritsch 2013). Importantly, the NPF seems well suited to comparative research (Linchbach and Zuckerman 2009) because the transportability of NPF concepts into other contexts and settings is by now established. Although the groundwork for the NPF has been laid in a variety of contexts, true concept comparative analyses using the NPF remain a ripe area of research. But we need more cross-country comparisons, comparisons of sectors within a single country, and narratives in the same policy sector across different countries.

Comparative studies are predominantly case studies, and as such lend themselves to what the NPF refers to as the mesolevel of analysis. For example, comparing policy actors' narratives in different country contexts sheds light on the policy process for crosscutting policy issues such as climate change or immigration. Comparing narratives at different time periods illuminate the role of narratives in time-sensitive episodes of policy change. One can argue that narratives evolve at a differential pace in the politics stream, the policy stream, and the problem stream of the Multiple Streams Framework (Kingdon 2003). However, NPF has well-developed microlevel propositions that, applied to comparative studies, could bring on a relatively underdeveloped genre of microlevel comparative experimental studies. For example, comparing the effects of particularly constructed narratives on individuals in different countries could be meaningful in understanding macrolevel policy debates.

In sum, systematic comparisons of the role of narratives in different policy process contexts at different levels of analysis contribute to specific understandings of that context and more importantly to a generalized understanding of narratives in the policy process.

Evidence in Narratives

In the context of the political challenges between evidence-based decision making (Pew-MacArthur Results First Initiative 2014) and science denial (Rosenau 2012), it is no surprise that many NPF studies include an examination of evidence (e.g., science and information statements) in policy narratives (for a comprehensive review of NPF studies and evidence, see Schlaufer 2016 and Smith-Walter et al. 2016). For example, Crow and Berggren (2014) examine the strategic use of science to support a narrative's policy preference. Gupta et al. (2014) find that winning groups use science in a way that demonstrates certainty in the status quo, whereas losing groups use science to show uncertainty about unwanted public policy. Nonnarrative science statements (i.e., no characters or policy preference) have been used as a control condition in experiments to test the effect of narrative on opinion (e.g., Jones 2014a; Shanahan et al. 2014). These studies have demonstrated the strategic use of science in policy narratives.

In their study of gun policy narratives disseminated by the NRA and the Brady Campaign, Smith-Walter et al. (2016) make an important advancement to the NPF's study of evidence by theoretically anchoring additional fine-scale categories of evidence within policy narratives: scientific studies, statistics, polls, *ipso dictum,* and legal. In a study of Swiss school policy debates, Schlaufer (2016) also advances the NPF's use of evidence in policy narratives by finding that evidence cannot be separated from the use of narrative elements such as setting, moral of the story, characters, and plot. Schlaufer (2016) challenges the NPF's tendency to treat evidence as an isolated narrative element and suggests focusing on the integration of evidence with other narrative elements to understand narrative effect. "Does the integration of evidence within different parts of a narrative make stories more or less convincing?" (Schlaufer 2016, 19). Whereas NPF studies focusing on evidence are proliferating, general conclusions about evidence within the NPF remain tentative.

Digital Media as Policy Narrative Data

NPF studies commonly derive policy narrative data from "public consumption documents"—the policy narratives disseminated by policy actors through newsletters, speeches, editorials, and sometimes media accounts (McBeth,

Shanahan, and Jones 2005). The proliferation of digital media and the relative ease with which these data can be collected have resulted in several mesolevel NPF studies that expressly explore whether policy narratives exist in these digital venues (e.g., YouTube, Twitter, blogs). Merry (2015) uses the NPF to study how the Brady Campaign and the NRA use social media to construct policy narratives. Using a nearly five-year time frame, Merry collected a total of 9,918 tweets from the two groups and used them in an innovative methodological way to effectively build a narrative. She examined tweets over a day or a week, finding this assessment of tweets leads to "more detailed narratives," and suggests that this is "a better reflection of the way individuals receive and process information from social media" (Merry 2016, 16). Her data indicated that the Brady Campaign focused on victims of gun violence and employed more evidence than the NRA did (11). In another study using tweets, Gupta et al. (2016) use the NPF to study narrative elements and strategies in debates on Twitter over nuclear energy. Furthermore, the NPF has been combined with the theory of Schneider and Ingram (1993) to the study of YouTube videos (e.g., Lybecker et al. 2015). Additional social media outlets such as Facebook and Reddit seem likely candidates for future NPF studies.

Policy Change in the NPF: Policy Narrative Learning

As a public policy theory, the NPF has focused most successfully on understanding how policy processes function according to narrative effects and proliferation at the micro-, meso-, and macrolevels. But what about the policy outcomes that result from these processes? Many policy scholars point to policy learning as a way to understand policy change. Certainly, policy learning has long been argued to play an important role in the policy process (see Radaelli and Dunlop 2013; Hall, 1993; Heclo 1974; Jenkins-Smith and Sabatier 1993; Heikkila and Gerlak 2013). For the NPF, "policy narrative learning" may be a way to begin linking policy processes to policy change.

Policy narrative learning occurs with the adoption of or convergence on a new narrative configuration (e.g., Roe's 1994 reflexivity or Schon and Rein's 1994 frame reflection). For example, one might argue that in the United States, states that have overturned their statutory bans on gay marriage have experienced policy narrative learning as the pro–gay marriage and anti–gay marriage narratives changed from combating each other as villains to sharing a common victim—that of sons, daughters, parents, friends, and relatives. There is at least some evidence that narratives can play a more powerful role influencing individual opinion compared with nonnarrative science statements (e.g., Hinyard and Kreuter 2007; Shanahan et al. 2014), and thus changes in underlying narratives may prompt policy learning (what we call policy narrative learning here) and hence policy change. To emphasize narrative learning as a potential driver of policy change we have removed the phrase "policy change and policy outcomes" from mesolevel H_6 and offer a new NPF hypothesis focusing on policy change:

H_1: *Policy narrative learning*: Sustained reconfigurations of narrative components within dominant policy narratives lead to policy change.

Unpacking and measuring the architecture and process involved with policy narrative learning and reliably linking such learning to policy change are not trivial endeavors.

CONCLUSION: IN THE END, THERE IS A NEW BEGINNING

The NPF seeks to answer questions about the role of policy narratives in the policy process. The NPF offers empirical measures of policy narratives (i.e., narrative elements and narrative strategies), which allows for hypothesis testing and perhaps prediction at some point in the future. Importantly, the NPF does not levy judgment on or seek to uncover the veracity of any specific policy narrative but rather operationalizes policy narratives in an empirical sense—capturing policy realities or what exists in the world as it is presented by people—and attempts to determine the effect.

In the last few years, we have seen a surge of policy process scholars take the lead on several new fronts for the NPF. NPF scholars have tested NPF hypotheses in different policy contexts (e.g., international, across substantive policy areas), critiqued and improved the NPF's theoretical scaffolding, expanded data sources, employed different methodologies, linked levels of analysis, and conveyed practical applications. Such new explorations of the NPF represent an engaged and growing community of scholars working to take aim at the NPF's central research question in innovative ways.

Although the NPF was developed and continues to flourish within the public policy process literature, the NPF is likely to be transportable to questions that cross subdisciplinary boundaries as well. For example, the NPF could be used to tackle some political science questions (e.g., narratives and campaigns; narratives and representation; narratives and institutional identity), some policy analysis questions (e.g., narratives and costs-benefits), and some governance questions (e.g., narratives and legitimacy claims; narratives and public opinion). The potential of the NPF to be applied in other areas of inquiry in policy and political science is ripe for fruitful collaborations and discoveries.

Having been developed over the better part of a decade, the NPF is reaching its teenage years. As such, we expect that we may come upon some disagreements among NPF scholars as we test and retest hypotheses, explore new directions in the science of the NPF, and investigate the portability of the NPF to other subdisciplines. But, like all scientific endeavors, work on the NPF is iterative; we must be patient. And, above all, we must be clear enough to move forward with the continued development of the NPF.

NOTES

1. Author ordering is the result of high intracoalition policy narrative cohesion. All authors contributed equally.

2. Indeed, the European Commission has a whole website dedicated to the "New Narrative for Europe": http://ec.europa.eu/culture/policy/new-narrative/index_en.htm.

3. Descriptions of NPF assumptions, conceptual definitions, three levels of analysis, and hypotheses also appear in Jones and McBeth (2010), Shanahan, Jones, and McBeth (2011), McBeth, Jones, and Shanahan (2014), Jones, McBeth, and Shanahan (2014), and Shanahan, Jones, and McBeth (2015). In the interest of consistency and clarity, the content across these publications has been kept as similar as possible, and in some cases where precision is essential the text is exactly the same. However, for the same purposes of precision and clarity, this chapter also explicitly updates the NPF and thus represents the most current theorizing of the NPF.

4. Since Jones and McBeth (2010), the NPF has used the terms *postpositivist* and *positivist*. This can be a confusing dichotomy because various contrasts are employed in other social sciences (e.g., Guba and Lincoln 1994 add critical theory and constructivism to the positivist and postpositivist discussion) and even in public policy (e.g., Smith and Larimer 2013 employ a rationalist and postpositivist distinction) to address issues of ontology and epistemology. Although we acknowledge public policy could leverage any number of categorical distinctions for these types of discussions (e.g., Moses and Knutsen's 2012 distinctions of constructivism and naturalism), we slightly amend the NPF's initial "positivist" nomenclature to "more positivist-oriented," as Sabatier (2000, 137) himself claimed that the ACF was not classically positivist, acknowledging the "normative elements" in policy processes. For a detailed discussion of the NPF's ontological and epistemological orientation, please see Jones and Radaelli (2015).

5. For a detailed account of the history of the NPF, see McBeth, Jones, and Shanahan (2014) in *Theories of the Policy Process*, 3rd edition, pp. 226–227 and McBeth (2014) in *The Science of Stories*, pp. xiii–xviii.

6. There has been some confusion on how the NPF invokes the term *structuralist*. By *structuralist*, we are referring to the structural approach to literary studies and *not* the structural approach depicted in classic social science discussions of structure and agency. See Jones and McBeth (2010), pp. 331–333 for a discussion of structuralism's relationship with the NPF.

7. Note that the NPF originally conceived of causal mechanisms as a narrative element (i.e., Shanahan, Jones, and McBeth 2011 and Shanahan et al. 2013) but later reclassified causal mechanisms as a narrative strategy (Shanahan et al. 2014).

8. Previous mesolevel NPF theorizing exclusively employed *coalitions* as the unit of analysis. It is important to note that we now intentionally account for a wider variety of ways in which policy actors organize at the mesolevel. Thus, our reference to *policy actors* is intended to represent these various organizational configurations in the agora.

9. The use of the term *framing* demonstrates that in the early formative years of the NPF, the researchers were not yet fully cognizant of the differences between framing and policy narratives. Several reviewers over the years have also questioned whether policy narratives and policy framing were different. We argue that they are, but we also realize that internal inconsistencies within the NPF might have contributed to this misunderstanding.

REFERENCES

Abell, Peter. 2004. "Narrative Explanation: An Alternative to Variable Centered Explanation?" *Annual Review of Sociology* 30:287–310. doi:10.1146/annurev.soc.29.010202 .100113

Berinsky, Adam J., and Donald R. Kinder. 2006. "Making Sense of Issues through Media Frames: Understanding the Kosovo Crisis." *Journal of Politics* 68 (3): 640–656.

Bernstein, Mary, and Verta Taylor. 2013. "Identity Politics." In *The Wiley-Blackwell Encyclopedia of Social and Political Movements,* edited by David A. Snow, Donatella della Porta, Bert Klandermans, and Doug McAdam, 1–4. Hoboken, NJ: Blackwell Publishing. doi:10.1002/9780470674871.wbespm104.

Brock, Timothy C., Jeffrey J. Strange, and Melanie C. Green. 2002. "Power Beyond Reckoning: An Introduction to Narrative Impact." In *Narrative Impact: Social and Cognitive Foundations,* edited by Melanie C. Green, Jeffrey J. Strange, and Timothy C. Brock, 1–15. Mahwah, NJ: Lawrence Erlbaum.

Choi, Junghwa. 2016. "Conduit or Contributor? The Role of Media in the California End-of-Life Option Act Policy Process." Master's thesis, Oregon State University, Corvallis.

Clemons, Randall S., and Mark K. McBeth. 2001. *Public Policy Praxis: Theory and Pragmatism: A Case Approach.* Englewood Cliffs, NJ: Prentice Hall.

Clemons, Randy S., Mark K. McBeth, and Elizabeth Kusko. 2012. "Understanding the Role of Policy Narratives and the Public Policy Arena: Obesity as a Lesson in Public Policy Development." *World Medical and Health Policy* 4 (2): 1–26. doi:10.1515/1948-4682.1220.

Cook, Brian J. 2014. *Bureaucracy and Self-Government: Reconsidering the Role of Public Administration in American Politics.* 2nd ed. Baltimore: John Hopkins University Press.

Crow, Deserai. 2012. "The Narrative Policy Framework: Broadening the Framework for Increased Relevance." Paper presented at the 2012 Midwest Political Science Association meetings, Chicago, April 12–15.

Crow, Deserai A., and John Berggren. 2014. "Using the Narrative Policy Framework to Understand Stakeholder Strategy and Effectiveness: A Multi-Case Analysis." In *The Science of Stories: Applications of the Narrative Policy Framework,* edited by Michael D. Jones, Elizabeth A. Shanahan, and Mark K. McBeth, 131–156. New York: Palgrave Macmillan.

Crow, Deserai A., John Berggren, Lydia A. Lawhon, Elizabeth A. Koebele, Adrianne Kroepsch, and Juhi Huda. 2016. "Local Media Coverage of Wildfire Disasters: An Analysis of Problems and Solutions in Policy Narratives." *Environment and Planning C: Government and Policy* (September): 1–23. doi:10.1177/0263774X16667302.

Crow, Deserai A., and Andrea Lawlor. 2016. "Media in the Policy Process: Using Framing and Narratives to Understand Policy Influences." *Review of Policy Research* 33 (5): 472–491. doi:10.1111/ropr.12187.

Danforth, Scot. 2016. "Social Justice and Technocracy: Tracing the Narratives of Inclusive Education in the USA." *Discourse: Studies in the Cultural Politics of Education* 37 (4): 582–599. doi:10.1080/01596306.2015.1073022.

Delahais, Thomas, and Jacques Toulemonde. 2012. "Applying Contribution Analysis: Lessons from Five Years of Practice." *Evaluation* 18 (3): 281–293. doi:10.1177/1356389012450810.

Ertas, Nevbahar. 2015. "Policy Narratives and Public Opinion Concerning Charter Schools." *Politics & Policy* 43 (3): 426–451. doi:10.1111/polp.12120.

Escalas, Judy E. 2004. "Imaging Yourself in the Product: Mental Simulation, Narrative Transportation, and Persuasion." *Journal of Advertising* 33 (2): 37–48. doi:10.1080/00913367.2004.10639163.

Exadaktylos, Theofanis, and Claudio M. Radaelli, eds. 2012. *Research Design in European Studies*. Basingstoke, UK: Palgrave Macmillan.

Fischer, Frank. 2003. *Reframing Public Policy: Discursive Politics and Deliberative Practices*. Oxford: Oxford University Press.

Fitzgerald, John L. 2013. "Supervised Injecting Facilities: A Case Study of Contrasting Narratives in a Contested Health Policy Arena." *Critical Public Health* 23 (1): 77–94. doi:10.1080/09581596.2012.735360.

Gray, Gary, and Michael D. Jones. 2016. "A Qualitative Narrative Policy Framework? Examining the Policy Narratives of US Campaign Finance Reform." *Public Policy and Administration* 31 (3): 193–220. doi:10.1177/0952076715623356.

Green, Melanie C., and Timothy C. Brock. 2005. "Persuasiveness of Narratives." In *Persuasion: Psychological Insights and Perspectives,* 2nd ed., edited by Timothy C. Brock and Melanie C. Green, 117–142. London: Sage Publications.

Guba, Egon G., and Yvonna S. Lincoln.1994. "Competing Paradigms in Qualitative Research." In *Handbook of Qualitative Research,* edited by Norman K. Denzin and Yvonna S. Lincoln, 105–117. Thousand Oaks, CA: Sage Publications.

Gupta, Kuhika. 2012. "Comparing Public Policy: Using the Comparative Method to Advance Our Understanding of the Policy Process." *Policy Studies Journal* 40 (1): 11–26. doi:10.1111/j.1541-0072.2012.00443.x.

Gupta, Kuhika, Joseph T. Ripberger, and Savannah Collins. 2014. "The Strategic Use of Policy Narratives: Jaitapur and the Politics of Siting a Nuclear Power Plant in India." In *The Science of Stories: Applications of the Narrative Policy Framework,* edited by Michael D. Jones, Elizabeth A. Shanahan, and Mark K. McBeth, 89–106. New York: Palgrave Macmillan.

Gupta, Kuhika, Joseph T. Ripberger, and Wesley Wehde. 2016. "Advocacy Group Messaging on Social Media: Using the Narrative Policy Framework to Study Twitter Messages about Nuclear Energy Policy in the United States." *Policy Studies Journal.* Published electronically August 20, 2016. doi:10.1111/psj.12176.

Hall, Peter A. 1993. "Policy Paradigms, Social Learning, and the State: The Case of Economic Policymaking in Britain." *Comparative Politics* 25 (3): 275–296.

Heclo, Hugh. 1974. *Modern Social Politics in Britain and Sweden: From Relief to Income Maintenance.* New Haven, CT: Yale University Press.

Heikkila, Tanya, and Andrea K. Gerlak. 2013. "Building a Conceptual Approach to Collective Learning: Lessons for Public Policy Scholars." *Policy Studies Journal* 41 (3): 484–512. doi:10.1111/psj.12026.

Heikkila, Tanya, Jonathan J. Pierce, Samuel Gallaher, Jennifer Kagan, Deserai A. Crow, and Christopher M. Weible. 2014. "Understanding a Period of Policy Change: The Case of Hydraulic Fracturing Disclosure Policy in Colorado." *Review of Policy Research* 31 (2): 65–87. doi:10.1111/ropr.12058.

Herman, David. 2002. *Story Logic: Problems and Possibilities of Narrative.* Lincoln: University of Nebraska Press.

———. 2003. "Stories as a Tool for Thinking." In *Narrative Theory and the Cognitive Sciences,* edited by David Herman, 163–192. Stanford, CA: CSLI Publications.

Hinyard, Leslie J., and Matthew W. Kreuter. 2007. "Using Narrative Communication as a Tool for Health Behavior Change: A Conceptual, Theoretical, and Empirical Overview." *Health Education and Behavior* 34 (5): 777–792. doi:10.1177/1090198106291963.

Husmann, Maria A. 2015. "Social Constructions of Obesity Target Population: An Empirical Look at Obesity Policy Narratives." *Policy Sciences* 48 (4): 415–442.

Iyengar, Shanto. 1990. "Framing Responsibility for Political Issues: The Case of Poverty." *Political Behavior* 12(1): 19–40.

Iyengar, Shanto, and Adam Simon. 1997. "News Coverage of the Gulf Crisis and Public Opinion: A Study of Agenda Setting, Priming, and Framing." In *Do the Media Govern? Politicians, Voters, and Reporters in America,* edited by Shanto Iyengar and Richard Reeves, 248–257. Thousand Oakes, CA: Sage Publications.

Jenkins-Smith, Hank C., and Paul A. Sabatier. 1993. "The Dynamics of Policy Oriented Learning." In *Policy Change and Learning: An Advocacy Coalition Approach,* edited by Paul A. Sabatier and Hank C. Jenkins-Smith, 41–56. Boulder, CO: Westview Press.

Jenkins-Smith, Hank C., Gilbert K. St. Clair, and Brian Woods. 1991. "Explaining Change in Policy Subsystems: Analysis of Coalition Stability and Defection over Time." *American Journal of Political Science* 35 (4): 851–880.

Jones, Bryan D. 2001. *Politics and the Architecture of Choice: Bounded Rationality and Governance.* Chicago: University of Chicago Press.

Jones, Michael D. 2010. *Heroes and Villains: Cultural Narratives, Mass Opinion, and Climate Change.* PhD diss., Harvard University, Cambridge, MA, http://works.bepress.com/mjones/6/.

———. 2014a. "Communicating Climate Change: Are Stories Better than 'Just the Facts'?" *Policy Studies Journal* 42 (4): 644–673. doi:10.1111/psj.12072.

———. 2014b. "Cultural Characters and Climate Change: How Heroes Shape Our Perceptions of Climate Science." *Social Science Quarterly* 95 (1): 1–39. doi:10.111/ssqu.12043.

Jones, Michael D., Kjersti Fløttum, and Øyvind Gjerstad. 2017. "Stories about Climate Change: The Influence of Language on Public Opinion." In *The Role of Language in the Climate Change Debate*, edited by Kjersti Fløttum, 49–68. New York: Routledge.

Jones, Michael D., and Hank Jenkins-Smith. 2009. "Trans-Subsystem Dynamics, Policy Topography, Mass Opinion, and Policy Change." *Policy Studies Journal* 37 (1): 37–58. doi:10.1111/j.1541-0072.2008.00294.x.

Jones, Michael D., and Mark K. McBeth. 2010. "A Narrative Policy Framework: Clear Enough to Be Wrong?" *Policy Studies Journal* 38 (2): 329–353. doi:10.1111/j.1541-0072 .2010.00364.x.

Jones, Michael D., Mark K. McBeth, and Elizabeth A. Shanahan. 2014. "Introducing the Narrative Policy Framework." In *The Science of Stories: Applications of the Narrative Policy Framework*, edited by Michael D. Jones, Elizabeth A. Shanahan, and Mark K. McBeth, 1–25. New York: Palgrave Macmillan.

Jones, Michael D., and Claudio M. Radaelli. 2015. "The Narrative Policy Framework: Child or Monster?" *Critical Policy Studies* 9 (3): 339–355. doi:10.1080/19460171.20 15.1053959.

Jones, Michael D., and Geoboo Song. 2014. "Making Sense of Climate Change: How Story Frames Shape Cognition." *Political Psychology* 35 (4): 447–595. doi:10.1111/pops .12057.

Jorgensen, Paul, Geoboo Song, and Michael D. Jones. 2017. "Public Support for Campaign Finance Reform: The Role of Policy Narratives, Cultural Predispositions, and Political Knowledge in Collective Policy Preference Formation." *Social Science Quarterly*.

Kahan, Dan M., and Donald Braman. 2006. "Cultural Cognition and Public Policy." *Yale Law & Policy Review* 24:147–170.

Kahan, Dan M., Donald Braman, John Gastil, Paul Slovic, and C. K. Mertz. 2007. "Culture and Identity-Protective Cognition: Explaining the White-Male Effect in Risk Perception." *Journal of Empirical Legal Studies* 4 (3): 465–505.

Kahneman, Daniel. 2011. *Thinking Fast and Slow*. New York: Farrar, Straus and Giroux.

Kamkhaji, Jonathan C., and Claudio M. Radaelli. 2016. "Crisis, Learning and Policy Change in the European Union." *Journal of European Public Policy*, 1–21. Published electronically April 20, 2016. doi:10.1080/13501763.2016.1164744.

Kingdon, John W. 2003. *Agendas, Alternatives, and Public Policies*. 2nd ed. New York: Longman.

Kunda, Ziva. 1990. "The Case for Motivated Reasoning." *Psychological Bulletin* 108 (3): 480–498.

Kurzban, Robert. 2010. *Why Everyone (Else) Is a Hypocrite: Evolution and the Modular Mind*. Princeton, NJ: Princeton University Press.

Kusko, Elizabeth. 2013. "Policy Narratives, Religious Politics, and the Salvadoran Civil War: The Implications of Narrative Framing on U.S. Foreign Policy in Central America." PhD diss., Department of Political Science, Idaho State University, Pocatello.

Lakoff, George. 2002. *Moral Politics: How Liberals and Conservatives Think.* Chicago: University of Chicago Press.

Lasswell, Harold. 1990. *Politics: Who Gets What, When, How.* Gloucester, MA: Peter Smith. First published 1936 by McGraw-Hill.

Lawton, Ricky N., and Murray A. Rudd. 2014. "A Narrative Policy Approach to Environmental Conservation." *AMBIO* 43:849–857. doi:10.1007/s13280-014-0497-8.

Leong, Ching. 2015. "Persistently Biased: The Devil Shift in Water Privatization in Jakarta." *Review of Policy Research* 32 (5): 600–621. doi:10.111/ropr.12138.

Lichbach, Mark Irving, and Alan S. Zuckerman, eds. 2009. *Comparative Politics: Rationality, Culture, and Structure.* New York: Cambridge University Press.

Lodge, Milton, and Charles S. Taber. 2005. "The Automaticity of Affect for Political Leaders, Groups, and Issues: An Experimental Test of the Hot Cognition Hypothesis." *Political Psychology* 26 (3):455–482. doi:10.1111/j.1467-9221.2005.00426.x.

———. 2007. "The Rationalizing Voter: Unconscious Thought in Political Information Processing." December 21, 2007. doi:http://dx.doi.org/10.2139/ssrn.1077972.

Lukes, Steven. 1974. *Power: A Radical View.* London: Macmillan.

———. 2005. *Power: A Radical View.* 2nd ed. New York: Palgrave Macmillan.

Lybecker, Donna L., Mark K. McBeth, Maria A. Husmann, and Nicholas Pelikan. 2015. "Do New Media Support New Policy Narratives? The Social Construction of the US–Mexico Border on YouTube." *Policy & Internet* 7 (4): 497–525. doi:10.1002/poi3.94.

Lybecker, Donna L., Mark K. McBeth, and Elizabeth Kusko. 2013. "Trash or Treasure: Recycling Narratives and Reducing Political Polarization." *Environmental Politics* 22 (2): 312–332. doi:10.1080/09644016.2012.692935.

Lybecker, Donna L., Mark K. McBeth, and James W. Stoutenborough. 2016. "Do We Understand What the Public Hears? Stakeholders' Preferred Communication Choices for Decision Makers When Discussing River Issues with the Public." *Review of Policy Research* 33 (4): 376–392. doi:10.1111/ropr.12182.

Lyotard, Jean-Francois. 1984. *The Postmodern Condition: A Report on Knowledge.* Translated by Geoff Bennington and Brian Massouri. Minneapolis: University of Minnesota Press.

Mattila, Anna S. 2000. "The Role of Narratives in the Advertising of Experiential Services." *Journal of Service Research* 3 (1): 35–45. doi:10.1177/109467050031003.

May, Peter J., and Ashley E. Jochim. 2013. "Policy Regime Perspectives: Policies, Politics, and Governing." *Policy Studies Journal* 41 (3): 426–452. doi:10.1111/psj.12024.

McBeth, Mark K. 2014. "Preface: The Portneuf School of Narrative." In *The Science of Stories: Applications of the Narrative Policy Framework,* edited by Michael D. Jones, Elizabeth A. Shanahan, and Mark K. McBeth, xiii–xviii. New York: Palgrave Macmillan.

McBeth, Mark K., Randy S. Clemons, Maria A. Husmann, Elizabeth Kusko, and Alethea Gaarden. 2013. "The Social Construction of a Crisis: Policy Narratives and

Contemporary U.S. Obesity Policy." *Risk, Hazards, and Crisis in Public Policy* 4 (3): 135–163. doi:10.1002/rhc3.12042.

McBeth, Mark K., Michael D. Jones, and Elizabeth A. Shanahan. 2014. "The Narrative Policy Framework." In *The Theories of the Policy Process*, 3rd ed., edited by Paul A. Sabatier and Christopher M. Weible, 225–266. Boulder, CO: Westview Press.

McBeth, Mark K., Donna L. Lybecker, and Kacee A. Garner. 2010. "The Story of Good Citizenship: Framing Public Policy in the Context of Duty-Based versus Engaged Citizenship." *Politics & Policy* 38 (1): 1–23. doi:10.1111/j.1747-1346.2009.00226.x.

McBeth, Mark K., Donna L. Lybecker, and Maria Husmann. 2014. "The Narrative Policy Framework and the Practitioner: Communicating Recycling Policy." In *The Science of Stories: Applications of the Narrative Policy Framework,* edited by Michael D. Jones, Elizabeth A. Shanahan, and Mark K. McBeth, 45–68. New York: Palgrave Macmillan.

McBeth, Mark K., Donna L. Lybecker, and James W. Stoutenborough. 2016. "Do Stakeholders Analyze Their Audience: The Communication Switch and Stakeholder Personal versus Public Communication Choices." *Policy Sciences,* 1–24. Published electronically May 19, 2016. doi:10.1007/s11077-016-9252-2.

McBeth, Mark K., and Elizabeth A. Shanahan. 2004. "Public Opinion for Sale: The Role of Policy Marketers in Greater Yellowstone Policy Conflict." *Policy Sciences* 37 (3): 319–338. doi:10.1007/s11077-005-8876-4.

McBeth, Mark K., Elizabeth A. Shanahan, Molly Anderson, and Barbara Rose. 2012. "Policy Story or Gory Story? Narrative Policy Framework, YouTube, and Indirect Lobbying in Greater Yellowstone." *Policy & Internet* 4 (3–4): 159–183. doi:10.1002/poi 3.15.

McBeth, Mark K., Elizabeth A. Shanahan, Ruth J. Arnell, and Paul L. Hathaway. 2007. "The Intersection of Narrative Policy Analysis and Policy Change Theory." *Policy Studies Journal* 35 (1): 87–108. doi:10.1111/j.1541-0072.2007.00208.x.

McBeth, Mark K., Elizabeth A. Shanahan, and Michael D. Jones. 2005. "The Science of Storytelling: Measuring Policy Beliefs in Greater Yellowstone." *Society and Natural Resources* 18 (May/June): 413–429. doi:10.1080/08941920590924765.

McBeth, Mark K., Elizabeth A. Shanahan, Linda E. Tigert, Paul L. Hathaway, and Lynette J. Sampson. 2010. "Buffalo Tales: Interest Group Policy Stories in Greater Yellowstone." *Policy Sciences* 43 (4): 391–409. doi:10.1007/s11077-010-9114-2.

Merry, Melissa K. 2015. "Constructing Policy Narratives in 140 Characters or Less: The Case of Gun Policy Organizations." *Policy Studies Journal* 44 (4): 373–395. doi:10.1111/psj.12142.

———. 2016. "Making Friends and Enemies on Social Media: The Case of Gun Policy Organizations." *Online Information Review* 40 (5): 624–642. doi:10.1108/OIR-10 -2015-0333.

Morris, James P., Nancy K. Squires, Charles S. Taber, and Milton Lodge. 2003. "Activation of Political Attitudes: A Psychophysiological Examination of the Hot Cognition Hypothesis." *Political Psychology* 24 (4): 727–745. doi:10.1046/j.1467-9221.2003 .00349.x.

Moses, Jonathon, and Torbjørn Knutsen. 2012. *Ways of Knowing: Competing Methodologies in Social and Political Research,* 2nd ed. New York: Palgrave Macmillan.

Ney, Steven. 2006. *Messy Issues, Policy Conflict and the Differentiated Polity: Analysing Contemporary Policy Responses to Complex, Uncertain and Transversal Policy Problems.* PhD diss., LOS Center for Bergen, Vienna.

———. 2014. "The Governance of Social Innovation: Connecting Mesi and Macros Levels of Analysis." In *The Science of Stories: Applications of the Narrative Policy Framework in Public Policy Analysis,* edited by Michael D. Jones, Elizabeth A. Shanahan, and Mark K. McBeth, 207–234. New York: Palgrave Macmillan.

Ney, Steven, and Michael Thompson. 2000. "Cultural Discourses in the Global Climate Change Debate." *Society, Behaviour, and Climate Change Mitigation* 8:65–92.

Niederdeppe, Jeff, Sungjong Roh, and Michael A. Shapiro. 2015. "Acknowledging Individual Responsibility While Emphasizing Social Determinants in Narratives to Promote Obesity-Reducing Public Policy: A Randomized Experiment." *PLOS ONE* 10 (2): e0117565. doi:10.1371/journal.pone.0117565.

O'Bryan, Tom, Claire A. Dunlop, and Claudio M. Radaelli. 2014. "Narrating the 'Arab Spring': Where Expertise Meets Heuristics in Legislative Hearings." In *The Science of Stories: Applications of the Narrative Policy Framework in Public Policy Analysis,* edited by Michael D. Jones, Elizabeth A. Shanahan, and Mark K. McBeth, 107–129. New York: Palgrave Macmillan.

Orvis, Stephen, and Carol Ann Drogus. 2014. *Introducing Comparative Politics: Concepts and Cases in Context.* 3rd ed. Thousand Oaks, CA: Sage Publications.

Ostrom, Elinor. 1999. "Institutional Rational Choice: An Assessment of the Institutional Analysis and Development Framework." In *Theories of the Policy Process,* edited by Paul A. Sabatier, 35–71. Boulder, CO: Westview Press.

Peltomaa, Juha, Mikael Hilden, and Suvi Huttunen 2016. "Translating Institutional Change—Forest Journals as Diverse Policy Actors." *Forest Policy and Economics* 70:172–180. doi:10.1016./j.forpol.2016.06.029.

Peterson, Holly P., and Michael D. Jones. 2016. "Making Sense of Complexity: The NPF and Agenda Setting." In *Handbook of Public Policy Agenda-Setting,* edited by Nikolaos Zahariadis, 106–131. Northampton, MA: Edward Elgar.

Pew-MacArthur Results First Initiative. 2014. *Evidence-Based Policymaking: A Guide for Effective Government.* Washington, DC: Pew Charitable Trusts and the John D. and Catherine T. MacArthur Foundation. http://www.pewtrusts.org/~/media/assets /2014/11/evidencebasedpolicymakingaguideforeffectivegovernment.pdf.

Polkinghorne, Donald. 1988. *Narrative Knowing and the Human Sciences.* Albany: SUNY Press.

Pralle, Sarah B. 2006. *Branching Out Digging In: Environmental Advocacy and Agenda Setting.* Washington, DC: Georgetown Press.

Radaelli, Claudio M., Claire A. Dunlop, and Oliver Fritsch. 2013. "Narrating Impact Assessment in the European Union." *European Political Science* 12: 500–521. doi:10.1057/eps.2013.26.

Redlawsk, David P. 2002. "Hot Cognition or Cool Consideration? Testing the Effects of Motivated Reasoning on Political Decision Making." *Journal of Politics* 64 (4): 1021–1044. doi:10.1111/1468-2508.00161.

Riker, William H. 1986. *The Art of Political Manipulation*. New Haven, CT: Yale University Press.

Roe, Emery. 1994. *Narrative Policy Analysis: Theory and Practice*. Durham, NC: Duke University Press.

———. 2000. "Clear Enough to Be Wrong." *Journal of European Public Policy* 7 (1): 135–140. doi:10.1080/135017600343304.

Rosenau, Joshua. 2012. "Science Denial: A Guide for Scientists." *Trends in Microbiology* 20 (12): 567–569. doi:10.1016/j.tim.2012.10.002.

Sabatier, Paul A., Susan Hunter, and Susan McLaughlin. 1987. "The Devil Shift: Perceptions and Misperceptions of Opponents." *Western Political Quarterly* 41:449–476.

Sabatier, Paul A., and Hank C. Jenkins-Smith, eds. 1993. *Policy Change and Learning: An Advocacy Coalition Approach*. Boulder, CO: Westview Press.

———. 1999. "The Advocacy Coalition Framework: An Assessment." In *Theories of the Policy Process*, edited by Paul A. Sabatier, 117–166. Boulder, CO: Westview Press.

Sabatier, Paul A., and Christopher M. Weible. 2007. "The Advocacy Coalition Framework: Innovations and Clarifications." In *Theories of the Policy Process*, 2nd ed., edited by Paul A. Sabatier, 189–220. Boulder, CO: Westview Press.

Schattschneider, E. E. 1960. *The Semi-Sovereign People*. New York: Holt, Rinehart and Winston.

Schlager, Edella. 1999. "A Comparison of Frameworks, Theories, and Models of Policy Processes." In *Theories of the Policy Process*, edited by Paul A. Sabatier, 233–260. Boulder, CO: Westview Press.

———. 2007. "A Comparison of Frameworks, Theories, and Models of Policy Processes." In *Theories of the Policy Process*, edited by Paul A. Sabatier, 293–320. Boulder, CO: Westview Press.

Schlaufer, Caroline. 2016. "The Narrative Uses of Evidence." *Policy Studies Journal*. Published electronically August 20, 2016. doi:10.1111/psj.12174.

Schneider, Anne Larason, and Helen Ingram. 1993. "Social Construction of Target Populations: Implications for Politics and Policy." *American Political Science Review* 87 (2): 334–347.

Schon, Donald, and Martin Rein. 1994. *Frame Reflection: Toward the Resolution of Intractable Policy Controversies*. New York: Basic Books.

Scott, W. Richard. 1995. *Institutions and Organizations*. Thousand Oaks, CA: Sage Publications.

———. 2008. *Institutions and Organizations: Ideas and Interests*. Thousand Oaks, CA: Sage Publications.

Shanahan, Elizabeth A., Stephanie M. Adams, Michael D. Jones, and Mark K. McBeth. 2014. "The Blame Game: Narrative Persuasiveness of Intentional Causal Mechanism." In *The Science of Stories: Applications of the Narrative Policy Framework in Public Policy Analysis,* edited by Michael D. Jones, Elizabeth A. Shanahan, and Mark K. McBeth, 69–88. New York: Palgrave Macmillan.

Shanahan, Elizabeth A., Michael D. Jones, and Mark K. McBeth. 2011. "Policy Narratives and Policy Processes." *Policy Studies Journal* 39 (3): 535–561. doi:10.1111/j.1541-0072.2011.00420.x.

———. 2015. "Narrative Policy Framework." In *The Encyclopedia of Public Administration and Public Policy,* 3rd ed., edited by Melvin Dubnick and Domonic Bearfield. New York: Taylor and Francis. doi:10.1081/E-EPAP3-120053656.

Shanahan, Elizabeth A., Michael D. Jones, Mark K. McBeth, and Ross R. Lane. 2013. "An Angel on the Wind: How Heroic Policy Narratives Shape Policy Realities." *Policy Studies Journal* 41 (3): 453–483. doi:10.1111/psj.12025.

Shanahan, Elizabeth A., Mark K. McBeth, Ruth J. Arnell, and Paul L. Hathaway. 2008. "Conduit or Contributor? The Role of Media in Policy Change Theory." *Policy Sciences* 41 (2): 115–138. doi:10.1007/s11077-008-9058-y.

Shanahan, Elizabeth A., Mark K. McBeth, and Paul L. Hathaway. 2011. "Narrative Policy Framework: The Influence of Media Policy Narratives on Public Opinion." *Politics & Policy* 39 (3): 373–400. doi:10.1111/j.1747-1346.2011.00295.x.

Shenhav, Shaul R. 2015. *Analyzing Social Narratives.* New York: Routledge.

Simon, Herbert A. 1947. *Administrative Behavior: A Study of Decision-Making Processes in Administrative Organization.* New York: Macmillan.

Smith, Kevin B., and Christopher W. Larimer. 2013. *The Public Policy Theory Primer.* 2nd ed. Boulder, CO: Westview Press.

———. 2015. *The Public Policy Theory Primer.* 3rd ed. Boulder, CO: Westview Press.

Smith-Walter, Aaron, Holly Peterson, Michael D. Jones, and Ashley Reynolds. 2016. "Gun Stories: How Evidence Shapes Firearm Policy in the United States." *Politics & Policy.* Published electronically December 18, 2016. doi:10.1111/polp.12187.

Somers, Margaret R. 1992. "Narrativity, Narrative Identity, and Social Action: Rethinking English Working-Class Formation." *Social Science History* 16 (4): 591–630. doi:10.1017/S0145553200016679.

Stone, Deborah. 2012. *Policy Paradox: The Art of Political Decision Making.* New York: W. W. Norton.

Stroud, Natalie Jomini. 2008. "Media Use and Political Predispositions: Revisiting the Concept of Selective Exposure." *Political Behavior* 30:341–366.

Taber, Charles S., and Martin Lodge. 2006. "Motivated Skepticism in the Evaluation of Political Beliefs." *American Journal of Political Science* 50 (3): 755–769.

Thompson, Michael, Richard Ellis, and Aaron Wildavsky. 1990. *Cultural Theory.* Boulder, CO: Westview Press.

van den Hende, Ellis A., Darren W. Dahl, Jan P. L. Schoormans, and Dirk Snelders. 2012. "Narrative Transportation in Concept Tests for Really New Products: The Moderating Effect of Reader-Protagonist Similarity Narrative Transportation in Concept Tests for Really New Products: The Moderating Effect of Reader-Protagonist Similarity." *Journal of Product Innovation Management* 29:157–170. doi:10.1111/j.1540-5885.2012.00961.x.

Verweij, Marco, Mary Douglas, Richard Ellis, Christoph Engel, Frank Hendriks, Susanne Lohmann, Steven Ney, Steve Rayner, and Michael Thompson. 2006. "Clumsy Solutions for Complex World: The Case of Climate Change." *Public Administration* 84 (4): 817–843. doi:10.1111/j.1540-8159.2005.09566.x-i1.

Veselkova, Marcela, and Miroslave Beblavy. 2014. "From Selectivity to Universalism: How Macro-Level Policy Narratives." Paper presented at the ECPR General Conference, Glasgow, September 3–6. http://ecpr.eu/Filestore/PaperProposal/a45e317e -3cfa-4d36-97d7-5a9d4b648cc1.pdf.

von Bertalanffy, Ludwig. 1968. *General System Theory: Essays on Its Foundation and Development.* Rev. ed. New York: George Braziller.

Weible, Christopher M., Kristin L. Olofsson, Daniel P. Costie, Juniper M. Katz, and Tanya Heikkila. 2016. "Enhancing Precision and Clarity in the Study of Policy Narratives: An Analysis of Climate and Air Issues in Delhi, India." *Review of Policy Research* 33 (4): 420–441. doi:10.1111/ropr.12181.

Weible, Christopher M., Paul A. Sabatier, and Kelly McQueen. 2009. "Themes and Variations: Taking Stock of the Advocacy Coalition Framework." *Policy Studies Journal* 37 (1): 121–140. doi:10.1111/j.1541-0072.2008.00299.x.

Weymouth, Lally. 2016. "Renzi: 'Today We Have the Europe of Austerity. We Need the Europe of Hope.'" Opinion section, *Washington Post.* September 22. https://www .washingtonpost.com/opinions/global-opinions/renzi-today-we-have-the-europe -of-austerity-we-need-the-europe-of-hope/2016/09/22/ec73028a-80dc-11e6-a52d -9a865a0ed0d4_story.html?utm_term=.b263625136d5.

6

The IAD Framework and the SES Framework: An Introduction and Assessment of the Ostrom Workshop Frameworks

EDELLA SCHLAGER AND MICHAEL COX[1]

The Institutional Analysis and Development (IAD) framework is conceptually simple, but theoretically rich. Conceptually, it consists of seven components—an action situation, actors, rules (in use), community attributes, physical and material attributes, outcomes—and evaluative criteria. It is most useful in developing theories and models that seek to explain the "logic, design and performance of institutional arrangements" (Ostrom 2014, 269). Theories most compatible with the framework are those that seek to explain how actors' behavior is guided and constrained by institutions and how, in turn, human behavior shapes and forms institutional arrangements. Besides the theories that were intentionally developed using the framework, local public economies, and common pool resources, it is compatible with others, such as covenantal theory (Lutz 1988; Allen 2005), federalism theory (Ostrom 1987, 1997, 2008; Bednar 2009), transactions cost theory (Williamson 1985), and game theory, among others. Compatibility means that these theories use variables representing different dimensions of the seven components making up the framework to explain the interactions between institutional arrangements and human behavior.

More recently, Elinor Ostrom developed a second, related framework, the Social-Ecological Systems (SES) framework, that consists of the seven objects, plus others, but that rests on a diagnostic logic. The diagnostic logic, because it focuses on identifying more limited sets of variables that account for an outcome, tends to highlight the important role of models in theory development, although its full potential to do so has barely been tapped. Furthermore, the role of institutional arrangements is not as prominent in the SES framework as it is in the IAD; rather, the SES emphasizes the interactions between actors and ecological systems (as mediated by governing arrangements).

In this chapter, we describe the frameworks and how they support the development of theories and models through scientific inquiry. We also compare the two frameworks, how they are similar, but different, and why that matters. Finally, we examine how they have been used for social science research before concluding with assessments and future developments of the frameworks.

FRAMEWORKS AND THEORIES

"A framework provides a shared orientation for studying, explaining, and understanding phenomena of interest" (Ostrom 2014, 269). A shared orientation occurs through the major categories of concepts that capture key variables and aspects of the dimension of the world under study. Having a shared set of concepts and variables allows scholars to develop a common language and common metrics, which in turn supports communication among scholars and the cumulation of knowledge. "In the case of the institutional analysis and development (IAD) framework, useful knowledge consists of understanding the logic, design, and performance of institutional arrangements in a wide variety of settings and at different scales" (Ostrom 2014, 269).

A framework is distinct from a theory, even though the two terms are often used interchangeably, as the astute reader of this volume will readily note. In contrast to a framework, a "theory consists of many variables and the relations among them that are used to explain and predict processes and outcomes" (Ostrom 2014, 269). For instance, common pool resource theories, which endeavor to explain how actors overcome diverse collective action dilemmas in order to sustainably govern shared resources, is the best known of the theories emerging directly from the IAD framework (Ostrom 1990). One of the more well-known common pool resource theories is Elinor Ostrom's design principles for long-enduring, self-governing arrangements (Ostrom 1990). The original eight design principles focus on institutional arrangements, including: (1) well-defined boundaries of the resource and resource users; (2) congruence between appropriation and provision rules and local conditions; (3) most individuals affected by operational rules can participate in modifying the operational rules; (4) monitors who are accountable to the appropriators; (5) use of graduated sanctions; (6) low-cost conflict resolution mechanisms; (7) minimal recognition of rights to organize; and (8) nested enterprises (Ostrom 1990, 90). The design principles identify institutional variables that interact to support long-enduring governance by users of common pool resources (CPRs). Considerable scholarly work generally provides support for the design principles (Poteete, Janssen, and Ostrom 2010; Cox, Arnold, and Villamayor-Tomas

2010), with recent work examining whether different types of common pool resources exhibit different patterns of design principles (Baggio et al. 2016).

Whereas framework and theory are distinct concepts, they closely interact. Frameworks provide structure for theories by identifying the key concepts and variables that scholars draw on. Scholars do not have to invent or reinvent concepts and variables, nor do they always have to invent or reinvent how the concepts and variables are operationalized and measured. Instead, they can draw from and contribute to the body of work developed around the framework. In turn, as theories are developed and tested, and as variables are developed or refined, they may be fed back into the framework. The IAD framework emerged from such a process. In 1971, Vincent and Elinor Ostrom published an article in *Public Administration Review* in which they sketched out an approach for studying governing arrangements in which they identify decision makers, "the world of events," "decision making arrangements," and evaluative criteria to be applied to outcomes.

Over the next decade, these foundational pieces of the IAD framework were further developed through empirical research programs, such as the study of the delivery of police services in metropolitan areas (Ostrom 1972, 1975; Ostrom, Whittaker, and Parks 1973; Ostrom and Smith 1976), which culminated in a theory of local public economies (Oakerson 1999). Drawing from this empirical work as well as game theory, Larry Kiser (an economist) and Elinor Ostrom published the IAD framework in 1982. "The Three Worlds of Action: A Metatheoretical Synthesis of Institutional Approaches" (Kiser and Ostrom 1982) represents the initial published attempt to identify the concepts and variables useful for scholars who are interested in how institutions affect the incentives confronting individuals and the individuals' resultant behavior. This first presentation of a more completely developed framework included the decision situation, which later was relabeled the action situation. Institutional arrangements were defined and identified as configurations of rules, and a rule typology was provided. Most importantly, the three worlds of action—operational, collective choice, and constitutional choice—were presented; these are explained in more depth below.

WORKING WITH THE INSTITUTIONAL ANALYSIS AND DEVELOPMENT FRAMEWORK

The IAD framework has a problem-solving orientation. The purpose of the IAD framework is to allow scholars to explore and explain how people use institutional arrangements to address shared problems and to understand the logic of institutional designs (Ostrom 1987). In understanding the how and why of institutional design, it is then possible to develop informed proposals for improving institutional performance. Thus, the starting point in applying the IAD framework is with a collective action problem. As E. Ostrom (1998, 1) stated in her presidential address to the American Political Science Association, "The theory of collective action is the *central* subject of political science." The outcome one actor realizes depends not only on the actor's choices and actions but also on the choices and actions of the other actors in the situation. This interdependence, both in actions and in outcomes, means that for actors to achieve desired outcomes they must take one another into account and cooperate or coordinate their actions and choices. Cooperation and coordination, however, cannot be taken for granted. Rather, individual interests and collective interests often diverge. The tension between individual and group is the core of collective action problems, and institutional arrangements are one tool used to try to align the two.

An Action Situation

The initial step in analyzing a collective action problem is to identify an action situation. An action situation bounds one or more collective action dilemmas. According to Ostrom (2005, 32), action situations are characterized by two or more individuals who face "a set of potential actions that jointly produce outcomes." The action situation is the focal unit of analysis. In most research projects using the IAD framework, multiple action situations are identified and compared. For instance, Tang (1994) identified forty-seven cases of irrigation systems and analyzed water allocation action situations, collective choice action situations, and monitoring action situations. Action situations consist of participants who hold positions and who take actions in light of information they have available to them. Outcomes are a function of individual sequences of

FIGURE 6.1 A Framework for Institutional Analysis

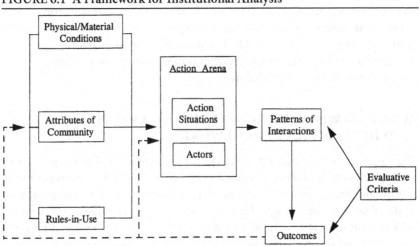

SOURCE: Adapted from E. Ostrom, Gardner, and Walker (1994, 37).

actions and the level of control each actor has over an action or choice. Furthermore, costs and benefits are assigned to actions and outcomes (see Figure 6.1).[2]

To more fully develop an action situation in order to analyze the choices, actions, and outcomes of actors, questions that correspond to the parts of an action situation need to be addressed. These questions (which may form the foundation of a coding instrument) are applied to each action situation studied. The left-hand column of Table 6.1, developed by Elinor Ostrom (2007b, 29–30), provides an illustrative set of questions oriented to studying common pool resources. For a fully developed set of coding forms and code books that guide analysts through the process of identifying action situations and operationalizing the components, see the SES Library (https://seslibrary.asu.edu/). As a conceptual object of a framework, an action situation can be applied to any situation in which the actors are interdependent, whether that is actors harvesting from a fishing ground, actors producing neighborhood security, or actors producing education in a university setting, for example. The action situation is not tied to a specific type of setting.

TABLE 6.1　Questions for Eliciting Information on Components of the Action Situation

Action Situation	Rules-in-Use Structuring an Action Situation
The set of participants: Who and how many individuals withdraw resource units (e.g., fish, water, fodder) from this resource system?	*Entry and exit rules:* Are the appropriators from this resource limited to local residents; one group defined by ethnicity, race, caste, gender, or family structure; those who win a lottery; those who have obtained a permit; those who own required assets (such as a fishing berth or land); or, in some other way, a class of individuals that is bounded? Is a new participant allowed to join a group by some kind of entry fee or initiation? Must an appropriator give up rights to harvest upon migrating to another location?
The positions: What positions exist (e.g., members of an irrigation association, water distributor-guards, and a chair)?	*Position rules:* How does someone move from being just a "member" of a group of appropriators to someone who has a specialized task, such as a water distributor-guard?
The set of allowable actions: Which types of harvesting technologies are used (e.g., are chainsaws used to harvest timber; are there open and closed seasons; do fishers return fish smaller than some limit to the water)?	*Choice rules:* What understandings do appropriators have about mandatory, authorized, or forbidden harvesting technologies? For fishers, must mesh size be of a particular dimension? Must forest users use some cutting tools and not others? What choices do various types of monitors have related to the actions they can take?

continues

TABLE 6.1 Questions for Eliciting Information on Components of the Action Situation *continued*

Action Situation	Rules-in-Use Structuring an Action Situation
The level of control over choice: Do appropriators take the above actions on their own initiative, or do they confer with others (e.g., before entering the forest to cut fodder, does an appropriator obtain a permit)?	*Aggregation rules:* What understandings exist concerning the rules affecting the choice of harvesting activities? Do certain actions require prior permission from, or agreement of, others?
The information available: How much information do appropriators have about the condition of the resource itself, about other appropriators' cost and benefit functions, and about how their actions cumulate into joint outcomes?	*Information rules:* What information must be held secret, and what information must be made public?
The potential outcomes: Which geographic region and which events in that region are affected by participants in these positions? What chain of events links actions to outcomes?	*Scope rules:* What understandings do these appropriators and others have about the authorized or forbidden geographic or functional domains? Do any maps exist showing who can appropriate from which region? Are there understandings about resource units that are "off-limits" (e.g., the historical rules in some sections of Africa that particular acacia trees could not be cut down even on land owned privately or communally)?
The costs and benefits of actions and outcomes: How costly are various actions to each type of appropriator, and what kinds of benefits can be achieved as a result of various group outcomes?	*Payoff rules:* How large are the sanctions that can be imposed for breaking any of the rules identified above? How is conformance to rules monitored? Who is responsible for sanctioning nonconformers? How reliably are sanctions imposed? Are any positive rewards offered to appropriators for any actions they can take (e.g., is someone who is an elected official relieved of labor duties)?

The Actor: Theories and Models of the Individual

In addition to identifying action situations and their constituent components, an analyst using the framework must also make explicit assumptions about how actors make choices. Actors animate action situations; it is their choices and actions that produce outcomes. Consequently, an analyst must make assumptions about (1) how and what participants value; (2) what their information-processing capabilities are; and (3) what internal mechanisms they use to decide upon strategies (Ostrom 2005). A more complete explanation of each category may be found in E. Ostrom (2005, chap. 4, "Animating Institutional Analysis"). How and what participants value refers to preferences and can range from utility maximizing to other regarding. In addition, norms also shape what participants value. Information processing focuses on the mental models of actors and the vividness and saliency of available information (Ostrom 2005, 109). Internal mechanisms used by actors to make decisions refer to the use of heuristics. Elinor Ostrom (2005, 119) provides guidance for analysts in deciding among the appropriate assumptions about human choice:

> What kind of goods and services are involved, what rules, and what kind of community surrounds a particular situation? We have to ask whether the situation is stable or changing, conveys substantial information about its structure and the behavior of participants, tends to invoke norms such as trust and reciprocity (or those of an eye for an eye), and allows participants to adapt more effective strategies over time?

Being explicit about how actors make choices serves important roles for theory building and policy analysis. First, scholars are prompted to carefully think through the appropriate model of choice for the action situations to be analyzed. One of the motivations behind Elinor Ostrom's common pool resource research program was to explore the mismatch between predictions derived from the models used to explain common pool resource settings and outcomes resources users achieved in practice (Ostrom 1990). The models, such as the tragedy of the commons (Hardin 1968), the prisoner's dilemma, and the logic of collective action (Olson 1965), predict that resource users pursue narrowly defined self-interest, resulting in no cooperation, free riding off of those who attempt to cooperate, and the eventual destruction of natural resources, or the failure to provide for public goods. These models clearly do not explain the hundreds of documented cases of resource users who through cooperation and coordination manage to avoid tragedy and instead devise workable institutional arrangements that support the long-term sustainable use of common pool resources (Poteete, Janssen, and Ostrom 2010). The purpose is not just to have scholars better capture "reality" in their models but to be aware of the settings and situations to which their theories and models are most applicable.

Second, by using models of choice better suited to the settings to be explained, more effective policies may be devised. Elinor Ostrom (1990, 1999, 2005) repeatedly noted that the policies derived from the tragedy of the commons model were not only incomplete but also possibly harmful. Placing a commons under private ownership or state ownership represents only two of many possibilities. Furthermore, assuming that people cannot or will not cooperate obviates the need to first understand the types of governing systems that are in place in a commons. Imposing private or state property systems often undermines locally devised governing arrangements (Coward 1977; Netting 1982; Lansing and Kremer 1993). With the emergence of behavioral economics, Ostrom's critique has been extended and sharpened. As Bowles (2008) argues in reviewing a number of findings from laboratory experiments, material incentives may work to undermine moral sentiments, crowding out cooperative behavior. Agrawal, Chhatre, and Gerber (2015) find evidence of crowding out in sustainable development programs based on material incentives, and other scholars have raised similar concerns regarding payment for ecosystem services (PES) (Hayes 2012).

Grounding a theory or model in explicit assumptions about human choice is not unique to the IAD framework. A number of the major theories of policy processes, such as the Advocacy Coalitions Framework (ACF) and Punctuated Equilibrium Theory (PET), are grounded in some form of bounded rationality. These theories assume that actors are goal seeking but are predominantly guided by belief systems, in the case of the ACF, or limits on what may be attended to at any given time, in the case of PET (Jenkins-Smith et al. 2017, see Chapter 4, this volume; Baumgartner, Jones, and Mortensen 2017, see Chapter 2, this volume). From specific assumptions about how actors value choices, process information, and select strategies, these scholars have developed and tested hypotheses ranging from the presence and stability of coalitions to system-level patterns of policy outputs.

The different models of choice foundational to theories of policymaking also highlight the extreme care that scholars should take in selecting and combining parts of different theories to explain phenomena of interest. Some concepts and variables may be portable across theories, but others may not be. Carefully attending to the model of decision making underlying a theory helps scholars determine which concepts are portable.

Evaluating Action Situations

Criteria used to evaluate the institutional arrangements, processes, and outcomes of action situations are similar to those used in many public policy analyses (Stone 2012; Weimer and Vining 2016). Effectiveness, efficiency, equity, and accountability are all commonly used evaluative criteria.

If frameworks support the accumulation of knowledge, then for the IAD framework an important "knowledge" category is whether actors engaged in an action situation resolve collective action dilemmas and realize desired outcomes. That is, did they develop effective responses? Dating back to the empirical work on local public economies in the 1970s and 1980s, effectiveness measures focus on physical and material conditions (described below), such as the quality of the public goods and common pool resources provided, and the resolution of collective action dilemmas (Ostrom and Bish 1977; Ostrom, Gardner, and Walker 1994). Effectiveness measures vary by context. Commonly used measures in irrigation studies include the distribution of water across a canal system, the timing and location of water shortages, cropping patterns, and irrigation infrastructure maintenance (Lam and Ostrom 2010). In contrast, for forests effectiveness often centers on forest cover, forest diversity, and forest density in addition to the design of institutional arrangements (Andersson, Benevides, and León 2013).

Evaluations of equity often take two forms. One is equity through fiscal equivalence, and one is redistributional equity. The first addresses the relationship between who bears the costs of providing a shared benefit and who receives or enjoys the flow of benefits. As Ostrom (2005) repeatedly noted, benefits relative to costs affect individuals' expressed preferences for public goods. Individuals are likely to overstate their preferences for benefits they do not pay for and understate their preferences if what they are asked to pay exceeds the benefits they are likely to receive. Fiscal equivalency also shapes individual behavior. Individuals may pursue strategies that minimize their contributions to a public good, even engaging in rule-breaking behavior, if they receive few benefits. Fiscal equivalency has received considerable attention in empirical work, and it appears in Ostrom design principles for long-enduring self-governing arrangements (Ostrom 1990). Design principle 2 is titled "proportional equivalence between benefits and costs," and in a comparative analysis of more than sixty common pool resource cases, Baggio et al. (2016) found that the design principle is a necessary, but not sufficient, condition for realizing sustainable use of resources.

Redistributional equity entails distributing resources to disadvantaged or marginalized actors. In the local public economies literature, redistributional equity is often explored in the context of polycentric arrangements, with higher levels of government redistributing resources among lower levels of government. In that literature, fiscal equivalence and redistributional equity are often used together to evaluate outcomes because using only one will give an incomplete understanding of equity. In the common pool resource literature, redistributional equity is used to evaluate the distribution of resource units among resource users, with special attention given to marginalized populations (Agrawal 2014). Accountability and responsiveness of governing officials to the actors subject to the rules and who make use of the public goods and common pool resources is another pair of evaluative criteria. *Accountability* refers to whether decision making authority has been exercised appropriately (Schlager and Blomquist 2008, 68). Who determines appropriateness has important implications for behavior. Ostrom design principle 4 posits monitors who are accountable to resource users. The assumption is that such monitors are more likely to be responsive to resource user needs and demands. In contrast, monitors who are accountable to hierarchical superiors are more likely to respond to a different set of demands that may not align with those of local-level resource users (Tang 1992). Accountability and responsiveness appear in local public economies as different mechanisms structuring relations among citizens and public officials, such as voting with one's feet or attending public meetings (Oakerson and Parks 2011). The mechanisms provide important information to public officials about citizens' preferences for public goods and services that public officials may respond to.

Most of these criteria are embedded in the two theories directly developed from the IAD framework—the theory of local public economies and common pool resource theory—and have been explained and illustrated through concrete examples. The criteria themselves, however, are more general and can be operationalized for a wide variety of contexts. That is, they appear in their more general form in the framework and take more concrete forms in the theories developed from the framework. For scholars interested in learning more about how the criteria have been operationalized, particularly for common pool resource settings, the original common pool resource coding forms may be found in the SES Library (https://seslibrary.asu.edu/). The coding forms used in the International Forestry Resources and Institutions (IFRI) project may be found at http://www.ifriresearch.net/.

FACTORS STRUCTURING ACTION SITUATIONS

Action situations are structured by physical and material conditions, rules (in use), and community characteristics. These three categories form the context of the action situation. As Anderies and Janssen (2013) note, in most applications of the IAD framework, what is compared and analyzed are action situations in context. For instance, typical common pool resource studies compare irrigation systems in distinct contexts (e.g., farmer managed versus government managed, Tang 1992; Lam 1998), or coastal fisheries in distinct contexts (Acheson, Wilson, and Staneck 1998), or diverse types of CPRs (Baggio et al. 2016). The structure, content, and dynamics of action situations are strongly determined by their context.

Physical and Material Conditions

In 1977, the Ostroms published a book chapter that remains foundational for describing physical and material conditions. The chapter, entitled "Public Goods and Public Choices," presents a two-by-two typology of goods based on costliness of excluding actors from a good and the subtractability or rivalrousness in the use of the good. By far, IAD scholars have paid most attention to common pool resources and public goods, both of which are characterized by costly exclusion. What distinguishes them from one another is subtractability. CPRs are characterized by subtractability, that is, what one actor consumes is not available for other actors; whereas public goods are characterized by nonsubtractability. Many actors may enjoy the good without interfering with others' enjoyment (Ostrom and Ostrom 1977).

Costliness of exclusion and subtractability lay the groundwork for collective action dilemmas, and consequently they have important policy implications. Recall that collective action dilemmas involve interdependent situations in which the outcomes realized by one actor depend on that actor's choices as well as the choices of others in the situation. The dilemma arises because of the tension between the interests of individual actors and those of the group. The failure to adequately address exclusion raises the specter of free riding off of the efforts of others to provide shared benefits. For instance, if controlling access to a common pool resource, such as a groundwater basin, is not addressed, those outside of the community of users may access it and pump water that members of the user community stored. Even if exclusion is adequately realized so that the group of users or beneficiaries of a CPR or public good is effectively restricted, another type of collective action dilemma may emerge in relation to use. Actors may degrade the good, such as overharvesting of a CPR, or interfere with one another's use. Thus, both access and use raise collective action dilemmas, and both must be carefully attended to if productive and sustainable provision and use of CPRs and public goods are to be realized.

Additional dimensions of public goods and common pool resources have been identified as raising challenges for resolving collective action dilemmas surrounding exclusion and subtractability. An initial effort to explain the variation in rules developed by resource users harvesting from different types of CPRs is Schlager, Blomquist, and Tang (1994). They explore the effects of mobility of resource units and the presence or absence of storage on the types of institutional arrangements resource users are likely to devise to govern their use of CPRs. For instance, whether resource users devise rules to directly allocate shares of resource flows or they instead devise rules that govern how, where, and when flows may be accessed is determined by mobility. Highly mobile flows, such as migrating fish stocks or water in rivers or streams, tend to be governed by time or technology rules. Stationary flows are more likely to be governed by quotas. Highly mobile resource flows mean that resource users exercise control over access, but not over the flows; thus, they do not attempt to allocate the flows. In contrast, resource users exercise control over more stationary flows and thus may attempt to allocate them.

Ostrom, Gardner, and Walker (1994) develop a typology of what they called CPR dilemmas. It represents an effort to identify and recognize a variety of dilemmas and not just overharvesting, as was common in the policy analysis literature at that time. The typology is a function of technology, resource patchiness, and time. If resource units are evenly distributed across a CPR and resource users deploy the same harvesting technology, then production externalities may arise. Users do not account for the harvesting externalities they impose on one another and thus harvest beyond what is economically efficient. If resource users deploy diverse forms of technology, then they may experience technological externalities as they directly interfere with each other's harvesting activities. If resource units are patchy, if they are unevenly distributed across a resource, then resource users may compete and conflict over the most productive spots, leading to assignment externalities or problems. Finally, Ostrom, Gardner, and Walker (1994) identify supply-side and demand-side CPR dilemmas, which may emerge over time. If access and use are not carefully regulated (demand side), or if investments are not undertaken to maintain or enhance the productivity of a resource, its longer-term productivity may be undermined.

More recently, Baggio et al. (2016) examined whether different types of CPRs (fisheries, forests, and irrigation systems) exhibit different patterns of Ostrom's design principles. In empirically examining over seventy CPR cases, they find that no matter the type of CPR, if fewer than five design principles are present, the outcomes realized by resource users and the condition of the resource are likely to be poor. In contrast, if more than five principles are present, outcomes are more positive. What is interesting is that the patterns of design principles found in more successful cases appear to vary by type of CPR. Baggio et al. (2016) speculate on what accounts for these patterns, proposing that a combination of the mobility of resource units and level of human built, hard infrastructure plays a key role.

The physical and material conditions of the IAD framework are strongly related to collective action dilemmas. It is the dimensions of the physical and material conditions, or what Ostrom and Ostrom (1971) initially referred to as "the world of events," that lead to collective action dilemmas that are captured by the IAD framework. The diverse features of common pool resources and public goods present distinct challenges to providers and users of public goods and common pool resources. How these problems are addressed (or not) is strongly affected by institutional arrangements.

The Concept of Rules

The IAD framework, at its core, is about institutions. Problems among actors may be sparked by a mismatch between material and physical conditions and institutional arrangements, or they may be resolved by the adoption of new institutional arrangements that better align individual interests with group interests. One of the values of the IAD framework is that it supports comparative *institutional* analyses.

What are institutions? According to Crawford and Ostrom (1995, 582), institutional arrangements are "enduring regularities of human action in situations structured by rules, norms, and shared strategies, as well as by the physical world." As prescriptions, institutional arrangements guide, constrain, and direct people's choices and actions. Thus, as E. Ostrom (2005, 219) noted, rules are tools, and they can be thought of as tools in a couple of different ways. They are tools used by people to resolve collective action dilemmas. Rules, if followed, support cooperation and allow people to coordinate their actions to realize valued outcomes that they could not otherwise achieve acting individually. In addition, the rule typology, first developed by Kiser and Ostrom (1982), can be used by scholars and policy analysts to understand and explain the processes and outcomes of action situations and can be used to revise action situations to obtain more desired outcomes.

Rule typology. Kiser and Ostrom (1982) make sense of what appears to be an infinite variety of rules by classifying rules according to the components of the action situation that they directly affect (see Figure 6.2). Ostrom (2007b, 38) provides a concise explanation of each type of rule:

> Entry and exit rules affect the number of participants, their attributes and resources, whether they can enter freely, and the conditions they face for leaving. Position rules establish positions in the situation. Authority rules assign sets of actions that participants in positions at particular nodes must, may, or may not take. Scope rules delimit the potential outcomes that can be affected and, working backward, the actions linked to specific outcomes.[3] Aggregation rules affect the level of control that a participant in a position exercises in the selection of an action. Information rules affect the knowledge-contingent information sets of participants. Payoff rules affect the benefits and costs that will be assigned to particular combinations of actions and outcomes, and they establish the incentives and deterrents for action.

Just as with each component of the action situation, a series of questions may be used to identify the rules-in-use that guide, direct, and define action situation components (see Table 6.1, right column).

In categorizing rules by the components of the action situation, Kiser and Ostrom (1982) made clear that for any given action situation, rules are configural and likely contingent. Furthermore, rules may have indirect effects on other components of an action situation. For instance, a choice rule may authorize a farmer, when it is his turn for water, to shut off his neighbor's diversion and to open his diversion. Such a choice rule affects the information that farmers possess about one another; for example, the farmer whose water is being shut off is likely to observe his neighbor's actions. Thus, it is unlikely, in many situations that changing a single rule will change the outcomes; conversely, it is rare to identify a single rule that leads to a particular outcome.

As E. Ostrom (2005) explains, once she realized that she would not find a rule, or the rule, that accounted for positive outcomes of resource user–governed common pool resources she turned to identifying design principles. Design principles are patterns, or configurations, of rules. For instance, design

FIGURE 6.2 Rules as Exogenous Variables Directly Affecting the Elements of
an Action Situation

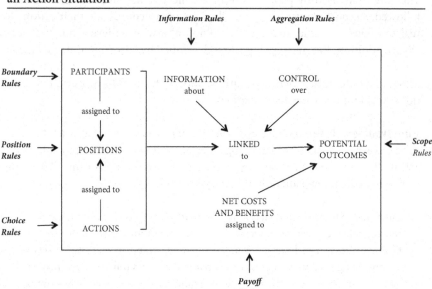

SOURCE: E. Ostrom (2005, 189). Used with permission from Princeton University Press.

principle 1—well-defined boundaries of the resource and resource users—in
many instances consists of multiple rules (Ostrom 1999). Or, in comparing
farmer-managed irrigation systems with government-managed irrigation systems, Tang (1992) argued that farmer-managed irrigation systems often exhibited design principle 2—rules well matched to the setting as evidenced by
configurations of choice and scope rules guiding the allocation of water depending on the water available. In contrast, government-managed irrigation
systems were much less likely to exhibit design principle 2, as evidenced by
the use of a single-choice rule for allocating water no matter the circumstances
(Schlager 2004).

The rule typology helps to bring order to what would otherwise be a very
disorderly and messy reality. But it is important to note that order is not the
same as simplicity. Configurations of rules and how rules interact to shape behavior may be quite complex.

Rules-in-use and rules-in-form. Most applications of the IAD framework involve identifying rules-in-use. Rules-in-use are the prescriptions that people
follow in practice and they are often not written down. Rules-in-use may be distinct from rules-in-form, which are the rules adopted through collective choice
venues and they are often written down. Rules-in-form are often the focus of

study by policy scholars who research public policies and elite behavior to the neglect of rules-in-use. IAD framework scholars, in contrast, overwhelmingly, but not exclusively, focus on rules-in-use to the neglect of rules-in-form.

Rules-in-use are identified by interviewing people and engaging in participant observation (Basurto 2005; Gibson, Williams, and Ostrom 2005; Coleman and Steed 2009; McCord et al. 2016). As E. Ostrom (2007b, 39) explained, rules-in-use are often understood implicitly by resource users, consequently "obtaining information about rules-in-use requires spending time at a site and learning how to ask nonthreatening, context-specific questions about rule configurations." The best example of identifying and measuring rules-in-use is from the International Forestry Resources and Institutions, where teams of researchers, having spent the day speaking with and observing forest users, would gather in the evenings to jointly complete coding instruments (Ostrom 2007b, 39).

The distinction between rules-in-use and rules-in-form is not simply a quaint convention practiced by IAD scholars. The recognition of rules-in-use forms the foundation for one of the major research programs coming out of the IAD framework—self-governance of common pool resources. In addition, examining the disjuncture between rules-in-use and rules-in-form has led to recognizing how rules-in-form can crowd out or crowd in cooperative behavior. By recognizing and encouraging the study of rules-in-use, the IAD framework has been used to extend the study of governance and democratic practices beyond the study of "the state" to include the often invisible practices of people collectively solving problems and providing shared benefits.

Grammar of institutions. A major theoretical and methodological extension of rules-in-use and rules-in-form occurred with the development of the grammar of institutions developed by Crawford and Ostrom (1995). The grammar provides a "theory that generates structural descriptions of institutional statements" (Crawford and Ostrom 1995, 583). The grammar consists of several components. The *attribute* identifies the doer of the action, the actor to whom the institutional statement applies. The *deontic* identifies whether the action is required, permitted, or forbidden. The *aim* is the verb of an institutional statement. It identifies the action of the attribute. The *condition* defines the what, when, where, and how of the action or outcome. The *or else* identifies a sanction if the institutional statement is violated. Later, an object category was added, which is the receiver of the action identified in the aim (Siddiki et al. 2011).

The grammar may be used to identify types of institutional statements. Statements that contain an attribute, aim, and conditions are strategies; statements that contain all but the or else are norms; and statements that contain all five of the original components are rules (Crawford and Ostrom 1995, 584). The grammar may also be used to analyze the content of institutional statements as well as how they may evolve over time. When the grammar is combined with a theory of action, a variety of questions that lie at the core of political science may be systematically explored, such as the legitimacy of institutions (Crawford and Ostrom 1995). Applications of the grammar have recently expanded; a team of researchers led by Chris Weible operationalized the grammar, coding rules-in-form, and analyzing the content and structure of laws and regulations (Basurto et al. 2010; Siddiki et al. 2011). Prior to this, Crawford and Ostrom (1995) had applied the grammar to develop and analyze games.

Institutional arrangements are the centerpiece of the framework. They are the tools used by people and by scholars to order action and to understand that order. However, E. Ostrom was always quick to point out that institutions can only be understood in context, in the context of other institutional statements, and in the context of physical and material conditions and attributes of the community.

Attributes of the Community

The category of concepts and variables that has received more limited attention than the others has consistently been labeled "attributes of the community." E. Ostrom variously points to "norms," "culture," and "world views" as constituting aspects of the community (Ostrom 1999, 2005; Poteete, Janssen, and Ostrom 2010). Most empirical work on this topic focuses on different attributes of groups of resource users. Important attributes of the group that have been examined for their effects on outcomes in action situations have included various types of heterogeneities (e.g., cultural or economic), socioeconomic status, dependence on a shared resource, group size, presence of accountable leadership, and levels of social capital (Poteete, Janssen, and Ostrom 2010; Cox et al. 2016). Agrawal (2003) has also argued for attention to levels of poverty, and Clement (2010), in incorporating into the framework discourses and attention to power, could have further developed the concepts by incorporating aspects of them into "attributes of the community." Although the category has received more limited attention than the others, it is well represented by numerous empirical articles and lively debates around the effects of group characteristics on collective action and outcomes.

LINKED ACTION SITUATIONS

Many applications of the IAD framework explicitly or implicitly involve linked action situations (McGinnis 2011). Action situations typically link through the outcomes of one situation directly affecting one or more of the components of another action situation. For instance, many studies of irrigation systems focus on three linked action situations—the production and maintenance of infrastructure (diversion dams, irrigation canals, etc.), the allocation of water, and the monitoring of rules (Coward 1977; Tang 1992; Lam 1998; Anderies and

Janssen 2013). The monitoring action situation directly links into the information that resource users possess about whether other resource users are contributing to infrastructure maintenance or are receiving agreed upon shares of water (Coward 1977). In turn, whether resource users are diverting water from canals at agreed upon times and places is affected by the actions taken around infrastructure maintenance (Anderies and Janssen 2013).

Regardless of whether it is irrigation systems, watersheds, aquifers, or forests, IAD scholars typically study linked action situations. In fact, one way of thinking of E. Ostrom's (1990) design principles is as a collection of linked action situations. The linking of action situations through the design principles is implicitly recognized in Figure 6.3, a fixture of this chapter through the several editions of this volume.

The Three Worlds of Action

Figure 6.3 links action situations through what Kiser and Ostrom (1982) call the three worlds of action, and what currently are called levels of analysis. The levels of analysis link action situations through the creation and application of rules. As Ostrom (2007b, 44) explained, "All rules are nested in another set of rules that define how the first set of rules can be changed." The operational level of action consists of the day-to-day activities people engage in, such as harvesting timber or diverting water from a canal or harvesting lobsters using lobster traps. The day-to-day activities are guided and constrained by operational-level rules. Operational-level rules emerge from collective choice and constitutional choice levels of action. Collective and constitutional choice levels of action entail activities related to rule making, rule following, and rule enforcing, as illustrated in Figure 6.3. Collective choice rules, which guide and constrain collective choice levels of action, define how operational-level rules are devised and adopted, how monitoring of operational-level actions is to occur, and so forth. Constitutional choice rules, which guide and constrain constitutional choice levels of action, define how collective choice rules are devised and adopted, how collective choice activities are monitored and enforced, and so forth. These levels of action, or levels of analysis, can include additional meta-constitutional levels of action and meta-meta-levels, if need be.

Levels of analysis are among the most difficult of the IAD concepts to work with and have led to considerable confusion, especially among graduate students who are just learning the framework or scholars who do not regularly work within the tradition. Part of the confusion stems from habitual thinking that regular, everyday people cannot also be rule creators, even though, at least in the United States, many rules governing day-to-day activities are collectively adopted by everyday people in their roles as part-time state legislators or part-time school board members. Some confusion can also stem from attempting to assign a level of government to a level of analysis. Cities define operational-level

FIGURE 6.3 Levels of Analysis and Outcomes

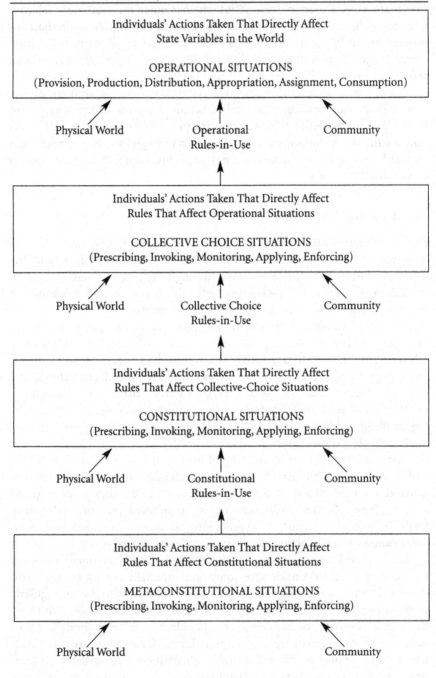

rules, states define collective choice rules, and the US Congress and Senate define constitutional choice rules. But much of the confusion comes from trying to apply complex concepts to messy, complex settings. It is difficult to do and easy to lose track of which level of analysis is the appropriate level. An initial cut is between activities that "directly affect state variables in the world" and rule-making, monitoring, and enforcing activities.

In regard to Figure 6.3, E. Ostrom identified categories of activities that occur at each level. The categories are not exhaustive, but they do identify the activities most commonly included and analyzed at each level. Beginning with operational situations at the top of the figure, provision, production, distribution, appropriation, assignment, and consumption are distinctive sets of activities. Examples include building dams and reservoirs, creating public safety, or education (production); distributing goods and services (distribution); harvesting or withdrawing units from a common pool resource (appropriation); and applying water to crops (consumption). The day-to-day activities most attended to through applications of the IAD framework are those that have the potential for creating collective action dilemmas that can be resolved through rule activities.

The rule activities identified in Figure 6.3 are varied as well. Although some of the language echoes that of Lasswell (1971) and his identification of decision processes, such as prescribing and invoking, the activities all relate in some way to creating and maintaining rules and rule-following behavior. Collective choice and constitutional choice situations are not restricted to rule making, that is, prescribing and invoking, but such situations also include rule monitoring, rule clarifying, and sanctioning of rule violations.

Most of the E. Ostrom design principles point to institutional arrangements and activities that occur at the collective choice and constitutional choice levels of action. Design principles three through eight deal with rule-making venues, monitoring, graduated sanctioning for rule violations, conflict resolution mechanisms, autonomy to engage in self-governance, and nesting of governing arrangements revolving around rule activities.

Paying attention to the three worlds of action is important given the centrality of institutions in the framework. The framework provides analysts with tools to engage in in-depth, substantive analysis of rules and rule activities and how those rule activities shape day-to-day, or operational-level, actions. In addition, the framework makes clear that rule activity is not delegated to a handful of actors, such as policy elites, or interest groups. Rather, rule activity may be engaged in by many actors.

COMPARING ACTION SITUATIONS IN CONTEXT

The problem-solving focus of the IAD framework and the emphasis on rules as tools for resolving collective action problems mean that the framework is well suited for organizing comparative institutional analyses (Cole 2013). Comparative institutional analyses require careful consideration of the settings to be compared and the evaluative criteria to be used. One of the cardinal mistakes in engaging in comparative institutional analysis is to fail to consistently apply the same set of evaluative criteria across settings. A classic example is Demsetz's (1967) comparison of common property with private property. Demsetz (1967) identifies high levels of transaction costs as the weakness of common property institutions and posits private property institutions as an alternative, without considering the transaction costs of such systems (Cole 2013). Consequently, private property institutions, according to Demsetz (1967), are a more effective means of governing natural resources. A complete institutional analysis of both types of property arrangements may have raised questions about the conditions under which each system is likely to perform better (for examples of comparative institutional analysis, see Netting 1982; Rose 2001; and Garrick 2015). As E. Ostrom (2007b, 26) noted, "Without the capacity to undertake systematic, comparative institutional assessments, recommendations of reform may be based on naïve ideas about which kinds of institutions are 'good' or 'bad' and not on an analysis of performance."

The IAD framework, as noted at various points in this chapter, provides scholars with sets of concepts, variables, and evaluative criteria to engage in systematic comparisons. Many empirical analyses seek to compare across two or more action situations in context to understand and explain the effects of particular variables on actions and outcomes. Whether it is exploring different "treatments" in experimental settings or field settings, much (but not all) of the empirical work grounded in the framework is comparative.

THE SOCIAL-ECOLOGICAL SYSTEMS (SES) FRAMEWORK

In 2007 Ostrom (2007a, 2009) introduced a novel framework that she labeled the Social-Ecological Systems (SES) framework. According to Anderies et al. (2004), "A SES is an ecological system intricately linked with and affected by one or more social systems." In her introduction, Ostrom stated that the "framework further elaborates the Institutional Analysis and Development (IAD) framework developed by scholars at Indiana University . . . and the framework developed by Anderies et al. . . . . for examining the robustness of SESs" (Ostrom 2007a, 15182). Figure 6.4 illustrates the primary elements of the SES framework. It shows a social-ecological system (SES) as consisting of four main types of components: governance systems, actors, resource systems, and resource units. The framework includes two other components as well: (1) social, economic, and political settings and (2) related ecosystems, although thus far these have received much less attention in the literature employing the framework.

FIGURE 6.4 The Core Subsystems in a Framework for Analyzing
Social-Ecological Systems

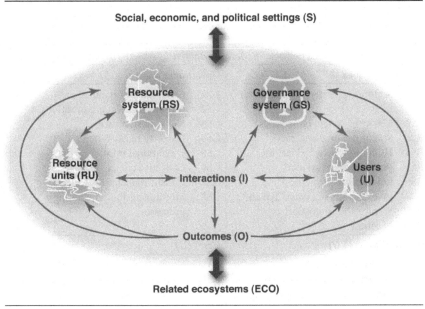

SOURCE: E. Ostrom (2009, 420). Used with permission from *Science*.

These components are described as constituting the first "tier"; the framework then associates each of them with a set of objects at what Ostrom labeled the second tier in a multitiered framework. We use the term *objects* here with respect to the second tier of the SES framework because of our opinion that the second-tier elements are not readily interpretable as variables, although they are frequently referred to as such. An additional task facing any potential user of the SES framework, then, is to take this step of turning the objects Ostrom provides into measurable variables. Table 6.2 illustrates this second tier.

Similarities between the Frameworks

As Elinor Ostrom initially stated, the SES framework was designed to build on the IAD framework, although how it does this is not immediately clear from the figures that are most commonly used to represent both frameworks. Nevertheless, the main components of the IAD framework may be mapped onto the SES framework. The most fundamental similarity is that each is oriented around a set of action situations, leading the analyst to unpack the elements that affect decision making in these social arenas. From here, we can map such elements between the two frameworks.

TABLE 6.2 Examples of Second-Level Variables under First-Level Core Subsystems (S, RS, GS, RU, U, I, O, and ECO) in a Framework for Analyzing Social-Ecological Systems

Social, economic, and political settings (S)	
S1 Economic development. S2 Demographic trends. S3 Political stability. S4 Government resource policies. S5 Market incentives. S6 Media organization.	

Resource systems (RS)	*Governance systems (GS)*
RS1 Sector (e.g., water, forests, pasture, fish)	GS1 Government organizations
RS2 Clarity of system boundaries	GS2 Nongovernment organizations
RS3 Size of resource system*	GS3 Network structure
RS4 Human-constructed facilities	GS4 Property rights systems
RS5 Productivity of system*	GS5 Operational rules
RS6 Equilibrium properties	GS6 Collective choice rules*
RS7 Predictability of system dynamics*	GS7 Constitutional rules
RS8 Storage characteristics	GS8 Monitoring and sanctioning
RS9 Location	processes

Resource units (RU)	*Users (U)*
RU1 Resource unit mobility*	U1 Number of users*
RU2 Growth or replacement rate	U2 Socioeconomic attributes of users
RU3 Interaction among resource units	U3 History of use
RU4 Economic value	U4 Location
RU5 Number of units	U5 Leadership/entrepreneurship*
RU6 Distinctive markings	U6 Norms/social capital*
RU7 Spatial and temporal distribution	U7 Knowledge of SES/mental models*
	U8 Importance of resource*
	U9 Technology used

Interactions (I) →	*Outcomes (O)*
I1 Harvesting levels of diverse users	O1 Social performance measures
I2 Information sharing among users	(e.g., efficiency, equity, accountability,
I3 Deliberation processes	sustainability)
I4 Conflicts among users	O2 Ecological performance measures
I5 Investment activities	(e.g., overharvested, resilience, biodiversity,
I6 Lobbying activities	sustainability)
I7 Self-organizing activities	O3 Externalities to other SESs
I8 Networking activities	

Related ecosystems (ECO)	
ECO1 Climate patterns. ECO2 Pollution patterns. ECO3 Flows into and out of focal SES.	

*Subset of variables found to be associated with self-organization.
NOTE: The framework does not list variables in an order of importance because their importance varies in different studies.
SOURCE: E. Ostrom (2009, 421).

To begin, the closest similarity between the two frameworks is the actors/community category, which is prominent in both and which plays essentially the same role. Here we describe important attributes of the relevant actor groups, such as group size or heterogeneity or another variable prominent in the CPR literature. That the SES framework is a direct descendant of the CPR literature is revealed by the fact that E. Ostrom (2007a) initially labeled this component the "user group" component.

With respect to the other components, the comparison is less direct. The "governance system" component in the SES framework is roughly analogous to the "rules" component in the IAD framework, although the objects listed under this component are not just rules. But each such object does have an institutional feel to it. From here we move to the biophysical elements that affect decision making, and there the comparison is more direct than it might seem. In the traditional account of the IAD framework, the biophysical (or just physical) attributes begin with the typology of goods (CPR, private, etc.) that is very popular in the CPR literature. Meanwhile, the two biophysical components in the SES framework (resource units and resource systems) and the distinction between them come directly out of the CPR literature. Indeed, going back as far as 1994, E. Ostrom, Gardner, and Walker (1994) describe a distinction between resource systems and resource units in their discussion of CPRs. They state that a CPR system "creates the conditions for the existence of a stock of resource units" (Ostrom, Gardner, and Walker 1994, 8). Thus the idea of a system producing a set of units has been with us for quite some time, even though it wasn't ever pictorially represented. So, the two frameworks have some similar content.

Differences between the Frameworks

Primary differences between the IAD framework and the SES framework are the novel diagnostic terminology and the associated tiered structure as well as inclusion of a list of second-tier objects in the SES framework. The literature on the IAD framework makes no reference to such ideas. The motivation behind this multitiered structure, from Ostrom's point of view, was to enable a diagnostic analysis of SESs, in which a scholar would retrieve the variables from the framework that were needed to examine his or her particular case or type of case, with the idea being that an analyst need not examine every possible variable for every possible case but should focus on those most appropriate for the type of system under study. (It's noteworthy that this is already somewhat standard practice in the field, although limitations on data availability likely play just as strong a role in variable selection.) To diagnose a problem or system, then, is to determine which variables are needed on the basis of some series of questions, to measure these, and then to explore relevant patterns of association to uncover important causal processes. There is a strong analogy here to medicinal practice, where a medical expert presumably prioritizes certain questions in ascertaining the causes of a condition in a patient. It also builds on language used by Young (2002) in his discussion of institutional fit. Indeed, Young has discussed the concept of diagnosis much more than any other institutional scholar, including Ostrom.

The basic idea, regardless of its precise implementation, is that the multi-tier structure enables such a process of variable selection because subsequent tiers beyond the second list objects that are increasingly specific to subtypes of systems. The lower (in number) a tier is, the more likely is each object in that tier to be relevant to any particular system. So, the components at the first tier are probably relevant for just about every type of system, whereas not all of the objects in the second tier would be, and objects in the third tier would be less likely still, and so on.

A second notable difference between the two frameworks is that the action situation does not feature as prominently as an obvious unit of analysis in the SES framework. Applications of the SES framework have generally not emphasized the action situation component as a focal unit of analysis (except see McGinnis 2011). Given that it has been applied by a larger range of researchers than the IAD framework has, it is not surprising that the SES framework has moved somewhat away from the collective action orientation of the action situation. The unit of analysis used in most applications of the SES framework is probably most correctly stated to be the SES itself, rather than individual decision making arenas contained within an SES.

A third difference between the two frameworks is their theoretical grounding. The IAD framework draws heavily on game theory. The action situation shares features with a game, such as actors holding positions, possessing information, and making choices (Ostrom 1990; Crawford and Ostrom 1995; Ostrom 2005). As such, the action situation represents, or captures, strategic interactions among individuals. The interactions are strategic in the sense that actors are taking one another into account as they choose actions aimed at achieving a particular outcome that is conditioned by all other actors' choices. The categories of variables that structure the action situation are also theoretically grounded. The material and physical conditions category, though seemingly simplistic compared to the SES categories of resources and resource units, is grounded in theories of goods from the economics and public choice literatures. Rules-in-use are grounded in theories of institutions and link with theories from institutional economics. Thus, scholars who work out of the IAD framework have not only the framework for guidance but also a variety of theories that fit comfortably with the framework. The IAD framework has a conceptual and theoretical coherency provided by its grounding in institutions.

This is not necessarily the case with the SES framework. How the tiered structure and diagnostic logic of the framework incorporate or work with theories has not been developed. In introducing the SES framework, E. Ostrom (2007a, 2009) used illustrative applications that represent models, such as the model of the tragedy of the commons (Ostrom 2007a). Furthermore, a number of the objects that appear in the second tier, particularly under governance, imply theories, such as networks, but network theories and the implications for selecting one theory rather than another have not been explored. Interestingly, Cox et al. (2016) implicitly use the SES framework to identify models and theories common in different fields. They identified sixty-three models and theories across eight fields that were compatible with the SES framework. This points to both the richness of the SES framework and its current limitations. It has the potential to support many diverse research programs across many natural and social science disciplines, but developing a consistency and coherency among the research programs is only likely to occur with decades of dedicated effort.

A fourth notable difference between the two frameworks flowing from the previous difference is the IAD framework's normative underpinnings. In previous work, E. Ostrom (2007a) used the terms *democracy* and *democratic rule*. One of the defining missions of the Ostrom Workshop is to study self-governance broadly construed and how rule-ordered relationships support or impede the realization of self-governance (Aligica 2013). The study of self-governance occurred at different scales, with Vincent Ostrom focused on constitutional design and federalism theory and Elinor Ostrom on regional and local-level forms of self-governance. Regardless of scale, the effort was to understand how people could exercise decision making authority over their own lives and in relation to others to realize productive patterns of order.

The SES framework, though related to the IAD framework, has distinctive features, such as its tiered system of objects that are organized and justified around a diagnostic logic. As discussed below, it is largely used in environmental and sustainability sciences to examine social-ecological systems. And its value is in providing well-defined categories of objects that can be operationalized and measured to explore dynamic interactions between social and ecological systems. The framework may be too young to expect it to be fully developed; its future trajectory is likely to be different from that of the IAD framework, even if a coalition of researchers coalesce around it and spend the next several decades realizing its full potential.

APPLICATIONS OF THE OSTROM FRAMEWORKS

The applications of the two frameworks are quite different, largely because of age. The IAD framework, which has been actively applied for over thirty-five years, has a longer track record than does the SES framework. Because of the different histories of the two frameworks, we examine applications separately. For the IAD framework, we highlight applications since the last version of this chapter, that is, applications between 2014 and 2016. In particular, we focus on special issues of journals and on books. In addition, we randomly sample 10 percent of journal articles that cite Elinor Ostrom's (2005) *Understanding Institutional Diversity* to develop a sense of how the IAD framework is being applied more generally, that is, by scholars who may not have had a close affiliation with the Ostroms or the Ostrom Workshop at Indiana University.

We take a different approach to the SES framework, with Cox conducting a systematic review and coding of all articles that cite to the two foundational pieces that present and explain the framework (Ostrom 2007a, 2009).

Applications of the IAD Framework

Between 2014 and 2016, eight special issues of journals grounded in or closely related to the IAD framework were published (see Table 6.3). Of those, two were prompted by the passing of Elinor and Vincent Ostrom in 2012, and the articles focus on their scholarly contributions to different social science disciplines. Of the remaining six, three focus on social dilemma experiments—one on laboratory experiments, one on field experiments conducted in Latin America, and one on both forms of experiments. Another consists of manuscripts that critically examine and extend common pool resource theory. The final two, both appearing in the *International Journal of the Commons*, focus on document coding and using the data to test common pool resource theory, with one examining historic commons; the other, contemporary common pool resource settings.

Several themes and arguments emerge from the special issues. First, polycentricity, and the contributions of V. Ostrom and E. Ostrom to its conceptualization and development, is motivating a new wave of empirical work around multilevel governance of common pool resources, including fracking (Arnold and Holahan 2014), forestry (Libman and Obydenkova 2014), and fisheries (Gruby and Basurto 2014). Second, formal modeling and experiments on social dilemmas and common pool resource dilemmas continue as a vibrant and expanding line of research. Topics explored range from examining the roles of norms, such as trust, in supporting cooperation and the role of shame as a form of punishment to investigating the influence of different forms of communication, including intergenerational transmission of information, and variations in the dynamics of the common pool resource system, such as different levels of scarcity, and the effects on cooperation. Third, systematic coding of secondary documents and of historical documents remains an important source of data for studying common pool resources. The two special issues of the *International Journal of the Commons* provide advice on coding best practices, datasets, and examples of how to analyze the data. The manuscripts appearing in the eight special issues provide a broad overview of the IAD framework, numerous empirical applications, and a good sense of ongoing research programs.

TABLE 6.3 Journal Special Issues and Books Published, 2014–2016

Special Issues
Bushouse, Brenda, Brent Never, and Robert Christensen. 2016. "Elinor Ostrom's Contribution to Nonprofit and Voluntary Action Studies." *Non-Profit and Voluntary Sector Quarterly* 45:7–174S.
Coleman, Erik, and Rick Wilson. 2016. "Elinor Ostrom and Social Dilemmas." *Journal of Theoretical Politics* 28 (1): 3–185.
Janssen, Marco, Therese Lindahl, and James Murphy. 2015. "Advancing the Understanding of Behavior in Social-Ecological Systems: Results from Lab and Field Experiments." *Ecology and Society* 20 (4): [34].
Kincaid, John. 2014. "The Federalism Scholarship of Elinor and Vincent Ostrom: Applications and Reflections." *Publius: The Journal of Federalism* 44 (2): 227–368.
Laborda-Peman, Miguel, and Tine de Moore. 2016. "Collective Action Institutions in a Long-Term Perspective." *International Journal of the Commons* 10 (2): 517–664.
Lejano, Raul, and Eduardo Araral, eds. 2014. "Interrogating the Commons." *Environmental Science & Policy* 36:1–92.
Muradian, Roldan, and Juan Campos Cardenas. 2015. "Collective Action and the Governance of the Commons in Latin America." *Ecological Economics* 120:358–450.
Schlager, Edella. 2016. "The Role of Context, Scale, and Interdependencies in Successful Commons Governance." *International Journal of the Commons* 10 (2): 405–516.
Books
Aligica, Paul Dragos. 2014. *Institutional Diversity and Political Economy: The Ostroms and Beyond*. New York: Oxford University Press.
Tarko, Vlad. Forthcoming. *Elinor Ostrom: An Intellectual Biography*. London: Rowman & Littlefield International.
Wall, Derek. 2014. *The Sustainable Economics of Elinor Ostrom: Commons, Contestation and Craft*. New York: Routledge.

The Web of Science was used to identify the English-language journal articles that cited E. Ostrom (2005) between 2014 and 2016, which corresponds with the period of time from the last edition of this volume to the present.[4] The 555 articles predominantly appear in environmental studies and the environmental sciences, with 57 percent of the articles appearing in these categories. Economics, ecology, and public administration categories are home to 31 percent of the articles, and the remaining 12 percent appear across a variety of categories, such as management and computer sciences. This distribution reflects the focus on common pool resources and social-ecological systems applications of the IAD framework.

Ten percent of the articles published each of the three years were randomly selected, and abstracts were inspected to determine whether each article represented an application of the IAD framework. Of the fifty-seven article abstracts examined, eleven, or 20 percent, directly applied or drew upon the framework. The remaining articles cited E. Ostrom (2005), with many of them centered on institutional arrangements and governance. Although the classic common pool resources, such as fisheries, irrigation, and grazing, are represented in the empirical studies, so, too, are housing cooperatives, local-level revenues, and landfills. Five of the eleven empirical applications are comparative, that is, the articles examine and compare more than a single case; four examined single cases, and two were conceptual and did not use empirical data. Finally, the cases were located in nine different countries on five continents. These empirical applications of the IAD framework are broadly representative of the empirical work on common pool resources developed by students and close associates of the Ostroms (see previous editions of this chapter). The work tends to focus on settings outside of North America and at the regional to local levels. In addition, comparative institutional analyses are common.

Applications of the SES Framework

To test the utility of the SES framework, that is, how it is being used and whether comparable data collection methods are being used, Cox conducted a meta-analysis of the studies that have cited either of the two articles in which Ostrom (2007a, 2009) originally presented the SES framework. These studies were obtained through two searches conducted in the Web of Science Database on February 2, 2014, and then again on October 1, 2014. The great majority of the studies found in these searches were examined. In addition, several articles from a very recent special issue of the *International Journal of the Commons* were added to this list and examined as well. Each of these articles was analyzed to infer values for a set of variables via a standard content analysis coding process.

To guide this process, a coding guide was developed that defined and described each of the variables being measured. Table 6.4 describes the variables that were coded. The first, second, and fourth columns here are fairly self-explanatory. The third column describes the type of study each variable was measured for. The first three variables were measured for all studies; the second two were measured only for empirical studies.

We found only 33 empirical studies in the 741 studies we coded. Of these empirical studies, 75 percent (25) explicitly implement the framework. In general, the research questions these explicit studies addressed reflect the literature on the commons and the management of common pool resources. A strong emphasis was frequently placed on outcomes for environmental common pool resources and related dynamics of collective action among commons users. There was also a frequent focus on the livelihoods of commons users and the issues of risk and vulnerability of these users and of the larger social-ecological

TABLE 6.4 Summary of Variables Coded in the Social-Ecological Framework Meta-Analysis

Name	Type	Studies	Variable Description
Methodology	Categorical	All	Records what type of methodology a study employs
Sector	Categorical	All	Records a study's primary sector (e.g., fisheries)
Empirical	Binary	All	Records whether a study empirically employs the framework
Explicit	Binary	Empirical	Records whether a study explicitly employs the framework
Protocol	Binary	Empirical	Records whether an empirical study used a common protocol

system of which they are a part. Eight of the empirical studies used a protocol that is shared by at least one other study. These eight can be broken down into a pair of studies by MacNeil and Cinner (2013) and Cinner et al. (2012) that use the same protocol for the framework, and a group of six studies from a common project known as the Social-Ecological Systems Meta-Analysis Database, or SESMAD, project (Cox 2014).

Table 6.5 breaks down all the studies as well as the empirical studies by methodology and sector. It shows that the majority of studies in the total sample are conceptual (not data-driven), with the second most common being case studies. By far the most common methodology used in the empirical studies is the case study. Turning to the sectors, roughly 41 percent of the studies were not associated with any individual sector. Fisheries is by far the most common sector in the total sample and is the most common in the empirical studies as well, although not by as much. Among both the larger set of cases and the empirical cases, the most common sectors are those that are also most common in the CPR management literature (fisheries, forests, and water governance, which includes irrigation cases). This is not surprising, given the network of scholars with whom Ostrom worked and her prominent position in this literature.

There were several trends in the ways in which the empirical studies did and did not use the framework. The most common pattern was for the authors to use the second-tier concepts as essentially a "checklist" of concepts from which they could draw to qualitatively or quantitatively measure their variables for the sake of case descriptions, case study comparisons, or statistical analyses. The overwhelming trend was for the studies to select from the list of second-tier concepts a subset that the researchers found, or predicted, to be more important for their particular analysis. With some exceptions (Basurto, Gelchich, and

TABLE 6.5 Results of the Social-Ecological Meta-Analysis by Methodology and Sector

Methodology	Total	Empirical	Sector	Total	Empirical
Conceptual study	285	0	None	310	3
Case study	201	21	Fisheries	131	11
Statistical analysis	86	5	Water governance	75	6
Synthesis	81	2	Other	89	7
Model	64	3	Forestry	56	4
Model/statistical analysis	9	1	Climate change	30	0
Biography	7	0	Agriculture	31	2
Field experiment	5	1	Health and disease	7	0
Lab experiment	3	0	Energy	6	0
			Social-technical system	6	0
Total	**741**	**33**	**Total**	**741**	**33**

NOTE: The following categories were used to code the methodology of the studies. Conceptual study: a study that contains a primarily abstract or theoretical argument; case study: a study that contains a detailed description of one or more cases; statistical analysis: a study that contains a statistical analysis of many cases; model: a study that contains a mathematical and/or simulation-based model; synthesis: a study that synthesizes the results of two or more others; model/statistical analysis: a study with a mathematical or simulation model that also implements a statistical analysis; biography: a study that describes Elinor Ostrom herself; field experiment: a study that takes place in a controlled field setting; lab experiment: a study that takes place in a controlled lab setting.

Ostrom 2013; Epstein et al. 2013), the empirical studies mostly did not engage with the "tiered" aspect of the framework to (1) develop new variables specific to their cases or types of cases, and (2) integrate these with existing components and concepts in the framework, which are the primary mechanisms through which the framework is supposed to enable a diagnostic approach to analysis.

Finally, as reflected in the Protocol variable, the empirical cases tended to use their own protocols for implementing the first and second tiers of the framework. With the exception of the eight cases mentioned earlier, none of the studies used the same protocol for operationalizing the second-tier concepts that Ostrom introduced. One primary weakness, then, of the empirical studies is their relatively ad hoc measurement methods of these concepts. The empirical studies generally do not provide details about how they decided to measure the concepts from the framework, making it difficult to impossible to characterize the validity of their measurement protocols or the consistency of these across applications.

Conclusions of the SES Framework Meta-Analysis

One of the purposes of examining studies citing the two foundational articles was to explore whether the SES framework was producing comparable results. In brief, the findings suggest the following:

1. The great majority of the studies that cited either of Ostrom's articles did not empirically implement the framework.
2. Out of the empirical studies, roughly 75 percent use the framework explicitly in a way that could produce comparable results.
3. However, with the exception of two groups of studies and eight in total, no common application or variable measurement protocol is used across the empirical studies.

These findings suggest that the framework has not succeeded in facilitating systematic comparative analyses of SESs similar to how the IAD framework has, at least not yet. There are relatively few empirical applications, and these are likely not producing comparable data because they are using idiosyncratic protocols to implement the framework. Why has the framework struggled in this way? As a leader in her field (and indeed in multiple fields) and with experience in framework development, E. Ostrom was well positioned to produce a highly successful framework. And based on the simple metric of citations mentioned above, the framework has been successful. However, the SES framework has not succeeded in important ways. There are several likely reasons for this, some resulting from the framework itself and some resulting from the challenges faced by any group of scientists who need to collaborate to produce generalizable findings. Regarding the framework itself, the most important factor is likely that there are no instructions to guide the user in how to implement it. Neither E. Ostrom nor her colleagues (a group to which we consider ourselves fortunate to have belonged) have ever provided definitions of the first-tier components (e.g., resource systems) or of the second-tier objects associated with these components. If the second-tier objects are to be interpreted as variables, then data comparability would require that users measure such variables in consistent ways.

In addition, the findings reflect a basic challenge facing collaborating scientists. In the same way that traditional CPR users face collective action problems in managing their resources, scientists in fact face a collective action problem in coordinating their efforts to produce comparable analyses (see Poteete, Janssen, and Ostrom 2010 for an in-depth discussion of this issue). Scaling up such collaboration is likewise very difficult: the transaction costs of scientific research increase as the size of the scientific group increases, inhibiting large-scale collaborative work.

These challenges are intertwined. Developing a set of coding forms and guidelines that validly and reliably measure the variables constituting the tiers will likely require a multidisciplinary team of scientists. For example, it took a team of five professors and graduate students more than two years to develop the original common pool resource coding forms (Ostrom et al. 1989). Following that, two additional sets of coding forms were developed, one set devoted to irrigation and one set to forestry. Both sets took research teams multiple years to develop and perfect. These three sets of forms and guidelines and the data collected using them represent the three largest common pool resource datasets, two of which are publicly available, at least partially. Unsurprisingly, E. Ostrom was involved in each one.[5] A promising locus of developing the SES framework may be a group of Ostrom's own former PhD students who have teamed up with several resilience alliance scholars to establish the SESMAD project (see http://sesmad.dartmouth.edu/) (Cox 2014).

A final challenge relates to theory. Arguably, one of the factors explaining the productivity of the IAD framework is its close association with theories, especially those developed through direct applications of the framework. One way to jump-start the use of the SES framework would be for a group of scholars to collaborate around a major research question and a shared understanding of the models and theories to be drawn upon to address the research question. Theory development and productivity demonstrate the value of the framework, encouraging more scholars to utilize it. Without that demonstration of value, encouraging scientific collaborations and widespread adoption of the framework is all the more challenging.

CONCLUSION

The concept and use of a framework are not widely recognized or used in the social sciences. Whereas most scholars and analysts are comfortable with theories and models, organizing knowledge at a more general level is rarely pursued. Its value, however, can be substantial, as demonstrated by the two frameworks discussed here and the several major research programs they support. The IAD framework is likely to continue to provide the infrastructure for research well into the future. It is well developed, stable, and embedded in ongoing research. Consequently, its future role will probably be in support of major research projects that use it to explore collective action dilemmas in new domains.

As we note above, the future development of the SES framework is uncertain. It awaits scientific collaborations that intentionally use it to organize major research programs. Meanwhile, and unlike in the social sciences, scholars studying social-ecological systems now have a diversity of frameworks to choose from (Binder et al. 2013). It is difficult to say whether this proliferation is scientifically healthy or not. Our hypothesis is that this current diversity has likely impeded the ability of scholars to coalesce around one or a few standard ways of conceiving of and analyzing social-ecological systems. We also hypothesize that these other SES frameworks suffer from the same problems that Ostrom's SES framework has faced.

One of the purposes of a framework is to support the accumulation of knowledge through a shared language that supports high comparability of research. One of the implications of accumulation is succession. Do frameworks and theories, especially in public policy studies, outlive their creators and their close colleagues and graduate students? Without succession, without generations of committed scholars devoted to continuing to develop theories in the context of a framework, the goal of accumulation is unlikely to be realized. In a way, this problem of intergenerational transfer of cumulated knowledge and joint personal-intellectual attachments to a particular research program mirrors some of the problems faced by communities of resource users the two frameworks we have discussed currently face themselves. In both cases we have seen the importance of leaders: prestigious individuals who are capable of rallying others to their perspective and activities. Conversely, we have also seen that the loss of an important leader such as Elinor Ostrom can greatly complicate this already challenging process.

NOTES

1. Although this chapter does not include Elinor Ostrom as an author, it is inspired by her life and her life's work. As we noted last time, the IAD framework is more than a tool for engaging in policy analysis; it also represents how the Ostroms and their many colleagues at the Workshop in Political Theory and Policy Analysis approach the world and conduct science. We were blessed to have Elinor Ostrom as a mentor and friend; and we will continue to be guided by her spirit and vision.

2. These are the common elements used in game theory to construct formal game models.

3. Authority rules, combined with the scientific laws about the relevant states of the world being acted upon, determine the shape of the decision tree, that is, the action-outcome linkages.

4. The Web of Science was accessed November 20, 2016.

5. The original common pool resource coding forms, guidelines, and data may be accessed through the SES Library (https://seslibrary.asu.edu/). The International Forestry Resources and Institutions (IFRI) project has made available its coding forms and manuals and limited portions of its data (http://www.ifriresearch.net/).

REFERENCES

Acheson, James, James Wilson, and Robert Steneck. 1998. "Managing Chaotic Fisheries." In *Linking Social and Ecological Systems: Management Systems and Social Mechanisms for Building Resilience,* edited by Fikret Berkes and Carl Folke, 390–413. New York: Cambridge University Press.

Agrawal, Arun. 2003. "Sustainable Governance of Common-Pool Resources: Context, Methods, and Politics." *Annual Review of Anthropology* 32:243–262.

———. 2014. "Studying the Commons, Governing Common-Pool Resource Outcomes: Some Concluding Thoughts." *Environmental Science & Policy* 36:86–91.

Agrawal, Arun, Ashwini Chhatre, and Elisabeth Gerber. 2015. "Motivational Crowding in Sustainable Development Interventions." *American Political Science Review* 109 (3): 470–487.

Aligica, Paul Dragos. 2013. *Institutional Diversity and Political Economy: The Ostroms and Beyond.* Oxford: Oxford University Press.

Allen, Barbara. 2005. *Tocqueville, Covenant, and the Democratic Revolution: Harmonizing Earth with Heaven.* Lanham, MD: Lexington Books.

Anderies, Marty, and Marco Janssen. 2013. "Robustness of Social Ecological Systems." *Policy Studies Journal* 41 (3): 513–536.

Anderies, Marty, Marco Janssen, and Elinor Ostrom. 2004. "A Framework to Analyze the Robustness of Social-Ecological Systems from an Institutional Perspective." *Ecology and Society* 9 (1): 18. http://www.ecologyandsociety.org/vol9/iss1/art18/.

Andersson, Krister, Jean Paul Benevides, and Rosario León. 2014. "Institutional Diversity and Local Forest Governance." *Environmental Science & Policy* 36:61–72.

Arnold, Gwen, and Robert Holahan. 2014. "The Federalism of Fracking: How the Locus of Policy-Making Affects Civic Engagement." *Publius* 44 (2): 344–368.

Baggio, Jacobo, Allain Barnett, Irene Perez-Ibarra, Ute Brady, Elicia Ratajczyk, Nathan Rollins, Cathy Rubinos, Hoon Shin, David Yu, Rimjhim Aggrawal, John Anderies, and Marco Janssen. 2016. "Explaining Success and Failure in the Commons: The Configural Nature of Ostrom's Institutional Design Principles." *International Journal of the Commons* 10 (2): 417–439.

Basurto, Xavier. 2005. "How Locally Designed Access and Use Controls Can Prevent the Tragedy of the Commons in a Mexican Small-Scale Fishing Community." *Society & Natural Resources* 18 (7): 643–659.

Basurto, Xavier, Stefan Gelcich, and Elinor Ostrom. 2013. "The Social–Ecological System Framework as a Knowledge Classificatory System for Benthic Small-Scale Fisheries." *Global Environmental Change* 23 (6): 1366–1380.

Basurto, Xavier, Gordon Kingsley, Kelly McQueen, Mshadoni Smith, and Christopher M. Weible. 2010. "A Systematic Approach to Institutional Analysis: Applying Crawford and Ostrom's Grammatical Syntax." *Political Research Quarterly* 63 (3): 523–537.

Baumgartner, Frank R., Bryan D. Jones, and Peter B. Mortensen. 2017. "Punctuated Equilibrium Theory: Explaining Stability and Change in Public Policymaking." In *Theories of the Policy Process,* 4th ed., edited by Christopher M. Weible and Paul A. Sabatier, 55–101. Boulder, CO: Westview Press.

Bednar, Jenna. 2009. *The Robust Federation: Principles of Design.* Cambridge: Cambridge University Press.

Binder, Claudia R., Jochen Hinkel, Pieter W. G. Bots, and Claudia Pahl-Wostl. 2013. "Comparison of Frameworks for Analyzing Social-Ecological Systems." *Ecology and Society* 18 (4): 26.

Bowles, Samuel. 2008. "Policies Designed for Self-Interested Citizens May Undermine the 'Moral Sentiments': Evidence from Economics Experiments." *Science* 320 (5883): 1605–1609.

Cinner, Joshua, Tim McClanahan, M. Aaron MacNeil, Nicholas Graham, Tim Daw, Ahmad Mukminin, David Feary, Ando L. Rabearisoa, Andrew Wamukota, Narriman Jiddawi, Stuart J. Campbell, Andrew H. Baird, Fraser A. Januchowski-Hartley, Salum Hamed, Rachael Lahari, Tau Morove, and John Kuange. 2012. "Comanagement of Coral Reef Social-Ecological Systems." *Proceedings of the National Academy of Sciences* 109 (14): 5219–5222.

Clement, Floriane. 2010. "Analyzing Decentralized Natural Resource Governance: Proposition for a Politicized Institutional Analysis and Development Framework." *Policy Sciences* 43:129–156.

Cole, Daniel. 2013. "The Varieties of Comparative Institutional Analysis." *Wisconsin Law Review,* 383–409.

Coleman, Eric, and Brian Steed. 2009. "Monitoring and Sanctioning in the Commons: An Application to Forestry." *Ecological Economics* 68 (7): 2106–2113.

Coward, E. Walter. 1977. "Irrigation Management Alternatives: Themes from Indigenous Irrigation Systems." *Agriculture Administration* 4:223–237.

Cox, Michael. 2014. "Understanding Large Social-Ecological Systems: Introducing the SESMAD Project." *International Journal of the Commons* 8 (2): 265–276.

Cox, Michael, Gwen Arnold, and Sergio Villamayor-Tomas. 2010. "A Review of Design Principles for Community-Based Natural Resource Management." *Ecology and Society* 15 (4): 38.

Cox, Michael, Sergio Villamayor-Tomas, Graham Epstein, Louisa Evans, Natalie C. Ban, Forrest Fleischman, Mateja Nenadovic, and Gustavo Garcia-Lopez. 2016. "Synthesizing Theories of Natural Resource Management and Governance." *Global Environmental Change* 39:45–56.

Crawford, Sue E. S., and Elinor Ostrom. 1995. "A Grammar of Institutions." *American Political Science Review* 89 (3): 582–600.

Demsetz, Harold. 1967. "Toward a Theory of Property Rights." *American Economic Review* 62:347–359.

Epstein, Graham, Jessica M. Vogt, Sarah K. Mincey, Michael Cox, and Burney Fischer. 2013. "Missing Ecology: Integrating Ecological Perspectives with the Social-Ecological System Framework." *International Journal of the Commons* 7 (2): 432–453.

Garrick, Dustin. 2015. *Water Allocation in Rivers under Pressure: Water Trading, Transaction Costs and Transboundary Governance in the Western US and Australia.* London: Edward Elgar.

Gibson, Clark, John Williams, and Elinor Ostrom. 2005. "Local Enforcement and Better Forests." *World Development* 33 (2): 273–284.

Gruby, Rebbeca, and Xavier Basurto. 2014. "Multi-Level Governance for Large Marine Commons: Politics and Polycentricity in Palau's Protected Area Network." *Environmental Science & Policy* 33:260–272.

Hardin, Garrett. 1968. "The Tragedy of the Commons." *Science* 162:1243–1248.

Hayes, Tanya. 2012. "Payment for Ecosystem Services, Sustained Behavioral Change, and Adaptive Management: Peasant Perspectives in the Colombian Andes." *Environmental Conservation* 39 (2): 144–153.

Jenkins-Smith, Hank C., Daniel Nohrstedt, Christopher M. Weible, and Karin Ingold. 2017. "The Advocacy Coalition Framework: An Overview of the Research Program." In *Theories of the Policy Process*, 4th ed., edited by Christopher M. Weible and Paul A. Sabatier, 135–171. Boulder, CO: Westview Press.

Kiser, Larry L., and Elinor Ostrom. 1982. "The Three Worlds of Action: A Metatheoretical Synthesis of Institutional Approaches." In *Strategies of Political Inquiry*, edited by Elinor Ostrom, 179–222. Beverly Hills, CA: Sage Publications.

Lam, Wai Fung. 1998. *Governing Irrigation Systems in Nepal: Institutions, Infrastructure, and Collective Action*. San Francisco: ICS Press.

Lam, Wai Fung, and Elinor Ostrom. 2010. "Analyzing the Dynamic Complexity of Development Interventions: Lessons from an Irrigation Experiment in Nepal." *Policy Sciences* 43 (1): 1–25.

Lansing, J. Stephen, and James Kremer. 1993. "Emergent Properties of Balinese Water Temple Networks: Coadaptation on a Rugged Fitness Landscape." *American Anthropologist* 95 (1): 97–114.

Lasswell, Harold D. 1971. *A Pre-View of the Policy Sciences*. New York: American Elsevier Publishing.

Libman, Alexander, and Anastassia Obydenkova. 2014. "Governance of Commons in Large Non-Democratic Country: The Case of Forestry in the Russian Federation." *Publius* 44 (2): 298–323.

Lutz, Donald. 1988. *The Origins of American Constitutionalism*. Baton Rouge: Louisiana State University Press.

MacNeil, Aaron, and Joshua E. Cinner. 2013. "Hierarchical Livelihood Outcomes among Co-Managed Fisheries." *Global Environmental Change* 23 (6): 1393–1401.

McCord, Paul, Jampel Dell'Angelo, Elizabeth Baldwin, and Tom Evans. 2016. "Polycentric Transformation in Kenyan Water Governance: A Dynamic Analysis of Institutional and Social-Ecological Change." *Policy Studies Journal*. Published electronically June 23, 2016. doi:10.1111/psj.12168.

McGinnis, Michael. 2011. "Networks of Adjacent Action Situations in Polycentric Governance." *Policy Studies Journal* 39 (1): 51–78.

Netting, Robert McC. 1982. "Territory, Property, and Tenure." In *Behavioral and Social Science Research: A National Resource, Part II*, edited by R. McC. Adams, N. J. Smelser, and D. J. Treiman, 446–501. Washington, DC: National Academy Press.

Oakerson, Ronald. 1999. *Governing Local Public Economies: Creating the Civic Metropolis*. Oakland, CA: ICS Press.

Oakerson, Ronald, and Roger Parks. 2011. "The Study of Local Public Economies: Multi-Organizational, Multi-Level Institutional Analysis and Development." *Policy Studies Journal* 39 (1): 147–167.

Olson, Mancur. 1965. *The Logic of Collective Action: Public Goods and the Theory of Groups*. Cambridge, MA: Harvard University Press.

Ostrom, Elinor. 1972. "A Metropolitan Reform: Propositions Derived from Two Traditions." *Social Science Quarterly* 53:474–493.

———. 1975. "The Design of Institutional Arrangements and the Responsiveness of the Police." In *People vs. Government: The Responsiveness of American Institutions,* edited by Leroy N. Rieselbach, 274–364. Bloomington: Indiana University Press.

———. 1990. *Governing the Commons: The Evolution of Institutions for Collective Action.* New York: Cambridge University Press.

———. 1998. "A Behavioral Approach to the Rational Choice Theory of Collective Action." *American Political Science Review* 92 (1): 1–22.

———. 1999. "Coping with the Tragedy of the Commons." *Annual Review of Political Science* 2:493–535.

———. 2005. *Understanding Institutional Diversity.* Princeton, NJ: Princeton University Press.

———. 2007a. "A Diagnostic Approach for Going Beyond Panaceas." *Proceedings of the National Academy of Sciences* 104:15181–15187.

———. 2007b. "Institutional Rational Choice: An Assessment of the Institutional Analysis and Development Framework." In *Theories of the Policy Process,* 2nd ed., edited by Paul Sabatier, 21–64. Boulder, CO: Westview Press.

———. 2009. "A General Framework for Analyzing Sustainability of Social-Ecological Systems." *Science* 325 (5939): 419–422.

———. 2014. "An Assessment of the Institutional Analysis and Development Framework and Introduction of the Social-Ecological Systems Framework." With Michael Cox and Edella Schlager. In *Theories of the Policy Process,* 3rd ed., edited by Paul Sabatier and Christopher Weible, 267–306. Boulder, CO: Westview Press.

Ostrom, Elinor, Arun Agrawal, William Blomquist, Edella Schlager, and Shui Yan Tang. 1989. *CPR Coding Manual.* Bloomington, IN: Workshop on Political Theory and Policy Analysis.

Ostrom, Elinor, Roy Gardner, and James Walker. 1994. *Rules, Games, and Common-Pool Resources.* Ann Arbor: University of Michigan Press.

Ostrom, Elinor, and Dennis Smith. 1976. "On the Fate of Lilliputs in Metropolitan Policing." *Public Administration Review* 36 (2): 192–200.

Ostrom, Elinor, Gordon Whitaker, and Roger Parks. 1973. "Do We Really Want to Consolidate Urban Police Forces? A Reappraisal of Some Old Assumptions." *Public Administration Review* 33 (September/October): 423–433.

Ostrom, Vincent. 1987. *The Political Theory of a Compound Republic: Designing the American Experiment.* Lincoln: University of Nebraska Press.

———. 1997. *The Meaning of Democracy and the Vulnerability of Democracies: A Response to Tocqueville's Challenge.* Ann Arbor: University of Michigan Press.

———. 2008. *The Intellectual Crisis in American Public Administration.* 3rd ed. Tuscaloosa: University of Alabama Press.

Ostrom, Vincent, and Elinor Ostrom. 1971. "Public Choice: A Different Approach to the Study of Public Administration." *Public Administration Review* 13:203–216.

———. 1977. "Public Goods and Public Choices." In *Alternatives for Delivering Public Services: Toward Improved Performance,* edited by E. S. Savas, 7–49. Boulder, CO: Westview Press.

Ostrom, Vincent, and Frances Pennell Bish, eds. 1977. *Comparing Urban Service Delivery Systems: Structure and Performance.* Beverly Hills, CA: Sage Publications.

Poteete, Amy, Marco Janssen, and Elinor Ostrom. 2010. *Working Together: Collective Action, the Commons, and Multiple Methods in Practice.* Princeton, NJ: Princeton University Press.

Rose, Carol. 2001. "Common Property, Regulatory Property and Environmental Protection." In *The Drama of the Commons,* Committee on the Human Dimensions of Global Change, edited by Elinor Ostrom, Thomas Dietz, Nives Dolšak, Paul Stern, Susan Stonich, and Elke Weber. Washington, DC: National Academy Press.

Schlager, Edella. 2004. "Local Governance of Common Pool Resources." In *Environmental Governance Reconsidered: Challenges, Choices, and Opportunities,* edited by Robert Durant, Dan Fiorino, and Rosemary O'Leary, 145–175. Cambridge, MA: MIT Press.

Schlager, Edella, and William Blomquist. 2008. *Explaining Watershed Politics.* Boulder, CO: University Press of Colorado.

Schlager, Edella, William Blomquist, and Shui Yan Tang. 1994. "Mobile Flows, Storage, and Self-Organized Institutions for Governing Common-Pool Resources." *Land Economics* 70 (3): 294–317.

Siddiki, Saba, Christopher M. Weible, Xavier Basurto, and John Calanni. 2011. "Dissecting Policy Designs: An Application of the Institutional Grammar Tool." *Policy Studies Journal* 39 (1): 79–103.

Stone, Deborah. 2012. *Policy Paradox: The Art of Political Decision Making.* New York: W. W. Norton.

Tang, Shui Yan. 1992. *Institutions and Collective Action: Self-Governance in Irrigation.* San Francisco: ICS Press.

———. 1994. "Institutions and Performance in Irrigation Systems." In *Rules, Games and Common Pool Resources,* edited by Elinor Ostrom, Roy Gardner, and James Walker, 225–245. Ann Arbor: University of Michigan Press.

Weimer, David, and Aiden Vining. 2016. *Policy Analysis: Concepts and Practice.* London: Routledge.

Williamson, Oliver. 1985. *The Economic Institutions of Capitalism.* New York: Free Press.

Young, Oran. 2002. *The Institutional Dimensions of Environmental Change.* Cambridge, MA: MIT Press.

7

Innovation and Diffusion Models in Policy Research

FRANCES STOKES BERRY AND WILLIAM D. BERRY

Although most actions by governments are incremental in that they marginally modify existing programs or practices, and much research about policymaking seeks to explain why it tends to be incremental, ultimately every government program can be traced back to some nonincremental *innovation*.[1] Thus, one cannot claim to understand policymaking unless one can explain the process through which governments adopt new programs. Recognizing this, public policy scholars have conducted extensive inquiry into policy innovation.

When people speak of innovation in common parlance, they usually refer to the introduction of something *new*. But when should a government program be termed "new"? The dominant practice in the policy innovation literature is to define an innovation as a program that is new to the government adopting it (Walker 1969, 881). This means that a governmental jurisdiction can innovate by adopting a program that numerous other jurisdictions established many years before. By embracing this definition, students of policy innovation explicitly choose not to study policy *invention*—the process through which *original* policy ideas are conceived. To flesh out the distinction via illustration, a single policy *invention* can prompt numerous governmental jurisdictions to *innovate*, some many years after others.

This chapter reviews the dominant theories of government innovation in the public policy literature.[2] However, we will show that these theories borrow heavily from others developed to explain innovative behavior by *individuals*: for example, teachers using a new method of instruction (studied by education scholars), farmers adopting hybrid seeds and fertilizers (studied by rural sociologists), and consumers purchasing new products (studied by marketing scholars).[3] We will also show that theories of government innovation share many commonalities with models that seek to explain *organizational* innovation.

Some studies of government innovation have been cross-national, investigating how countries develop new programs and how such programs have diffused across countries (Heclo 1974; Collier and Messick 1975; Brown et al. 1979; Tolbert and Zucker 1983; Kraemer, Gurbaxani, and King 1992; Simmons 2000; Simmons and Elkins 2004; Weyland 2004; Brooks 2005; Gilardi 2005, 2010; Meseguer 2005; Baturo and Gray 2009; Lee, Chang, and Berry 2011; Jensen and Lindstädt 2012; Hughes, Krook, and Paxton 2015). Many other studies focus on American states (e.g., Walker 1969; Gray 1973a; Canon and Baum 1981; Berry and Berry 1990; Mooney and Lee 1995; Mintrom 1997; Ka and Teske 2002; Berry and Baybeck 2005; Volden 2006; Shipan and Volden 2008; Pacheco 2012). Still other studies have focused on innovation by local or regional governments within the United States (Crain 1966; Aiken and Alford 1970; Bingham 1977; Midlarsky 1978; Lubell et al. 2002; Moon and Norris 2005; Shipan and Volden 2006) or local or regional governments in other nations (Ito 2001; Walker 2006; Walker, Avellaneda, and Berry 2011).[4]

Despite the extensive number of studies of government innovation, at a general level, there are two principal explanations for the adoption of a new program by a government: *internal determinants* and *diffusion* (Berry and Berry 1990). Internal determinants explanations posit that the factors leading a jurisdiction to innovate are political, economic, or social characteristics internal to the jurisdiction. By contrast, diffusion explanations are inherently intergovernmental; they view government adoptions of policies as emulations of previous adoptions by other governments. Walker's (1969) seminal study of state government innovation across a wide range of policy areas introduced both types of explanations to political scientists.[5] In the years following the publication of Walker's article, the volume of research on policy innovation has grown enormously. This growth is documented in Figure 7.1, which shows the number of books and articles about policy innovation published in political science, public administration, or public policy journals in each year between 1966 and 2012 (as identified with a JSTOR search).

This chapter begins with separate discussions of the central features of internal determinants and diffusion explanations for the adoption of a policy. We then turn to the methodologies that have been used to test them. Although most scholars have acknowledged that few policy adoptions can be explained purely as a function of (1) internal determinants (with no diffusion effects) or (2) policy diffusion (with no impact by internal factors), most *empirical* research conducted before 1990 focused on one type of process or the other. At the time of their introduction during the late 1960s and early 1970s, the "single-explanation" methodologies were highly creative approaches using

FIGURE 7.1 Growth in Published Research on Policy Innovation, 1966–2012

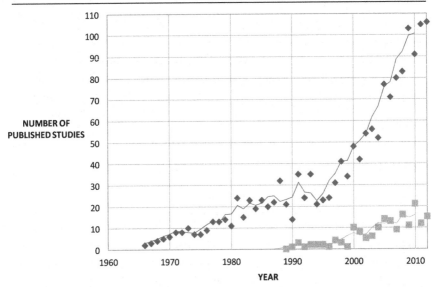

◆ Number of published books & articles about policy innovation

NOTE: Each value plotted is the number of books and articles about policy innovation published in political science, public administration, or public policy journals in a year (as identified with a JSTOR search in November 2013). The JSTOR search command yielding the values plotted on the top curve is as follows:

((("policy innovation") OR ("policy diffusion")) AND ((cty:(journal)
AND ty:(fla)) OR cty:(book))) AND (year:####) AND disc:(politicalscience
-discipline OR publicpolicy-discipline)

where #### indicates the year being searched. The search command yielding the values plotted on the bottom curve is as follows:

(((policy innovation) OR ("policy diffusion")) AND (("event history analysis") OR ("proportional hazards") OR ("survival analysis") OR ("Cox model") OR ("Cox proportional"))) AND ((cty:(journal) AND ty:(fla)) OR cty:(book)) AND (year:####) AND disc:(politicalscience-discipline OR publicpolicy-discipline)

Each fitted curve reflects a three-year moving average of plotted values.

state-of-the-art quantitative techniques. However, more recent research has shown that these traditional methodologies are severely flawed (Berry 1994b). In 1990, Berry and Berry presented a model of American state lottery adoptions reflecting the simultaneous effects of both internal determinants and policy diffusion on state adoption behavior and employed *event history analysis* (hereafter, EHA) to test their model. By allowing scholars to test models reflecting the effects of both internal determinants and policy diffusion, the introduction of EHA to the set of empirical techniques available to policy innovation scholars seems to have prompted a dramatic expansion in research over the last quarter century.[6] As this expansion has occurred, the EHA approach has been extended to a highly diverse set of policy contexts (for a list of some of the published studies of policy innovation relying on EHA, see www.westviewpress .com/weible4e). Moreover, as large numbers of scholars have employed EHA in policy innovation research, the methodology has been refined and improved.

Because this chapter does not do justice to the wide range of scholarship on policy innovation, you can find a short list of suggested readings for exploring the literature more widely on the book's website at www.westviewpress.com /weible4e.

DIFFUSION EXPLANATIONS FOR POLICY ADOPTION

Rogers (1995, 35) defines diffusion as "the process by which an innovation is communicated through certain channels over time among the members of a social system." Students of government policy innovation positing diffusion models conceive of a set of governmental jurisdictions (e.g., the fifty states in the United States, or the twenty-eight countries of the European Union) as a social system and maintain that the pattern of policy adoptions by member governments results from one member emulating the behavior of other members. More generally, we can say that policy diffusion occurs if the probability of adoption of a policy by one governmental jurisdiction is influenced by the policy choices of other governments in the system. However, theorists have identified a variety of alternative *mechanisms* by which the policy choices in one jurisdiction can influence the choices of other governments. At least five mechanisms have been discerned: learning, imitation, normative pressure, competition, and coercion.[7]

Alternative Mechanisms for Diffusion

Learning. Learning occurs when policymakers in one jurisdiction derive information about the effectiveness (or success) of a policy from previously adopting governments (Levy 1994; Braun and Gilardi 2006). Therefore, we say that a policy diffuses as a result of learning when the probability that one government— say, A—will adopt a policy is influenced by the perceptions of policymakers in A about the effectiveness of the policy in jurisdictions that have previously adopted.[8] Note that effectiveness need not be conceived narrowly; it can include success not only in meeting policy objectives but also in achieving political goals such as winning reelection or higher office (Shipan and Volden 2008; Gilardi 2010; Seljan and Weller 2011).

Some theories (e.g., Bayesian updating models from economics) assume that policymakers are rational and that learning is complete; each government observes all information about the effectiveness of a policy in every jurisdiction in which it has been adopted and is capable of processing all this information (Simmons, Dobbin, and Garrett 2006). Other theories assume that gathering and processing information about policy effectively are costly, and thus policymakers are "bounded" (or constrained) in their ability to obtain and analyze information (March and Simon 1993; Meseguer 2005; Weyland 2007). These constraints lead policymakers to take shortcuts, perhaps by restricting attention to only a subset of previous adopters. Officials may be assumed to limit their attention to contiguous—or nearby—jurisdictions (Berry and Baybeck 2005) or to governments they perceive as "leaders" or as peers (Meseguer 2004). Moreover, theorists need not assume that all jurisdictions are equally constrained; in some theories, governments vary in their *capacity* to learn, by virtue of the types and amounts of resources they possess (Desmarais, Harden, and Boehmke 2015). For example, it has been hypothesized that the level of expertise of a jurisdiction's legislators influences the jurisdiction's ability to learn from the experiences of other governments (Shipan and Volden 2006, 2014).

Imitation. Government *A imitates* government *B* when *A* adopts a policy adopted by *B* simply "in order to look like [*B*]" (Shipan and Volden 2008, 842–843). Imitation occurs because policymakers in *A* perceive *B* as worthy of emulation, prompting *A* to adopt any policy that *B* adopts independently of any evaluation of the character of the policy or its effectiveness (Simmons, Dobbin, and Garrett 2006; Meseguer 2006; Karch 2007). The types of jurisdictions that a government seeks to imitate may vary. In some conceptions, policymakers look to "leader" governments; these leaders may be large or wealthy jurisdictions or jurisdictions that have earned strong reputations or high levels of credibility (Walker 1969; Grupp and Richards 1975). In other conceptions, the governments imitated share characteristics that make them particularly valuable role models or peers (Simmons and Elkins 2004; Weyland 2004; Brooks 2005). For example, Volden (2006; see also Grossback, Nicholson-Crotty, and Peterson 2004) finds that policymakers tend to emulate policy adoptions of jurisdictions that share similar partisan and ideological orientations. In a useful clarification of the essential differences among mechanisms, Shipan and Volden (2008, 842–843) note that the major distinction between learning and imitation "is that learning focuses on the *action* (i.e., the policy being adopted by another government), while imitation focuses on the *actor* (i.e., the other government that is adopting the policy)."[9]

Normative pressure. Government *A* succumbs to *normative pressure* when *A* adopts a policy, not because it is imitating any particular government or learning from the experience of other adopters but rather because it observes that the policy is being widely adopted by other governments and, because of shared norms, *A* chooses to conform (DiMaggio and Powell 1983; Sugiyama 2012). Such shared norms can emerge across societies, allowing some policies (e.g., women's suffrage) to achieve a status of "taken-for-grantedness" (Braun and Gilardi 2006, 311). Some have pointed to the role of experts (or "epistemic communities") in forging a consensus on norms (Haas 1992). For example, Simmons, Dobbin, and Garrett (2006) note that the diffusion of economic liberalization in Latin America was facilitated by the advocacy of "expert" American economists, which molded views about appropriate economic policies. For policies made by administrative agencies rather than legislatures, the shared norms that facilitate diffusion have been argued to be a product of professionalization. Agency personnel—regardless of the jurisdiction in which they serve— develop a shared understanding of "good" policy by virtue of their common professional training and accreditation (Teodoro 2009). This shared conception of good policy leads agencies to be receptive to adopting policies thought to be "best practices" adopted elsewhere (Walker, Avellaneda, and Berry 2011). Shared norms across jurisdictions are often reinforced by the participation of agency personnel in intergovernmental professional associations that constitute networks across which policies can diffuse (DiMaggio and Powell 1983; Majone 1997).

Competition. A policy diffuses via *competition* when a government's decision about whether to adopt the policy is motivated by the desire of its officials to achieve an economic advantage over other jurisdictions or, equivalently, to prevent other jurisdictions from securing an advantage over it. In diffusion via learning, other governments' adoptions generate new data about the payoffs (costs and benefits) of adopting. In contrast, in diffusion via competition, other governments' adoptions actually change the payoffs of adopting (Simmons, Dobbin, and Garrett 2006). At least two distinct types of competition mechanisms have been described in the literature; we refer to them as *location-choice competition* and *spillover-induced competition*.

In location-choice competition, governments seek to influence the location choices of individuals (persons or firms) who are in position to acquire some good in more than one jurisdiction—usually their own and at least one other (Meseguer and Gilardi 2009). With this type of diffusion, jurisdiction A adopts a policy (e.g., a lottery or a restrictive labor immigration policy) to encourage individuals to (1) acquire within A a good that is beneficial for A to provide, or (2) go elsewhere to obtain a good that is costly for A to provide. Some policies of the US states that have been hypothesized to diffuse as a result of location-choice competition include the lottery (Berry and Baybeck 2005; Baybeck, Berry, and Siegel 2011), casino legalization (Calcagno, Walker, and Jackson 2010), restaurant smoking bans (Shipan and Volden 2008), welfare benefits (Peterson and Rom 1990; Volden 2002; Berry, Fording, and Hanson 2003; Bailey and Rom 2004), various business regulations (Mossberger 1999), and individual or corporate tax rates (Berry and Berry 1992) or sales tax adoptions (Burge and Piper 2012). Crossing national boundaries is certainly more costly for individuals and firms than crossing state boundaries in the United States. Nevertheless, location-choice competition is relevant in the international setting for policies designed to influence a variety of choices of individuals or firms, including business location, individual and corporate purchasing decisions, and migration (Oates 2001; Genschel 2002).

In spillover-induced competition, an adoption by government *B* has a (positive or negative) externality effect on government *A* that changes *A*'s expected net benefit from adopting. For example, *B* might adopt a pollution abatement project that would reduce pollution in both *B* and *A*; this positive spillover would encourage *A* to "free-ride" on *B*'s adoption, thereby lowering *A*'s incentive to adopt. Other policies that might diffuse via spillover-induced competition involve trade (Elkins, Guzman, and Simmons 2006), military mobilization or conflict (Most and Starr 1980), and commercial standards (e.g., standards trucks must meet to travel in neighboring jurisdictions).

Coercion. Government *A* is *coerced* into adopting a policy when a more powerful government, *B*, takes action that increases *A*'s incentive to adopt or, in the extreme case, forces *A* to adopt. Students of cross-national diffusion have identified cases of *horizontal* coercion, in which a powerful country encourages a weaker country to adopt a policy, sometimes by threatening action if the weaker nation does not capitulate (Simmons, Dobbin, and Garrett 2006). In other cases, one or more countries take actions that create an incentive for another country to adopt a policy. For example, Bush (2011) finds that a developing country becomes more likely to adopt a gender quota for its legislature as the country's dependence on foreign aid from developed Western countries increases or when the country is exposed to international election monitors.

Researchers studying diffusion in the American federal system are more likely to focus on *vertical* coercion, that is, diffusion across levels of government. In some cases, the national government can simply mandate certain activities by states (e.g., the National Voter Registration Act, which required states to allow people to register to vote at the same time they register their motor vehicles), or the Supreme Court can make rulings that constrain state policy choices (Hoekstra 2009; Hinkle 2015). In other cases, the national government uses a "carrot" rather than a "stick," by creating an incentive for a state to adopt a policy. One common vehicle for federal influence is a grant-in-aid creating a financial motivation for a state to adopt. In one example, Derthick (1970) shows how the Social Security Act of 1935 shaped state welfare programs through the Aid to Families with Dependent Children (AFDC) grant to the states (see also Welch and Thompson 1980; Soss et al. 2001; Allen, Pettus, and Haider-Markel 2004). Indeed, international organizations such as the International Monetary Fund (IMF) and the World Bank can play a similar coercive role by requiring a country to adopt some policy as a condition for financial aid (e.g., Weyland 2007; Simmons and Elkins 2004; Barrett and Tsui 1999). McCann, Shipan, and

Volden (2015) found that holding congressional hearings on antismoking laws influenced state policy choices, indicating that activities of the national government can influence state policy even in the absence of formal "carrots" or "sticks."

Complicating matters, multiple mechanisms may underlie a policy's diffusion. For example, at the same time location-choice competition may increase a state's probability of adopting a lottery if its neighboring states adopt one, the state may learn by observing positive consequences of neighbors' lotteries, also increasing its probability of adopting. Moreover, the mechanism responsible for a policy's diffusion may vary in a number of ways depending on the context. First, the mechanism can vary with characteristics of a state. For example, Stone (1999, 54) argues that an "economic recession or crisis, or defeat in war" makes a country more vulnerable to coercion. Also, Shipan and Volden (2008), in their study of the diffusion of antismoking policies, hypothesize that a city's size has a positive effect on its likelihood of learning from other cities and a negative effect on its probability of imitating or competing with other cities or being coerced by its state. Second, the mechanism underlying policy diffusion can vary over time. In one example, Gilardi, Füglister, and Luyet (2009)—who study the diffusion of hospital financing reforms across countries—find that the countries become more prone to learn over time as the quality of information available about the effects of other countries' adoptions increases. Finally, the mechanism by which a policy diffuses can be influenced by the nature of the policy. For instance, Makse and Volden (2011)—focusing on five attributes of policies identified by Rogers—posit that learning becomes more likely as a policy's relative advantage, compatibility, and observability rise and as the policy's complexity and trialability decline.

As we review various diffusion models developed in the policy innovation literature, each focusing on a different channel of communication and influence across government jurisdictions, we will show that each model relies on one or more of the five mechanisms described above to justify why governments emulate other governments when making public policy.

We now turn our attention to three models that dominated early scholarship on policy innovation. One—the *national interaction* model—assumes that policy diffuses because of learning. The others—the *regional diffusion* model and the *leader-laggard* model—are consistent with multiple mechanisms for diffusion.

The National Interaction Model

This learning model was developed and formalized by communication theorists analyzing the diffusion of an innovation through a social system (assumed to be of fixed size) consisting of individuals (Rogers 1995). In equation form, the model can be expressed as:

$$\Delta N_t = N_t - N_{t-1} = bN_{t-1}\,[L-N_{t-1}]\ \text{[Equation 7.1]}$$

In this model, L is the proportion of individuals in the social system who are potential adopters (a value assumed to remain constant over time) and serves as a ceiling on possible adoptions. If every person in the system is unconstrained and may adopt, L equals 1. N_t is the cumulative proportion of adopters in the social system at the end of time period t, N_{t-1} is the cumulative proportion at the end of the previous period, and thus ΔN_t is the proportion of new adopters during period t.[10] With some algebraic manipulation, the terms in Equation 7.1 can be rearranged to yield:

$$N_t = (bL + 1)\,N_{t-1} - bN^2_{t-1}\ \text{[Equation 7.2]}$$

Then, because Equation 7.2 is linear, given data on the timing of adoptions by all potential adopters, the parameters b and L can be estimated by regressing N_t on N_{t-1} and N^2_{t-1}.[11] When the cumulative proportion of adopters is graphed against time, Equation 7.1 yields an S-shaped curve, like that reflected in Figure 7.2. Early in the diffusion process, adoptions occur relatively infrequently. The rate of adoptions then increases dramatically but begins to taper off again as the pool of potential adopters becomes small.

FIGURE 7.2 S-Shaped Curve Consistent with National Interaction Model (Equation 7.1)

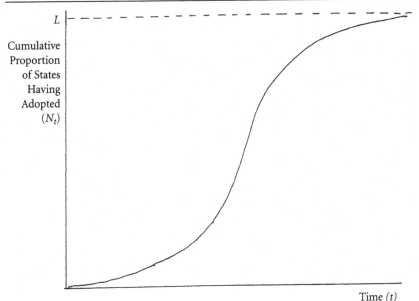

In an important early effort to enhance the theoretical precision of policy innovation research, Virginia Gray (1973a; see also Menzel and Feller 1977; Glick and Hays 1991; Boushey 2012) employs Equation 2, setting the time period as the calendar year and assuming that (1) the social system is the community of American states, and (2) the innovation diffusing is one of several state policies—including AFDC, education policies, and civil rights laws. Gray's model assumes a national communication network among state officials in which officials learn about programs from their peers in other states. The model presumes that officials from states that have already adopted a program interact freely and mix thoroughly with officials from states that have not yet adopted it, and that each contact by a not-yet-adopting state with a previous adopter provides an additional stimulus for the former to adopt. There are, indeed, formal institutional arrangements that encourage the thorough mixing of states. Chief among these are various associations of state officials that allow individuals with similar positions across the fifty states to meet periodically in national conferences. These include associations of elected "generalist" officials such as the National Governors Association and the National Conference of State Legislatures, each of which has numerous committees on specific policy areas as well as organizations of functionalist officials such as the National Association of State Chief Administrators.

But several factors limit the utility of the national interaction model—as traditionally conceived in Equations 1 and 2—for students of government innovation. First, the model assumes that, during any time period, all potential adopters that have not yet adopted are equally likely to do so; the only variable influencing the probability that a potential adopter will adopt during any time period is the cumulative number of adopters prior to that period. Indeed, the model treats all potential adopters as totally undifferentiated actors who interact "randomly," that is, who are equally likely to have contact with the members of the social system. Thus, the theory is well suited for when the social system is a large society of individuals and the scholarly interest is in a macrolevel description of the diffusion process. Although certainly in any society friendships and work and family relations guarantee that an individual's interactions with other members of the society are nonrandom, when studying the diffusion of a new consumer product through a large society, for instance, it may suffice to employ a model assuming random interaction. But when studying the diffusion of a policy through the fifty states, it seems less reasonable to treat the states as undifferentiated units; we know that Mississippi differs in many ways from New York, and our theory should probably take some of these differences into account. It is also likely that contacts between officials from different states are patterned rather than random.[12] It makes sense, for example, that politicians and bureaucrats in New York will have more contact with their counterparts in New Jersey than with officials in Mississippi.

Recently, the logic underlying the national interaction model has been modified to reflect a recognition that the professional associations encouraging interaction among state officials involve some states more than others, thereby prompting probabilities of policy adoption that vary across states. For example, Balla (2001) hypothesizes that states whose insurance commissioners sat on a committee of the National Association of Insurance Commissioners with jurisdiction over the regulation of health maintenance organizations (HMOs) were more likely than others to adopt model legislation proposed by the committee as a result of the greater centrality of commissioners in the informational networks surrounding the proposed legislation.

The Regional Diffusion Model

The regional diffusion model posits that governments are influenced primarily by other governments that are geographically proximate. Most of these models assume that governments are influenced exclusively by those jurisdictions with which they share a border; as such, we call them *neighbor* models. Specifically, these models hypothesize that the probability that a government will adopt a policy is positively related to the number (or proportion) of jurisdictions bordering it that have already adopted it (e.g., Berry and Berry 1990; Mintrom 1997; Balla 2001). Other models, which we term *fixed-region* models, assume that some collectivity of jurisdictions (e.g., the states in the United States, the countries in Latin America) is divided into multiple regions and that governments within the same region tend to emulate each other's policies (e.g., Mooney and Lee 1995).

Although fixed-region and neighbor models are similar in that they emphasize the emulation of nearby jurisdictions, the models are subtly different in their specified channels of influence. Fixed-region models presume (if only implicitly) that all governments within the same region experience the same channels of influence. In contrast, neighbor models—by avoiding fixed regional groupings of jurisdictions and instead pointing to the influence of all bordering jurisdictions—assume that each government has a unique set of reference jurisdictions for cues on public sector innovations. Although one can discern policies where a neighbor model makes more sense than a fixed-region formulation (e.g., in the case of lottery adoptions), and vice versa, neither pure model is entirely realistic. Fixed-region models imply implausibly that some jurisdictions—those bordering another region—are completely unaffected by some of their neighbors. Neighbor models assume that jurisdictions that are close but that share no border (e.g., Vermont and Maine) have no influence on one another. A more realistic regional diffusion model might assume that jurisdictions are influenced most by their neighbors but also by other jurisdictions that are nearby. One simple specification consistent with this assumption is that the level of influence of one jurisdiction over another is inversely related to the distance between the two.

There is strong theoretical justification for expecting that some policy diffusion is regional, and there is much empirical evidence of regional diffusion across jurisdictions (Berry and Berry 1990; Boehmke and Witmer 2004). However, a weakness of the regional diffusion model is that multiple mechanisms for diffusion can be the basis for an expectation that diffusion channels are regional. For example, governments may be more likely to learn from nearby jurisdictions than from those far away because governments can more easily "analogize" to proximate jurisdictions, which tend to share economic and social problems and have environments similar enough so that policy actions may have similar effects (Mooney and Lee 1995; Elazar 1972). Also, because of constraints on the mobility of most individuals and firms, governments are more likely to engage in location-choice competition with nearby jurisdictions than with those far away. For example, US states worried about losing revenue—especially those with large population centers near a border—are likely to be very concerned about whether their immediate neighbors have lotteries but unconcerned about remote states. Similarly, a state fearful of becoming a "welfare magnet" may match reductions in welfare benefits by neighboring states with large concentrations of poor people near its border but may be unresponsive to benefit adjustments in far-away states (Berry and Baybeck 2005).[13]

Leader-Laggard Model

The leader-laggard model assumes that certain jurisdictions are pioneers in the adoption of a policy and that other jurisdictions emulate these leaders (Walker 1969, 893). Most often, scholars presume that leadership is regional, with states taking cues from one or more pioneer jurisdictions within their geographical region (Walker 1969, 1973; Grupp and Richards 1975; Foster 1978). This model can be modified easily, however, to reflect the notion of a national leader among US states or an international leader among countries: a jurisdiction that, when it adopts a new program, increases the likelihood that other jurisdictions, regardless of their geographical location, will adopt.

Like the regional diffusion model, the leader-laggard model can be motivated by multiple mechanisms for diffusion. For instance, the leader-laggard model is compatible with learning. Policymakers in some governments may be more risk acceptant than officials in other jurisdictions, making the former governments most likely to be "leaders" that are willing to adopt a new untested policy. Jurisdictions in which policymakers are more risk averse may prefer not to adopt until they are able to observe the degree of success of the policy in jurisdictions that adopted early. However, the leader-laggard model is also compatible with imitation. For example, in some issue areas, officials in one jurisdiction may be more highly regarded by their peers than other jurisdictions' officials, making policymakers more likely to turn to that jurisdiction for cues.[14]

Although there are certainly strong reasons to expect leader jurisdictions to emerge, thereby forming the groundwork for leader-laggard diffusion, such models are often flawed by their failure to identify a priori (1) the jurisdictions (or even types of jurisdictions) that are expected to be pioneers, and (2) the predicted order of adoption of the governments expected to follow. Indeed, without an a priori theoretical prediction of which jurisdiction will lead and the order in which the remaining jurisdictions will follow, a leader-laggard model is virtually nontestable; any adoption pattern will involve one jurisdiction (which ex post facto could be designated the pioneer) adopting a policy first and other governments adopting afterward.

One leader-laggard model that clearly specifies the channels of diffusion is the *hierarchical* model developed by Collier and Messick (1975). Studying the pattern of social security adoptions by nations around the world, these authors hypothesize that the pioneers in social security were highly (economically) developed nations and that social security programs diffused down a hierarchy of nations from most to least developed.[15] Such a hypothesis specifies (in a testable fashion) the characteristics of leaders (high economic development) and a clear ordering of successive adoptions (from most- to least-developed countries). But note that, although the hierarchical model specifically posits diffusion of a policy across jurisdictions, its empirical prediction of a strong relationship between economic development and earliness of adoption is indistinguishable from that of an internal determinants model, which assumes no influence of jurisdictions on one another and instead posits that the sole determinant of the propensity of a government to adopt is its level of development. We turn now to consider the internal determinants explanation for policy adoption.

INTERNAL DETERMINANTS EXPLANATIONS
FOR POLICY ADOPTION

Internal determinants models presume that the factors causing a government to adopt a new program or policy are political, economic, and social characteristics of the jurisdiction. Thus, in their pure form, these models preclude diffusion effects in which a government is influenced by the actions of other governments. Certainly, once a policy is adopted by one jurisdiction, it is extremely unlikely that another jurisdiction's adoption would be *completely* independent from the previous one. Unless the two governments arrived at the same (or very similar) policy via a highly improbable coincidence, at a minimum there must have been diffusion from one government to the other of the *idea* for the policy. Thus, we believe that internal determinants models must acknowledge that, when a government adopts a policy new to the world, media coverage and institutionalized channels of communication among governments make it likely that knowledge of the policy spreads to other jurisdictions.[16] However, internal determinants models assume that once a jurisdiction's policymakers are aware of a new policy, the jurisdiction's internal characteristics, rather than pressure created by other governments' adoptions or explicit evaluations of the impacts of the policy in earlier-adopting jurisdictions, determine its probability of adoption.

The Choice of a Dependent Variable

One important theoretical issue in the construction of internal determinants models is how the dependent variable—the propensity of a government to adopt a policy or a set of policies—is defined. In research prior to the 1990s, most internal determinants models made the American state the unit of analysis and employed a dependent variable that assumed that the earlier a state adopted, the greater its "innovativeness." Empirical analysis was cross-sectional, and the dependent variable was generally measured at the interval level by the year of adoption (or some linear transformation thereof) or at the ordinal level by the rank of a state when states were ordered by their time of adoption (Canon and Baum 1981; Glick 1981; Gray 1973a; Walker 1969). However, a dichotomous version of this variable, which indicates whether a state had adopted a policy by a specified date, was also used (Filer, Moak, and Uze 1988; Glick 1981; Regens 1980).

More recent research generally conceptualizes the propensity of a jurisdiction to adopt a policy differently. The unit of analysis is now the jurisdiction in a particular year. More precisely, the unit of analysis is the jurisdiction in a year in which it has not previously adopted the policy and, thus, is still eligible to adopt in a particular year.[17] The dependent variable is the probability that a jurisdiction eligible to adopt will do so during that year (e.g., Berry and Berry 1990, 1992; Hays and Glick 1997; Mintrom 1997). Empirical analysis is pooled (cross-sectional/time-series), where a set of jurisdictions is observed over multiple years.

One important distinction between the two dependent variables is that the probability of adoption is a concept that is (1) defined for each jurisdiction at any point in time and (2) free to change over time, whereas the earliness of adoption takes on a single fixed value for each jurisdiction, determined by the year it adopts. A second distinction is that, although the timing of a government's adoption relative to other governments' adoptions is fundamental to the government's score on the "earliness of adoption" variable, relative timing is not necessarily relevant to a determination of a jurisdiction's propensity to adopt when a "probability of adoption" conception is utilized. A jurisdiction adopting a policy decades later than most other jurisdictions is not necessarily deemed as having had a (stable) low propensity to adopt; it is possible that the jurisdiction had a low probability for many years but that changing conditions led to an increased probability of adoption.

Although we are reluctant to declare either of these dependent variables—earliness of adoption or probability of adoption—as unambiguously the best one for internal determinants models, we believe that greater advances have come from models using the latter dependent variable, a position on which we elaborate below. Furthermore, our discussion of the theory underlying internal determinants models in this section emphasizes conceptualizations in which the dependent variable is the probability of adoption.

When propensity to adopt is conceived of as the probability of adoption, the focus of research must be a single policy.[18] However, in the study of the innovativeness of jurisdictions as reflected by their earliness of adoption, attention can focus on either one policy or a set of policies. At one extreme are studies designed to explain jurisdictions' adoptions of a single policy or program (e.g., Hays and Glick's 1997 research on state living wills). Other internal determinants models have focused on multiple policy instruments in a single issue area (e.g., Sigelman and Smith's 1980 research on consumer protection, covering twenty-eight different kinds of consumer legislation). At the other extreme is Walker's (1969; see also Savage 1978) analysis of the innovativeness of American states using an index reflecting the earliness of adoption of a set of eighty-eight policies spanning a wide range of economic and social issue areas. Boehmke and Skinner (2012) constructed a new measure of state innovativeness—also based on dates of adoptions of numerous policies—designed to overcome methodological shortcomings of Walker's measure. Ma (2016) recently developed an index of state government innovativeness based not on dates of adoption but rather on the frequency with which the states are recognized by the Innovations in American Government Awards (IAGA) program created by Harvard's Kennedy School of Government.

Implicit in the Walker measure of innovativeness is that it is reasonable to conceive of a general proclivity of a government to innovate across a wide range of issue areas. Some are skeptical of this claim; in a classic exchange with Walker, Gray (1973a, 1973b) claims that governments can be highly innovative in one program area but less so in others, rendering any general innovativeness score useless. Of course, whether governments are innovative generally and across a range of policy areas is an empirical question, and if the evidence is supportive, it is useful to develop models explaining generic innovativeness.

But even the variation already documented in state innovativeness across issue areas makes it obvious that, for any individual policy, the propensity of states to adopt the policy cannot be explained fully by a general proclivity to innovate (Gray 1973a). For this reason, even if generic innovativeness is a useful concept, we still ought not to treat it as the ultimate dependent variable. A good alternative is to take the course of Mooney and Lee (1995), Hays and Glick

(1997), and Soule and Earl (2001), who conceive of a jurisdiction's general proclivity to innovate as just one of a set of independent variables that influence the probability that a jurisdiction will adopt a particular policy. The idea is that governments vary in their general receptivity to new ideas and that this is one factor that accounts for their differential probabilities of adopting any specific program. The strength of the role played by general receptivity relative to other specific determinants of the probability of adoption is assessed empirically.

Hypotheses from Internal Determinants Models

Much of the theory underlying internal determinants models of government innovation can be traced to research about the causes of innovativeness at the individual level. For example, a tremendous level of support has been generated for the proposition that persons with greater socioeconomic status— higher levels of education, income, and wealth—are more likely to innovate than persons with less status.[19] A high level of education provides individuals access to knowledge about innovative practices and an openness to new ideas. Many innovations cost money or involve financial risks for those who adopt them; greater income and wealth provide people the resources necessary to absorb these costs. Similar hypotheses have been developed about innovation in organizations. Organizations of greater size and with greater levels of "slack resources" are assumed to be more innovative than smaller organizations and those with fewer resources (Cyert and March 1963; Rogers 1995; Berry 1994a; Ma 2013). In turn, Walker (1969, 883–884) explicitly draws on these organizational-level propositions to support the hypothesis that larger, wealthier, and more economically developed American states are more innovative.

Indeed, we can turn to the literature on organizational innovation for a framework useful for assessing the variety of internal determinants likely to influence the probability that a government will innovate. Lawrence Mohr (1969, 114) proposes that the probability that an organization will innovate is inversely related to the strength of obstacles to innovation and directly related to (1) the motivation to innovate, and (2) the availability of resources for overcoming obstacles. This proposition suggests a valuable organizational device because among the hypotheses frequently reflected in internal determinants models are those concerning the motivation to innovate as well as the obstacles to innovation and the resources available to surmount them.

We review these hypotheses, emphasizing those that seem applicable to a wide range of policies. However, we recognize that explaining the adoption of any specific policy is likely to require attention to a set of variables that are ad hoc from the point of view of innovation theory but critical given the character of the politics surrounding the issue area in question. For example, US states with strong teacher unions are less likely to adopt school choice reforms (Mintrom 1997), and states with large fundamentalist populations are less likely to adopt several policies considered immoral by many fundamentalists: state reforms (in the pre-*Roe* period) making abortions more accessible and state lotteries (Berry and Berry 1990; Mooney and Lee 1995; Roh and Berry 2008). A strong presence of religious fundamentalists in a state does not diminish the likelihood of adoptions of every policy, just those raising moral issues central to this group's religious beliefs.

An explanation of the adoption of any specific policy also is likely to require independent variables that are relevant not because they are determinants of the propensity of a government to adopt a new policy but because they influence the preferences of policymakers concerning the substantive issues raised by the new policy. For instance, a state legislator's response to a proposal for a new welfare program should be driven partially by the same factors determining the legislator's reaction to a proposal for an incremental change in existing welfare programs, such as increasing benefit levels. In another example, research by Berry and Berry (1992, 1994) on state tax policy finds that the factors explaining states' adoptions of new tax instruments are virtually identical to the variables accounting for decisions to increase the rates in existing taxes—despite the fact that the imposition of a tax new to a state can unambiguously be termed a policy innovation, whereas an increase in the rate for an existing tax would probably be viewed as an incremental policy choice. The unpopularity of taxes seems to drive the politics of taxation in the American states, and this unpopularity affects both tax adoptions and tax increases.[20]

Our review of hypotheses from internal determinants theories of government innovation emphasizes variables that seem especially relevant for explaining the adoption of new programs. This means that we do not discuss a wide range of factors widely believed to influence both innovative and routine policymaking. For example, citizen and elite ideologies are frequently hypothesized to influence the adoption of many programs that reflect traditional liberal-conservative cleavages (e.g., Mooney and Lee 1995; Berry and Berry 1992; Sapat 2004; Doan and McFarlane 2012). But their influence is not relevant to an understanding of policy innovation per se because ideology is widely perceived to influence routine or incremental policy choices as well (Hill, Leighly, and Hinton-Andersson 1995; Clingermayer and Wood 1995).[21]

Factors reflecting the motivation to innovate. Numerous scholars have hypothesized that problem severity is an important determinant of the motivation to innovate. Problem severity can influence the motivation of government officials to adopt a policy directly, by clarifying the need for the policy, or indirectly, by stimulating demand for the policy by societal groups. For instance, Allard (2004, 529) maintains that poor economic conditions contributed to the adoption of mothers' aid programs by increasing "demand and need for assistance." Similarly, Stream (1999) proposes that the rate of uninsurance among a state's population influences the likelihood that the state will adopt a set of health insurance reforms. Also, Mintrom and Vergari (1998, 135) argue that the greater the ratio of state education funding to local funding, the more likely a state legislature will be to consider "systemic reform like school choice."

Social scientists often assume that the principal goal of elected officials is to win reelection (e.g., Mayhew 1974; Kiewiet and McCubbins 1985). Although this assumption suggests that elected officials should be responsive to public opinion when deciding whether to adopt a new policy, their responses should vary with their level of electoral security. The more insecure they feel, the more likely they will be to adopt new policies that are popular with the electorate, and the less likely they will be to adopt new policies that are widely unpopular, or at least sufficiently unpopular with some segment of the electorate to be deemed controversial. Two corollaries of this proposition have frequently been introduced in the literature. One relates to interparty competition. Walker (1969) argues that politicians anticipating closely contested elections are especially likely to embrace new programs to try to broaden their electoral support. Implicit in this hypothesis is that the new programs are popular with the public. In the case of unpopular programs (like the imposition of a new tax), electoral competition is likely to reduce the probability that politicians will support the program.

Politicians' levels of electoral security also vary with the amount of time until the next election. Reasoning similar to the above suggests that the closer it is to the next election, the more likely a government is to adopt a new popular program and the less likely it is to adopt an unpopular or highly controversial new policy. This proposition has received support in the case of highly popular state lotteries (Berry and Berry 1990), very unpopular mandatory taxes (Mikesell 1978; Berry and Berry 1992), and controversial school choice initiatives (Mintrom 1997). However, contrary to expectation, Boushey (2016) finds that the timing of elections does not influence the probability that a state will adopt popular "law and order" policies.

Obstacles to innovation and the resources available to overcome them. Theories of individual and organizational innovation have stressed the importance of financial resources (i.e., wealth and income levels for individuals and slack resources for organizations) and other characteristics (e.g., a high level of education for an individual and large size for an organization) reflecting the capability of the potential adopter to innovate. Similar kinds of resources are often held to be critical for government innovation.

Some new government programs require major expenditures, and therefore the availability of financial resources is a prerequisite for adoption. Thus, one can hypothesize that the fiscal health of a government often has a positive impact on its propensity to adopt a new policy (Allard 2004; Lowry 2005; Aidt and Jensen 2009).[22] Analogous to the notion of highly capable individuals or organizations is the concept of governments with strong capacity. Walker (1969), Sigelman and Smith (1980), Andrews (2000), and McLendon, Heller, and Young (2005) maintain that American states with legislatures that give their members generous staff support and extensive research facilities should be more likely to adopt new policies than states with less professionalized legislatures, and Brooks (2005) posits that the level of party fragmentation in a country is inversely related to the country's likelihood of innovation.[23] Alternatively, it can be argued that the capacity of a jurisdiction's economy to finance extensive public services is the ultimate determinant of the jurisdiction's propensity to innovate (Daley and Garand 2005). Such capacity is reflected by several measures of economic development common in the literature, including per capita income, gross domestic product, and level of urbanization.

Walker (1969, 884) suggests that jurisdictions with high levels of economic development have a greater probability of adopting even those policies that do not require large budgets (e.g., enabling legislation for zoning in cities or a state council on the arts), partly because of their greater adaptivity and tolerance for change. Furthermore, Wagner (1877; see also Mann 1980; Berry and Lowery 1987) hypothesizes that economic development prompts increased demand for government services. Greater personal income among a jurisdiction's citizens leads them to demand governmental services that might be considered luxuries when personal income is low. Similarly, greater urbanization and industrialization lead to social problems that often require "collective" governmental solutions (Hofferbert 1966).

Others have argued that, although adequate financial resources are a prerequisite for government innovation, individuals who advocate policy ideas and who are willing to devote their energies to pushing these ideas can be critical to the adoption of a new policy. Most of the scholarly attention to the importance of so-called policy entrepreneurs, both inside and outside of government, has focused on their role in agenda setting (Kingdon 1984; Baumgartner and Jones 1993; Schneider, Teske, and Mintrom 1995). However, Mintrom (1997; see also Mintrom and Vergari 1996) offers evidence of the importance of policy entrepreneurs in facilitating the adoption of school choice initiatives in the American states.[24] Similarly, Sabatier and Weible (2007) argue that advocacy coalitions— coordinated groups of government officials, activists, journalists, researchers, and policy analysts—can be crucial in paving the way for policy adoptions.[25]

Indeed, several theorists, recognizing the rarity of government innovation, have argued that innovation can be expected to occur only in the unusual case wherein various independent conditions happen to occur simultaneously. Kingdon (1984, chap. 8) speaks of policy windows—rare periods of opportunity for innovation—that are created when a new political executive takes office, an important congressional committee chair changes hands, or some event or crisis generates an unusual level of public attention to some problem.

He argues that policy entrepreneurs consciously wait for such windows of opportunity to press their policy demands. In their study of tax adoptions, Berry and Berry (1992; see also Hansen 1983) argue that taxes tend to be adopted when several political and fiscal conditions converge to create a rare "political opportunity"—like a fiscal crisis in government occurring when the next election is not near and when one or more neighboring jurisdictions have recently adopted a new tax.

A UNIFIED MODEL OF GOVERNMENT INNOVATION REFLECTING BOTH INTERNAL DETERMINANTS AND DIFFUSION

We propose that models of government innovation should take the following general form:

$$ADOPTi,t = f(MOTIVATIONi,t, RESOURCES/OBSTACLESi,t,$$
$$OTHERPOLICIESi,t, EXTERNALi,t). \text{ [Equation 3]}$$

The unit of analysis for this equation is the jurisdiction i eligible to adopt a policy (i.e., the jurisdiction that has not yet adopted the policy) in a particular year t. The dependent variable—$ADOPTi,t$—is the probability that jurisdiction i will adopt the policy in year t. $EXTERNALi,t$ denotes variables reflecting diffusion effects on jurisdiction i at time t; thus, these variables would measure the behavior of other jurisdictions at time t, or in the recent past.

The remainder of the terms in the function f are internal determinants. $MOTIVATIONi,t$ represents variables indicating the motivation of public officials in jurisdiction i at time t to adopt the policy; these variables would include the severity of the problem motivating consideration of the policy, the character of public opinion and electoral competition in the jurisdiction, and other ad hoc motivation factors. $RESOURCES/OBSTACLESi,t$ denotes variables reflecting obstacles to innovation and the resources available for overcoming them. For many policies, the government's level of economic development and the professionalism of its legislature would be among the variables included. Factors indicating the presence (and skill) of interested policy entrepreneurs, or the strength of advocacy coalitions, in a jurisdiction could also be included.[26] Finally, $OTHERPOLICIESi,t$ is a set of variables indicating the presence or absence in jurisdiction i of other policies that have implications for the likelihood that the jurisdiction will adopt the new policy.

The impacts of previous policy choices on the probability of adopting a new policy have all but been ignored in the empirical literature on government innovation, but we contend that models of policy innovation must recognize the effects of one policy choice on another. Mahajan and Peterson (1985, 39–40) identify four types of "innovation interrelationships": innovations may be (1) independent, (2) complementary, (3) contingent, or (4) substitutes. This typology has relevance for explaining policy adoptions.

If we are seeking to explain the adoption of policy *B*, and policy *A* is largely *independent* of *B* (in the sense that a jurisdiction's probability of adopting *B* is unaffected by whether it has already adopted *A*), obviously we need not concern ourselves at all with policy *A*. But policies of the other three types are not so safely ignored. Sometimes two policies are *complementary*: the adoption of policy *A* increases the probability that a government will adopt policy *B*. For example, a US state that has previously chosen to license one type of auxiliary medical practitioner (e.g., physician assistants) may have created a precedent that makes it more likely that advocates of licensing other auxiliary personnel (e.g., nurse practitioners) will be successful.

Note that a positive relationship between the probability of adoption of policy *B* and the presence of policy *A* can exist without *A* and *B* being complementary if the relationship is spurious—resulting from both policies' adoptions being influenced by a common set of variables. For example, if the probability that an American state will adopt one type of welfare reform is positively related to the presence of another similar type of reform, yet that relationship is exclusively due to the fact that the same kinds of causal forces are at work in the adoption of both policies, the two welfare reforms should not be viewed as complementary. Only when the adoption of one policy changes conditions in a jurisdiction so as to make the jurisdiction more receptive to the other policy would we term the two policies complementary.

Another possibility is that policy *B*'s adoption is *contingent* on the previous adoption of policy *A*, in which case the probability that a jurisdiction will adopt *B* is zero until the jurisdiction adopts *A*. Brace and Barrilleaux (1995) present a theory of state policy reform designed to explain changes in existing programs in a variety of policy areas. The adoption of many of these policy changes is contingent on a state's previous adoption of the program being reformed.

A final alternative is that policy *A* is a *substitute* for policy *B*. When *A* is an *exact* substitute for *B*, *A*'s adoption completely precludes the possibility of adopting *B*. However, exact policy substitutes are rare; partial substitutes are more likely. In the case of partial substitutes, the adoption of *A* does not preclude the adoption of *B*; it only reduces its likelihood. For instance, it may be that different school choice plans considered by US states are partial substitutes. One possibility is that states create charter schools in an attempt to diminish the prospects that a more "radical" program—such as school vouchers—will be adopted. In this case, a state's previous adoption of a charter school program would lower the probability that the state would establish a voucher program.[27] In all these instances—in which policy *B* is complementary to, contingent on, or a substitute for policy *A*—a variable indicating whether a jurisdiction has adopted policy *A* should be included in the model explaining jurisdictions' adoptions of policy *B*.

EARLY APPROACHES TO TESTING INTERNAL DETERMINANTS AND DIFFUSION MODELS

Prior to 1990, the literature on government innovation was dominated by empirical research testing (1) internal determinants explanations that assume no diffusion occurs, or (2) diffusion models that assume no effects of internal determinants. Berry (1994b) argues that each of three models of government innovation discussed above—internal determinants, national interaction, and regional diffusion—is associated with a distinct methodology for empirical testing and explores the ability of these techniques to detect the true innovation process underlying policy adoptions. She does this by applying the methodologies to data generated from simulated innovation processes with known characteristics. Berry's results, which we summarize here, paint a very pessimistic picture of the ability of the traditional methodologies to help us understand government innovation.[28]

Testing Internal Determinants Models

Internal determinants models were traditionally tested with cross-sectional regression (or probit or discriminant) analysis (e.g., Regens 1980; Glick 1981; Canon and Baum 1981; Filer, Moak, and Uze 1988). The dependent variable was a measure of how early a government adopted one or more policies (or whether or not some policy had been adopted by a certain date), whereas the independent variables were political and socioeconomic characteristics of jurisdictions.

Several problems with this cross-sectional regression strategy are immediately apparent. The first pertains to the year for observing independent variables. If one measures the independent variables in a year that is later than some jurisdictions' adoptions, one winds up attempting to account for the behaviors of these jurisdictions with variables measured after the behavior has occurred. Thus, the only logical alternative is to measure the independent variables in the year that the first jurisdiction adopts (or some earlier year). But when adoptions of the policy are spread over many years, this approach requires an implausible assumption that late-adopting governments' behavior can be explained by the characteristics of those jurisdictions many years prior. Moreover, the cross-sectional approach to testing an internal determinants model does not permit an assessment of the effects of variables that change substantially over time; each jurisdiction is a single case in the analysis, having a fixed value for each independent variable. Finally, although the cross-sectional approach is suitable for testing an internal determinants model in which the propensity to adopt is defined as the "earliness of adoption," a cross-sectional model cannot be used if the dependent variable is conceptualized as the probability of adoption in a particular year.

In addition to these limitations, Berry finds that the cross-sectional approach to testing internal determinants models cannot be trusted to discern whether the adoptions of a policy by governments are actually generated by internal determinants. She finds, for example, that simulated policy adoptions generated out of a pure regional diffusion process—with no impact at all by internal characteristics of a jurisdiction—tend to exhibit evidence of internal determinants when a traditional cross-sectional model containing independent variables frequently used in the literature is estimated. The empirical problem is that jurisdictions near each other tend to have similar values on many political and socioeconomic characteristics. Thus, policies that diffuse regionally—say, by being passed to bordering jurisdictions—tend to yield an order of adoption by jurisdictions that correlates highly with these internal characteristics.

Testing the National Interaction Model

As noted earlier, the national interaction model was traditionally tested using time-series regression to estimate a model in the form of Equation 2. However, Berry finds that this regression approach cannot reliably discern whether a policy's adoptions are the result of national interaction. In particular, when data for simulated policy adoptions generated either (1) by a pure regional diffusion process, or (2) solely as a result of internal determinants are used to estimate Equation 2, the results often support the hypothesis that the policies spread via a national interaction process.

The empirical problem here is that, for any policy for which a graph of the cumulative proportion of states having adopted against time approximates an S shape similar to that shown in Figure 7.2, the regression approach will generate support for the national interaction model. Unfortunately, this S shape will result from any process that produces a period of infrequent adoptions followed by a period of more frequent adoptions (which is inevitably followed by a tapering off in the rate of adoptions as the number of remaining potential adopters declines). Policies that diffuse regionally can produce this adoption pattern. Even policies that are adopted as independent responses to internal state conditions can. Consider, for example, a policy that is most likely to be adopted by states with healthy economies; if a national economic boom cycle lifts the economies of all states, adoptions by many states may be clumped together to produce a period of frequent adoptions sandwiched by periods with less frequent adoptions.

Testing Regional Diffusion Models

The classic approach to testing regional diffusion models was Walker's (1969; see also Canon and Baum 1981) factor analytic technique. Walker used factor analysis to isolate groupings of American states with similar orders of adoption for eighty-eight policies. He then observed that the groupings coincided with regional clusters of states, which he interpreted as empirical evidence for regional diffusion.

Berry simulates state adoptions of 144 policies, each diffusing regionally based on a pure neighbor model. When the data for these 144 policies are factor analyzed according to Walker's procedure, there is strong support for the regional diffusion proposition. Thus, Berry finds evidence that Walker's methodology correctly identifies neighbor-to-neighbor diffusion when it exists. Our hunch is that the methodology also successfully shows support for the regional diffusion hypothesis when employed with policies that diffuse via fixed-region diffusion. If we are correct, the good news would be that factor analysis reliably detects diffusion when it exists in either of two prototypic forms: neighbor to neighbor, or in fixed regions. But the bad news would be that the technique is not able to distinguish the two similar—but still distinct—types of regional diffusion. Even more troublingly, Berry finds that Walker's methodology yields support for the regional diffusion hypothesis when applied to simulated policies known to diffuse via a pure national interaction model with no regional element whatsoever. She also finds evidence that policy adoptions generated purely as a result of internal determinants can indicate the presence of regional diffusion when an alternative "single-explanation methodology" is used[29] (see also Volden, Ting, and Carpenter 2008).

TESTING THE UNIFIED MODEL OF GOVERNMENT INNOVATION USING EVENT HISTORY ANALYSIS

As we have seen, Berry's (1994b) simulation results show that the early compartmentalized approach to testing the various explanations of government innovation calls into question the empirical evidence for these explanations from this era. Berry finds no evidence of false negatives, that is, no reason to believe that the early tests for the presence of regional diffusion, national interaction, and the impact of internal determinants fail to discern these processes when they are present. But she does find a disturbing pattern of false positives—a tendency for the methodologies to *find* regional diffusion, national interaction, or the effect of internal determinants when no such influence actually exists. In 1990, Berry and Berry developed a model of the adoption of lotteries by US states taking the form of Equation 3, positing that a state's propensity to adopt a lottery is influenced by forces both internal and external to the state, and they tested it using event history analysis (EHA). In the next section, we summarize their EHA model. Then we examine a variety of important refinements that other scholars have introduced as the literature has developed. Since 1990—but especially since the turn of the century—EHA has been employed across a wide variety of policy arenas to test models of government innovation reflecting both internal determinants and intergovernmental diffusion.

Berry and Berry's Event History Analysis Model

EHA is an ideal methodology for estimating the coefficients of an innovation model taking the form of Equation 3 (Box-Steffensmeier and Jones 2004). In EHA, we conceive of a risk set, the jurisdictions that (at any point) are at risk of adopting the policy in question. In a discrete-time model, the period of analysis is divided into a set of discrete periods, typically years. The dependent variable—the probability that a jurisdiction in the risk set will adopt during year t—is not directly observable. However, we can observe for each jurisdiction in the risk set whether the jurisdiction adopts the policy (typically coded 1) or not (scored 0). It is assumed that once a jurisdiction adopts a policy, it falls out of the risk set; thus, for each jurisdiction that adopts during the period of analysis, the time-series for the dependent variable is a string of zeros followed by a single 1 in the year of adoption. Given data for the jurisdictions in the risk set over a period of years, the EHA model, having a dichotomous observed variable, can be estimated using logit or probit maximum likelihood techniques.[30]

The maximum likelihood estimates of the coefficients for the independent variables in the EHA model offer information on the predicted impacts of these variables on the propensity of jurisdictions in the risk set to adopt the policy. Using procedures common in the analysis of probit and logit results, the coefficient estimates can, in turn, be used to generate predictions of the probability that a jurisdiction with any specified combination of values on the independent variables will adopt the policy in a given year. Furthermore, one can estimate the change in the probability of adoption associated with a specified increase in the value of any independent variable when the remaining independent variables are held constant at specified values (Tomz, Wittenberg, and King 2003). Such estimated changes in probability yield easily interpretable estimates of the magnitude of the effect of the independent variable.

Berry and Berry (1990) employed EHA to test a model of state lottery adoptions. Their model includes internal determinants reflecting the motivation of politicians to adopt a lottery (e.g., the proximity to elections), the obstacles to innovation (e.g., the presence of a sizable population of religious fundamentalists), and the presence of resources for overcoming obstacles (e.g., whether there is unified political party control of government), as well as a variable specifying interstate diffusion—the number of previously adopting neighboring states.

Recent Refinements to Event History
Modeling of Government Policy Innovation

Berry and Berry's (1990) initial application of EHA to the study of policy innovation assumed that the probability of adoption is constant over time. Yet,
it is unlikely that the true policy process conforms to this assumption. For instance, the pressure to adopt a new policy—hence the probability of adoption—
can increase gradually over time as coalitions designed to promote the policy
are built. Similarly, when intense efforts to secure adoption of a policy fail in
a year, the probability of adoption may be reduced the year following as advocates of the policy tire of the battle and decide to marshal their resources for the
future. More recent studies have allowed the probability of adoption to vary
over time (i.e., have allowed for "duration dependence") using strategies suggested by Beck, Katz, and Tucker (1998) and Buckley and Westerland (2004);
these include using dummy variables for time periods or a time counter (or
some transformation of time, such as the natural logarithm or cubic smoothing
splines) among the independent variables.

However, the most important refinements of Berry and Berry's EHA approach over the last two decades have been modifications to accommodate a
variety of different forms of diffusion. Recall that, to specify diffusion, Berry
and Berry include among the independent variables in their model the number
of contiguous jurisdictions that have previously adopted. Including the number (or percentage) of contiguous jurisdictions that have previously adopted
remains the most common specification of diffusion to this day (e.g., Mintrom
1997; Hill 2000; Balla 2001; Allard 2004; Chamberlain and Haider-Markel 2005;
Langer and Brace 2005; Allen 2005). But some EHA studies have introduced
alternative diffusion specifications. Mooney and Lee (1995), Andrews (2000),
and Allen, Pettus, and Haider-Markel (2004) have modeled fixed-region diffusion in the United States by defining regions of the country and including a
measure of the percentage (or number) of states from a state's region that have
previously adopted. Balla (2001) includes a measure of whether a state's insurance commissioner sat on a committee with jurisdiction over the regulation of
HMOs in a model predicting the adoption of model legislation proposed by the
committee. Allen, Pettus, and Haider-Markel's (2004) study of the adoption of
truth-in-sentencing laws in the United States specifies vertical influence, with a
variable indicating whether the national government had passed legislation in
1994 creating financial incentives for states to adopt.

Indeed, EHA is flexible enough to model other forms of policy diffusion as
well. Our earlier suggestion to assume that a jurisdiction i is influenced most
by its neighbors yet is subject to some influence by more distant jurisdictions
(an effect that diminishes with the distance from i) can be operationalized by
constructing a dummy variable for each jurisdiction (1 if a jurisdiction has
adopted the policy, 0 if not) and taking a weighted average of these dummies

across jurisdictions, where the weights are proportional to the distance from jurisdiction i. Leader-laggard diffusion can be modeled with a dummy variable indicating whether jurisdiction i's presumed "leader" has already adopted the policy. Even the thorough mixing of US states assumed by the national interaction model can be specified in an EHA model; the independent variables would include the percentage of the fifty states that have previously adopted the policy. However, we do not recommend this approach, preferring that scholars develop more realistic formulations of national interaction.

The "unified" model of government innovation—Equation 3—includes a set of variables ($OTHERPOLICIESi,t$) indicating the presence or absence of other policies that influence the likelihood that a government will adopt a new policy. The earliest applications of EHA did not incorporate this aspect of Equation 3. However, some more recent studies have tested models incorporating the impacts of other policies. Baturo and Gray (2009) test whether the probability that a country will adopt a flat tax is influenced by whether the country has previously adopted other economic reforms. Similarly, Balla's (2001) analysis of the adoption of the HMO Model Act by US states includes a variable indicating whether a state had previously adopted another model act assumed complementary to the HMO legislation.

Berry and Berry (1990) introduce a regional diffusion hypothesis predicting that the probability that an American state without a lottery will adopt one is positively related to the number of contiguous states that have already adopted. They defend this expectation by arguing both that lotteries in nearby states provide information about the consequences of adopting a lottery and that when the residents of a state without a lottery can easily cross the border and play other states' lotteries the state fears losing revenue to these other states. As such, Berry and Berry justify their regional diffusion hypothesis by arguing that states learn from one another and that they engage in location-choice competition for lottery sales to individuals living near a common border. Although this indicates the authors' recognition that policies can diffuse via multiple mechanisms, their empirical analysis was designed to answer the question "Does a policy diffuse?" but not the question "By what mechanism does the policy diffuse?" This inattention to isolating the mechanism underlying a policy's diffusion also characterizes the many other empirical studies of policy diffusion relying on EHA in the quarter century following the publication of Berry and Berry's 1990 paper.

We believe that the most important development in the study of policy innovation in the last decade is the shift in focus to the mechanism for diffusion and the corresponding development of theories about alternative mechanisms. The question "By what mechanism does a policy diffuse?" is much more interesting to those seeking to understand the policymaking process than is the question "Does a policy diffuse?" Accordingly, we applaud the shift in research focus to identifying the mechanism for diffusion and believe that developing

methods for detecting the presence of specific mechanisms—thereby allowing our tools for empirical analysis to catch up with advances in theory—is
the most important task on the agenda of scholars of policy innovation and
diffusion.

Assume that an analyst has competing plausible theories about the mechanism by which a policy diffuses—for example, it diffuses via learning or via
competition. She should evaluate each theory with as strong a test as possible
by deriving from each as many observable implications as possible, then conducting empirical analysis to determine whether each predicted implication
holds. Most importantly, some of the identified observable implications should
allow for a critical test of the competing theories: if the policy diffuses via learning, implication *A* will occur and *B* will not, but if the policy diffuses via competition, *B* will occur and *A* will not.

Berry and Baybeck (2005) try to determine whether the diffusion of the
lottery across American states detected by Berry and Berry (1990) was due
to learning or location-choice competition. Berry and Baybeck argue that if
the lottery diffuses because of competition—that is, a state adopts a lottery to
prevent a loss of revenues when its residents cross state borders to play other
states' lotteries—a state's response to neighboring states' adoptions would vary
depending on the distance of its residents from other states with lotteries (and,
thus, the ease with which residents can travel to the other states). By contrast,
if the lottery diffuses because of learning from neighboring states, a state's response to contiguous states' adoptions would be the same regardless of the distance of its residents to other states with lotteries.

Berry and Baybeck use geographic information systems (GIS) software to
calculate for each state *s* in each year *t* the population in state *s* living near another state with a lottery relative to the total population of state *s*—a quantity
that measures *s*'s concern that residents will play other states' lotteries.[31] They
contend that if the lottery diffuses owing to location-choice competition among
states, for any state *s* without a lottery, *s*'s concern that residents will play other
states' lotteries should have a positive effect on *s*'s probability of adopting a
lottery; but if the lottery diffuses owing to learning, there should be no relationship between *s*'s fear that residents will play other states' lotteries and *s*'s
probability of adopting. The authors further maintain that if the lottery diffuses
as a result of learning from neighboring states, the number of states bordering *s*
that have previously adopted a lottery should have a positive effect on the probability that *s* will adopt a lottery; if the lottery diffuses as a result of competition,
however, there should be no relationship between number of previously adopting neighboring states and a state's probability of adopting (after statistically
controlling for a state's fear that residents will play other states' lotteries).

Berry and Baybeck estimate an EHA model that includes as independent
variables both the number of previously adopting neighboring states and a
measure of a state's degree of concern that its residents will play other states'

lotteries. Their results indicate that concern that residents will play other states' lotteries has a positive effect on the probability of a lottery adoption, whereas the number of previously adopting neighbors has little impact on the probability of adoption. This leads Berry and Baybeck (2005, 515) to conclude that "there is compelling evidence that the interstate influence leading to the diffusion of the lottery results from competition—fear by state officials of losing revenues to neighboring states—rather than policy learning."

Readers can judge for themselves whether Berry and Baybeck's empirical analysis constitutes a strong critical test of their competing competition and learning hypotheses. Two points, however, seem clear. First, the variable Berry and Baybeck construct to tap location-choice competition (based on counting population living near a state's border and, therefore, having easy access to another state's lottery) is more directly tied to the mechanism being operationalized than is the variable they use to tap learning from neighboring states: the number of previously adopting neighboring states. The number of s's neighbors that have previously adopted a lottery does measure s's opportunity to learn from its neighbors' experiences with a lottery, which makes the variable a plausible proxy for tapping learning from neighbors. But constructing a variable taking into account the consequences of a lottery adoption in previously adopting neighboring states would constitute a more direct, and more valid, way to tap learning from neighbors.[32] Second, it is clear that Berry and Baybeck's lack of empirical evidence of learning from neighboring states is insufficient to rule out the presence of either other forms of learning in which states obtain information about the consequences of adopting a lottery from states that are not contiguous or some mechanism not involving learning—such as imitation.[33] Additional empirical analysis would be needed to eliminate the possibility that these other mechanisms are at work.

Probably the most systematic effort to test for the presence of competing mechanisms for diffusion is Shipan and Volden's (2008) study of US local governments' adoptions of antismoking policies. The authors rely on EHA and include independent variables chosen to identify: (1) whether a local government learns from other cities in a state (the proportion of one state's population that lives in a city that has previously adopted smoking restrictions); (2) whether a city competes on the basis of a fear that its smoking residents will abandon local businesses and patronize businesses in nearby cities without smoking restrictions (the total population in nearby cities that do not have restrictions relative to a city's own population); (3) whether a city imitates larger cities (a dummy variable measuring whether the nearest larger city has adopted); (4) whether a city is coerced by its state to adopt (dummy variables measuring whether one's state has adopted a smoking restriction, reducing the city's incentive to act); and (5) whether a city is explicitly prohibited by its state from adopting.

There is insufficient space for us to provide lengthy descriptions of the large number of studies of policy diffusion over the last decade that have

sought to develop tests of competing theories about the mechanisms underlying diffusion. Boehmke and Witmer's (2004) study of Indian gaming policy
and Baybeck, Berry, and Siegel's (2011) analysis of lottery adoptions include
some research on interstate diffusion in the United States. But there has been
even more cross-national research in this vein, including Henisz, Zelner, and
Guillén's (2005) study of market-oriented reforms; Elkins, Guzman, and Simmons's (2006) study of bilateral investment treaties; Cao's (2010) and Jensen
and Lindstädt's (2102) analyses of corporate tax rates; Sugiyama's (2012) study
of conditional cash transfer programs; and Lee, Chang, and Berry's (2011)
research on e-government and e-democracy. A key challenge for researchers
in the decade ahead is to continue to conduct empirical research seeking to
identify the mechanism(s) underlying policy diffusion but to focus attention
on developing better empirical indicators for the presence of specific mechanisms. For each diffusion mechanism—learning, imitation, competition, coercion, and normative pressure—the goal should be to construct indicators for
the presence of the mechanism that can not only successfully detect this mechanism when it is present (avoiding false negatives) but also fail to detect the
mechanism when it is not present (avoiding false positives).

RESEARCH BEYOND THE BOUNDS
OF THE "UNIFIED" MODEL

Although the "unified" model (Equation 3) is sufficiently flexible to serve as
a framework for studies of numerous aspects of policy diffusion, some interesting and important avenues for research require modifying, or even aban-
doning, the unified model. The unit of analysis for the unified model is a
jurisdiction that has not yet adopted some policy, the conceptual dependent
variable is the probability that the jurisdiction will adopt the policy in a year,
and the observed dependent variable is whether the jurisdiction adopts in the
year. However, sometimes a policy adoption is a repeatable event so that a jurisdiction stays at risk of adopting a policy even in a year after it has previously
adopted. Berry and Berry (1992) offer an example of this situation in their
study of tax innovation by American states, in which the dependent variable
is the probability that a state will adopt *any* new tax in a year, making it so that
each state is eligible to adopt in each year regardless of how many taxes it has
previously adopted.[34]

In other situations, it is useful to abandon the unified model's binary observed dependent variable—adopt or not in a year—in favor of an alternative
dependent variable. Often, policies can be conceived as having multiple components, and a jurisdiction can choose to adopt none, one, or multiple components; moreover, the jurisdiction may adopt all the components it desires in
a single year or stretch adoptions over a longer period. For example, in studying the diffusion of antismoking policies across US cities, Shipan and Volden

(2006) identify three distinct components of such policies: limitations on (1) smoking in government buildings, (2) smoking in restaurants, and (3) out-of-package sales. Boehmke (2009a) reviews a variety of options for studying innovation and diffusion of policies with multiple components, discussing the strengths and weaknesses of each. Some of these approaches—for example, a separate analysis of each component or pooled analysis of all components—are compatible with EHA. But it is also possible to treat the number of components a jurisdiction adopts as the dependent variable of interest and to use an event count model for estimation.

Sometimes it might be best to conceive of a government's policy choice not as involving a binary choice (adopt or not)—or a set of binary choices regarding multiple components of a policy—but instead to view the choice as among three or more distinct alternatives. For example, Berry and Berry (1992) studied the adoption of sales and income taxes separately, assuming for each that states without the tax might choose to adopt or not in any year. But it may more accurately reflect the process of decision making to conceptualize states that have neither tax in any year as having four choices: adopt a sales tax, adopt an income tax, adopt neither, or adopt both.[35]

Another limitation of the unified model's conception of the policy choice confronting a government as binary is that the model ignores potential variation among adopters in the "depth" or "extent" of innovation. Glick and Hays (1991, 836; see also Downs and Mohr 1976) distinguish between "superficial" and "deep" adoption. For example, two governments might adopt an antidiscrimination program (in housing or the workplace), yet one adoption may be largely symbolic, whereas the other may involve an extensive commitment of resources through investigatory and enforcement actions. Calling them both antidiscrimination programs and treating them as functionally equivalent may mask variation essential to understanding the innovation process at work. Boehmke and Witmer (2004) specify an innovation model in which multiple events—a state signing an Indian gaming compact—may occur in the same year and the number of adoptions by a state in a year yields information about the depth of innovation. Boehmke and Witmer estimate their model with generalized event count regression.

Some of the variation in the depth of a policy adoption may be the result of what Glick and Hays (1991; see also Clark 1985) call policy *reinvention* or what Karch and Cravens (2014) call policy *modification*.[36] Implicit in the notion of reinvention is an assumption that learning is the mechanism for diffusion. This learning model assumes that governments use information about the impacts of a policy in other jurisdictions not only to assist them in deciding whether to adopt the policy but also to help them refine the policy in light of the other governments' experiences. In turn, early adopters can reform their policies to take advantage of the experiences of late adopters who passed a modified version of the initial policy.

It can also be useful to move away from the unified model's focus on the adoption stage of the policymaking process and to turn attention to explaining how new policies make their way onto a government's agenda for consideration.[37] Specifically, researchers can develop innovation-diffusion models that explain whether a policy is on the legislative agenda in a jurisdiction (i.e., given serious consideration by its legislature) in a year. The most obvious empirical indicator of whether a policy is on the legislative agenda is whether it is introduced as legislation. However, "introduction" is not a perfect indicator of "serious consideration" because some bill introductions in a legislature are symbolic acts, with a given bill's sponsors having no expectation that the legislation will pass or even be assigned to committee for consideration. Mintrom (1997) illustrates the potential value of a focus on agenda setting in his study of education reform by American states. He conducts EHA with a model predicting the probability that a state's legislature will *consider* a school choice proposal in a year (see also Karch 2012; Karch, Nicholson-Crotty, and Woods 2016).[38]

One final important avenue for research incompatible with the unified model is shifting the unit of analysis from a government jurisdiction—as in the unified model—to a pair of jurisdictions. Volden (2006; see also Gilardi 2010; Füglister 2012; Hinkle 2015; Nicholson-Crotty and Carley 2016; Volden 2016) recently introduced *directed-dyad event history analysis* into the study of government policy innovation. In traditional EHA, the unit of analysis is the jurisdiction-year, and each jurisdiction is included in the dataset during each year it is at risk of adopting the policy. With directed-dyad EHA, the unit of analysis is the dyad-year—where *dyad* refers to a pair of jurisdictions—and the dependent variable measures whether one jurisdiction in the pair emulates the policy of the other. Gilardi and Füglister (2008) and Boehmke (2009b) help refine Volden's dyadic approach by investigating a variety of modeling issues one faces when conducting dyadic analysis. At this point, there is insufficient research relying on directed-dyad EHA to fairly evaluate the technique's contribution to research on policy innovation. However, the potential for directed-dyad EHA is great because the technique would seem to be enormously valuable in tracing the way a policy diffuses from one jurisdiction to another. For example, Volden's (2006) research finds that a state having a successful policy has a higher probability of being emulated than a state with a failing policy.

NOTES

1. For a review of the literature on incremental decision making, see Berry (1990).

2. Note that much of the text of this chapter is drawn from our chapter in the third edition (2014) of this volume.

3. Rogers (1995, chap. 2) discusses numerous examples of research on innovation at the individual level.

4. Graham, Shipan, and Volden (2013) note that research on policy diffusion is done within each major subfield of political science—American politics, comparative politics, and international relations—and persuasively argue that scholarship on diffusion would benefit from researchers in each subfield paying more attention to diffusion research done in other subfields.

5. Walker calls what we term his "internal determinants" explanation an analysis of the "correlates of innovation."

6. As Figure 7.1 shows, there was a sudden and dramatic increase in the frequency of published research in the mid-1990s—as evidenced by the abrupt change at this time in the slope of the top curve for the number of published studies of policy innovation in a year. This change occurred just a few years after EHA's introduction in 1990 and about the same time as a substantial increase in the frequency of research relying on EHA (see the bottom fitted curve).

7. For other lists of alternative mechanisms of diffusion, see DiMaggio and Powell (1983), Simmons, Dobbin, and Garrett (2006), Karch (2007), Shipan and Volden (2008), Meseguer and Gilardi (2009), and Walker, Avellaneda, and Berry (2011).

8. Pacheco (2012) posits a "social contagion model" in which the public in one state *A* learns about a policy when it is adopted by a neighboring state *B*, and then the public in *A* presses its own officials to adopt the policy.

9. Alternatively, one might conceive of imitation not as a mechanism distinct from learning but as a form of *bounded* learning in which policymakers lacking comprehensive information about the effectiveness of a policy rationally choose to emulate its adoption by a jurisdiction regarded as worthy of emulation based on a track record of effectiveness.

10. Since ΔN_t denotes the proportion of new adopters during time period *t* and $L - N_{t-1}$ is the proportion of potential adopters who have not adopted by the beginning of time period *t*, bN_{t-1} must represent the proportion of remaining potential adopters that actually adopt in time period *t*. Alternatively, bN_{t-1} can be viewed as the probability that an individual who has not yet adopted prior to time period *t* will do so during *t*. Those familiar with calculus should note that Equation 1 can be cast in continuous terms by defining $N(t)$ as the cumulative number of adopters at time *t*, defining *L* as the total number of potential adopters, and specifying (see Mahajan and Peterson 1985) that $dN(t) / dt = bN(t - 1) [L - N(t)]$.

11. Because there is no constant term in Equation 2, the model predicts that the regression intercept is zero.

12. Gray (1973b) recognizes that the national interaction model's assumption of a thorough mixing of states is unrealistic, but she adopts a position of methodological nominalism (Friedman 1953), arguing that the essential issue is not whether the assumption is realistic but whether it sufficiently approximates reality to be useful for explanation.

13. Regional diffusion may also be due to spillover-induced competition—when the externalities of a policy accrue primarily to nearby jurisdictions—or to governments coercing geographically proximate jurisdictions to adopt.

14. This "inequality of esteem" across states was observed by Grupp and Richards (1975) in their survey of upper-level administrators in US states. The leader-laggard model is certainly also compatible with a normative pressure mechanism in that laggards may be states that delay adopting a policy until it has been widely adopted by other governments.

15. Similarly, Clark (2013) hypothesizes that developed countries tended to pass legislation responding to the HIV/AIDS epidemic earlier than developing nations. Hierarchical models—based on population rather than economic development—originated in geographers' theories of the diffusion of product and cultural innovations among individuals. The models predicted that such innovations tend to flow from more populated cities to less populated rural areas (Hagerstrand 1967; Blaikie 1978).

16. Rogers (1995, 162) views *knowledge* as the first stage in the "innovation decision-process."

17. Using the traditional terminology of EHA, the unit of analysis is the jurisdiction *at risk* of adopting.

18. This is also true of diffusion models, which by their very nature focus on the spread of a single policy.

19. For a review of the research on the determinants of individual innovativeness, see Rogers (1995, chap. 7).

20. Taxation may be unique in this regard. Adopting a new tax instrument may be closer to routine policymaking than adopting most other major new policies because most proposals for new policies face the difficult task of finding a spot on a crowded governmental agenda; governments' need for revenue gives the issue of tax policy a permanent place on the agenda.

21. Moreover, the effect of ideology on innovation varies across policies. For example, a high level of liberalism should promote the adoption of new social welfare initiatives but impede the adoption of conservative criminal justice programs inconsistent with liberal ideology.

22. Brooks (2005) advances a similar proposition in a cross-national study of pension privatization. Yet, for some policies, it is actually *poor* fiscal health that contributes to an increase in the likelihood of adoption. Such situations have occurred with state taxes (Berry and Berry 1992) and industrial policies designed to attract new business to a state (Gray and Lowery 1990). For conceptual and operational definitions of "fiscal health," see Reeves (1986), Ladd and Yinger (1989), and Berry and Berry (1990).

23. Similarly, Sapat (2004) hypothesizes that a state agency's level of administrative professionalism influences its probability of adopting environmental policy innovations, and Kim and Gerber (2005) propose that the capacity of a state public utility commission—as reflected by the amount of discretion granted to the commission—influences its probability of adopting regulatory reforms.

24. Note also Soule and Earl's (2001) research on the impact of the presence of the Anti-Defamation League in a US state on the prospects for adoption of hate crime legislation, Allard's (2004) analysis of the impact of women's group activities on the adoption of state mothers' aid programs in the United States in the early 1900s, Toshkov's

(2013) study of the impact of the tobacco industry on adoption of smoking bans in Europe, and Dolšak's (2013) study of the role of domestic nongovernmental organizations (NGOs) on countries' adoption of the Kyoto Protocol.

25. In the United States, the character and activities of advocacy coalitions—which are presumed to consist of numerous individuals across the American states—might be conceived as factors influencing state government innovation that are neither purely "internal" nor "external" to states.

26. Some might argue that it is not feasible to accurately measure the presence or strength of entrepreneurs and advocacy coalitions when doing a fifty-state analysis. But Mintrom (1997) develops such measures for school choice entrepreneurs in the American states.

27. An alternative proposition is that a charter school program and a school voucher policy are complementary: when a state adopts one type of school choice reform, the political environment is changed, and the state becomes more amenable to other school choice initiatives. Presumably, empirical analysis could resolve these competing hypotheses.

28. The rest of this section draws extensively from Berry's (1994b) results.

29. The method is an EHA model (like those described in the next section of this chapter) with a single independent variable: the number of bordering states that have previously adopted.

30. For a more detailed discussion of EHA, see Box-Steffensmeier and Jones (2004), Allison (1984), or Buckley and Westerland (2004).

31. This description oversimplifies Berry and Baybeck's measure; the actual measure weights individuals by their distance from a state that has a lottery.

32. One other weakness of using the number of previously adopting states to tap the opportunity to *learn* from other states is that this variable could also plausibly be conceived as reflecting the opportunity of a state to *imitate* other states, the potential for a state to experience *normative pressure* to adopt, or the incentive of a state to *compete* with other states.

33. Indeed, Grossback, Nicholson-Crotty, and Peterson (2004) contend that the lottery diffuses via a mechanism in which states learn from ideologically similar states, which may or may not be contiguous. Moreover, it seems plausible that a state may *imitate* lottery adoptions by other states because its officials perceive those other states as reliable role models independent of any information about the consequences of these states' adoptions.

34. EHA can be modified to allow for the analysis of a repeatable event (Jones and Branton 2005; Box-Steffensmeier, De Boef, and Joyce 2007).

35. Innovation processes that allow for a choice among three or more policies can be specified using a multinomial logit model (Greene 1993) or a variant of a Cox duration model (Jones and Branton 2005).

36. Volden (2016) studies the diffusion of the most extreme form of policy modification: the abandonment of a failing policy.

37. Gilardi (2016) argues that diffusion research should be extended to an analysis of the implementation or enforcement of policies.

38. Mintrom's model includes a second equation predicting the probability that a state considering the proposal will actually *adopt* it. In essence, Mintrom assumes that policy adoption is contingent on preliminary policy consideration.

REFERENCES

Aidt, Toke S., and Peter S. Jensen. 2009. "The Taxman Tools Up: An Event History Study of the Introduction of the Personal Income Tax." *Journal of Public Economics* 93:160–75.

Aiken, Michael, and Robert R. Alford. 1970. "Community Structure and Innovation: The Case of Public Housing." *American Political Science Review* 64:843–864.

Allard, Scott W. 2004. "Competitive Pressures and the Emergence of Mothers' Aid Programs in the United States." *Policy Studies Journal* 32:521–544.

Allen, Mahalley D. 2005. "Laying Down the Law? Interest Group Influence on State Adoption of Animal Cruelty Felony Laws." *Policy Studies Journal* 33:443–457.

Allen, Mahalley D., Carrie Pettus, and Donald Haider-Markel. 2004. "Making the National Local: Specifying the Conditions for National Government Influence on State Policymaking." *State Politics and Policy Quarterly* 4:318–344.

Allison, Paul D. 1984. *Event History Analysis Data.* Beverly Hills, CA: Sage Publications.

Andrews, Clinton J. 2000. "Diffusion Pathways for Electricity Deregulation." *Publius* 30:17–34.

Bailey, Michael A., and Mark Carl Rom. 2004. "A Wider Race: Interstate Competition Across Health and Welfare Programs." *Journal of Politics* 66:326–347.

Balla, Steven J. 2001. "Interstate Professional Associations and the Diffusion of Policy Innovations." *American Politics Research* 29:221–245.

Barrett, Deborah, and Amy Ong Tsui. 1999. "Policy as Symbolic Statement: International Response to National Population Policies." *Social Forces* 78:213–233.

Baturo, Alexander, and Julia Gray. 2009. "Flatliners: Ideology and Rational Learning in the Adoption of the Flat Tax." *European Journal of Political Research* 48:130–159.

Baumgartner, Frank R., and Bryan D. Jones. 1993. *Agendas and Instability in American Politics.* Chicago: University of Chicago Press.

Baybeck, Brady, William D. Berry, and David Siegel. 2011. "A Strategic Theory of Policy Diffusion via Intergovernmental Competition." *Journal of Politics* 73:232–247.

Beck, Nathaniel, Jonathan N. Katz, and Richard Tucker. 1998. "Taking Time Seriously: Time Series–Cross-Section Analysis with a Binary Dependent Variable." *American Journal of Political Science* 42:1260–1288.

Berry, Frances Stokes. 1994a. "Innovation in Public Management: The Adoption of State Strategic Planning." *Public Administration Review* 54:322–329.

——. 1994b. "Sizing Up State Policy Innovation Research." *Policy Studies Journal* 22:442–456.

Berry, Frances Stokes, and William D. Berry. 1990. "State Lottery Adoptions as Policy Innovations: An Event History Analysis." *American Political Science Review* 84:395–415.

————. 1992. "Tax Innovation in the States: Capitalizing on Political Opportunity." *American Journal of Political Science* 36:715–742.

————. 1994. "The Politics of Tax Increases in the States." *American Journal of Political Science* 38:855–859.

Berry, William D. 1990. "The Confusing Case of Budgetary Incrementalism: Too Many Meanings for a Single Concept?" *Journal of Politics* 52:167–196.

Berry, William D., and Brady Baybeck. 2005. "Using Geographic Information Systems to Study Interstate Competition." *American Political Science Review* 99:505–519.

Berry, William D., Richard C. Fording, and Russell L. Hanson. 2003. "Reassessing the 'Race to the Bottom' in State Welfare Policy: Resolving the Conflict between Individual-Level and Aggregate Research." *Journal of Politics* 65:327–349.

Berry, William D., and David Lowery. 1987. *Understanding United States Government Growth: An Empirical Assessment of the Postwar Era.* New York: Praeger.

Bingham, Richard D. 1977. "The Diffusion of Innovation among Local Governments." *Urban Affairs Quarterly* 13:223–232.

Blaikie, P. 1978. "The Theory of the Spatial Diffusion of Innovativeness: A Spacious Cul de Sac." *Progress in Human Geography* 2:268–295.

Boehmke, Frederick J. 2009a. "Approaches to Modeling the Adoption and Diffusion of Policies with Multiple Components." *State Politics and Policy Quarterly* 9:229–252.

————. 2009b. "Policy Emulation or Policy Convergence? Potential Ambiguities in the Dyadic Event History Approach to State Policy Emulation." *Journal of Politics* 71:1125–1140.

Boehmke, Frederick J., and Paul Skinner. 2012. "State Policy Innovativeness Revisited." *State Politics and Policy Quarterly* 12:303–329.

Boehmke, Frederick J., and Richard Witmer. 2004. "Disentangling Diffusion: The Effects of Social Learning and Economic Competition on State Policy Innovation and Expansion." *Political Research Quarterly* 57:39–51.

Boushey, Graeme. 2012. "Punctuated Equilibrium Theory and the Diffusion of Innovations." *Policy Studies Journal* 40:127–146.

————. 2016. "Targeted for Diffusion? How the Use and Acceptance of Stereotypes Shape the Diffusion of Criminal Justice Policy Innovations in the American States." *American Political Science Review* 110:198–214.

Box-Steffensmeier, Janet M., Suzanna De Boef, and Kyle A. Joyce. 2007. "Event Dependence and Heterogeneity in Duration Models: The Conditional Frailty Model." *Political Analysis* 15:237–256.

Box-Steffensmeier, Janet M., and Bradford S. Jones. 2004. *Event History Modeling: A Guide for Social Scientists.* Cambridge: Cambridge University Press.

Brace, Paul, and Charles Barrilleaux. 1995. "A Model of Policy Reform in the American States." Paper presented at the annual meeting of the American Political Science Association, Chicago.

Braun, Dietmar, and Fabrizio Gilardi. 2006. "Taking 'Galton's Problem' Seriously: Towards a Theory of Policy Diffusion." *Journal of Theoretical Politics* 18:298–322.

Brooks, Sarah M. 2005. "Interdependent and Domestic Foundations of Policy Change: The Diffusion of Pension Privatization Around the World." *International Studies Quarterly* 49:273–294.

Brown, L., R. Schneider, M. Harvey, and B. Ridell. 1979. "Innovation Diffusion and Development in a Third World Setting: The Cooperative Movement in Sierra Leone." *Social Science Quarterly* 60:249–268.

Buckley, Jack, and Chad Westerland. 2004. "Duration Dependence, Functional Form, and Correct Standard Errors: Improving EHA Models of State Policy Diffusion." *State Politics and Policy Quarterly* 4:94–114.

Burge, Gregory S., and Brian Piper. 2012. "Strategic Fiscal Interdependence: County and Municipal Adoptions of Local Option Sales Taxes." *National Tax Journal* 65:387–416.

Bush, Sarah Sunn. 2011. "International Politics and the Spread of Quotas for Women in Legislatures." *International Organization* 65:103–137.

Calcagno, Peter T., Douglas M. Walker, and John D. Jackson. 2010. "Determinants of the Probability and Timing of Commercial Casino Legalization in the United States." *Public Choice* 142:69–90.

Canon, Bradley C., and Lawrence Baum. 1981. "Patterns of Adoption of Tort Law Innovations." *American Political Science Review* 75:975–987.

Cao, Xun. 2010. "Networks as Channels of Policy Diffusion: Explaining Worldwide Changes in Capital Taxation, 1998–2006." *International Studies Quarterly* 54:823–854.

Chamberlain, Robert, and Donald P. Haider-Markel. 2005. "'Lien on Me': State Policy Innovation in Response to Paper Terrorism." *Political Research Quarterly* 58:449–460.

Clark, Benjamin Y. 2013. "Multilateral, Regional, and National Determinants of Policy Adoption: The Case of HIV/AIDS Legislative Action." *International Journal of Public Health* 58:285–293.

Clark, Jill. 1985. "Policy Diffusion and Program Scope: Research Directions." *Publius* 15:61–70.

Clingermayer, James, and B. Dan Wood. 1995. "Disentangling Patterns of State Debt Financing." *American Political Science Review* 89:108–120.

Collier, David, and Richard E. Messick. 1975. "Prerequisites versus Diffusion: Testing Explanations of Social Security Adoption." *American Political Science Review* 69:1299–1315.

Crain, Robert L. 1966. "Fluoridation: The Diffusion of Innovation Among Cities." *Social Forces* 44:467–476.

Cyert, Richard M., and James G. March. 1963. *A Behavioral Theory of the Firm.* Englewood Cliffs, NJ: Prentice Hall.

Daley, Dorothy M., and James C. Garand. 2005. "Horizontal Diffusion, Vertical Diffusion, and Internal Pressure in State Environmental Policymaking, 1989–1998." *American Politics Research* 33:615–644.

Derthick, Martha. 1970. *The Influence of Federal Grants.* Cambridge, MA: Harvard University Press.

Desmarais, Bruce A., Jeff Harden, and Frederick J. Boehmke. 2015. "Persistent Policy Pathways: Inferring Diffusion Networks in the American States." *American Political Science Review* 109:392–406.

DiMaggio, Paul J., and W. W. Powell. 1983. "The Iron Cage Revisited: Institutionalism and Collective Rationality in Organizational Fields." *American Sociological Review* 48:147–160.

Doan, Alesha E., and Deborah R. McFarlane. 2012. "Saying No to Abstinence-Only Education: An Analysis of State Decision-Making." *Publius* 42:613–635.

Dolšak, Nives. 2013. "Climate Change Policies in the Transitional Economies of Europe and Eurasia: The Role of NGOs." *Voluntas* 24:382–402.

Downs, George W., Jr., and Lawrence B. Mohr. 1976. "Conceptual Issues in the Study of Innovation." *Administrative Science Quarterly* 21:700–713.

Elazar, Daniel. 1972. *American Federalism: A View from the States*. New York: Thomas Crowell.

Elkins, Zachary, Andrew T. Guzman, and Beth A. Simmons. 2006. "Competing for Capital: The Diffusion of Bilateral Investment Treaties, 1960–2000." *International Organization* 60:811–846.

Filer, John E., Donald L. Moak, and Barry Uze. 1988. "Why Some States Adopt Lotteries and Others Don't." *Public Finance Quarterly* 16:259–283.

Foster, John. 1978. "Regionalism and Innovation in the American States." *Journal of Politics* 40:179–187.

Friedman, Milton. 1953. *Essays in Positive Economics*. Chicago: University of Chicago Press.

Füglister, Katharina. 2012. "Where Does Learning Take Place? The Role of Intergovernmental Cooperation in Policy Diffusion." *European Journal of Political Research* 51:316–349.

Genschel, Philipp. 2002. "Globalization, Tax Competition, and the Welfare State." *Politics and Society* 30:245–275.

Gilardi, Fabrizio. 2005. "The Institutional Foundations of Regulatory Capitalism: The Diffusion of Independent Regulatory Agencies in Western Europe." *Annals of the American Academy of Social and Political Sciences* 598: 84–101.

———. 2010. "Who Learns from What in Policy Diffusion Processes?" *American Journal of Political Science* 5:650–666.

———. 2016. "Four Ways We Can Improve Policy Diffusion Research." *State Politics and Policy Quarterly* 16:8–21.

Gilardi, Fabrizio, and Katharina Füglister. 2008. "Empirical Modeling of Policy Diffusion in Federal States: The Dyadic Approach." *Swiss Political Science Review* 14:413–450.

Gilardi, Fabrizio, Katharina Füglister, and Stéphane Luyet. 2009. "Learning from Others: The Diffusion of Hospital Financing Reforms in OECD Countries." *Comparative Political Studies* 42:549–573.

Glick, Henry R. 1981. "Innovation in State Judicial Administration: Effects on Court Management and Organization." *American Politics Quarterly* 9:49–69.

Glick, Henry R., and Scott P. Hays. 1991. "Innovation and Reinvention in State Policymaking: Theory and the Evolution of Living Will Laws." *Journal of Politics* 53:835–850.

Graham, Erin R., Charles R. Shipan, and Craig Volden. 2013. "The Diffusion of Policy Diffusion Research in Political Science." *British Journal of Political Science* 43:673–701.

Gray, Virginia. 1973a. "Innovation in the States: A Diffusion Study." *American Political Science Review* 67:1174–1185.

———. 1973b. "Rejoinder to 'Comment' by Jack L. Walker." *American Political Science Review* 67:1192–1193.

Gray, Virginia, and David Lowery. 1990. "The Corporatist Foundations of State Industrial Policy." *Social Science Quarterly* 71:3–24.

Greene, William H. 1993. *Econometric Analysis.* 2nd ed. New York: Macmillan.

Grossback, Lawrence J., Sean Nicholson-Crotty, and David A. M. Peterson. 2004. "Ideology and Learning in Policy Diffusion." *American Politics Research* 32:521–545.

Grupp, Fred W., Jr., and Alan R. Richards. 1975. "Variations in Elite Perceptions of American States as Referents for Public Policy Making." *American Political Science Review* 69:850–858.

Haas, Peter M. 1992. "Introduction: Epistemic Communities and International Policy Coordination." *International Organization* 46:1–35.

Hagerstrand, T. 1967. *Innovation Diffusion as a Spatial Process.* Chicago: University of Chicago Press.

Hansen, Susan. 1983. *The Politics of Taxation.* Westport, CT: Praeger.

Hays, Scott P., and Henry R. Glick. 1997. "The Role of Agenda Setting in Policy Innovation: An Event History Analysis of Living Will Laws." *American Politics Quarterly* 25:497–516.

Heclo, Hugh. 1974. *Modern Social Politics in Britain and Sweden.* New Haven, CT: Yale University Press.

Henisz, Witold J., Bennet A. Zelner, and Mauro F. Guillén. 2005. "The Worldwide Diffusion of Market-Oriented Infrastructure Reform, 1977–1999." *American Sociological Review* 70:871–897.

Hill, Kim Quaile, Jan Leighly, and Angela Hinton-Andersson. 1995. "Lower Class Mobilization and Policy Linkage in the United States." *American Journal of Political Science* 39:75–86.

Hill, Twyla J. 2000. "Legally Extending the Family: An Event History Analysis of Grandparent Visitation Rights Laws." *Journal of Family Issues* 21:246–261.

Hinkle, Rachael. 2015. "Into the Words: Using Statutory Text to Explore the Impact of Federal Courts on State Policy Diffusion." *American Journal of Political Science* 59:1002–1021.

Hoekstra, Valerie. 2009. "The Pendulum of Precedent: U.S. State Legislative Response to Supreme Court Decisions on Minimum Wage Legislation for Women." *State Politics and Policy Quarterly* 9:257–283.

Hofferbert, Richard. 1966. "The Relation between Public Policy and Some Structural and Environmental Variables in the American States." *American Political Science Review* 60:83–92.

Hughes, Melanie M., Mona Lena Krook, and Pamela Paxton. 2015. "Transnational Women's Activism and the Global Diffusion of Gender Quotas." *International Studies Quarterly* 59:357–372.

Ito, Shuichiro. 2001. "Shaping Policy Diffusion: Event History Analyses of Regional Laws in Japanese Prefectures." *Japanese Journal of Political Science* 2:211–235.

Jensen, Nathan M., and René Lindstädt. 2012. "Leaning Right and Learning from the Left: Diffusion of Corporate Tax Policy across Borders." *Comparative Political Studies* 45:283–311.

Jones, Bradford S., and Regina P. Branton. 2005. "Beyond Logit and Probit: Cox Duration Models of Single, Repeating and Competing Events for State Policy Adoption." *State Politics and Policy Quarterly* 5:420–443.

Ka, Sangjoon, and Paul Teske. 2002. "Ideology and Professionalism: Electricity Regulation and Deregulation over Time in the American States." *American Politics Research* 30:323–343.

Karch, Andrew. 2007. "Emerging Issues and Future Directions in State Policy Diffusion Research." *State Politics and Policy Quarterly* 7:54–80.

———. 2012. "Vertical Diffusion and the Policy-Making Process: The Politics of Embryonic Stem Cell Research." *Political Research Quarterly* 65:48–61.

Karch, Andrew, and Matthew Cravens. 2014. "Rapid Diffusion and Policy Reform: The Adoption and Modification of Three Strikes Laws." *State Politics and Policy Quarterly* 14:461–491.

Karch, Andrew, Sean C. Nicholson-Crotty, and Neal D. Woods. 2016. "Policy Diffusion and the Pro-Innovation Bias." *Political Research Quarterly* 69:83–95.

Kiewiet, D. Roderick, and Matthew D. McCubbins. 1985. "Congressional Appropriations and the Electoral Connection." *Journal of Politics* 47:59–82.

Kim, Junseok, and Brian Gerber. 2005. "Bureaucratic Leverage over Policy Choice: Explaining the Dynamics of State-Level Reforms in Telecommunications Regulation." *Policy Studies Journal* 33:613–633.

Kingdon, John W. 1984. *Agendas, Alternatives, and Public Policies.* Boston: Little, Brown.

Kraemer, Kenneth I., Vijay Gurbaxani, and John Leslie King. 1992. "Economic Development, Government Policy, and the Diffusion of Computing in Asia-Pacific Countries." *Public Administration Review* 52:146–156.

Ladd, Helen F., and John L. Yinger. 1989. *America's Ailing Cities: Fiscal Health and the Design of Urban Policy.* Baltimore: Johns Hopkins University Press.

Langer, Laura, and Paul Brace. 2005. "The Preemptive Power of State Supreme Courts: Adoption of Abortion and Death Penalty Legislation." *Policy Studies Journal* 33:317–340.

Lee, Chung-Pin, Kaiju Chang, and Frances Stokes Berry. 2011. "Testing the Development and Diffusion of E-Government and E-Democracy: A Global Perspective." *Public Administration Review* 71:444–454.

Levy, Jack S. 1994. "Learning and Foreign Policy: Sweeping a Conceptual Minefield." *International Organization* 48:279–312.

Lowry, William R. 2005. "Policy Reversal and Changing Politics: State Governments and Dam Removals." *State Politics and Policy Quarterly* 5:394–419.

Lubell, Mark, Mark Schneider, John T. Scholz, and Mihriye Mete. 2002. "Watershed Partnerships and the Emergence of Collective Action Institutions." *American Journal of Political Science* 46:148–163.

Ma, Liang. 2013. "The Diffusion of Government Microblogging: Evidence from Chinese Municipal Police Bureaus." *Public Management Review* 15:288–309.

———. 2016. "Political Ideology, Social Capital and Government Innovativeness: Evidence from the US States." *Public Management Review*. Published electronically May 12, 2016. http://dx.doi.org/10.1080/14719037.2016.1177108.

Mahajan, V., and R. A. Peterson. 1985. *Models for Innovation Diffusion*. Beverly Hills, CA: Sage Publications.

Majone, Giandomenico. 1997. "The New European Agencies: Regulation by Information." *Journal of European Public Policy* 4:262–275.

Makse, Todd, and Craig Volden. 2011. "The Role of Policy Attributes in the Diffusion of Innovations." *Journal of Politics* 73:108–124.

Mann, Arthur J. 1980. "Wagner's Law: An Econometric Test for Mexico: 1925–1976." *National Tax Journal* 33:189–201.

March, James G., and Herbert A. Simon. 1993. *Organizations*. 2nd ed. Cambridge, MA: Blackwell.

Mayhew, David. 1974. *Congress: The Electoral Connection*. New Haven, CT: Yale University Press.

McCann, Pamela Clouser, Charles Shipan, and Craig Volden. 2015. "Top Down Federalism: State Policy Responses to National Government Discussions." *Publius* 45:495–525.

McLendon, Michael K., Donald E. Heller, and Steven P. Young. 2005. "State Postsecondary Policy Innovation: Politics, Competition, and the Interstate Migration of Policy Ideas." *Journal of Higher Education* 76:363–382.

Menzel, Donald C., and Irwin Feller. 1977. "Leadership and Interaction Patterns in the Diffusion of Innovations among the American States." *Western Political Quarterly* 30:528–536.

Meseguer, Covadonga. 2004. "What Role for Learning? The Diffusion of Privatisation in OECD and Latin American Countries." *Journal of Public Policy* 24:299–325.

———. 2005. "Policy Learning, Policy Diffusion, and the Making of a New Order." *Annals of the American Academy of Political and Social Science* 598:67–81.

———. 2006. "Learning and Economic Policy Choices." *European Journal of Political Economy* 22:156–178.

Meseguer, Covadonga, and Fabrizio Gilardi. 2009. "What Is New in the Study of Policy Diffusion?" *Review of International Political Economy* 16:527–543.

Midlarsky, Manus I. 1978. "Analyzing Diffusion and Contagion Effects: The Urban Disorders of the 1960s." *American Political Science Review* 72:996–1008.

Mikesell, John L. 1978. "Election Periods and State Tax Policy Cycles." *Public Choice* 33:99–105.

Mintrom, Michael. 1997. "Policy Entrepreneurs and the Diffusion of Innovation." *American Journal of Political Science* 41:738–770.

Mintrom, Michael, and Sandra Vergari. 1996. "Advocacy Coalitions, Policy Entrepreneurs, and Policy Change." *Policy Studies Journal* 24:420–434.

———. 1998. "Policy Networks and Innovation Diffusion: The Case of State Education Reforms." *Journal of Politics* 60:126–148.

Mohr, Lawrence. 1969. "Determinants of Innovation in Organizations." *American Political Science Review* 75:111–126.

Moon, Jae, and Donald Norris. 2005. "Advancing E-Government at the Grassroots: Tortoise or Hare?" *Public Administration Review* 65:64–75.

Mooney, Christopher Z., and Mei-Hsien Lee. 1995. "Legislating Morality in the American States: The Case of Pre-Roe Abortion Regulation Reform." *American Journal of Political Science* 39:599–627.

Mossberger, Karen. 1999. "State-Federal Diffusion and Policy Learning: From Enterprise Zones to Empowerment Zones." *Publius* 29:31–50.

Most, Benjamin A., and Harvey Starr. 1980. "Diffusion, Reinforcement, Geopolitics, and the Spread of War." *American Political Science Review* 74:932–946.

Nicholson-Crotty, Sean, and Sanya Carley. 2016. "Effectiveness, Implementation and Policy Diffusion: Or 'Can We Make That Work for Us?'" *State Politics and Policy Quarterly* 16:78–97.

Oates, Wallace E. 2001. "Fiscal Competition or Harmonization? Some Reflections." *National Tax Journal* 54:507–512.

Pacheco, Julianna. 2012. "The Social Contagion Model: Exploring the Role of Public Opinion on the Diffusion of Antismoking Legislation across the American States." *Journal of Politics* 74:187–202.

Peterson, Paul E., and Mark C. Rom. 1990. *Welfare Magnets*. Washington, DC: Brookings Institution.

Reeves, H. Clyde. 1986. *Measuring Fiscal Capacity*. Boston: Oelgeschlager, Gunn & Hain.

Regens, James L. 1980. "State Policy Responses to the Energy Issue." *Social Science Quarterly* 61:44–57.

Rogers, Everett M. 1995. *Diffusion of Innovations*. 4th ed. New York: Free Press.

Roh, Jongho, and Frances S. Berry. 2008. "Modeling the Outcomes of State Abortion Funding Referenda: Morality or Redistributive Policy, or Both?" *State Politics and Policy Quarterly* 8:66–87.

Sabatier, Paul A., and Christopher M. Weible. 2007. "The Advocacy Coalition Framework: Innovations and Clarifications." In *Theories of the Policy Process,* edited by Paul A. Sabatier, chap. 7. Boulder, CO: Westview Press.

Sapat, Alka. 2004. "Devolution and Innovation: The Adoption of State Environmental Policy Innovations by Administrative Agencies." *Public Administration Review* 64:141–151.

Savage, Robert L. 1978. "Policy Innovativeness as a Trait of American States." *Journal of Politics* 40:212–224.

Schneider, Mark, Paul Teske, and Michael Mintrom. 1995. *Public Entrepreneurs*. Princeton, NJ: Princeton University Press.

Seljan, Ellen C., and Nicholas Weller. 2011. "Diffusion in Direct Democracy: The Effect of Political Information on Proposals for Tax and Expenditure Limits in the US States." *State Politics and Policy Quarterly* 11:348–368.

Shipan, Charles, and Craig Volden. 2006. "Bottom-Up Federalism: The Diffusion of Antismoking Laws from U.S. Cities to States." *American Journal of Political Science* 50:825–843.

———. 2008. "The Mechanisms of Policy Diffusion." *American Journal of Political Science* 52:840–857.

———. 2014. "When the Smoke Clears: Expertise, Learning and Policy Diffusion." *Journal of Public Policy* 34:357–387.

Sigelman, Lee, and Roland E. Smith. 1980. "Consumer Legislation in the American States: An Attempt at Explanation." *Social Science Quarterly* 61:58–69.

Simmons, Beth A. 2000. "International Law and State Behavior: Commitment and Compliance in International Monetary Affairs." *American Political Science Review* 94:819–835.

Simmons, Beth A., Frank Dobbin, and Geoffrey Garrett. 2006. "Introduction: The International Diffusion of Liberalism." *International Organization* 60:781–810.

Simmons, Beth A., and Zachary Elkins. 2004. "The Globalization of Liberalization: Policy Diffusion in the International Political Economy." *American Political Science Review* 98:171–189.

Soss, Joe, Sanford F. Schram, Thomas P. Vartanian, and Erin O'Brien. 2001. "Setting the Terms of Relief: Explaining State Policy Choices in the Devolution Revolution." *American Journal of Political Science* 45:378–395.

Soule, Sarah A., and Jennifer Earl. 2001. "The Enactment of State-Level Hate Crime Law in the United States: Intrastate and Interstate Factors." *Sociological Perspectives* 44:281–305.

Stone, Diane. 1999. "Learning Lessons and Transferring Policy across Time, Space and Disciplines." *Politics* 19:51–59.

Stream, Christopher. 1999. "Health Reform in the States: A Model of State Small Group Health Insurance Market Reform." *Political Research Quarterly* 52:499–525.

Sugiyama, Natasha Borges. 2012. "Bottom-Up Policy Diffusion: National Emulation of a Conditional Cash." *Publius* 42:25–51.

Teodoro, Manuel P. 2009. "Bureaucratic Job Mobility and the Diffusion of Innovations." *American Journal of Political Science* 53:175–189.

Tolbert, Pamela, and Lynne Zucker. 1983. "Institutional Sources of Change in the Formal Structure of Organizations: The Diffusion of Civil Service Reform, 1880–1935." *Administrative Science Quarterly* 28:22–39.

Tomz, Michael, Jason Wittenberg, and Gary King. 2003. "CLARIFY: Software for Interpreting and Presenting Statistical Results." Version 2.1. Stanford University, University of Wisconsin, and Harvard University. http://gking.harvard.edu.

Toshkov, Dimiter. 2013. "Policy-Making Beyond Political Ideology: The Adoption of Smoking Bans in Europe." *Public Administration* 91:448–468.

Volden, Craig. 2002. "The Politics of Competitive Federalism: A Race to the Bottom in Welfare Benefits?" *American Journal of Political Science* 46:352–363.

———. 2006. "States as Policy Laboratories: Emulating Success in the Children's Health Insurance Program." *American Journal of Political Science* 50:294–312.

———. 2016. "Failures: Diffusion, Learning and Policy Abandonment." *State Politics and Policy Quarterly* 16:44–77.

Volden, Craig, Michael M. Ting, and Daniel P. Carpenter. 2008. "A Formal Model of Learning and Policy Diffusion." *American Political Science Review* 102:319–332.

Wagner, Adolph. 1877. *Finanzwissenshaft.* Pt. 1. Leipzig: C. F. Winter.

Walker, Jack L. 1969. "The Diffusion of Innovations among the American States." *American Political Science Review* 63:880–899.

———. 1973. "Comment." *American Political Science Review* 67:1186–1191.

Walker, Richard M. 2006. "Innovation Type and Diffusion: An Empirical Analysis of Local Government." *Public Administration* 84:311–335.

Walker, Richard M., Claudia N. Avellaneda, and Frances Stokes Berry. 2011. "The Diffusion of Innovation: A Longitudinal Empirical Test of the Berry and Berry Model." *Public Management Review* 13:95–125.

Welch, Susan, and Kay Thompson. 1980. "The Impact of Federal Incentives on State Policy Innovations." *American Journal of Political Science* 24:715–729.

Weyland, Kurt, ed. 2004. *Learning from Foreign Models in Latin American Policy Reform.* Washington, DC: Woodrow Wilson Center Press.

———. 2007. *Bounded Rationality and Policy Diffusion: Social Sector Reform in Latin America.* Princeton, NJ: Princeton University Press.

PART II

Comparisons and Conclusions

8

Comparison of Theories of the Policy Process

TANYA HEIKKILA AND PAUL CAIRNEY

Scholars compare theories, frameworks, and models (or generally "theoretical approaches") to consider how to combine their insights or accept some and reject others (Sabatier 2007a, 330). They often do this implicitly or in an ad hoc way. Our aim is to add some rigor to this process by examining three of the criteria used by Weible (2017, see Introduction in this volume):

1. To what extent does the approach cover the basic elements of a theoretical approach, such as a shared vocabulary and defined concepts?
2. Are the scholars who are applying the theoretical approach developing an active research program?
3. Does the theoretical approach explain a large part of the policy process?

Using these criteria, our aim is to make the theoretical approaches presented in this volume comparable by identifying their key concepts, their strengths and weaknesses for understanding the policy process and advancing knowledge, and the similarities and differences in what these theories explain and what shared knowledge can be gleaned across them.[1]

This takes place in the context of a policy theory field that is not conducive to systematic comparison. The literature contains a complicated mix of frameworks, theories, and models (Schlager 1999, 2007). The major theories and frameworks have generally been produced independently of each other and were not designed with these comparisons in mind. They contain different frames of reference, foci, and concepts. Some are used to produce a parsimonious understanding of a large number of cases; others tend to emphasize in-depth understanding of single cases. Their assumptions and findings may complement or contradict each other. They may attach different meanings to the same concepts (Cairney 2013a, 7). They may require extensive training to understand fully. So, a systematic comparison is an important aim in itself—to foster broad agreement on how we, as a group of scholars, can understand and judge different approaches. This is as much a practical requirement as a scientific statement: we need to know what information to pay attention to and what to ignore and to ensure that the information we receive can be meaningfully compared with our own. Although we recognize that some of the approaches identified in this book may operate more at the level of broader frameworks, or more narrowly as models (see Schlager 1999, 2007 for further discussion), for the remainder of this chapter we use the term *theory* in a generic sense for ease of description.

HOW SHOULD WE COMPARE THEORETICAL APPROACHES? THREE CRITERIA

The first criterion is the extent to which the basic elements of a theory are covered. Following Weible (2017, see Introduction, this volume), we consider the extent to which each has (1) a defined scope and levels of analysis, (2) a shared vocabulary and defined concepts, (3) explicit assumptions, (4) identified relationships among key concepts or variables, and (5) a model of the individual grounding the theory. People making choices are at the heart of policy studies, but not all theories conceptualize this process extensively.

The second criterion is the development of an active research program. We consider four indicators of this criterion: (1) the degree to which the approach has been employed actively by researchers and published as journal articles and books; (2) whether it has been tested in multiple contexts, inclusive of diverse policy issues and different political systems, and with multiple methods; (3) whether scholars involved in employing the theory have made an attempt to actively develop shared research protocols, methods, or approaches; and (4) how the theory has been adapted or modified over time.

Developing indicators of the third criterion—whether the theory explains a large part of the policy process—is the most challenging because we know that the policy process is complex and there is no "general theory" (Smith and Larimer 2009, 15–19). This prompts us to consider a fundamental question: Given that we must simplify a complex world to understand it, which elements do policy scholars treat as crucial to explanation? These crucial elements are identified in similar ways (see, e.g., Weible 2014; John 2003; Cairney 2012b; Schlager 2007).

We are interested in how each theory describes the following elements and explains the interactions between them to provide an overall explanation of policymaking systems:

1. *Actors making choices:* The policymaking world may include thousands of people. To simplify, policy theories often categorize and describe key actors. Actors can be individuals or collectives, and collectives can range from private companies to interest groups to governments bodies (Weible 2017, see Introduction, this volume).

2. *Institutions:* These are the rules, norms, practices, and relationships that influence individual and collective behavior. The choices of actors are explained partly by their understanding of and adherence to rules. Rules can be formal and widely understood, such as when enshrined in law or a constitution, or informal and only understood in particular organizations. Institutions at one level (e.g., constitutional) can also shape activity at another (e.g., legislative or regulatory), establish the types of venues where policy decisions are made, and make the rules that allow particular types of actors or ideas to enter the policy process.

3. *Networks or subsystems:* These are the relationships between actors responsible for policy decisions and the "pressure participants" (Jordan, Halpin, and Maloney 2004), such as interest groups with which they consult and negotiate. Senior policymakers delegate responsibility for policymaking to bureaucrats, who seek information and advice from groups. Groups exchange information for access to and potential influence within government. Bureaucracies and other public bodies (or forums for collective choice) may have operating procedures that favor particular sources of evidence and some participants over others.

4. *Ideas or beliefs:* This broad category captures how theories deal with ways of thinking or the knowledge that plays a role in the policy process. This category may include beliefs, knowledge, worldviews, and shared definitions of policy problems, images, and solutions within groups, organizations, networks, and political systems. Some ideas or beliefs may be taken for granted or rarely questioned—such as core beliefs, values, or paradigms. Others may be more malleable, such as proposed solutions to policy problems.

5. *Policy context:* This category describes the wide array of features of the policymaking environment that can influence policy decisions. It can refer to the often-changing policy conditions that policymakers take into account when identifying problems and deciding how to address them, such as a political system's geography, biophysical and demographic profile, economy, and mass attitudes and behavior (Hofferbert 1974). It can also refer to a sense of policymaker "inheritance"—of laws, rules, institutions, and programs—on entry into office (Rose 1990).

6. *Events:* Events can be routine and anticipated, such as elections that produce limited change or introduce new actors with different ideas. Or they can be unanticipated incidents, including social or natural crises or major scientific breakthroughs and technological changes (Weible 2017, see Introduction, this volume). Their unpredictability makes them difficult to theorize, and they can often be treated as "errors" or external factors providing an additional source of explanation. Or they can be incorporated within theories that focus on how actors interpret and respond to events.

The main complication is that policy theories do not treat these concepts in the same way. First, these terms are ambiguous, producing debate about their meaning and most useful applications. For example, there are at least five major approaches to studies of institutionalism (rational choice, historical, sociological, constructivist, and feminist), and it is still difficult to place many texts within those categories (Lowndes 2010, 65; Hall and Taylor 1996, 939–940; Peters 2005, 108; Cairney 2012b, 77). These problems are compounded when we try to connect terms and use a range of other ambiguous concepts—such as power, evolution, punctuated equilibrium, and policy entrepreneurs—to provide a complete explanation (Cairney 2012b, 271–273). Additionally, each of the elements we identified above includes multiple subelements, and scholars may debate whether the subelements can be combined or form part of the same overarching concept.

Second, the boundaries between terms are fluid. As one example, institutions are defined primarily as rules and norms, which make them difficult to disentangle from ideas or networks. In particular, "constructivist institutionalism" challenges the suggestion that institutions represent fixed structures (Hay 2006, 65; Béland and Cox 2010, 4; Cairney 2012b, 83–84). Other studies identify shared rules and norms as the main explanation for network or subsystem stability (Jordan and Maloney 1997). Similarly, one person's event or context is another person's idea, particularly if events only become important when important people pay attention to them.

Third, theories explore these processes at the level of the individual, network, or system. The metaphor of the telescope is useful: (1) zooming in to see individuals, then zooming out to see groups and organizations, networks, and political systems (Cairney 2012b, 346); and (2) shifting one's focus from the "top" to the "bottom" or from one organization to another. Further, not all theories focus on all aspects of the policy process. Some focus on a small number of these terms—partly because trade-offs exist between explaining either one element in depth or the whole process. So, we should not assume that each theory refers to each term in the same way or shares the same focus. Rather, we consider how each theory uses these elements of the policy process and describes their interaction to produce an explanation of a significant part of the policy process.

COMPARATIVE CRITERION 1: ELEMENTS OF A THEORY

To help organize our comparison, Table 8.1 presents a brief summary of the indicators we use to explore our first criterion: key elements of a theory. These indicators include: (1) a defined scope and levels of analysis; (2) shared vocabulary and defined concepts; (3) defined assumptions; (4) the model of the individual; and (5) identified relationships among key concepts.

Scope and levels of analysis. Each of the approaches in this volume has a relatively well-defined scope and provides a different lens on the policy process. They all, to some degree, address questions related to policy formulation and change within their scope. The Multiple Streams Framework (MSF), Punctuated Equilibrium Theory (PET), and innovation and diffusion models (IDM) tend to emphasize particular stages of the policy process more than the other theories, although each poses distinct questions. MSF explores how agenda setting and policymaking occur under conditions of ambiguity (see Chapter 1). PET explains why and how political systems, generally characterized by stability and incrementalism, occasionally produce large-scale departures from the past (see Chapter 2). The IDM consider what explains the adoption of new policies and how they diffuse across states and other jurisdictions (see Chapter 7). The Narrative Policy Framework (NPF) and Advocacy Coalition Framework (ACF) place a premium on studying questions related to policy formulation and change but also the importance of the cognitive biases that make storytelling and coalition formation so important. The ACF digs into questions around coalition formation and policy learning, for example (see Chapter 4). The NPF looks at how narratives influence public opinion, how these narratives are structured, and how they reflect policy beliefs (see Chapter 5). Although Policy Feedback Theory (PFT; see Chapter 3) addresses policy formulation and change, it focuses more on questions of policy design and dynamics, such as the feedback of policies into society. The Institutional Analysis and Development (IAD) framework and its related Social-Ecological Systems (SES) framework differ from the other theories in that they are explicitly more generic frameworks. The IAD framework is aimed at guiding inquiry of how institutions, which include public policies, shape human interactions as well as how they are designed and perform. As noted by Schlager and Cox (2017, see Chapter 6 in this volume), the starting point for the IAD framework is typically a collective action problem, and scholars have applied a diverse set of theories and models in studying different collective action problems.

For many of the approaches covered in this volume, the level of analysis, or where conclusions from the research are drawn or inferred, is a policy system or subsystem. However, it is important to differentiate between the level of analysis and the unit of observation. Often researchers applying the theories rely on units of observation that differ from the primary level of analysis. For

TABLE 8.1 What Elements of a Theoretical Approach Are Included?

	MSF	PET	PFT	ACF	NPF	IAD Framework	IDM
Scope and levels of analysis	Scope: Policy choice under ambiguity Level: System, but implicit, and focus is on actors coupling streams	Scope: Political system toward stability and periodic major change Level: System	Scope: How policies shape politics and subsequent policymaking Level: System, but implicit	Scope: Advocacy coalition interaction, learning, and policy change Levels: Coalitions and subsystems	Scope: Influence of narratives on public opinion, policy dialogue, agenda setting, policy change Levels: Individual, coalition, societal	Scope: How people devise institutions and the outcomes of those processes Level: The action situation may be broadly interpreted	Scope: Policy diffusion and innovation Levels: Policymaking venues/governments
Shared vocabulary and defined concepts	Primarily the five structural elements of the framework	Numerous key concepts such as institutional friction	Primarily policy feedback and the types of effects	Numerous key concepts	Numerous key concepts, some borrowed	Numerous key concepts, expanded further by Social-Ecological Systems (SES) framework	Primarily policy adoption and diffusion and key concepts explaining diffusion or adoption
Assumptions	Explicitly defined	Included, for example, logic of decision making, but not explicitly labeled as assumptions	Implicitly defined assumptions underlying the rationale for effects	Explicitly defined	Explicitly defined	Defined, but very generally at the framework level	Some assumptions explicitly defined for the models
Model of the individual	Challenges assumptions of comprehensive rationality; focus on ambiguity	Bounded rationality, particularly relating to attention	Not explicitly discussed in this volume; suggests individual choice is shaped by policies and institutions	Boundedly rational, emphasis that individuals are motivated by beliefs and prone to devil shift	Homo narrans, builds on bounded rationality recognizing the role of heuristics, primacy of affect, hot cognition, selective exposure, primacy of groups, identity protective cognition, narrative cognition	Multiple are compatible, but the researcher must be explicit with the model	Not explicit, but recognizes that both bounded rationality and rational choice models may be compatible
Relationships among key concepts	Generally identifies three streams that come together during windows of opportunity to cause major policy change; specific hypotheses recently added	Describes factors that lead to major policy change and those that constrain change or produce incrementalism; offers specific hypotheses for empirical testing	General emphasis on effects of public policy on the meaning of citizenship, form of governance, power of groups, political agendas—all of which affect future policy; hypotheses in empirical applications	General relationships shaping subsystem at framework level; specific factors that influence coalition formation, policy learning, and policy change via hypotheses	Hypotheses at microlevel and mesolevel on influence of narrative elements on individual persuasion, how narratives are used in coalitional strategies, policy learning	General relationships at the framework level, and more specific at theory and model levels, for example, conditions that lead to collective action and principles of robust common pool resource governance	General model of innovation identified; specific determinants of policy diffusion and adoption identified in alternative models in empirical applications

example, ACF studies typically use individuals or organizations as the unit of observation to draw conclusions about coalitions or subsystems, whereas PET is explicitly a system-level analysis.

Some theories are more explicit than others about what levels of analysis are of interest. The NPF directs researchers to three possible levels of analysis (macro/societal, meso/subsystem, micro/individual), whereas the ACF identifies and defines two levels of analysis (policy subsystems and coalitions). PET discusses the nature of decision making in policy systems but does not define policy systems as directly as the ACF. The MSF and PFT also explore questions related to policy systems but do not pay close attention to the boundaries of those systems. IDM studies look at policymaking venues or governments for the level of analysis. Still, the IDM draw inferences about how policies diffuse across a system or collection of states (i.e., a political system made up of states, such as the United States or European Union). The primary level of analysis in the IAD framework also diverges from the others in that it looks at action situations. However, the breadth of the concept of the action situation means that it could be viewed as a coalition, network, or other type of collective action venue, depending on the research question addressed. Decision making within the action situation can also operate at constitutional, collective, and operational levels.

Shared vocabulary and defined concepts. All of the theories or frameworks presented have developed shared vocabulary and a set of concepts that inform the research scope. Most are explicit about their definitions and have incorporated the primary key concepts into principal diagrams and figures that represent the scope of the theory. The IAD and the SES frameworks may have the most extensive set of shared vocabulary, likely the result of their broad scope. By contrast, the MSF, although it presents a set of shared key concepts and general definitions, would benefit from more consistent and clear operationalization of its core concepts, as recognized by Herweg, Zahariadis, and Zohlnhöfer in this volume (2017, see Chapter 1), Jones et al. (2016), and Cairney and Jones (2016). Although clear conceptualization can aid analysts by providing opportunities for more precise measurement, especially across research contexts, an overly complex, or precisely defined, set of concepts may inhibit widespread appeal of the applicability of the theory. Additionally, the set of key concepts identified within these theories can evolve, or the theory may incorporate new concepts or shift their emphasis. We discuss some of these changes below in our examination of research program coherence.

Defined assumptions. All of the theories in this volume offer at least implicit assumptions that underlie their theoretical logic. The IAD framework's assumptions are the most general and least specified at the framework level. For example, in laying out the components of an action situation, or identifying a typology of rules and the levels where collective action occurs (operational, collective choice, constitutional), the IAD framework includes assumptions about the factors that are critical to understanding collective decision making. ACF provides more explicit assumptions, such as its emphasis on a long time period to study policy change. MSF is also explicit with its assumptions, focusing on the ambiguity of decision making, the time constraints facing policymakers, problematic preferences of actors in policy processes, unclear technology within political systems, fluid participation in decision making bodies, and stream independence. PET draws on similar assumptions about bounded rationality and agenda setting but adds the expectation that policy systems exhibit exogenous and endogenous drivers of positive and negative feedback. The ACF assumes that the focus of policymaking activity is the subsystem. The NPF also recognizes the subsystem as a key level of activity at the mesolevel but also explicitly assumes that policy narratives operate across micro-, meso-, and macrolevels. The NPF further assumes that the world is (to a great extent) socially constructed, but those constructions are susceptible to manipulation by actors telling stories. The MSF similarly suggests that the problem stream is socially constructed but does not include this in its set of explicit assumptions.

Model of the individual. The model of the individual in many theories is part of the stated assumptions. Most theories in this book adopt a broad focus on bounded rationality. People do not have the time, resources, and cognitive ability to consider all issues and act optimally, so they use informational shortcuts and other heuristics or emotional cues to produce what they perceive to be good-enough decisions. However, bounded rationality on its own is little more than a truism, and each approach has to make sense of its implications in relation to other key concepts. So, despite its widespread recognition among the theories, we find different emphases in the models of the individual.

For instance, the NPF emphasizes the role of emotions and narration on human decision making in establishing its model of *homo narrans*: actors tell stories to manipulate the bounded rationality of others. PET focuses on the need for individual actors to consider issues serially (one issue at a time), whereas organizations can parallel process, producing limited attention to most issues, but continuous potential for major shifts in attention. The theories also differ in their recommendations about how to work with the model of the individual. The IAD framework accepts that it can accommodate differing models of the individual; some models make the assumption of comprehensive rationality, whereas others explore bounded rationality. What is critical in the IAD framework is that analysts are explicit about their assumptions about individual values, their information-processing abilities, and their internal decision making mechanism. IDM also recognize that both bounded rationality and rational choice models may be compatible with the theory. The NPF seeks to synthesize approximately ten ideas about rationality and decision making to produce a model that is more nuanced, but it is difficult to connect the specific elements of the model to the rationale underlying the theory's hypotheses. On the opposite end of the spectrum, PFT is the least explicit about its model of the individual. Like the other theories, however, PFT suggests that individuals are not perfectly rational because their choices and understanding of the political world are influenced by policy designs.

We argue there is a trade-off in the level of specificity underlying the model of the individual. On the one hand, more detailed models of the individual are likely to offer more accurate representations of the underlying drivers of human decision making. Moreover, adding nuances to the simplified "boundedly rational" models of the individual can open up new questions about how actors engage and interact in policy processes as well as whether and under what conditions policy learning occurs. For example, different emphases on the model of the individual have opened up questions about how problem framing occurs (MSF), how attention to policy problems shift (PET, MSF), why collective action is possible under certain conditions (IAD framework), and the ways in which coalitions demonize their opponents (ACF, NPF). Expanding individual models further or adopting insights from other models may add areas for future theoretical development. On the other hand, adding too many layers of complexity to models of the individual may lead to problems of internal inconsistencies with parent theories and can make it difficult to establish clear linkages or rationale for the hypotheses or models that they should inform. It is also difficult, if not impossible, to present system-wide analysis without a simple model of individual behavior.

Relationships among key concepts. Each body of literature presents relationships among key variables that build on the logic of the theory's assumptions and models of the individual—often in the form of explicit hypotheses or propositions. Most often these relationships explore how different factors (e.g., contextual variables, narratives, coalitional structures, institutional venues, or framing of target populations) affect an outcome within the policy process (e.g., major or minor policy change, public opinion of policies, policy efficacy). In some cases, these relationships are broadly implied. For example, the main argument of the MSF is that three "streams" (problems, policies, politics) come together, often through the efforts of policy entrepreneurs, during "windows of opportunity" to set policy agendas and effect policy change. Yet, new exponents of the MSF also offer a set of more specific hypotheses in this volume of the book (see Chapter 1, Tables 1.1 and 1.2). These lay out the conditions under which the key elements of the framework are more likely to lead to agenda setting and policy decision making. PET also lays out general expectations and more precise hypotheses. It identifies institutional, subsystem, and decision making factors that lead to major policy change as well as those that constrain change or produce incrementalism. Within its models, PET further develops more precise hypotheses, such as explanations of the distribution of budget changes over time, and focuses on levels of institutional friction to explain the size or frequency of punctuations. Similarly, IDM refer to highly specified variables of both internal and external "determinants" that aim to explain why a policymaking venue is likely to adopt a new policy. NPF also develops a number of hypotheses that detail how persuasive policy narratives will be on individuals, how narratives are used in coalitional strategies, and how narrative strategies can affect public opinion and policy outcomes. PFT does not present specific hypotheses in the overview chapter in this volume, but individual studies that examine policy feedback have explored how different types of policy designs influence outcomes, such as the power of groups and political agendas. PFT research also seeks to examine the mechanisms that drive these relationships.

Both the ACF and the IAD and SES frameworks are open to tackling diverse sets of relationships among key concepts or variables. They present these relationships both at the general framework level, identifying the broad categories of factors that can influence policy processes (or action situations in the case of the IAD framework), and at the theory level in explaining more precise phenomena within the policy process. The ACF's theory-level explanations address the nature of coalitions, policy learning, and policy change. The IAD framework is less explicit about its hypotheses at the theory level than the ACF, but it does lay out the conditions that lead to collective action around common pool resource governance as well as the principles or factors associated with robust common pool resource institutions. Game theory models employed by IAD scholars have been used to identify more specific relationships about collective action.

Not all of the theories offer causal or explanatory hypotheses; rather, some present descriptive hypotheses. These include the ACF's propositions on coalitions and PET's propositions about the frequency and characterization of budget distributions. At the same time, some propositions stem directly from their assumptions, such as the ACF's ordering of beliefs. PET's assumptions also appear as propositions or hypotheses. For instance, PET argues that bounded rationality produces disproportionate attention and that ambiguity leads to reframing or institutional friction that may produce punctuations. These propositions or hypotheses explicitly help explain system-wide effects rather than try to predict which issues will receive most attention and which policy areas are subject to most punctuations.

COMPARATIVE CRITERION 2: ACTIVENESS OF RESEARCH PROGRAMS AND THEIR COHERENCE

Table 8.2 presents a summary of our assessment of the theories' levels of research activity and coherence. Most have produced publications in the hundreds, with the exception of the relatively new NPF and PFT, whose applications appear to

TABLE 8.2 How Active and Coherent Are the Research Programs?

	MSF	PET	PFT	ACF	NPF	IAD Framework	IDM
Extent of publications	Kingdon's two editions plus numerous applications	Extensive and growing rapidly; almost 400 publications in web annex	Numerous applications, including books and journal articles	Numerous applications; 224 listed between 1987–2013	Fewer than others, but growing	Numerous, especially common pool resource applications	Numerous with rapid growth; over 100 per year since 2010
Tested in multiple contexts and/ or with multiple methods	Applications: Diverse policy domains, including subnational, national, and international levels Methods: Mostly case studies	Applications: Budgets and agendas in diverse policy domains, both national and international Method: Mostly quantitative	Applications: Social welfare policies and case studies, but more attention to other policy areas Methods: Mostly case studies and some quantitative	Applications: Multiple countries and settings, but with initial bias toward US and environmental policy Methods: Mixed, for example, surveys, case studies, document analyses, interviews	Applications: Mostly United States in a few policy contexts, but still new Methods: Mixed, for example, case study, document coding, experiments, surveys	Applications: Mostly common pool resources around the world, but other policy domains, too Methods: Mixed, for example, meta-analyses, field research, experiments	Applications: Multiple policy topics, often US state level, but also national Methods: Mostly quantitative
Shared research protocols, methods, approaches	Unclear, but studies appear to be inspired by broad, intuitive concepts	Shared models of budget changes, agenda change Shared datasets, website, etc.	Unclear, but publications highlight common research agendas among the diverse community of scholars	Coding forms and surveys often available as appendices Many ACF survey questions replicated, but application of protocols not always consistent	Shared codebooks and methods for identifying narratives, with several modifications and adaptations	Framework is the shared approach with a large and active network; a number of shared datasets and models; less guidance on Social-Ecological Systems (SES) framework	Key methods and variables and unified model of policy innovation identified; common use of event history analysis
Change or adaptation to the theory over time	Scholars such as Durant and Diehl and Zahariadis have modified the theory to apply to foreign policy or European cases, but not as part of a core program.	Hypotheses added, concepts modified, methods advanced. Major shift from case study focus on the United States, to a general punctuation hypothesis applied in new contexts (e.g., the Comparative Agendas Project).	Some evolution of the underlying theory of feedback and mechanisms. The most recent innovations have been methodological.	Hard core of the theory maintained, with multiple revisions, including 1993 (major edited book), 1998 (European focus), and 2007 (clarifying shocks).	Has updated hypotheses and connections to related policy theories as NPF is tested and critiqued.	Has evolved since the 1980s, clarifying vocabulary and concepts, and links to theory and models; addition of the SES framework is the main adaptation.	Diffusion mechanism has been made more explicit and tested more explicitly and rigorously in the models.

be growing steadily. As the number of applications of each of the theories has grown, so, too, has the diversity of contexts within which they are applied (for example, only 36 percent of PET studies since 2005 are from the United States). Still, the majority of applications across the theories covered here have been made in the United States or Europe, often across national or state levels, with few at local levels. The IAD framework and its companion SES framework are the exceptions. Some tend to employ quantitative methods with sophisticated modeling techniques (e.g., PET and IDM); others have relied more heavily on qualitative or case study applications (e.g., MSF and PFT). Others, such as the ACF, IAD framework, and NPF, have emphasized both quantitative and qualitative approaches and multiple types of data sources, such as surveys, document coding, and experiments.

Across the theories, we find strengths and weaknesses in how each advances its research program in terms of the extent and diversity of the research applications, the shared research protocols, and adaptations to the theory over time. When the MSF is applied, its strength is also its weakness. Its core concepts have broad intuitive appeal, which may make it feasible to apply without being immersed in the research program over a long period (Cairney and Jones, 2016). It also has been modified to make it more readily applicable outside the United States. Most applications have been case studies that use the concepts of contingency and ambiguity to focus in detail on why key decisions at particular stages were made in particular places at particular times. The explanations are impressive but difficult to generalize. A recent meta-analysis of the MSF, for example, has found that the coherence of the research program remains limited, particularly because of the inconsistencies in the operationalization of MSA's core concepts and the lack of integration of new subcomponents into the MSF's hypotheses (Jones et al. 2016).

Compared to MSF studies, PET research generally has treated its core concepts and their interaction consistently and coherently. Some concepts have been modified, and methods have advanced over time. There is potential for reduced clarity as the Comparative Agendas Project expands and new scholars (with different backgrounds and less training in PET) become involved, although PET's history of shared datasets and methods may help. When applied, PET has two major strengths. The original work produced in-depth case studies combining qualitative and quantitative methods of postwar policy continuity and change. The general punctuation hypothesis extended the analysis to a quantitative account of stability and instability in budgets and legislative outputs. This has helped shift the focus from agenda setting to the broader process (although the original work, covering decades, examined policy continuity and change over several "cycles"). The explanations are increasingly generalizable, across levels of US government and in multiple countries (particularly budget distributions), although this expansion has prompted some debate about methods and measurement among the core team (Dowding, Hindmoor, and Martin 2016; Jones 2016).

PFT has tended to emphasize in-depth case studies, especially on social welfare policy topics in the United States. The research has begun to expand in recent years to include large-*n* datasets and experiments and applications outside the United States. Mettler and SoRelle (2017, see Chapter 3 in this book) discuss many recent examples of rigorous applications. However, it is not directly apparent that there is a coordinated and coherent research program promoting shared research protocols or approaches.

As with the PET, the ACF's core studies treat key concepts and their interaction consistently and coherently—but with considerable scope for independent scholars to use the ACF very loosely, without testing any of its hypotheses (which may, in part, contribute to its extensive use). The framework's authors describe its strength in explaining "high-conflict situations at the subsystem level of analysis," with theoretical emphases on coalitions, policy learning, and policy change (see Chapter 4, pp. 135–171). It is increasingly applied beyond the United States and environmental policy, prompting its key authors to adapt the framework to make it more generalizable and to coordinate comparative applications (e.g., Weible et al. 2016). ACF also has shared approaches and protocols that are commonly made available to scholars, but the consistency in application of these protocols is less clear. The framework has maintained its basic assumptions, but hypotheses and concepts have been modified on occasion to reflect new empirical and theoretical insights.

The NPF's attempt to advance "postpositivist" accounts by making the role of narratives in the policy process measurable and more conducive to testable hypotheses has led NPF scholars to develop shared codebooks and methods for identifying and quantifying the nature and effect of narratives. Some inconsistencies remain across the applications in terms of how the elements of narratives are operationalized. Yet, continued efforts to refine and adapt the methodologies, modify (or eliminate) some hypotheses, and extend the research outside of the United States suggest growth in the research program (albeit while facing some friction when building on insights from positivist *and* postpositivist accounts; see Jones and Radaelli 2016). Because it is still a relatively young research program, some hypotheses have yet to be tested, and applicability to a wide array of policy contexts remains somewhat limited.

The IAD framework's long-standing research program has been structured around a shared approach for a large and cohesive network of scholars as well as the development of shared datasets, models, and methods (see Poteete, Janssen, and Ostrom 2010). These trends in diverse methods and applications continue, as evidenced by the recent special issues of journals and books that Schlager and Cox identify in Chapter 6, including many applications using formal modeling and experimental work as well as comparative studies from around the world. Its most prominent strength is in the study of common pool resources, with Ostrom winning the Nobel Prize in Economics in 2009 for demonstrating how people can create and enforce rules to ward off common pool resource exhaustion. Recent efforts to apply some of the IAD framework's early work on polycentric governance to common pool resource studies have taken this research in new directions. The IAD's sister framework, the SES, continues to evolve, although the number of empirical SES applications remains somewhat limited and application is inconsistent. As we noted in our 2014 chapter in this volume, however, it would be beneficial to see more development of IAD framework–related research on public policy issues and collective action dilemmas outside of the environmental domain.

IDM have exhibited substantial growth in recent years, in terms of the number of applications and advancements in the methods and models. The research approaches and methods have also been relatively cohesive over time. Walker (1969) set the agenda, and core authors such as F. Berry and W. Berry have continued to extend the research. Early models focused primarily on communication and learning (the voluntary adoption of policies), and later models have devised a mix of five explanations for diffusion. Berry and Berry (2017, see Chapter 7, this volume) identify a major shift in the last ten years, from asking whether a policy diffuses to investigating how and why policy innovation occurs. By integrating lessons from the diverse empirical applications of diffusion and innovation, they have further established a generic unified model of government innovation that includes diffusion and internal determinants variables. Traditionally, the focus has been on the US states, but recent work has also applied IDM to European contexts.

COMPARATIVE CRITERION 3:
HOW DOES EACH THEORETICAL APPROACH
EXPLAIN "THE POLICY PROCESS"?

Table 8.3 identifies how each theory describes the six key elements of the policy process and explains how they interact to produce policies.

Multiple streams analysis. Kingdon's (1984) focus was on the interaction between two kinds of ideas: the type of policy solution that could draw attention and catch on quickly and the established set of beliefs in a policy community that would slow a policy solution's progress. Government attention may lurch quickly to a problem, but a feasible solution (i.e., one acceptable to the community) takes much longer to produce. This highlights the role of relatively open networks—the interaction among wide groups of actors in a policy community to refine a solution—and actors, who include the policy entrepreneurs trying to find the right time to propose solutions (when attention is high) and the policymakers needing the motive and opportunity to adopt them. The role of

TABLE 8.3 What Elements of the Policy Process Are Explained or Emphasized?

	MSF	PET	PFT	ACF	NPF	IAD Framework	IDM
Actors making choices	Policy entrepreneurs and policymakers	Broadly, policymakers, interest groups and other organizations, and individuals within groups and different venues	Implicitly actors who are affected by policy may in turn become policy actors	Policy actors who form coalitions, act strategically, learn, etc.	Actors and groups interested in policies use narratives strategically to influence public opinion and decisions	Actors, primarily individuals, who make choices	Policymakers, experts, entrepreneurs
Institutions as rules or venues of decision making	Informal rules and formal venues, recognized but institutions not emphasized	Institutional venues and their rules, which cause more or less friction	Policies institutionalized in rules and programs	Types of policy venues and rules in the broader context, but less directly	Part of context	Institutions as rules and norms that shape behavior; and typology of rules	Indirectly, institutionalized channels of communication
Networks/ subsystems	A broad policy community of actors, with relatively little focus on insulated subsystems	Subsystems as sources of stability and power	Groups mobilizing to protect or challenge programs	Subsystems and coalitions	Modifies the ACF's flow diagram on subsystems and explores the idea of focusing on regimes	Networks within action situation, but no explicit attention to subsystems	Loosely, information networks
Ideas or beliefs	Policy solutions proposed and amended over time to become acceptable to a policy community	Monopoly of understandings in established subsystem; and new solutions or ideas that break through	Ideas about policy benefits and political attitudes via interpretive effects of policy	Belief systems that drive policy actor behavior	Narrative strategies, grounded in belief systems and ways of thinking that are embedded in cultures	Shared preferences or norms of actors, but not explicit	Policy solutions emulated, or the perceived norms of policy adoption that influence policy borrowers
Context	National mood, policy conditions, pressure groups, admin turnover, etc.	Endogenous subsystem context; wider policy environment	Past policy decisions and broader context	Stable parameters—social, cultural, economic, physical, and institutions structuring the subsystem	Not a core part of NPF, but recognizes legal, constitutional parameters, geography, etc., as important	Physical and material conditions, community characteristics, preexisting institutions	Socioeconomic, conditions, education, ideology, religion, etc.
Events	Focusing events draw attention to problems	Events shift the macropolitical agenda	Not directly addressed	External events and internal events (e.g., shocks, change to governing coalition)	Not directly addressed, but may combine with narratives to focus attention	Not directly addressed	Indirectly addressed, for example, crises, but part of context

institutions in the MSF comes from the framework's recognition of policy venues and can be inferred from the recognition of informal rules in each political system, such as when to introduce a bill in Congress (see Chapter 1 in this book and Zahariadis 2014), and the MSF chapter in this volume (Chapter 1) offers further suggestions for advancing insights on the role of institutions in agenda setting and decision making. Focusing events can be important to shift levels of attention to a problem, but the MSF is about the need for other processes to occur before the event has more than a fleeting importance. Key sources of context include the "national mood," interpreted by policymakers, and the policy conditions in each case, such as levels of congestion, fuel availability, and pollution when policymakers consider transport policy. We can tease out the interactions among all elements, but a lack of clarity in some aspects may produce studies describing this interaction in different ways.

Punctuated Equilibrium Theory. The PET emphasizes the interaction between two types of ideas: (1) the "monopoly of understandings" underpinning established subsystem relationships, and (2) the new solutions that could "catch fire" following successful venue shopping or prompt endogenous change (when attention shifts and issues are reframed). Subsystems are a source of stability, power, and policy continuity for long periods (decades in some cases). Instability and major change can come from the interactions among institutions, such as venues with different rules and understandings, or the interactions between the policy subsystem and the macropolitical system (a conceptualization also found in some evolutionary and complexity theories; Cairney 2013b). The latter is unpredictable: lurches of macropolitical attention can destabilize subsystems, but most subsystems can remain unaffected for long periods.

The concept of institutional friction describes the amount of effort required to overcome established rules. High friction suggests that a major or cumulative effort is required to secure institutional change, which may produce a pressure-dam effect and a major policy punctuation. Major events, such as wars that change budget patterns, as well as sustained and cumulative attention to minor events may also cause punctuations. Different sequences of events help explain different processes across countries. However, the focus is on serial attention to events. Although *events* can include elections, PET studies increasingly discuss political parties to show that agendas seem more likely to shift in relation to the policymaking environment than parties of government. Context is important, but the focus of the PET is often the endogenous change in subsystems in the absence of similar change in the wider policy environment. Overall, the PET covers all the major elements of the policy process.

Policy Feedback Theory. The PFT has its roots in historical institutionalism, which suggests that policy commitments made in the past produce increasing returns and make it costly to choose a different path (Pierson 2000; Cairney

2012b, 76). When a policy becomes established and resources are devoted to programs, it helps structure current activity and provides advantages for some groups more than for others (Mettler and SoRelle 2017, see Chapter 3 in this book).

Although PFT may not directly conceptualize many elements of the policy process, we can identify a broad focus on actors, networks, and ideas. Actors are present when policies assign different citizen rights to groups, influencing their ability and incentive to mobilize and engage. Networks are implied when government agencies mobilize support for, and groups mobilize to protect, programs. Ideas appear in the PFT because established policies and rules represent institutionalized beliefs or dominant policy frames (public opinion on programs may also shift after they have been introduced). Further, in historical institutionalism, "sensitivity to initial conditions" describes a particular sequence of past decisions that sets the broad context for current policy, and "critical juncture" highlights the major event that may be required to prompt institutional change when policies are "locked in" (Cairney 2012b, 84). Consequently, using our identified elements, we can infer that various elements of the policy process underlie or inform the PFT.

Advocacy Coalition Framework. According to the ACF, people engage in politics to translate their beliefs into action (Chapter 4). There are three main types of beliefs: core, policy core, and secondary. Actors with similar beliefs become part of the same advocacy coalition, and coalitions compete with each other. We can identify a role for institutions as venues when coalitions compete for influence in multiple arenas. However, the main focus of the ACF is the subsystem, which represents a key venue (with particular rules of engagement) for coalition interaction. The ACF's conceptualization of subsystems is distinctive, focusing on actors beyond government and interest groups, to include, for example, academics and analysts. The ACF flow diagram identifies spillover effects from other policy subsystems and events, such as a change in government or a shift in governmental priorities, on subsystems. However, its focus is on how coalitions interpret and respond to events—as external or internal shocks. Major responses to shocks are far less frequent than policy learning and the revision of secondary aspects of coalition beliefs. Overall, the ACF covers all the major elements of the policy process as well as interactions among these elements, although the role of institutions is addressed less directly than the other elements.

Narrative Policy Framework. The NPF seeks to measure how actors both use narratives and are influenced by narratives in policymaking. Narratives are stylized accounts of the origins, aims, and likely impacts of policies. They are used strategically to reinforce or oppose policy measures. Thus, actors making choices, as influenced by particular types of policy ideas (or narratives), are the core focus of the NPF. Subsystems are also a cornerstone of the NPF's mesolevel of analysis. This framework has adapted the ACF to identify how advocacy coalitions compete through narratives or how subsystem-level actors can dominate narratives. Context is also important in the NPF through the policy setting. Context includes the factors that actors have to account for when constructing narratives (e.g., legal and constitutional parameters, geography, scientific evidence, economic conditions, and agreed-upon norms). However, NPF hypotheses and empirical analyses have not explored the role of context in shaping narratives or their influence on policy in much detail. Institutions are addressed more indirectly in the NPF through the context and by arguing that successful narratives may become embedded in the culture, or institutionalized, in policy systems at the macrolevel.[2] Events are treated primarily as resources, used to construct focusing events and apportion blame, but also are not central to the framework. Overall, the NPF pays attention to all six elements, but actors and ideas dominate the approach.

Institutional Analysis and Development framework. The IAD framework focuses on the ways in which actors make choices within institutional environments that structure (or at least help explain) their behavior, namely, when engaged in collective action dilemmas. The focus is on providing tools to explore how different sets of actors and institutions produce different outcomes, often evaluated in terms of trade-offs among efficiency, equity, accountability, and other criteria such as robustness. The IAD framework contains a typology of rules regarding, for example, who can take part, how extensive their involvement can be, who is in charge, how to share information, and how to punish defectors—but it notes that many rules are implicit and difficult to identify in practice. One set of operational rules is nested in a set of rules on collective action, which in turn is nested in constitutional rules.

The institutional context is underpinned by physical and material conditions that affect how people can act and which rules can be set. This wider context may produce the incentives for people to act selfishly or cooperatively or to produce public goods. This context influences the rules that people generate to regulate individual behavior. The IAD framework does not discuss ideas explicitly, but shared preferences or norms underpin the production of rules. For example, an institutional solution in the United States, with its tradition of market-based solutions, will likely differ significantly from one in China, with its tradition of state-based solutions. Similarly, subsystems are not theorized, but the role of networks (the interaction of actors in venues with specific rules) is important within the concept of the action situation (Ostrom 2009) and is recognized in the SES framework (Schlager and Cox 2017, see Chapter 6, this volume). Overall, the IAD framework focuses explicitly on actors, institutions, and context and more implicitly on ideas and networks or subsystems.

Innovation and diffusion models. Innovation is the adoption of a policy that is new to the individual government, and both determinants that are internal to a government and external—via diffusion—factor into innovation, according to IDM's unified model. Substantial effort has been put into modeling both internal determinants and diffusion sources of innovation. Through these efforts the IDM tend to emphasize the role of context, events, and ideas in explaining policy change. With respect to context and events, IDM have recognized that economic crises or unsuccessful wars make government more vulnerable to coercion, larger cities are more likely to learn, and diffusion is dependent on information technology. Some models also use proximity to explain adoption, from physical proximity (regional models) to a wider similarity between states (ideology, biophysical properties, social composition, attitudes, etc.). Leader-laggard and other models partly explain innovation in terms of context (e.g., levels of economic development, education, "slack resources," and research capabilities). With respect to ideas, diffusion models recognize that "the probability of adoption of a policy by one governmental jurisdiction is influenced by the policy choices of other governments in the system" (see Chapter 7, p. 256, this volume). In other words, diffusion often follows policymakers' perceptions of the benefits of adopted policies in neighboring jurisdictions or of their need to keep up with norms or competitive pressures. The properties of policy solutions may also influence the extent to which the solutions receive attention. However, diffusion is also something to be explained in terms of how attractive policy solutions are to policymakers. Internal determinants models express the roles of perception and demand most strongly.

Regarding actors, IDM tend to focus on the policy choices of actors at the "collective level" (i.e., by a state or jurisdiction). However, the broader policy transfer literature identifies the "usual suspects" within each state (including elected policymakers, officials, and interest groups), plus actors who operate across states, including supranational or federal organizations, multinational corporations, epistemic communities containing networks of experts (Haas 1992), and entrepreneurs selling policies from one government to another (Cairney 2012b, 263). Institutions are conceptualized minimally, in terms of organizations exchanging information, without a discussion of rule-based action. Networks are defined loosely as information networks, not the more regular and systematic patterns of behavior in subsystems.

COMPARING THEORIES: WHERE DO WE GO FROM HERE?

In the third edition of this book, we focused on the extent to which these theories should be treated as complementary or contradictory (Cairney and Heikkila 2014). The former is tempting as a way to explain the policy process as fully as possible. For example, actors form coalitions to cooperate with each other and compete with their opponents (ACF); they exploit cultural stereotypes and cognitive biases to tell stories with heroes and a policy moral (NPF); the policy system dampens the effect of most stories and amplifies some (PET); the small number of amplified issues prompt policy change during a window of opportunity (MSF); and subsequent policies create feedback, or the rules that constrain and facilitate future coalition activity (PFT). Yet, theories rarely examine the same cases and, when individual studies try to combine insights and apply them to specific cases, they face major terminological and methodological obstacles (Cairney 2013a). The alternative, to focus on a small number of discrete theories and reject others, is what we do as professional scholars (e.g., through peer review and editorial discretion), often on the basis of widespread adherence to certain scientific principles (Sabatier 1999, 2007b; Eller and Krutz 2009). Or this occurs without fully agreeing on the rules for inclusion (Cairney 2013a), and without being sure that different theories using different concepts to explain different things actually compete with each other (Dowding 2015).

In that context, we highlight where we see the strengths and weaknesses, broadly speaking, when we look across the chapters in this volume using our three overarching criteria: (1) inclusion of basic elements of a theoretical approach (i.e., well-defined scope and levels of analysis, shared vocabulary, clear assumptions, model of the individual, and relationships among key variables); (2) development of an active and coherent research program (inclusive of broad substantive and geographic applications); and (3) explanation of a large part of the policy process (i.e., coverage of actors, institutions, networks/subsystems, ideas/beliefs, context, and events).

With respect to the first criterion, we find that the theoretical approaches discussed in this book all largely include the basic elements we identified. Of course, there is variation within and across the theories. All do well in clearly defining their scope/levels of analysis and establishing clear vocabulary, although some are more expansive (i.e., the IAD framework) or perhaps more consistent than others. Some (PFT, IAD, IDM) leave their assumptions more implicitly stated or leave their model of the individual more implicit (PFT, IDM) and could provide more clarity for theory consumers and potential users on those fronts. All of the theories have defined relationships among key variables, with wide variation in how these are described. Occasionally, theories present more general relationships through a visual framework or flow diagram (ACF, IAD) or through a generalized model (IDM). Others focus on describing these general relationships verbally (MSF, PET, PFT). All, except the IAD framework, also lay out more specific hypotheses that have been identified theoretically or empirically; the IAD framework explores more precise relationships through related modeling, such as game theory and laboratory experiments. A few are more limited, however, in the extent to which some of their theoretical hypotheses have been empirically tested across a diversity of contexts (i.e., MSF, NPF). Overall, we argue that the theories in this book, as well as other policy theories, can continue to improve on particular elements of theory building and can learn from those that are more well developed in their explication of these elements.

In comparing the theories on the second criterion, we find an impressive level of activity with respect to the extent of publications and adaptation of the theories over time. Whereas most have well-developed research protocols and methods, some have room to develop on this front (MSF, PFT). Others may struggle with consistency in the application of their theories and concepts (ACF, NPF, IAD/SES framework) or with the application of sophisticated data collection or modeling (PET, IDM), especially when scholars from outside of the core research community look to apply these theories. This is a critical challenge for all of the theories if we expect to see continued growth and expansion. Yet it points to the need for ongoing training opportunities (e.g., conference workshops) and more transparent and easily accessible research protocols (i.e., appendices to journal articles, online manuals). These points are also critical for expanding the empirical applications of these theories to new policy settings (e.g., even more diversity outside of the environmental arena for the ACF, NPF, and IAD framework) or to more non-Western contexts. The IAD framework is largely the exception in terms of its applicability outside of Western democracies. Efforts to develop a global network of scholars have been part of the IAD framework through the Ostrom Workshop in political theory and policy analysis for more than three decades. Such efforts may provide a useful example of how to broaden the contexts where a research program is applied, although this requires resources and dedicated leadership that may not be available to each of these theories.

Finally, in examining how the theories meet our third criterion, we find that most at least pay attention to the six major elements of the policy process we included as part of their explanations of policy processes. However, the emphasis on specific factors varies on the basis of the scope of each theory in terms of which primary phenomenon the theory seeks to explain or which key factor it considers important in shaping policy outcomes. This is typical of theories. No single theory can adequately explain all of the elements of policy processes—such an attempt would likely render it either overly complex or overly superficial. Consumers and users of theories should pay attention to the foci of theories and ensure that applications are appropriate for the question at hand. At the same time, to advance the theories, it may be useful to consider whether more attention to the elements of policy processes that are not addressed (e.g., the PFT or IDM incorporating more attention to events or the NPF delving more into institutions) could offer new theoretical insights, at least within the scope and assumptions of the theory.

We offer the above assessments with a note of caution. That is, we need to keep examining why we use such criteria, and not others, and the implications these criteria have for promoting certain theories and rejecting others.

Other legitimate criteria are available. Alongside narrow scientific criteria (e.g., whether a theoretical approach has core elements of a theory or an active scientific research program) are explanatory criteria (e.g., the extent a theory adequately explains the complexity of policy processes) and practical or normative criteria (e.g., how a theory helps us solve real-world policy problems). We may want all three but face major trade-offs, which force us to prioritize one over the others.

The theories described in this book prioritize scientific criteria (see the Introduction for the rationale for theory selection in this volume). To prioritize the explanation of complex policymaking, without as much clarity of exposition but with more focus on the practical political implications, might prompt us to include studies of multilevel governance and complexity theory (Cairney 2012a). To prioritize normative issues would prompt us to include the social construction and policy design (SCPD) framework, which has more than a hundred applications since 1993 (Pierce et al. 2014). Most of the SCPD studies identify degenerative politics in which the distribution of government benefits to target populations is highly unequal, reflecting and reinforcing inequalities in society and producing policy designs that contribute to low levels of civic and political participation (Schneider, Ingram, and deLeon 2014). Many of these concerns overlap with the PFT, but perhaps with SCPD focusing primarily on the fate of deviant populations and the PFT on the wider effects of policy feedback on policymakers, policy agendas, interest groups, *and* citizens. The latter may replace the former because of scientific criteria—for example, PFT's scope is wider, and its propositions are more general—rather than the normative importance of the questions it raises.

If they focus primarily on scientific criteria, other policy theories may offer only the *untapped potential* to help explain and evaluate such normative issues. Or, if the normative criteria become more important, such concerns may represent a small, but growing, feature of key theories. For example, PET now focuses more on the potential links between policymaking pathologies and punctuated equilibrium. Major change may emerge after long periods of resistance to change and limited information gathering, eventually with the help of major events or pressure. Although these developments were previously linked to a healthy US democratic process, studies of China, for example, highlight comparable processes in authoritarian regimes and prompt us to consider how centralist are key organizations in less authoritarian regimes. These concerns, aided partly by more comparative studies of democratic and authoritarian regimes, are also raised by the ACF, whereas the NPF raises the prospect of stories used to reinforce inequalities in political power. However, the value of SCPD has been to identify pressing normative issues in the United States even when, for comparative purposes, US policymaking would be treated relatively positively.

CONCLUSIONS AND REFLECTIONS ON OUR CRITERIA

The theories, frameworks, and models presented in this volume are indicative of the depth and vibrancy of the field. The literature is growing, and there are many significant overlaps between theories that aid the study of the policy process, but also important differences. How we evaluate the theoretical approaches allows us to see some of the differences, similarities, strengths, and weaknesses across the different theories, which we hope can help guide researchers and students who want to apply, test, or perhaps even attempt to integrate some of them. Our criteria allowed for comparison across some key scientific principles (e.g., elements of a theory). They also helped us evaluate the development of research programs and understand the breadth or coverage of the theories, frameworks, and models in terms of how they incorporate or address some critical elements of the policy process.

In applying the criteria we selected, our goal was not to identify the best theory or framework. Moreover, these criteria would be limited in their ability to do so if that were one's goal. One reason is the difficulty of simultaneously meeting all of the criteria or the indicators we selected; meeting one criterion may impose trade-offs on another. For example, in our criteria for research program development we explored (1) whether the theories use multiple methods, and (2) whether they have developed shared research protocols and methods. Establishing standardized approaches to data collection and analysis within a research program, using well-developed and replicable instruments, takes time and energy. Such investments could therefore make it challenging to engage in a diversity of methods, at least initially.

Additionally, the criteria we selected by no means encompass the full range of possible evaluative or comparative criteria for theories. We did not explore the quality of the explanatory or causal arguments made by the theories and models, such as their generalizability, coherence, parsimony, relevance, or precision (e.g., Gerring 2012). Also, Schlager (1999, 2007) organized her evaluation of the theories in the first and second editions of this book to highlight comparisons across theories, frameworks, and models more directly, which was valuable for identifying differences in research programs and scientific advancements. In terms of the policy process elements, we did not compare how the theories address key outcomes of the policy process, such as policy change or collective action, as examined by Schlager. Nor did we examine the extent to which the theories are applicable to various stages of policymaking, including implementation and evaluation, or to different policy venues (e.g., regulatory/administrative, legislative, judicial, or even informal collaborative processes).

In sum, we encourage scholars to be open to multiple and alternative criteria in their comparisons and evaluations of theories, frameworks, and models of the policy process and to make their criteria transparent. We see this as fitting with the call to explain methods, define concepts clearly, and clearly set out the causal processes, which is the conventional wisdom used to warn scholars against obfuscation, confirmation bias, and a generally defensive approach to their results. In this context we introduced a range of criteria—not to adjudicate between theories and solve unequivocally the problem of which are worthiest of our resources but to generate some level of agreement within the discipline about which frameworks and theories are clear enough to be proven wrong and which show a sufficient amount of payoff from the investment of scholars.

NOTES

1. For brevity, we use the following acronyms: MSF for Multiple Streams Framework, PET for Punctuated Equilibrium Theory, PFT for Policy Feedback Theory, ACF for Advocacy Coalition Framework, NPF for Narrative Policy Framework, IAD for Institutional Analysis and Development framework, and IDM for innovation and diffusion models.

2. Although there is some scope for confusion because they describe subsystems as systems—effectively moving the ACF flow diagram's external processes into one subsystem box—or they describe regimes as collections of interlocked subsystems without fully explaining their reasoning.

REFERENCES

Béland, Daniel, and Robert Henry Cox. 2010. "Introduction: Ideas and Politics." In *Ideas and Politics in Social Science Research,* edited by Daniel Béland and Robert Henry Cox. Oxford: Oxford University Press.

Berry, Frances Stokes, and William D. Berry. 2017. "Innovation and Diffusion Models in Policy Research." In *Theories of the Policy Process,* 4th ed., edited by Christopher M. Weible and Paul A. Sabatier, 253–297. Boulder, CO: Westview Press.

Cairney, Paul. 2012a. "'Public Administration in an Age of Austerity': Positive Lessons from Policy Studies." *Public Policy and Administration* 27 (3): 230–247.

———. 2012b. *Understanding Public Policy.* Basingstoke, UK: Palgrave.

———. 2013a. "Standing on the Shoulders of Giants: How Do We Combine the Insights of Multiple Theories in Public Policy Studies?" *Policy Studies Journal* 41 (1): 1–21.

———. 2013b. "What Is Evolutionary Theory and How Does It Inform Policy Studies?" *Policy and Politics* 41 (2): 279–298.

Cairney, Paul, and Tanya Heikkila. 2014. "A Comparison of Theories of the Policy Process." In *Theories of the Policy Process,* 3rd ed., edited by Paul A. Sabatier and Christopher M. Weible, 363–390. Boulder, CO: Westview Press.

Cairney, Paul, and Michael D. Jones. 2016. "Kingdon's Multiple Streams Approach: What Is the Empirical Impact of This Universal Theory?" *Policy Studies Journal* 44 (1): 37–58.

Dowding, Keith. 2015. *The Philosophy and Methods of Political Science.* Basingstoke, UK: Palgrave Macmillan.

Dowding, Keith, Andrew Hindmoor, and Aaron Martin. 2016. "The Comparative Policy Agenda Project: Theory, Measurement and Findings." *Journal of Public Policy* 36 (1): 3–25.

Eller, Warren, and Glen Krutz. 2009. "Editor's Notes: Policy Process, Scholarship and the Road Ahead: An Introduction to the 2008 Policy Shootout!" *Policy Studies Journal* 37 (1): 1–4.

Gerring, John. 2012. *Social Science Methodology: A Unified Framework: Strategies for Social Inquiry.* 2nd ed. Cambridge: Cambridge University Press.

Haas, Peter M. 1992. "Introduction: Epistemic Communities and International Policy Coordination." *International Organization* 46 (1): 1–35.

Hall, Peter A., and Rosemary C. R. Taylor. 1996. "Political Science and the Three New Institutionalisms." *Political Studies* 44 (4): 936–957.

Hay, Colin. 2006. "Constructivist Institutionalism." In *The Oxford Handbook of Political Institutions,* edited by R. Rhodes, S. Binder, and B. Rockman. Oxford: Oxford University Press.

Herweg, Nicole, Nikolaos Zahariadis, and Reimut Zohlnhöfer. 2017. "The Multiple Streams Framework: Foundations, Refinements, and Empirical Applications." In *Theories of the Policy Process,* 4th ed., edited by Christopher M. Weible and Paul A. Sabatier, 17–53. Boulder, CO: Westview Press.

Hofferbert, Richard I. 1974. *The Study of Public Policy.* Indianapolis: Bobbs-Merrill.

John, Peter. 2003. "Is There Life After Policy Streams, Advocacy Coalitions, and Punctuations: Using Evolutionary Theory to Explain Policy Change?" *Policy Studies Journal* 31 (4): 481–498.

Jones, Bryan D. 2016. "The Comparative Policy Agendas Projects as Measurement Systems: Response to Dowding, Hindmoor and Martin." *Journal of Public Policy* 36 (1): 31–46.

Jones, Michael D., Holly L. Peterson, Jonathan J. Pierce, Nicole J. Herweg, Amiel Bernal, Holly Lamberta Raney, and Nikolaos Zahariadis. 2016. "A River Runs Through It: A Multiple Streams Meta-Review." *Policy Studies Journal* 44 (1): 13–36.

Jones, Michael D., and Claudio M. Radaelli. 2016. "The Narrative Policy Framework's Call for Interpretivists." *Critical Policy Studies* 10 (1): 117–120.

Jordan, Grant, Darren Halpin, and William Maloney. 2004. "Defining Interests: Disambiguation and the Need for New Distinctions?" *British Journal of Politics and International Relations* 6 (2): 195–212.

Jordan, Grant, and William A. Maloney. 1997. "Accounting for Subgovernments: Explaining the Persistence of Policy Communities." *Administration and Society* 29 (5): 557–583.

Kingdon, John. 1984. *Agendas, Alternatives, and Public Policies.* New York: HarperCollins.

Lowndes, Vivien. 2010. "The Institutional Approach." In *Theory and Methods in Political Science,* edited by D. Marsh and G. Stoker, 90–108. Basingstoke, UK: Palgrave Macmillan.

Mettler, Suzanne, and Mallory SoRelle. 2017. "Policy Feedback Theory." In *Theories of the Policy Process*, 4th ed., edited by Christopher M. Weible and Paul A. Sabatier, 103–134. Boulder, CO: Westview Press.

Ostrom, Elinor. 2009. "A General Framework for Analyzing Sustainability of Social-Ecological Systems." *Science* 325:419–422.

Peters, Guy B. 2005. *Institutional Theory in Political Science: The "New Institutionalism."* 2nd ed. London: Continuum.

Pierce, Jonathan J., Saba Siddiki, Michael D. Jones, Kristin Schumacher, Andrew Pattison, and Holly Peterson. 2014. "Social Construction and Policy Design: A Review of Past Applications." *Policy Studies Journal* 42 (1): 1–29.

Pierson, Paul. 2000. "Increasing Returns, Path Dependence, and the Study of Politics." *American Political Science Review* 94 (2): 251–267.

Poteete, Amy, Marco Janssen, and Elinor Ostrom. 2010. *Working Together: Collective Action, the Commons and Multiple Methods in Practice*. Princeton, NJ: Princeton University Press.

Rose, Richard. 1990. "Inheritance Before Choice in Public Policy." *Journal of Theoretical Politics* 2 (3): 263–291.

Sabatier, Paul., ed. 1999. *Theories of the Policy Process*. Boulder, CO: Westview Press.

———. 2007a. "Fostering the Development of Policy Theory." In *Theories of the Policy Process*, 2nd ed., edited by Paul A. Sabatier, 321–36. Boulder, CO: Westview Press.

———, ed. 2007b. *Theories of the Policy Process*. 2nd ed. Boulder, CO: Westview Press.

Schlager, Edella. 1999. "A Comparison of Frameworks, Theories, and Models of Policy Processes." In *Theories of the Policy Process*, edited by Paul A. Sabatier, 233–260. Boulder, CO: Westview Press.

———. 2007. "A Comparison of Frameworks, Theories, and Models of Policy Processes Theory." In *Theories of the Policy Process*, 2nd ed., edited by Paul A. Sabatier, 293–319. Boulder, CO: Westview Press.

Schlager, Edella, and Michael Cox. 2017. "The IAD Framework and the SES Framework: An Introduction and Assessment of the Ostrom Workshop Frameworks." In *Theories of the Policy Process*, 4th ed., edited by Christopher M. Weible and Paul A. Sabatier, 215–252. Boulder, CO: Westview Press.

Schneider, Anne L., Helen Ingram, and Peter deLeon. 2014. "Democratic Policy Design: Social Construction of Target Populations." In *Theories of the Policy Process*, 3rd ed., edited by Paul A. Sabatier and Christopher M. Weible, 105–150. Boulder, CO: Westview Press.

Smith, Kevin, and Christopher W. Larimer. 2009. *The Public Policy Theory Primer*. Boulder, CO: Westview Press.

Walker, Jack L. 1969. "The Diffusion of Innovations among the American States." *American Political Science Review* 63 (3): 880–899.

Weible, Christopher M. 2014. "Introducing the Scope and Focus of Policy Process Research and Theory." In *Theories of the Policy Process*, 3rd ed., edited by Paul A. Sabatier and Christopher M. Weible, 3–21. Boulder, CO: Westview Press.

————. 2017. "Introduction: The Scope and Focus of Policy Process Research and Theory." In *Theories of the Policy Process*, 4th ed., edited by Christopher M. Weible and Paul A. Sabatier, 1–13. Boulder, CO: Westview Press.

Weible, Christopher M., Tanya Heikkila, Karin Ingold, and Manuel Fischer, eds. 2016. *Policy Debates on Hydraulic Fracturing: Comparing Coalition Politics in North America and Europe*. New York: Palgrave Macmillan.

Zahariadis, Nikoloas. 2014. "Ambiguity and Multiple Streams." In *Theories of the Policy Process*, 3rd ed., edited by Paul A. Sabatier and Christopher M. Weible, 25–57. Boulder, CO: Westview Press.

9

Struggle and Triumph in Fusing Policy Process and Comparative Research

JALE TOSUN AND SAMUEL WORKMAN

Policymaking is characterized by general patterns not restricted to one or a few jurisdictions, policy domains, or institutional constellations. This chapter concentrates on a specific subgroup of this literature—comparative research drawing on the theories of the policy process—and strives to discuss its challenges and opportunities. This is an important endeavor because good science demands examination of the generalizability of theories and their findings to other institutional and political contexts. For scholars and practitioners alike, it is crucial to understand the conditions that bound hypotheses developed from the theories. It is likewise important to understand the major implications of theories for understanding comparative politics and public policy. Just as the past decades of research have taught us much about these bounding conditions, they have also offered a wealth of broad and well-founded generalizations that chip away the country-specific exceptionalism common in comparative policy studies.

The field of public policy has witnessed tremendous growth in the last thirty years, and much of the recent growth has been in developing and testing comparative extensions of the theories. These extensions were triggered by improved availability of data and innovative ways for gathering and analyzing data, for instance, by means of multimethod designs (e.g., Wolf 2010) and the adoption of concepts and methodologies from neighboring disciplines such as behavioral and communication sciences (e.g., Shafir 2013; Jones 2003). This has moved public policy closer to adjacent fields such as comparative and international political economy and, more recently, political psychology. Tsebelis's (2002) concept of institutional veto players has been particularly important for strengthening the comparative perspective on public policy. In the

Western European context, political parties and the assessment of their policy preferences—which concurs with Tsebelis's veto player theory—have been the focal explanatory variables of many studies and the bridge to comparative politics, which became further strengthened by the Comparative Agendas Project (see Baumgartner, Green-Pedersen, and Jones 2006; Green-Pedersen and Walgrave 2014).

This chapter offers an entrée to comparative policy process research. It begins by explicating the fundamental challenges of theoretical and empirical extensions of the policy process theories. The theories have followed unique trajectories in addressing institutions, interest group politics and advocacy, and issue-specific politics in comparative perspective. These unique trajectories deepen our understanding of issues, interests, and institutions and their impact on the dynamics of public policy (May, Sapotichne, and Workman 2006). We argue, however, that the comparative policy processes approach has arrived at a precipice where we can now make several generalizations about how institutions influence policy dynamics, the sets of issues that governments of all types face, and the form of politics within substantively specific issue areas. The comparative policy process theories owe their successes in large part to an expansive conception of what constitutes comparative research. The array of approaches yields useful lessons for the development of policy process theorizing in classic country-comparative studies. On the one hand, the approaches facilitate a more demanding empirical test of the causal mechanisms underlying policy process theories and therefore help to increase confidence in their analytical merits. On the other, the concepts and findings challenge existing theories and potentially further develop studies of the policy process. This chapter also addresses what we have learned and what is left to do.

CONCEPTUAL AND THEORETICAL CHALLENGES

For a straightforward structuring of this treatise, we follow Weible's (2017) introductory chapter in this book and the definition of policy process research he gives, which is "the study of the interactions that occur over time between public policies and surrounding actors, events, contexts, and outcomes." Working from this definition, we can identify and discuss a set of conceptual categories that group the various challenges in conducting comparative policy process research.

Public Policies

From the literature, one might suspect that there is no debate about what public policies actually are. Yet the first and perhaps most fundamental challenge in comparative policy process research remains identifying what will be compared. Will the same policy be compared across different contexts or different points in time? Will different policies be compared in similar contexts, or will the same outcomes from different public policies be compared? And so forth.

Comparative public policy research has adopted a pragmatic approach to the question of what constitutes a public policy; there is agreement that the *content* rather than the *form* matters. It is rarely the case that comparative analyses systematically differentiate whether a public policy is an executive or a legislative act—both forms are treated as policies. In most cases, it is assumed that the causal mechanism responsible for the way a given policy outcome cuts is partisan ideology (e.g., Schmidt 1996; Huber and Stephens 2001), which should matter in the same way as a heuristic devise for choosing among different policy options regardless of the type of legal act adopted (but see Fankhauser, Gennaioli, and Collins 2015, 2016). In other cases, a variable captures the institutional arrangements leading to a public policy.

In contrast, court decisions are usually treated as instances of political agenda setting or triggers of policy change (e.g., Black and Owens 2009), but not as policies in the narrow sense. Nonetheless, the implications are the same: the involvement of courts is captured conceptually and empirically—if not when assessing the dependent variable, then when developing the conceptual model and identifying the relevant explanatory variables.

Concern for the form of public policy versus the substantive content of public policy is reflected in, and motivates, the process theories under consideration here. One could, in fact, arrange the theories in terms of their attention to the form, institutional configuration, or substance of public policies. At one end of the continuum would fall the Institutional Analysis and Development (IAD) framework, which emphasizes the institutional configuration and form of public policies. Such institutional configurations are often studied through different arrangements of the rule typology, as rules-in-form in written public policies or as rules-in-use (see Ostrom 2011; Schlager and Cox 2017, Chapter 6 in this volume). Although the IAD framework has often been adapted to public goods, particularly common pool resource issues, the framework emphasizes the institutional configurations that arise from decision dependency and repeated social interactions that promote institutional rules and norms that structure policy outputs.

The Punctuated Equilibrium Theory (PET) occupies the middle ground. It attempts to mesh together an understanding of institutional forms, particularly delegation and organization in policymaking systems, and the substantive content of issue agendas (see Baumgartner and Jones 1993; Baumgartner, Jones, and Mortensen 2017, Chapter 2, this volume). With regard to the latter, substantive content has been measured by means of budgets for specific policy areas (e.g., Jones et al. 2009) as well as for issues included in the political agendas of policymakers or the mass media (e.g., Walgrave, Soroka, and Nuytemans 2008). In PET, the institutional arrangements are often the driving force in the various degrees of leptokurtosis in agenda and policy dynamics across political systems.

Anchoring the other end of the continuum are the Advocacy Coalition Framework (ACF) and Multiple Streams Framework (MSF), both of which devote much more attention to understanding the role of particular actors and the competition among actors as they intersect with issue-specific policy problems. These theories focus much less on institutional forms and organization, assuming their effects lie in the background, with actor characteristics (e.g., beliefs) brought to the theoretical foreground. In fact, one could argue that the MSF strives to overcome the notion of the structuring role of institutions for interactions between actors. As Herweg, Zahariadis, and Zohlnhöfer (2017, Chapter 1, this volume) argue, the MSF is based on the idea of fluid participation, which means that the composition of decision making bodies is subject to constant change. From this perspective, institutions are thought to play a less prominent role in policymaking compared with actors. By the same token, MSF pays considerable attention to the content of policies, as indicated by one of the three streams being denoted the policy stream.

The individual policy process theories emphasize the form or the institutions to varying degrees when explaining the outcomes of policymaking. However, this leaves the question of how to define public policy in a way that is conducive to comparative research. An approach adopted by many comparative studies is the conceptual framework put forward by Hall (1993), who differentiates between policy instruments, their settings, and the hierarchy of goals behind policies, also known as policy paradigms. Despite the existence of this widely embraced approach (e.g., Knill, Schulze, and Tosun 2012), defining what exactly a policy is continues to pose a challenge for comparative research.

Time

The temporal perspective is prominent in comparative public policy and is predominantly taken up by the ACF, the PET, the MSF, and the policy subsystem adjustment model proposed by Howlett and Ramesh (2002).

Policy change requires the assessment of policy arrangements at two or more points in time. For a more nuanced conceptualization of policy change, many studies draw on the influential work of Hall (1993), who suggested differentiating between three orders of change. Changes in instrument settings correspond to first-order changes and can be attributed to "incrementalism, satisficing, and routinized decision making" (Hall 1993, 280). The adoption of a new policy instrument represents second-order change and is likely to be the outcome of strategic action. Third-order changes are changes in policy paradigms and are associated with experimentation with new policies and lesson drawing from policy failures. Knill, Schulze, and Tosun (2012) added a fourth category that denotes the scope of a policy instrument, that is, how it governs its target groups. These categories have been used to empirically assess how policies expanded and contracted over time (Bauer et al. 2012; Knill, Schulze, and Tosun 2012; Jordan, Bauer, and Green-Pedersen 2013). It should be noted that a key contribution of policy process theorizing is raising the question of whether the dynamics of policy change are similar at all levels of change or whether different dynamics characterize change at different levels (Baumgartner 2013).

More recently, a second conceptualization, which was originally developed to assess forms of institutional change, has become popular. Streeck and Thelen (2005) propose five forms of gradual institutional changes: displacement, layering, drift, conversion, and exhaustion. Displacement is about new organizational models emerging and spreading, which then challenge the existing models. Layering is when new elements are added to existing models, creating new models that over time can expel or supplant the original ones. Drift is about organizational changes brought about by nondecisions, that is, lacking the capacity or willingness to adapt to new goals or roles. Conversion is related to the redirection of organizations to new goals or roles. Exhaustion is a gradual institutional breakdown. An application of the theoretical debate on institutional change to policy research can be found in Béland's (2007) study of three major social policy episodes in the United States: enactment of the 1939 amendments, the first mandate of the Nixon administration, and Social Security privatization during the 1990s.

Similar to policy change, the study of policy diffusion would not be possible without taking into account the temporal perspective. Policy diffusion is generally defined as the socially mediated spread of policies across and within political systems (Berry and Berry 2017, Chapter 7, this volume). The first studies of policy diffusion were descriptive and concentrated on its shape, that is, they described the adoption patterns on the basis of the cumulative number of countries that have adopted a given policy by time *t*. In most cases, this produces an S-shaped curve, implying that adoption is slow at first, then rapid, and finally levels off as saturation is reached (Gray 1973; Boushey 2010).

Policy diffusion might result in policy convergence, which can be defined as "any increase in the similarity between one or more characteristics of a certain policy (e.g., policy objectives, policy instruments, policy settings) across a given set of political jurisdictions (supra-national institutions, states, regions, local authorities) over a given period of time" (Knill 2005, 768).

In regard to the comparative perspective they adopt, there is one fundamental difference between studies that are interested in policy change—and hence are closely linked to policy process theories—and those that explore policy diffusion and convergence. Studies of policy change compare the same policy or policies over time in the same context, whereas studies of policy diffusion and convergence compare the same policy over time in different contexts. The feature they share is that all three concepts concentrate on the same policy, but research on diffusion and convergence is more comparative than studies examining policy change. From this, it follows that capturing the temporal dimension is critical to studies of policy change because it constitutes the main comparative aspect. Studies of policy diffusion and convergence can additionally exploit the comparative potential of different contexts. Therefore, policy research seeking to explain policy change must cope with the challenge of reasonably selecting the observation period.

Actors

In the last few years, the dominant trend in theorizing in comparative and political economy has certainly been to emphasize the characteristics and strategies of individual or collective actors. For example, actor-centered institutionalism, which brings the actors to the fore, is an influential theoretical perspective that appeared in 1990s policy research (see Scharpf 1997). Among the policy process theories, four pay close attention to actors: the ACF, the MSF, the Narrative Policy Framework (NPF), and the IAD framework.

In the ACF, any policy subsystem includes a set of actors, who are persons "regularly attempting to influence subsystem affairs" (Jenkins-Smith et al. 2017, Chapter 4, this volume). The merit of the ACF is that it embraces this more generic definition of actors, which has been abstracted from the classic perspective in comparative politics that an individual or a system of government agencies and interest groups matters. The concept of actors significantly broadens the understanding of who in a given political system can exercise influence on policy decisions. This conceptualization of actors makes the ACF, particularly, and the MSF and NPF suitable for comparative research. The interaction between actors or actor coalitions, rather than an understanding of institutions, lies at the heart of the research endeavor. In the end, policy subsystems vary by the actors involved in them and their influence on policies.

Although the ACF broadly considers the question of who matters for policymaking, it rests on sophisticated assumptions about actors' belief system structures. Actors have deep core beliefs (i.e., fundamental normative values and ontological axioms), policy core beliefs (i.e., beliefs specific to the respective policy subsystem), and secondary beliefs (i.e., specific instrumental means for achieving the goals underlying the policy core beliefs). The notion of beliefs indicates the ACF—similar to the PET, the MSF, and the NPF—proposes that individuals possess a limited ability to process information, that is, they are boundedly rational. From this, it follows that individuals have goals but face uncertainty in achieving those goals. Further, they have limited cognitive abilities, which make their belief systems relevant to their formulating and pursuing policy demands.

Thus, individuals' beliefs, not their ability to process information, motivate them to support or oppose certain policies. Similarity in belief systems determines which actors form coalitions, and competition between these "advocacy coalitions" has an impact on policy change.

The MSF locates actors in the politics and problem streams (Herweg, Zahariadis, and Zohlnhöfer 2017, Chapter 1, this volume). Policy change is attained when a policy entrepreneur strategizes the confluence of the three streams (Zohlnhöfer 2016), yielding agenda and policy change when coupling occurs. The next actor in the MSF, associated with the problem stream, is denoted as the problem broker and helps define the conditions of problems; this person may be identical to the policy broker. The main difference between these actors is that the "problem broker only argues that something must be done about a specific condition while the policy entrepreneur suggests solutions to the problem" (Herweg, Zahariadis, and Zohlnhöfer 2017, this volume).

Relatedly, the NPF concentrates on how policy narratives affect individuals' preferences, risk perceptions, and attitudes about certain policies (Shanahan et al. 2017, Chapter 5, this volume). The IAD framework conceives of actors as individuals or groups in an action situation, which, again, is a sophisticated conceptualization because it presumes that actors and institutions are holistic entities (Schlager and Cox 2017, Chapter 6, this volume).

These frameworks have in common that they rest on complex conceptualizations of actors and their characteristics and how they may influence the policy process. Whereas this represents a strength for analyzing a given policy-making situation, particularly specific substantive policy issues, it complicates the adoption of a comparative approach to the study of the policy process. It also makes understanding institutions and governing systems problematic. The more nuanced a concept and its empirical application, the more difficult we will find applying it for comparative research, which becomes feasible by deliberately abstracting away from details (see Newton and van Deth 2016, 392).

Events

Events have been the central analytical concept used in studies of risk and uncertainty and policy change, diffusion, and convergence. In most theoretical approaches, events are conceived as focusing events, that is, both expected and unexpected occurrences that attract the attention of the public or policymakers for a certain period of time. Birkland (1997) differentiates between natural and manmade disasters as focusing events, whereas Cobb and Elder (1972) and Kingdon (1984), for instance, regard political alignments as focusing events or, at a minimum, as windows of opportunity.

Studies comparing policymaking over time have typically treated changes in the partisan composition of governments as events that have an impact on the dynamics and outcomes of policymaking (e.g., Walgrave and Varone 2008). Studies that compare the same policy in different contexts—cross-country comparisons—have adopted the concept of focusing events and more political variants. A typical example of a comparative study that draws on focusing events is an analysis of how accidents in nuclear power plants affect the decision to phase out nuclear power (e.g., Jahn and Korolczuk 2012). Event-focused research questions in comparative public policy are about how regional or global economic crises such as the 1970s oil shock or the 2007–2008 financial and economic crises affect policymaking (Starke, Kaasch, and Van Hooren 2014).

Research on focusing events typically concerns major policy shifts that, as many studies argue, would not have been feasible without the attention directed to a given issue for a limited period of time. Many studies of focusing events implicitly or explicitly hypothesize that these events neutralize other political forces. When events are endogenous to the system, forces such as the partisan ideology of policymakers must be taken into account (e.g., economic crisis). In marked contrast to focusing events, enabling factors—events such as party changes or changes in the socioeconomic situation of societies—are triggers for policymaking.

Comparative research is more straightforward in the case of focusing events versus other events for two reasons. First, focusing events are easier to define, which facilitates case selection. Second, focusing events are considered to be powerful enough to dominate domestic politics (but see, e.g., Nohrstedt 2005), which means the comparative research design can be simplified. More resources can be allocated to characterizing the origin, nature, and perception of the focusing events than is the case with other events. It follows that policy process theories stressing the role of systemic, or endogenous, events are more likely to pose challenges in comparative designs. For example, are changes in partisan composition of a government as relevant in one country as in another? Or does comparison require concentrating on the specific partisan composition of government? These questions illustrate the need for further reflection when incorporating systemic or endogenous events in comparative policy research.

Contexts

An important component of policy process theories is context. For example, in the NPF *context* refers to the macrolevel of analysis and to institutions or culture (see Shanahan et al. 2017, this volume). It is clear that the context in which policy processes take place matters a great deal to the outcomes and does not necessarily prevent comparative analyses. As noted above, comparative research can either exploit variation while holding the context constant (e.g., by comparing policies over time or comparing different policies) or create variation by allowing the context to vary. Policy process theories that draw on the notion of policy subsystems (e.g., NPF and ACF) find it easier to adopt the first option, whereas theories like the policy diffusion model tend to adopt the second.

Comparative studies can theoretically and methodologically deal with context. Theoretically, one needs to identify which macrolevel factors matter for explaining policy dynamics. In the case of comparing policies that address risk and uncertainty, for example, the general institutional arrangements are less important for explaining differences or similarities between countries than risk cultures are (Douglas and Wildavsky 1983). Many observers would agree that Germany and Sweden share many similarities—relative to other countries—regarding institutional setup, socioeconomic development level, and integration in Europe. Despite these similarities, the majority of Germans oppose the production of nuclear power (e.g., Jahn and Korolczuk 2012), whereas the majority of Swedes are supportive of nuclear power (e.g., Nohrstedt 2005). It follows that German policymakers have adopted a more restrictive—if not to say prohibitive—stance on the production of nuclear power than policymakers in Sweden. Relevant contextual factors should be dependent on theory; otherwise, analyses devolve into residual explanations.

Theoretical considerations naturally have implications for research design. Qualitative comparative policy research designs can keep the context factors as similar as possible (i.e., most-similar-systems design) or allow them to vary (i.e., most-different-systems design) across countries (see Newton and van Deth 2016, 388–389). Although both designs have merit, in the literature we mostly observe country-comparative studies based on the logic of the most-similar-systems design.

Institutions provide perhaps the most relevant conceptualization of context. Handling of institutions in comparative policy process research has varied greatly, in part owing to the conception of institutions in the original theories. Extant theories of comparative politics are grounded in firm understandings of institutions. The theories of the policy process offer a rich and varied conceptualization of political institutions. Standard theories of comparative politics depict institutions as transaction costs. The veto player model as put forward by Tsebelis (2002) is a prime example of institutions as transaction costs. This conceptualization allows the veto player model to assess the policy effects of political institutions from a unified theoretical perspective, which is appealing to scholars in both comparative politics and public policy (see Ganghof 2003).

The more varied conceptualization in policy processes has its costs. For instance, comparing institutional hypotheses from the theories is difficult, even in similar problems. This lack of convergence is more problematic when we consider that understanding the effects of political institutions is a core concern in political science generally, and not just in the study of public policy.

The policy process theories gain leverage in their conceptualization and examination of political institutions by holding key elements of policy substance, and thus the range of positions and actors, stable. Where the theories, particularly the ACF and IAD framework, address particular policy problems cross-nationally, their substantive focus allows for isolating how institutional arrangements shape not only policy but also the opportunity structures faced by coalitions of actors (e.g., Gupta 2014). So, one set of institutional hypotheses derived from the policy process theories is issue dependent.

In contrast, scholars working in the PET tradition have conceptualized institutions as decision making systems for processing information and generating particular patterns of policy dynamics. For these scholars, processes of delegation, organization, and sequencing are just as important as the particular form taken by institutional structures or the substantive nature of the policy problem. Institutions are important both in prioritizing issues on the policy agenda and in determining the dynamics of policy outputs over time (Jones et al. 2009).

Development is helped along by a common system of measurement for issue agendas and in-depth work on political budgeting. This is important because it ties the front end and back end of the policy process together via generalizations about political processes (i.e., agenda setting, budgeting, or regulatory politics) and common patterns of policy dynamics. Thus, emphasis is not on comparing, say, parliaments directly to the US Congress but on comparing issue agendas and patterns of policy change. This notion of having a common measurement system leads directly to a discussion of the methodological challenges posed by comparative applications of the policy process theories.

Outcomes

Despite addressing public policy from different perspectives, studies in policy processes have in common that they largely address policy outputs and not the effects—policy outcomes. With the exception of the budgeting tradition in PET, comparative policy research has paid relatively scant attention to comparing policy outcomes. More precisely, it has hardly examined similar outcomes (e.g., reduction in poverty) as being achieved by different public policies across different contexts.

On the one hand, the concentration of policy process research on policy outputs is reasonable because these are most likely to be affected by the interactions of actors in a given institutional setting. Policy outcomes can be regarded as a type of policy feedback, which can start a new policy process. From this perspective, conceiving of the outcomes of previous policy decisions as explanatory variables concurs with the most general logic of policy process theories.

An adjacent literature strand concentrating explicitly on policy outcomes is political economy and, more precisely, studies drawing on the varieties of capitalism approach. According to Hall and Soskice (2001), the degree of coordination within the economy distinguishes between two ideal types: liberal market economies (LMEs) and coordinated market economies (CMEs). Both ideal types represent the extremes of a spectrum of pure market powers and a strong coordination of market forces in which political economies can be classified. In LMEs strong market forces dominate; in CMEs coordination mechanisms play a major role between the various market participants. In LMEs, companies coordinate their activities in all subsystems of the economy primarily by orientation on price signals, free competition in the market, and marginal cost. In CMEs, however, non-market-based relations play a major role and are crucial for the development of corporate core competencies. Corresponding research shows that CMEs produce policies that help them mitigate the adverse effects of crises more effectively than LMEs.

Interim Conclusions

We have discussed how policy process theories conceive of public policies, their temporal dimension, and the role they assign to actors, events, and context and have examined how they deal with policy outcomes. The overview shows that there exist established definitions of public policy and its elements that are, in principle, suitable for comparative analysis. Analyzing policy decisions in the same context at different points in time represents a form of comparative analysis that is implicitly and explicitly addressed in policy studies. However, there exists policy research that is comparative with regard to policy decisions and the context in which they are formulated.

The main limitation in comparative policy research is the conceptualization and systematic analysis of policy outcomes. It makes sense that policy outcomes do not represent the main subject of interest of policy process theories because they are not only affected by strategic interactions between actors but also by a whole range of additional factors (see Knill, Schulze, and Tosun 2012). Nonetheless, policy outcomes could be conceptualized as policy feedbacks (see Mettler and SoRelle 2017, Chapter 3, this volume) that—together with other factors—trigger policy change. This idea is particularly interesting because policy outcomes can be measured in ways that allow for comparison across units, time, and policy areas.

All in all, the field of comparative policy process contains several conceptual and theoretical starting points for research. Yet we also need to take into account empirical and methodological considerations before formulating a comparative policy research agenda.

EMPIRICAL AND METHODOLOGICAL CHALLENGES

In general, the research designs for applying the policy process theories comparatively are . . . comparative. Leaving this higher-order design problem aside, issues of measurement and methods still plague applications of the theories, as we have already indicated. Methodologically, one of the theories in this volume has achieved a much greater level of standardization in both measurement and methods.

The PET uses a common system for measuring the issue agendas of political institutions or systems (see Jones 2016). This system was developed early on, and subsequent developments in the theory have retained this concern for issue agendas and measuring them in a reliable, backward-compatible way. What this yields is standardization and a common metric for testing hypotheses generated across countries, institutions, and governing systems generally. This common base of measurement not only provides a common vernacular among the group but also fosters the generation of cross-national hypotheses that are very general.

This common metric has also allowed a common mode of analysis. In particular, the theory makes use of distributional and stochastic process methods, from which the general punctuation hypothesis is explored. The central notion of the PET is that individual and institutional cognition, constrained by limited attention, leads to disproportionate information processing. That is to say, policy change is characterized by lots of small, incremental changes punctuated by large, dramatic change. This dynamic leads to the characteristic "fat tails" in agenda and policy change distributions, where the distribution of change over time is leptokurtic. This hypothesis has proved particularly powerful in describing policy dynamics in political institutions and, moreover, across countries and political systems.

The PET has made thorough use of government budgets for which country-comparative data are available (especially for advanced market economies). For example, using data for annual changes in government budgets in six nations, Jones et al. (2009) managed to identify a general empirical law of budget punctuations. This law suggests that budget processes are leptokurtic in general. More specifically, the law suggests that budgetary decreases are more punctuated than increases and that local governments are less punctuated compared to central governments.

This common metric and set of methods is largely absent from studies applying the ACF, the MSF, or the NPF. Of course, these theories have different analytical interests as well. Whereas the PET is concerned with identifying and explaining broader policy patterns on the basis of limited attention and institutional friction, the ACF, the MSF, and the NPF attach greater importance to specific policy substance. Specificity requires a more varied approach to analysis. As concerns the analytical interests of these theories and the concepts on which they draw, the above discussion shows that they are conducive to comparative research. However, they are confronted with empirical limitations that stem from key analytical concepts.

For these reasons, PET presents a more standardized approach and vocabulary for rapidly generating comparative hypotheses. To their credit, the ACF, MSF, and NPF see measuring policy change as more problematic than it at first appears, and they tend to attempt to incorporate directional measures of policy advocacy and policy change not captured in the PET's focus on attention (though the exception is in budgetary processes, where directionality is clear and easily assessed). This more varied, or at least less settled, approach to measurement and analysis in these theories comes with a cost in development. Because all these theories are well on in years, a considerable amount of time is needed to study the theories at a level that allows systematic assessment of their hypotheses. This situation is made more acute in comparative applications.

POLICY PROCESS RESEARCH
AND COMPARATIVE POLITICS

The classic policy analysis literature acknowledged the relationship between policies and politics. The main claim in Lowi's (1964) influential work is that "policy determines politics" in the sense that policy types entail varying degrees of costs and opposition to attempts to change the status quo. On the basis of this reasoning, Lowi put forward a typology that distinguishes among *distributive policies* (measures that affect the distribution of resources from the government to particular recipients), *redistributive policies* (measures on the transfer of resources from one societal group to another), *regulatory policies* (measures that define conditions and constraints for individual or collective behavior), and *constituent policies* (measures that create or modify the states' institutions).

More recent research has attempted to reverse this relationship and to understand how concepts from politics can be used to explain policy decisions (e.g., Knill and Tosun 2012, 2017). The main motivation for integrating concepts from politics in policy studies stems from the success of comparative politics (see Newton and van Deth 2016). The comparative politics literature can draw on established concepts and datasets on the positions of political parties (e.g., Volkens et al. 2013), corporatism (e.g., Kenworthy 2003), and veto players (e.g., Jahn 2011), which enable comparative research.

A key interest in comparative politics is to explain the development of modern states, which includes processes of transitions toward democracy and—as increasingly happens in the last few years—autocracy (e.g., Croissant et al. 2015). The second analytical focus lies on the characteristics and effects of structures and institutions. It is within this research perspective that there exists a sizable literature addressing policymaking in executives and legislatures, which is, for instance, interested in whether government or opposition parties propose certain policies and how long the policymaking process takes given certain constellations such as grand coalition governments or minority governments (e.g., Manow and Burkhart 2008). Another key topic in the comparative politics approach to policymaking is the role of political ideologies and how states perform in the sense of solving problems by means of policymaking (e.g., Bale et al. 2010). A third major area of interest of comparative politics scholars is citizens' attitudes and their political participation (e.g., Soroka and Wlezien 2009) and the role of various actor groups, including pressure groups, social movements, mass media, and political parties (e.g., Baumgartner et al. 2009; Tosun and Schaub 2017; Walgrave, Soroka, and Nuytemans 2008; Walgrave and Varone 2008).

The integration of policy research with comparative politics research has been realized in two ways. First, studies seeking to explain policy decisions make use of the isolated factors presented above. For example, Knill, Debus, and Heichel (2010) are interested in explaining environmental policy change, but instead of relying on the policy process theories that concentrate on policy change, the authors focus on the impact of the electoral strength of political parties. Second, studies using policy process theories incorporate concepts from comparative politics. The PET is perhaps the process theory that has the most visible connection with comparative politics, which is also reflected in the background of the scholars contributing to this body of research.

To illustrate this point, note the volume on the comparative approach to agenda setting edited by Green-Pedersen and Walgrave (2014). Both editors have a background in comparative politics, with Green-Pedersen's other research concentrating on party politics and party competition (e.g., Green-Pedersen and Krogstrup 2008) and Walgrave's research revolving around the role of mass media in politics (e.g., Walgrave, Soroka, and Nuytemans 2008). The great majority of other researchers contributing to that volume—including the inventors of the PET (Baumgartner and Jones 1993; Baumgartner, Jones, and Mortensen 2017, this volume)—are comparative politics scholars working on institutions, parties, and representation (e.g., Bevan and Jennings 2014). The PET lends itself particularly well to incorporating concepts from comparative politics because of the role institutional arrangements play therein. As Baumgartner, Jones, and Mortensen (2017, this volume) explain, institutional arrangements characterized by institutional separation often work to reinforce policy stability, but sometimes they can be conducive to policy change by working to "wash away existing policy subsystems." We argue that it is the prominence of institutional arrangements and the fact that these scholars can build on the insights existing scholarship in comparative politics yields that has helped strengthen the comparative approach to PET.

Turning to actor-centered policy process theories like the ACF, we can note that these deviate from studies in comparative politics. They do not concentrate on individual actor groups but are interested in actor coalitions and their respective beliefs and resources. These are in turn a product of their long-term coalition opportunity structures and short-term constraints and resources. It is the complexity of the relationship between the individual actors forming a coalition, the importance of the relationship of different actor coalitions within policy subsystems, and the additional factors influencing them that reduces the compatibility between the ACF and comparative politics research. From this perspective, the ACF—like most other policy process theories—can make limited use of the insights offered by comparative politics owing to its sophisticated and particularly refined approach to modeling how advocacy coalitions structure policy change.

For example, Shanahan et al. (2011) use the NPF to analyze the effect of policy narratives on public opinion. To this end, the authors treat a group of students with two media accounts that reflect divergent advocacy coalitions and assess how this affects their opinion on the policy issue concerning snowmobile access to Yellowstone National Park. To transform this study into one that could guide comparative research, the focus would need to be one actor group, most likely government actors, whose policy narrative could then be explained by comparative data on how political ideology determines positions on nature protection.

Summing up, scholars in comparative politics have agreed in many areas on levels of analysis that allow for comparative measurement, which has helped this literature to become prolific. The concepts from comparative politics have migrated to some varieties of policy process research and have paved the way for comparative analysis there. Because the institution-centered process theories such as the PET can be more easily divided into specific components, they have benefited more from concepts and data originating from comparative politics than actor-centered theories, which tend to be more complex. Yet this does not mean that comparative research that draws on policy process theories does not exist, and it certainly does not preclude more comparative studies. We elaborate on this point in the next section.

POLICY PROCESS RESEARCH IN COMPARATIVE PERSPECTIVE

In this section, we characterize the comparative research that has already been undertaken or that is under way applying the theories of the policy process. We argue that the comparative extensions of the policy process theories need not be nation-comparative only but can include insights from comparing political institutions, subnational units, and different stages of the policy process (e.g., agenda setting vs. policy adoption). Our discussion of the comparative research in these theoretical traditions sets the stage for considering what we have learned, what is left undone, and what opportunities are presented by these more recent comparative extensions of the theories and concepts presented in this volume. These opportunities encompass theoretical, conceptual, and methodological possibilities.

Multiple Streams Framework

As it is the case with many policy process theories, the MSF was developed under the impression of policy dynamics in the institutional setting of the United States. Therefore, for a long time, this approach was applied to the US context, and no attempts were made to develop it further conceptually or empirically. Recently, however, studies have applied the MSF to different institutional contexts (see Herweg, Zahariadis, and Zohlnhöfer 2017, this volume; Jones et al. 2016), and conceptual efforts have been made to develop a comparative approach to MSF.

In this context, Zohlnhöfer, Herweg, and Huß (2016) argue that the MSF could be transformed to become more conducive to comparative research by paying enhanced attention to formal political institutions. This suggestion is particularly remarkable given our discussion of the natural relationship between institution-centered policy process theories and comparative politics and how this proximity has helped promote comparative policy process research. From this perspective, the proposal by Zohlnhöfer, Herweg, and Huß (2016) points at exactly the same dimension, namely, to explore possibilities for exploiting the analytical tools supplied by comparative politics. Remarkably, the need to concentrate more specifically on institutional factors is supported by a conceptual piece by Béland (2016). Also focusing on the conceptual dimension, Howlett, McConnell, and Perl (2015) advance the argument that a combination of the MSF with other policy process theories would increase its fit with comparative logic.

An example of a country-comparative application of the MSF is offered by Spohr (2016), who examines reforms of labor market policies in Germany and Sweden emphasizing the role of policy entrepreneurs. More broadly, although the comparative insights provided by the MSF are limited, we must acknowledge that isolated components of this approach have been used for comparative research. The most frequently used concepts are—such as in Spohr's (2016) study—policy entrepreneurs and focusing events (Béland and Howlett 2016, 224). For example, trade disputes, mostly in the context of the World Trade Organization, have been regarded as focusing events that trigger policy change (e.g., Ackrill and Kay 2011). Policy entrepreneurs, in particular, conceptually travel easily across the most diverse institutional settings. The same holds true for policy brokers, the notion of which has been adopted by comparative studies of the relationship between science and public policy. The concept used by these studies is related to the policy broker but refers to scientific actors as "honest brokers" (Pielke 2007).

It is interesting to see that the conceptual treatises on strengthening the comparative perspective of the MSF make a plea for emphasizing formal political institutions, whereas the existing empirical studies have chosen to concentrate on the two components that are detached from the institutional context. We can conclude that attempts to make the MSF more comparative can choose between adopting the whole approach and then concentrating on institutions and selecting isolated concepts and abstracting from institutional arrangements.

Punctuated Equilibrium Theory

PET scholars have devoted a considerable amount of effort to understanding human decision making and taking seriously the lessons of behavioral psychology and economics (Jones 1994, 2001). For this reason, the PET has been influential by itself and has stimulated other conceptual models. Building on Baumgartner and Jones (1993) and Schattschneider (1960), Engeli, Green-Pedersen, and Larsen (2012) highlight the importance of four elements: attention, actors, images, and institutional venues. The assumption of this model is that the policy process is determined by the underlying political conflicts over a given issue. In this context, the first factor that needs to be taken into account is the level of both public and political attention given to certain issues. The higher the level of attention, the more controversial the policy process that follows initial agenda setting.

Attention to individual cognition and its implications for how institutions process information and prioritize problems has led to a plethora of studies of comparative political institutions. These studies include US state governors' institutional powers (Breunig and Koski 2009), budgeting in Western democracies (Breunig, Koski, and Mortensen 2010; Jones et al. 2009), bureaucratic and regulatory policymaking (Bevan 2015; May, Workman, and Jones 2008; Workman 2015), and the relationship between the news media and parliamentary agenda setting (Vliegenthart et al. 2016).

Attention is closely connected to the number and types of actors that are involved in the problem definition of an issue (May, Sapotichne, and Workman 2006). Usually, issues of low attention are characterized by the participation of a limited group of actors in the policy process, and politicized issues are characterized by the involvement of more actors. Different types of actors typically have different preferences regarding the outcome of the policy process, which leads to controversial politics.

One area that presents tremendous possibilities in comparative policy process research is the concept of problem definitions. Stone (1989) provides a frequently used concept of problem definition: a causal story that identifies harm, describes what causes the harm, assigns blame to those causing it, and claims that the government is responsible for stopping the activity in question. Put simply, issue images are about a certain perspective from which issues are seen and about the exclusion of alternative views (Engeli, Green-Pedersen, and Larsen 2012).

The PET, with its attention to individual and organizational cognition, offers an alternative version of problem definition as the dimensions of a problem that are relevant for choice. For instance, climate change could be said to embody substantive dimensions involving trade policy, environmental policy, agricultural policy, and energy policy, among others. Climate change policy defined as energy policy has very different implications, regardless of cause and effect, than climate change policy defined as an environmental problem (see Elgin and Weible 2013). Borrowing from work on cognition, the PET sees problem definition as akin to problem representation. Choice requires the construction of a problem representation (Newell and Simon 1972; Jones 2001) before solutions can be generated and evaluated in terms of preferences or beliefs. Problem definition, then, is an indispensable precursor to choice.

Another alternative is Dery's (1984, 4–27) conceptualization of problem definitions as "gaps" or "opportunities." Policymakers compare the current policy to current conditions and define that discrepancy as either a gap in policy that needs filling or as an opportunity to expand policymaking in a given area. Using the twin notions of problem definition as dimensions of choice and as an opportunity for steering policy agendas, Workman (2015) identifies bureaucratic and administrative units as key to understanding how the governing system comes to understand given policy problems and how policy agendas are structured.

Policy Feedback Theory

The most prominent theory of policy feedback examines how current policies constrain the types of policies available in the future in a theory attentive to history and institutional development (Pierson 2004). The early policy feedback literature in particular was strongly influenced by historical institutionalism, which explores the impact of institutions on political behavior and policymaking dynamics (Béland 2010, 570). This approach is, however, different from the classic version of historical institutionalism to the extent that it has an explicit behavioral component, and as a result this theory is based on a microfoundation that allows for a more complete explanation of policy processes.

In empirical terms, this approach has been especially useful in comparative public policy for the study of the welfare state (Hacker 2002) and inequality (Hacker and Pierson 2011). Most empirical applications of the Policy Feedback Theory (PFT) draw on the concept of incrementalism and share similarities with the forms of institutional change identified by Streeck and Thelen (2005).

More broadly, the early literature paid particular attention to processes of state building, interest groups, and lock-in effects. More recently, scholars have focused on private benefits and institutions, the role of political behavior, and ideational and symbolic components of policy feedback (Béland 2010, 576). However, the design of policies can have feedback effects on individuals, not only in terms of the way they view the particular policy but also more broadly with implications on their attitudes toward politics and the political system in general (e.g., Mettler and Soss 2004). Policies that focus on broad segments of the population can pique interest in politics, for example, because political outcomes may create personal stakes and thus influence how attentive individuals are to the political process (see Shore 2016).

This scholarship mostly connects public policy to future policy change or individual behavior through the mechanism of positive feedback. However, considerable work in mass opinion makes similar connections through the mechanism of negative feedback. The thermostatic model of mass opinion posits that governments pursue policies in a left or right fashion, progressively farther away from the general preferences of the public (Wlezien and Soroka 2012). Once beyond some threshold, citizen preferences serve as negative feedback on governing party choices, even so far as being replaced if necessary. The thermostatic model is remarkably resilient across substantive policy issues and governing systems. A slightly different application of the PFT concerns the strategic use of policy decisions as a tool to move public opinion (see Soss and Schram 2007).

Weaver (2010) regards the turn to negative feedback as a correction to the emphasis historical institutionalism and path dependency literature placed on positive feedback. Positive feedback from these perspectives is associated with stability; negative feedback, with policy change. Therefore, the burgeoning attention paid to negative feedback concurs with the general increase in interest in the comparative empirical assessment and explanation of policy change.

In all, the PFT displays an affinity for comparative politics research, and therefore extending it to comparative research is a fruitful endeavor. Yet, existing studies that explicitly draw on this approach are mostly context-specific, although the accumulation of individual studies provides a relatively robust empirical picture. Nevertheless, the empirical potential of this approach has not been exploited for comparative policy process research and represents an avenue worth exploring in future research.

The Advocacy Coalition Framework and the Narrative Policy Framework

The ACF (Sabatier and Jenkins-Smith 1993, 1999; Sabatier 1998; Sabatier and Weible 2007; Weible, Sabatier, and McQueen 2009) is one of the most influential approaches to policy change. Essentially, it views policymaking as the result of the competition between coalitions of actors who advocate beliefs about certain policy options. This competition between advocacy groups takes place within policy subsystems. The framework further argues that actors process information according to a variety of cognitive heuristics that provide guidance in complex decision making situations. In this regard, belief systems give guidance about how a social problem is structured and how it could be remedied.

Against this background, policy change may principally result from two sources. First, policy change can occur as a result of learning processes, which induces a hegemonic advocacy coalition to transform its beliefs in response to experience or new information. Second, external events may lead to changes in the power distribution among advocacy coalitions. The revision of the Advocacy Coalition Framework by Sabatier and Weible (2007) identifies two more sources of policy change. One source is endogenous events that occur within the subsystem and that highlight failures in current subsystem practices. The other source is cross-coalition learning, where professional forums provide an institutional setting that allows coalitions to safely negotiate and implement agreements.

Scholars working within the ACF have just begun to leverage the power of comparative research designs in understanding variation in coalitional structure, competition, and resulting policy outputs. Weible et al. (2016) examine policy debates surrounding hydraulic fracturing in seven countries. They find that coalition makeup and intercoalitional structure vary greatly across different types of political systems. There remains a need to understand how coalitions, processes of learning, and policy change differ by policy topics, events, and actor constellations, especially in diverse institutional contexts. Federal versus unitary systems, for instance, structure who may and may not be part of the coalition addressing a particular issue.

One point of comparative advantage in applying the ACF might be institutional jurisdictions and how these structure coalitions and coalition formation. In the United States, for instance, issue jurisdictions are a point of competition among not only subsystem actors but also federal agencies addressing these problems (Workman 2015). This is less the case in unitary, central governments such as that of the United Kingdom, with clearer lines of demarcation. The ACF promises to be particularly powerful in understanding policy change pursuant to this variation.

The key challenges for the ACF in comparative perspective are empirical and methodological. Although the ACF maintains an empirical and methodological pluralism that enables it to be widely adapted to diverse contextual policy problems, this same pluralism strains the logic of comparative research design. A systematic effort to standardize some of these diverse empirical and methodological approaches would be a boon to comparative applications of the theory, allowing scholars to test some of these broader hypotheses before digging deeper into the nuances of policy change.

The NPF is similar to the ACF but also more complex in terms of the analytical concepts it uses (e.g., Jones and Radaelli 2015). As a result, empirical studies drawing on the NPF exist (e.g., Shanahan, McBeth, and Hathaway 2011), but the empirical work concentrates on comparing policy narratives used by different advocacy coalitions in the same institutional contexts. There are no indications that this literature seeks to adopt a comparative approach that would be different from comparing policy narratives. Do narratives differ fundamentally across national borders? This would be a useful extension of this line of research. If differences exist, researchers could then ask whether the comparative differences are important for understanding policy change.

The Institutional Analysis and Development Framework

The IAD framework offers an analytical tool focused on action situations and recognizes institutional settings (Blomquist and deLeon 2011). The institutional dimension of this framework makes it particularly useful for comparative analyses, especially in the study of overharvesting in common pool resource situations. Again, similar to the PFT, the actions are systematically connected to cost-benefit analyses of individuals, which strengthen the connection of this approach to comparative politics research. The comparative dimension of this approach is explicitly acknowledged by Schlager and Cox (2017, this volume). They state that its application allows for the production of data according to the same measurement standards.

An empirical application of the IAD framework is provided by Andersson (2006), who analyzes the determinants of success of decentralized policy regimes on common pool resources. To this end, the author gathered data on forest-sector activities in municipal governments in Bolivia, which show that local governance systems are more successful when information is exchanged and learning processes are facilitated. Another insightful example is the study by Imperial and Yandle (2005) on the effect of institutions on fisheries policy. This study is worth noting because it adopted a rather unusual comparative perspective. It uses institutional arrangements to manage fisheries, namely, bureaucracy, markets, community, and comanagement. Bureaucracy is characterized by the government holding the property rights to fish and a focus on regulation that maintains fish stocks at sustainable levels; markets use trading systems that allocate property rights to vessel owners or fishers using tradable permits. If communities hold property rights to fish, they use social norms, rules, and sanctions to govern fisher behavior. With comanagement, there is shared responsibility between government and user groups. The authors offer a conceptual discussion concerning implications of these institutional arrangements for efficiency, equity, accountability, and adaptability.

Despite the existence of comparative research, Clement (2010) states that the literature based on this approach mostly studies local communities and not higher institutional levels. This observation is accurate for the empirical study of Andersson (2006) and holds true more generally because most analyses concentrate on decentralization of policy regimes and the effectiveness of local-level governance. Clement (2010) gives an interesting conceptual reason for the empirical limitation of the IAD framework: its lack of attention to power mechanisms stemming from the political and economic structures that shape power distribution. Clement further argues that institutions are not neutral but rather emerge, sustain, or collapse in political-economic contexts. It follows that the challenge in comparative analysis using the IAD framework is studying more complicated governing arrangements (e.g., at the subsystem or political system level where the rule typology and description of action situations become unwieldy).

In this way, the IAD framework tends to face the opposite set of challenges as the ACF. The ACF's methodological pluralism allows it to adapt to diverse policy problems yet makes comparative research design difficult, at least empirically and methodologically. In contrast, the IAD framework's standardized approach to empirical and methodological design is useful in comparative designs but is not widely adaptable to diverse types of policy problems.

The Diffusion of Innovation Model

The diffusion literature is comparative by definition and benefits from the availability of a common set of explanatory variables—learning, imitation, economic competition, and coercion—and metrics (see Berry and Berry 2017, this volume). Although these variables are sometimes labeled differently, the underlying causal mechanisms are the same and can be summarized as follows.

Transnational learning can be roughly defined as a process in which governments search for solutions to a problem, which they find in another jurisdiction. Emulation is the desire of policymakers to attain international acceptance by demonstrating conformity with the behavior of states that are considered leaders. Coercion is based on the assumption that there is a power asymmetry between two jurisdictions in which the more powerful one can force the other to adopt certain policy measures. Economic competition induces policymakers to adopt policies in place elsewhere if these are expected to affect the national industry's ability to compete in the global market (Vogel and Kagan 2004).

There exists an impressive amount of policy diffusion research that concentrates on the most diverse policy areas (e.g., Holzinger, Knill, and Arts 2008). However, there also exists work concentrating on diffusion processes at the subnational level. For example, Boushey (2010) uses research in agenda setting and epidemiology to characterize the process of policy diffusion among the American states. This research refutes the notion that diffusion is a thought-out, incremental process; instead, it embodies the characteristics of an outbreak of disease. The theory posits interest groups as key to the "spread" of policies. Tosun and Shikano (2016) analyzed the spread of regions in Europe that declared they would not grow genetically modified organisms. By comparing diffusion processes within and across countries, the authors illustrate that intracountry diffusion dominates intercountry diffusion, which is an important finding because it shows that diffusion processes at the subnational level may be triggered by decision making at higher levels of government.

In addition to the agreement of a similar set of explanatory variables and their measurement, the proliferation of diffusion studies also stems from the agreement on how to measure the dependent variable. Typically, the dependent variable is binary. The similarity and simplicity in data coding have produced a remarkably coherent body of research that offers many comparative insights for processes of vertical diffusion (i.e., when a policy from a lower level of government diffuses to higher levels) and horizontal diffusion (i.e., when the policy spreads across the same levels of government, but in a number of jurisdictions). What is also characteristic for this literature is that it recognizes the importance of domestic politics and, because it is comparative by definition, it relies on concepts and measurements common in comparative politics. Thus, we have another policy process theory that has a close relationship with comparative politics and can incorporate analytical tools from that literature.

Perhaps the most robust empirical finding refers to the diffusion of environmental standards (e.g., air quality standards) in both developed and developing states. In environmental policy, the impact of economic interests on the definition of regulatory standards has been thoroughly discussed in relation to "races to the bottom." Here, the main mechanism relates to footloose investors relocating their polluting industries to "pollution havens" in parts of the world where the environmental standards are less strict. According to the theory, this can induce governments to deliberately lower their standards to a level below what is possible given the available technology. Empirically, however, there is a remarkable coherence in the absence of such dynamics (Holzinger, Knill, and Arts 2008; Tosun 2013), which means that there is no indication that governments adopt less stringent environmental standards when confronted with competitive pressure. What can be observed is the opposite scenario, known as the "race to the top," where developing countries adopt increasingly strict environmental standards (Vogel and Kagan 2004).

WHAT WE HAVE LEARNED FROM COMPARATIVE POLICY PROCESS RESEARCH

Theories of the policy process adapt well to the comparative perspective. This is particularly the case with the policy diffusion method and the IAD framework, which were developed as comparative approaches. The NPF is about comparing policy narratives created by individual advocacy coalitions. Scholars using the MSF have begun to explore the possibilities of comparative research, involving both theoretical (e.g., Howlett, McConnell, and Perl 2015; Zohlnhöfer, Herweg, and Huß 2016) and empirical work (e.g., Spohr 2016). Scholarship on PET has completed the comparative turn both by encompassing myriad political systems and their institutions and by adopting the perspective that *dynamics*, or changes in time, are necessary for understanding public policy.

The ACF has been applied to a great number of cases and already allows for drawing some comparative conclusions. In particular, we have learned that stable coalitional structures that oppose one another operate in much the same way across issue areas and governing systems. The structure, stability, and impact of advocacy coalitions vary across political contexts, but whether there exist stable patterns we do not know yet. Thus, seeking to go one step further, Weible et al. (2016) recently outlined a framework for comparative ACF research. The PFT has tremendous untapped, comparative potential.

Though much work remains to be done in developing theories that accommodate comparative research designs, some generalizable lessons can be drawn from applications of policy process theories in comparative contexts. These relate to the behavior of citizens and mass publics, institutional information processing, the types of issues governments face, and the importance of coalitional politics within substantive policy issues.

First, within the set of Western-style democracies, citizens behave and evaluate public policy in remarkably similar ways. In general, the lessons of this work are that governments attend to citizen demands for attention to substantive policy issues; what citizens think is important, governments also think important (Jones and Baumgartner 2004). This is not to say that lawmaking approximates public opinion in all cases, but there is tremendous congruence between public priorities and institutional policy agendas. Likewise, the thermostatic model (Soroka and Wlezien 2009) is explicitly comparative in design and establishes that democratic systems are successful in representation and responsiveness, though with some variation associated with institutional configurations across Western democracies. Policy process theories such as the MSF have recently started to pay more attention to the institutional differences, and judging from the insights yielded from existing research this appears to be a promising perspective for future research.

Second, the nature and types of issues and problems that governments face are similar, and this finding spans Western democracies, developing nations, and authoritarian regimes. The Comparative Agendas Project has emerged as a useful measurement system for understanding the types of problems characterizing the agendas of diverse governing systems (Jones 2016). Using this policy topic coding scheme, scholars have demonstrated systematic similarities in the number and nature of problems confronting Western democracies and, increasingly, other types of governments as well.

Third, the dynamics of policy change are similar across governing systems, across political institutions within governing systems, and even across policymaking within substantive issues. The characteristic slip-stick dynamics, with long periods of incrementalism punctuated by bursts of larger-scale policy change, have nearly become empirical law in policy dynamics (Jones et al. 2009). The shape of change derives from the shifting nature of political attention, institutional differences, and the dependencies and trade-offs implicit in the limited nature of attention and in public budgets (Breunig and Busemeyer 2012). The more recent expansions of this research link similar causal mechanisms, such as institutional friction and limited attention, to the same dynamics even in authoritarian regimes. These consistencies allow some powerful lessons to be drawn about the operation of institutions, the dynamics of policy change, and the issue agendas of governments the world over.

Fourth, within particular substantive issues, ACF scholars have shown that how nations ply coalitional politics and advocacy is similar across countries. These insights move our thinking from generalizable systemic statements about policy change to a more nuanced perspective on particular issues across countries. The IAD framework makes possible similar types of generalizations, concentrating on actors in institutional settings rather than on advocacy. Taken together, the policy process theories have generated a set of generalizations that span institutions and behavior, types of political systems, and substantive issues. Still, much is left to be done. In future comparative policy process research, there are considerable opportunities for theoretical, conceptual, and empirical advancement in understanding policy dynamics.

CONCLUSIONS AND THE WAY FORWARD

Subdisciplines of political science have made great progress in the last few years as a result of pursuing comparative research and applying comparative research designs. The goal of this chapter was to scrutinize the progress policy process research has made in applying a comparative perspective. Our systematic overview of the literature drawing on the policy process theories yielded two overarching findings.

First, policy process research has been carried out for a growing number of cases, which allows for identifying general empirical patterns and a more demanding test of theoretical expectations. Second, theoretical perspectives in policy process research have become noticeably comparative, including classic comparative approaches such as cross-country studies and newer ones such as comparisons of different policy sectors in one country. Moreover, our analysis suggests that the body of comparative policy process research will expand even further in the near future.

Among the various theories, the PET forms the basis of a literature that has developed the most visible comparative dimension, albeit the IAD framework has also produced a number of comparative studies. Diffusion research holds a specific position because this research is comparative by definition. Nevertheless, even diffusion research has developed in a fashion that includes larger samples as well as the inclusion of additional dimensions, such as policy sectors, for comparison. A group of international MSF scholars discuss at a conceptual level how the MSF can be adapted to comparative research, and a few empirical studies have applied it. In regard to the ACF, comparative insights are possible as a result of the sheer number of contexts to which this perspective has been applied. This saturation has illuminated the value of conceptual evenness and highlighted the struggles of empirical and methodological pluralism.

Thus, all in all, much comparative policy process research is occurring, and the analytical perspectives adopted so far are diverse and insightful. Yet we must bear in mind that the comparative dimensions of the policy process theories depend on the adoption of a broad definition of comparative design.

In strengthening the comparative dimension of policy process research, several avenues appear worth pursuing in future research. The first relates to the PET and why it has been so successful in mastering the comparative turn. By concentrating on individual theoretical components, researchers involved in the comparative study of political agendas bring to bear their expertise and knowledge of how to measure key concepts and what data could be used for this purpose, especially comparatively. Interestingly, Béland and Howlett (2016) seem to dismiss this disaggregated approach to adapting the MSF to the comparative logic, but from our perspective starting with isolated components enables the research to benefit from the expertise of authors and allows for mutual learning and cumulative knowledge. Our first suggestion for making policy process research more comparative is to concentrate on individual conceptual components and to make these suitable for comparative research.

Our second point is about the need for systematic data gathering and coding to strengthen comparative policy process research. Again, the PET is a good example of how this can be attained: data collection and coding are systematized and standardized, which allows for producing data that facilitate comparative research. It follows that comparative research must be accompanied by efforts to produce (better) data, which can be attained by individual research groups or by forming research networks and benefiting from a coordinated approach. The availability of reliable and valid data is critical for pushing further the comparative dimension in policy process research.

Third, formal political institutions offer a possibility for conceptually and empirically advancing comparative policy process research. Our reasoning builds on institutions as a key concept in comparative politics (and political science generally): they offer a methodological tool box and data that can be used by policy process research. Institutions can be incorporated into comparative policy process research in two ways. First, institutions can be regarded as the context in which decisions are made. Second, arguably the more ambitious approach, is to identify the role institutions play in the individual theories and then to address them in a more systematic fashion. This is a dimension on which the PET and the IAD framework were found to have a competitive advantage over the other theoretical approaches. At any rate, policy process theories offer added value in their treatment of institutions because they attend to how institutions structure and shape the relationships between actors more than approaches in comparative politics do.

Comparative research both widens and deepens our understanding of political processes. However, when we decide to compare we need to develop ideas about how to collect the appropriate evidence to test the empirical implications of the theoretical models. This leads to the question of what we should compare, and this is not an easy one to answer. In this chapter we showed that comparative research is not limited to country-comparative research. Nonetheless, we must avoid thinking that comparisons yield insights in all circumstances. To provide meaningful and novel insights, comparisons must be carefully considered and justified, so even comparative research must start with conceptual work.

REFERENCES

Ackrill, Robert, and Adrian Kay. 2011. "Multiple Streams in EU Policy-Making: The Case of the 2005 Sugar Reform." *Journal of European Public Policy* 18 (1): 72–89.

Andersson, Krister. 2006. "Understanding Decentralized Forest Governance: An Application of the Institutional Analysis and Development Framework." *Sustainability: Science, Practice, & Policy* 2 (1): 25–35.

Bale, Tim, Christoffer Green-Pedersen, André Krouwel, Kurt Luther, and Nick Sitter. 2010. "If You Can't Beat Them, Join Them? Explaining Social Democratic Responses to the Challenge from the Populist Radical Right in Western Europe." *Political Studies* 58 (3): 410–426.

Bauer, Michael W., Christoffer Green-Pedersen, Adrienne Héritier, and Andrew Jordan, eds. 2012. *Dismantling Public Policy: Preferences, Strategies, and Effects*. Oxford: Oxford University Press.

Baumgartner, Frank R. 2013. "Ideas and Policy Change." *Governance* 26 (2): 239–258.

Baumgartner, Frank R., Jeffrey M. Berry, Marie Hojnacki, Beth L. Leech, and David C. Kimball. 2009. *Lobbying and Policy Change: Who Wins, Who Loses, and Why*. Chicago: University of Chicago Press.

Baumgartner, Frank R., Christoffer Green-Pedersen, and Bryan D. Jones. 2006. "Comparative Studies of Policy Agendas." *Journal of European Public Policy* 13 (7): 959–974.

Baumgartner, Frank R., and Bryan D. Jones. 1993. *Agendas and Instability in American Politics*. Chicago: University of Chicago Press.

Baumgartner, Frank R., Bryan D. Jones, and Peter B. Mortensen. 2017. "Punctuated Equilibrium Theory: Explaining Stability and Change in Public Policymaking." In *Theories of the Policy Process*, 4th ed., edited by Christopher M. Weible and Paul A. Sabatier, 55–101. Boulder, CO: Westview Press.

Béland, Daniel. 2007. "Ideas and Institutional Change in Social Security: Conversion, Layering, and Policy Drift." *Social Science Quarterly* 88 (1): 20–38.

———. 2010. "Reconsidering Policy Feedback." *Administration and Society* 42 (5): 568–590.

———. 2016. "Kingdon Reconsidered: Ideas, Interests and Institutions in Comparative Policy Analysis." *Journal of Comparative Policy Analysis* 18 (3): 228–242.

Béland, Daniel, and Michael Howlett. 2016. "The Role and Impact of the Multiple-Streams Approach in Comparative Policy Analysis." *Journal of Comparative Policy Analysis* 18 (3): 221–227.

Berry, Frances Stokes, and William D. Berry. 2017. "Innovation and Diffusion Models in Policy Research." In *Theories of the Policy Process*, 4th ed., edited by Christopher M. Weible and Paul A. Sabatier, 253–297. Boulder, CO: Westview Press.

Bevan, Shaun. 2015. "Bureaucratic Responsiveness: Effects of Elected Government, Public Agendas and European Attention on the UK Bureaucracy." *Public Administration* 93 (1): 139–158.

Bevan, Shaun, and Will Jennings. 2014. "Representation, Agendas and Institutions." *European Journal of Political Research* 53 (1): 37–56.

Birkland, Thomas A. 1997. *After Disaster: Agenda Setting, Public Policy, and Focusing Events*. Washington, DC: Georgetown University Press.

Black, Ryan C., and Ryan J. Owens. 2009. "Agenda Setting in the Supreme Court: The Collision of Policy and Jurisprudence." *Journal of Politics* 71 (3): 1062–1075.

Blomquist, William, and Peter deLeon. 2011. "The Design and Promise of the Institutional Analysis and Development Framework." *Policy Studies Journal* 39 (1): 1–6.

Boushey, Graeme. 2010. *Policy Diffusion Dynamics in America*. Cambridge: Cambridge University Press.

Breunig, Christian, and Marius R. Busemeyer. 2012. "Fiscal Austerity and the Trade-Off between Public Investment and Social Spending." *Journal of European Public Policy* 19 (6): 921–938.

Breunig, Christian, and Chris Koski. 2009. "Punctuated Budgets and Governors' Institutional Powers." *American Politics Research* 37 (6): 1116–1138.

Breunig, Christian, Chris Koski, and Peter B. Mortensen. 2010. "Stability and Punctuations in Public Spending: A Comparative Study of Budget Functions." *Journal of Public Administration Research and Theory* 20 (3): 703–722.

Clement, Floriane. 2010. "Analysing Decentralised Natural Resource Governance: Proposition for a 'Politicised' Institutional Analysis and Development Framework." *Policy Sciences* 43 (2): 129–156.

Cobb, Roger W., and Charles D. Elder. 1972. "Individual Orientations in the Study of Political Symbolism." *Social Science Quarterly* 53 (1): 79–90.

Croissant, Aurel, Steffen Kailitz, Patrick Koellner, and Stefan Wurster, eds. 2015. *Comparing Autocracies in the Early Twenty-First Century: Volume 1: Unpacking Autocracies—Explaining Similarity and Difference*. London: Routledge.

Dery, David. 1984. *Problem Definition in Policy Analysis*. Lawrence: University Press of Kansas.

Douglas, Mary, and Aaron Wildavsky. 1983. *Risk and Culture: An Essay on the Selection of Technological and Environmental Dangers.* Berkeley: University of California Press.

Elgin, Dallas J., and Christopher M. Weible. 2013. "A Stakeholder Analysis of Colorado Climate and Energy Issues Using Policy Analytical Capacity and the Advocacy Coalition Framework." *Review of Policy Research* 30 (1): 114–133.

Engeli, Isabelle, Christoffer Green-Pedersen, and Lars T. Larsen. 2012. "Theoretical Perspectives on Morality Politics." In *Morality Politics in Western Europe,* edited by Isabelle Engeli, Christoffer Green-Pedersen, and Lars T. Larsen, 5–26. Basingstoke, UK: Palgrave Macmillan.

Fankhauser, Sam, Caterina Gennaioli, and Murray Collins. 2015. "The Political Economy of Passing Climate Change Legislation: Evidence from a Survey." *Global Environmental Change* 35:52–61.

———. 2016. "Do International Factors Influence the Passage of Climate Change Legislation?" *Climate Policy* 16 (3): 318–331.

Ganghof, Steffen. 2003. "Promises and Pitfalls of Veto Player Analysis." *Swiss Political Science Review* 9 (2): 1–25.

Gray, Virginia. 1973. "Innovation in the States: A Diffusion Study." *American Political Science Review* 67 (04): 1174–1185.

Green-Pedersen, Christoffer, and Jesper Krogstrup. 2008. "Immigration as a Political Issue in Denmark and Sweden." *European Journal of Political Research* 47 (5): 610–634.

Green-Pedersen, Christoffer, and Stefaan Walgrave, eds. 2014. *Agenda Setting, Policies, and Political Systems: A Comparative Approach.* Chicago: University of Chicago Press.

Gupta, Kuhika. 2014. "A Comparative Policy Analysis of Coalition Strategies: Case Studies of Nuclear Energy and Forest Management in India." *Journal of Comparative Policy Analysis: Research and Practice* 16 (4): 356–372.

Hacker, Jacob S. 2002. *The Divided Welfare State: The Battle over Public and Private Social Benefits in the United States.* Cambridge: Cambridge University Press.

Hacker, Jacob S., and Paul Pierson. 2011. *Winner-Take-All Politics: How Washington Made the Rich Richer—and Turned Its Back on the Middle Class.* New York: Simon and Schuster.

Hall, Peter A. 1993. "Policy Paradigms, Social Learning, and the State: The Case of Economic Policymaking in Britain." *Comparative Politics* 25 (3): 275–296.

Hall, Peter A., and David Soskice, eds. 2001. *Varieties of Capitalism: The Institutional Foundations of Comparative Advantage.* Oxford: Oxford University Press.

Herweg, Nicole, Nikolaos Zahariadis, and Reimut Zohlnhöfer. 2017. "The Multiple Streams Framework: Foundations, Refinements, and Empirical Applications." In *Theories of the Policy Process,* 4th ed., edited by Christopher M. Weible and Paul A. Sabatier, 17–53. Boulder, CO: Westview Press.

Holzinger, Katharina, Christoph Knill, and Bas Arts, eds. 2008. *Environmental Policy Convergence in Europe: The Impact of International Institutions and Trade.* Cambridge: Cambridge University Press.

Howlett, Michael, Allan McConnell, and Anthony Perl. 2015. "Streams and Stages: Reconciling Kingdon and Policy Process Theory." *European Journal of Political Research* 54 (3): 419–434.

Howlett, Michael, and M. Ramesh. 2002. "The Policy Effects of Internationalization: A Subsystem Adjustment Analysis of Policy Change." *Journal of Comparative Policy Analysis* 4 (1): 31–50.

Huber, Evelyne, and John D. Stephens. 2001. *Development and Crisis of the Welfare State: Parties and Policies in Global Markets.* Chicago: University of Chicago Press.

Imperial, Mark T., and Tracy Yandle. 2005. "Taking Institutions Seriously: Using the IAD Framework to Analyze Fisheries Policy." *Society and Natural Resources* 18 (6): 493–509.

Jahn, Detlef. 2011. "The Veto Player Approach in Macro-Comparative Politics: Concepts and Measurement." In *Reform Processes and Policy Change,* edited by Thomas König, George Tsebelis, and Marc Debus, 43–68. New York: Springer.

Jahn, Detlef, and Sebastian Korolczuk. 2012. "German Exceptionalism: The End of Nuclear Energy in Germany!" *Environmental Politics* 21 (1): 159–164.

Jenkins-Smith, Hank C., Daniel Nohrstedt, Christopher M. Weible, and Karin Ingold. 2017. "The Advocacy Coalition Framework: An Overview of the Research Program." In *Theories of the Policy Process,* 4th ed., edited by Christopher M. Weible and Paul A. Sabatier, 135–171. Boulder, CO: Westview Press.

Jones, Bryan D. 1994. *Reconceiving Decision-Making in Democratic Politics: Attention, Choice, and Public Policy.* Chicago: University of Chicago Press.

———. 2001. *Politics and the Architecture of Choice.* Chicago: University of Chicago Press.

———. 2003. "Bounded Rationality in Political Science: Lessons from Public Administration and Public Policy." *Journal of Public Administration Research and Theory* 13 (4): 395–412.

———. 2016. "The Comparative Policy Agendas Projects as Measurement Systems: Response to Dowding, Hindmoor, and Martin." *Journal of Public Policy* 36 (1): 31–46.

Jones, Bryan D., and Frank R. Baumgartner. 2004. "Representation and Agenda Setting." *Policy Studies Journal* 32 (1): 1–24.

Jones, Bryan D., Frank R. Baumgartner, Christian Breunig, Christopher Wlezien, Stuart Soroka, Martial Foucault, Abel François, Christoffer Green-Pederson, Chris Koski, Peter John, Peter B. Mortensen, Frédéric Varone, and Stefaan Walgrave. 2009. "A General Empirical Law of Public Budgets: A Comparative Analysis." *American Journal of Political Science* 53 (3): 855–873.

Jones, Michael D., Holly L. Peterson, Jonathan J. Pierce, Nicole Herweg, Amiel Bernal, Holly Lamberta Raney, and Nikolaos Zahariadis. 2016. "A River Runs Through It: A Multiple Streams Meta-Review." *Policy Studies Journal* 44 (1): 13–36.

Jones, Michael. D., and Claudio M. Radaelli. 2015. "The Narrative Policy Framework: Child or Monster?" *Critical Policy Studies* 9 (3): 339–355.

Jordan, Andrew, Michael W. Bauer, and Christoffer Green-Pedersen. 2013. "Policy Dismantling." *Journal of European Public Policy* 20 (5): 795–805.

Kenworthy, Lane. 2003. "Quantitative Indicators of Corporatism." *International Journal of Sociology* 33 (3): 10–44.

Kingdon, John. 1984. *Agendas, Alternatives, and Public Policies.* 2nd ed. Boston: Little, Brown.

Knill, Christoph. 2005. "Introduction: Cross-National Policy Convergence: Concepts, Approaches and Explanatory Factors." *Journal of European Public Policy* 12 (5): 764–774.

Knill, Christoph, Marc Debus, and Stephan Heichel. 2010. "Do Parties Matter in Internationalised Policy Areas? The Impact of Political Parties on Environmental Policy Outputs in 18 OECD Countries, 1970–2000." *European Journal of Political Research* 49 (3): 301–336.

Knill, Christoph, Kai Schulze, and Jale Tosun. 2012. "Regulatory Policy Outputs and Impacts: Exploring a Complex Relationship." *Regulation & Governance* 6 (4): 427–444.

Knill, Christoph, and Jale Tosun. 2012. *Public Policy: A New Introduction.* Basingstoke, United Kingdom: Palgrave Macmillan.

———. 2017. "Policy Making." In *Comparative Politics,* 4th ed., edited by D. Caramani. Oxford: Oxford University Press.

Lowi, Theodore J. 1964. "American Business, Public Policy, Case-Studies, and Political Theory." *World Politics* 16 (4): 677–715.

Manow, Philip, and Simone Burkhart. 2008. "Delay as a Political Technique under Divided Government? Empirical Evidence from Germany, 1976–2005." *German Politics* 17 (3): 353–366.

May, Peter J., Joshua Sapotichne, and Samuel Workman. 2006. "Policy Coherence and Policy Domains." *Policy Studies Journal* 34 (3): 381–403.

May, Peter J., Samuel Workman, and Bryan D. Jones. 2008. "Organizing Attention: Responses of the Bureaucracy to Agenda Disruption." *Journal of Public Administration Research and Theory* 18 (4): 517–541.

Mettler, Suzanne, and Mallory SoRelle. 2017. "Policy Feedback Theory." In *Theories of the Policy Process,* 4th ed., edited by Christopher M. Weible and Paul A. Sabatier, 103–134. Boulder, CO: Westview Press.

Mettler, Suzanne, and Joe Soss. 2004. "The Consequences of Public Policy for Democratic Citizenship: Bridging Policy Studies and Mass Politics." *Perspectives on Politics* 2 (1): 55–73.

Newell, Allen, and Herbert A. Simon. 1972. *Human Problem Solving.* Englewood Cliffs, NJ: Prentice Hall.

Newton, Kenneth, and Jan W. van Deth. 2016. *Foundations of Comparative Politics.* Cambridge: Cambridge University Press.

Nohrstedt, Daniel. 2005. "External Shocks and Policy Change: Three Mile Island and Swedish Nuclear Energy Policy." *Journal of European Public Policy* 12 (6): 1041–1059.

Ostrom, Elinore. 2011. "Background on the Institutional Analysis and Development Framework." *Policy Studies Journal* 39 (1): 7–27.

Pielke, Roger A., Jr. 2007. *The Honest Broker: Making Sense of Science in Policy and Politics.* Cambridge: Cambridge University Press.

Pierson, Paul. 2004. *Politics in Time: History, Institutions, and Social Analysis.* Princeton, NJ: Princeton University Press.

Sabatier, Paul A. 1998. "The Advocacy Coalition Framework: Revisions and Relevance for Europe." *Journal of European Public Policy* 5 (1): 98–130.

Sabatier, Paul A., and Hank C. Jenkins-Smith, eds. 1993. *Policy Change and Learning: An Advocacy Coalition Approach.* Boulder, CO: Westview Press.

———. 1999. "The Advocacy Coalition Framework: An Assessment." In *Theories of the Policy Process,* edited by Paul A. Sabatier, 117–166. Boulder, CO: Westview Press.

Sabatier, Paul A., and Christopher M. Weible. 2007. "The Advocacy Coalition Framework: Innovations and Clarifications." In *Theories of the Policy Process,* edited by Paul A. Sabatier, 189–220. Boulder, CO: Westview Press.

Scharpf, Fritz W. 1997. *Games Real Actors Play: Actor Centered Institutionalism in Policy Research.* Boulder, CO: Westview Press.

Schattschneider, Elmer. 1960. *The Semi-Sovereign People.* New York: Holt, Rinehart and Winston.

Schlager, Edella, and Michael Cox. 2017. "The IAD Framework and the SES Framework: An Introduction and Assessment of the Ostrom Workshop Frameworks." In *Theories of the Policy Process,* 4th ed., edited by Christopher M. Weible and Paul A. Sabatier, 215–252. Boulder, CO: Westview Press.

Schmidt, Manfred G. 1996. "When Parties Matter: A Review of the Possibilities and Limits of Partisan Influence on Public Policy." *European Journal of Political Research* 30 (2): 155–183.

Shafir, Eldar, ed. 2013. *The Behavioral Foundations of Public Policy.* Princeton, NJ: Princeton University Press.

Shanahan, Elizabeth A., Michael D. Jones, Mark K. McBeth, and Claudio M. Radaelli. 2017. "The Narrative Policy Framework." In *Theories of the Policy Process,* 4th ed., edited by Christopher M. Weible and Paul A. Sabatier, 173–213. Boulder, CO: Westview Press.

Shanahan, Elizabeth A., Mark K. McBeth, and Paul L. Hathaway. 2011. "Narrative Policy Framework: The Influence of Media Policy Narratives on Public Opinion." *Politics & Policy* 39 (3): 373–400.

Shore, Jennifer E. 2016. "Political Inequality: Origins, Consequences, and Ways Ahead." In *Understanding Inequality: Social Costs and Benefits,* edited by A. Machin and N. Stehr, 247–265. Wiesbaden, Germany: Springer VS.

Soroka, Stuart N., and Christopher Wlezien. 2009. *Degrees of Democracy: Politics, Public Opinion, and Policy.* Cambridge: Cambridge University Press.

Soss, Joe, and Sanford F. Schram. 2007. "A Public Transformed? Welfare Reform as Policy Feedback." *American Political Science Review* 101 (1): 111–127.

Spohr, Florian. 2016. "Explaining Path Dependency and Deviation by Combining Multiple Streams Framework and Historical Institutionalism: A Comparative Analysis of German and Swedish Labor Market Policies." *Journal of Comparative Policy Analysis* 18 (3): 257–272.

Starke, Peter, Alexandra Kaasch, and Franca Van Hooren. 2014. "Political Parties and Social Policy Responses to Global Economic Crises: Constrained Partisanship in Mature Welfare States." *Journal of Social Policy* 43 (2): 225–246.

Stone, Deborah A. 1989. "Causal Stories and the Formation of Policy Agendas." *Political Science Quarterly* 104 (2): 281–300.

Streeck, Wolfgang, and Kathleen Thelen. 2005. "Introduction: Institutional Change in Advanced Political Economies." In *Beyond Continuity: Institutional Change in Advanced Capitalist Economies,* edited by Wolfgang Streeck and Kathleen Thelen, 1–39. Oxford: Oxford University Press.

Tosun, Jale. 2013. *Environmental Policy Change in Emerging Market Democracies: Eastern Europe and Latin America Compared.* Toronto: University of Toronto Press.

Tosun, Jale, and Simon Schaub. 2017. "Mobilization in the European Public Sphere: The Struggle over GMOs." *Review of Policy Research.* Published electronically February 22, 2017. doi:10.1111/ropr.12235.

Tosun, Jale, and Susumu Shikano. 2016. "GMO-Free Regions in Europe: An Analysis of Diffusion Patterns." *Journal of Risk Research* 19 (6): 743–759.

Tsebelis, George 2002. *Veto Players—How Political Institutions Work.* Princeton, NJ: Princeton University Press.

Vliegenthart, Rens, Stefaan Walgrave, Frank R. Baumgartner, Shaun Bevan, Christian Breunig, Sylvain Brouard, Laura Chaqués Bonafont, Emiliano Grossman, Will Jennings, Peter B. Mortensen, Anna M. Palau, Pascal Sciarini, and Anke Tresch. 2016. "Do the Media Set the Parliamentary Agenda? A Comparative Study in Seven Countries." *European Journal of Political Research* 55 (2): 283–301.

Vogel, David, and Robert A. Kagan. 2004. *Dynamics of Regulatory Change: How Globalization Affects National Regulatory Policies.* Berkeley: University of California Press.

Volkens, Andrea, Pola Lehmann, Nicolas Merz, Sven Regel, Annika Werner, and Henrike Schultze. 2013. *The Manifesto Data Collection. Manifesto Project (MRG/CMP/MARPOR).* Version 2013b. Berlin: Wissenschaftszentrum Berlin für Sozialforschung.

Walgrave, Stefaan, Stuart Soroka, and Michiel Nuytemans. 2008. "The Mass Media's Political Agenda-Setting Power: A Longitudinal Analysis of Media, Parliament, and Government in Belgium (1993 to 2000)." *Comparative Political Studies* 41 (6): 814–836.

Walgrave, S., and F. Varone. 2008. "Punctuated Equilibrium and Agenda-Setting: Bringing Parties Back In: Policy Change After the Dutroux Crisis in Belgium." *Governance* 21 (3): 365–395.

Weaver, R. Kent. 2010. "Paths and Forks or Chutes and Ladders: Negative Feedbacks and Policy Regime Change." *Journal of Public Policy* 30 (2): 137–162.

Weible, Christopher M. 2017. "Introduction: The Scope and Focus of Policy Process Research and Theory." In *Theories of the Policy Process,* 4th ed., edited by Christopher M. Weible and Paul A. Sabatier, 1–13. Boulder, CO: Westview Press.

Weible, Christopher M., Karin Ingold, Manuel Fischer, and Tanya Heikkila, eds. 2016. *Policy Debates on Hydraulic Fracturing: Comparing Coalition Politics in North America and Europe.* Basingstoke, UK: Palgrave Macmillan.

Weible, Christopher M., Paul A. Sabatier, and Kelly McQueen. 2009. "Themes and Variations: Taking Stock of the Advocacy Coalition Framework." *Policy Studies Journal* 37 (1): 121–140.

Wlezien, Christopher, and Stuart N. Soroka. 2012. "Political Institutions and the Opinion–Policy Link." *West European Politics* 35 (6): 1407–1432.

Wolf, Frieder. 2010. "Enlightened Eclecticism or Hazardous Hotchpotch? Mixed Methods and Triangulation Strategies in Comparative Public Policy Research." *Journal of Mixed Methods Research* 4 (2): 144–167.

Workman, Samuel. 2015. *The Dynamics of Bureaucracy in the US Government: How Congress and Federal Agencies Process Information and Solve Problems*. Cambridge: Cambridge University Press.

Zohlnhöfer, Reimut. 2016. "Putting Together the Pieces of the Puzzle: Explaining German Labor Market Reforms with a Modified Multiple-Streams Approach." *Policy Studies Journal* 44 (1): 83–107.

Zohlnhöfer, Reimut, Nicole Herweg, and Christian Huß. 2016. "Bringing Formal Political Institutions into the Multiple Streams Framework: An Analytical Proposal for Comparative Policy Analysis." *Journal of Comparative Policy Analysis* 18 (3): 243–256.

10

Moving Forward and Climbing Upward: Advancing Policy Process Research

CHRISTOPHER M. WEIBLE

The policy process is best imagined as a complex phenomenon of continuous interactions involving public policy and its context, events, actors, and outcomes. These interactions are the source of major questions defining policy process research. Broad in scope and salient for society, such questions include, among many others, how policies affect politics and vice versa, what factors explain policy change, how policy designs affect implementation and performance, what institutional arrangements help overcome threats to collective action, and why people mobilize to support or oppose policy decisions. Given innumerable interactions involving public policy, theories have been, and continue to be, essential to the study of policy processes.[1]

This volume presents the most established and utilized theories of the policy process circa 2017. These theories include the Multiple Streams Framework, Punctuated Equilibrium Theory, Policy Feedback Theory, the Advocacy Coalition Framework, the Narrative Policy Framework, the Institutional Analysis and Development framework, and innovation and diffusion models. The theories in this volume were not the first to populate the field. If this volume had been published in 1977, the contributing chapters might have covered a combination of the following: incrementalism (Lindblom 1959), structural functionalism (Almond and Coleman 1960), arenas of power (Lowi 1964, 1972), group theory and elite theory (Truman 1951; Mills 1957; Dahl 1961), system theory (Easton 1953), public choice (Buchanan and Tullock 1962), the funnel of causality (Hofferbert 1974), the policy cycle (Jones 1970), agenda building (Cobb and Elder 1972), the issue-attention cycle (Downs 1972), and the Policy Sciences Framework (Lasswell 1971).[2]

The plausible existence of a 1977 volume is one indication that the need for and use of theories in the study of policy processes is nothing new. Since the early 1950s, when the field began as a conscious area of study, scholars have recognized the intractability of the topic and a need for simplification, common scope and purpose, shared language, clearly defined concepts, and explicit specification of interactions between concepts (Lasswell and Kaplan 1950; Lasswell 1951; Easton 1953; Lowi 1964; Ranney 1968; Froman 1968; Mitchell and Mitchell 1969; Lindblom 1968; Lasswell 1971). If anything has endured regarding the study of policy processes, it has been an understanding that these phenomena are messy and that theory is necessary to help disentangle them.[3]

THE NEEDS OF THE POLICY STUDIES FIELD

Commonality with the past does not suggest stagnation in the present. Consider two of the perceived needs for advancing the field mentioned more than two decades ago by Sabatier (1991). The first was the need to develop better theories. Compared to the past, the theories in this volume are better at describing and explaining the policy process and are supported by an unparalleled number of empirical applications. Punctuated Equilibrium Theory and innovation and diffusion models offer far more theoretical insights and are supported by far more empirical data than incrementalism (Lindblom 1959) and the funnel of causality (Hofferbert 1974). The Advocacy Coalition Framework offers a comprehensive approach with more empirical support for understanding and explaining coalitions, learning, and policy change than the policy cycle (Jones 1970), iron triangles (Freeman 1955), issue networks (Heclo 1978), and top-down and bottom-up approaches to implementation (Mazmanian and Sabatier 1983; Hjern and Hull 1982). The contributions of Elinor Ostrom and colleagues under the Institutional Analysis and Development framework have fundamentally altered our conception of self-governance and institutional designs, especially in the context of common pool resource theory, resulting in the Nobel Prize in Economics awarded to Ostrom in 2009. Additionally, beyond this volume, the field of policy processes continues to develop and explore new policy process theories (Schlager and Weible 2013). Although there can always be better theories, and challenges certainly remain regarding the quality of empirical applications, the current theories of the policy process are at least adequate to motivate a high number of empirical applications, offer original insight, and receive recognition from outside the field.

The second need was for a journal dedicated to theory-based policy process research. Since the *Policy Studies Journal* of the Policy Studies Organization became the journal of the Public Policy Section of the American Political Science Association in August 2003, it has become the leading outlet for theory-based policy process research. In recent years, the journal has published one issue featuring the established theories of the policy process (Eller and Krutz 2009); four theory-focused issues, including the Institutional Analysis and Development framework (Blomquist and deLeon 2011), the Advocacy Coalition Framework (Weible et al. 2011), the Punctuated Equilibrium Theory (Jones and Baumgartner 2012), and the Multiple Streams Framework (Weible and Schlager, 2016); and an issue featuring a compilation of new theories of the policy process (Schlager and Weible 2013). Moreover, theory-based policy process research is frequently published in other journals, including the *Journal of Public Administration Research and Theory*, *Policy Sciences*, the *Journal of Public Policy*, *Public Administration*, and the *Journal of European Public Policy*. Although the quality of scholarship and impact of these journals can improve, scholars today have more legitimate choices than ever before for publishing manuscripts that seek to make theoretical contributions to policy process research.

Despite these indicators of progress, the field continues to face challenges that have the potential to impede future progress. These include issues related to applying theories in a comparative world, dealing with theoretical silos, navigating a field populated by many established and new theories, and achieving broad impacts. The following sections explore each challenge through a set of questions and preliminary answers.

APPLYING THEORIES IN A COMPARATIVE WORLD

A large portion of policy process research is implicitly or explicitly comparative (Dodds 2013). One indication of the comparative approach is the hundreds of empirical applications of policy process theory that now span the globe and cover a wide range of public policy topics. Some questions of the past have been answered, including whether scholars can apply theories of the policy process outside the United States or only to a limited range of topics.[4] Instead, given the spread and growth in empirical applications, questions about how to leverage the comparative approach need answering:[5]

Should theories be applied outside their typical scope and, if so, how? Each theory can be thought of as a tool originally designed for a particular scope that includes a preferred range of research questions, research designs, and contextual settings. Depending on the scope of the research, one theory usually offers more utility than another in helping guide a project, and sometimes a theory will offer no utility at all. Theoretical fit matters, and applying a single theory to all research questions, designs, and contexts is a flawed strategy.

Although theoretical fit matters, practical insights and theoretical lessons can sometimes be gained by applying a theory outside its original scope. If we assume that theories are similar to any human artifact with an internal structure (e.g., the concepts and stipulated relations) and a function to understand and explain a part of the world (i.e., a policy context), then one reason for applying a theory outside its scope is to learn something new about its strengths and limitations. As Simon (1996, 12) states, "In a benign environment we would learn from the motor [policy process theory] only what it had been called upon to do; in a taxing environment we would learn something about its internal structure—especially about those aspects of the internal structure that were chiefly instrumental in limiting performance."

There are, however, nontrivial risks in applying a theory outside its scope. Theories are lenses designed to see some aspects of the policy process and ignore others. Studying a theory outside its scope may inadvertently lead a researcher to force observations into predefined conceptual categories, ignore vital aspects of the policy process, and misinterpret the magnitude and constancy of interactions. To address these risks is to approach the theories in this volume as malleable tools that are somewhat adaptable to the needs of analysts.

For what purposes should theories be applied? Theories exist for a variety of reasons and can serve multiple audiences. Not every application needs to contribute to refining and improving the theory for academic audiences. The purpose of some theoretical applications may be to describe and explain the intricacies of a case study. Other applications of theory can also provide client-oriented advice for a policy decision. The contributions to the literature will thus vary by how the theory is used in a particular application. Applications with a practical emphasis are more likely to result in informative policy implications, whereas applications with a theoretical emphasis will likely contribute more to theory development as part of a comparative research agenda. Both theoretical and practical applications of theory are legitimate uses. Regardless of the purpose, scholars need to be clear about the intent of the application, target the appropriate outlets for publication, and write for the appropriate audience.

Are there, and should there be, best practices for applying each of the different theories? Leveraging the advantages of conducting research in a comparative world requires some common methodological techniques for applying the theories. Unfortunately, explicit best practices for applying most of the theories in this volume are often nonexistent or primarily accessible only to the network of scholars specializing in developing a particular theory (Heikkila and Cairney 2017, Chapter 8, this volume). For people using a theory for the first time, the methods best suited for applying a policy process theory are often a mystery. Although the development of new and better theories remains an admirable endeavor, such a goal overshadows a far more pressing need to develop best practices for applying each theory.

The research question, design, and context are the first considerations in selecting as well as applying a theory. Yet best practices can inform both the appropriateness of a theory for a research project and ideas and concerns about its application. Communication of best practices can be accomplished by offering generic instruments for concept measurement, suggestions for data collection, lessons learned from previous applications, and recommendations for modeling and analyzing data. Obviously, best practices for applying theory should not be thoughtlessly adopted to guide any research project and rather should be available for initial consideration.

Best practices can also be communicated through workshops, conference panels, and publications. One example has been the Comparative Agendas Project organized by Bryan Jones and Frank Baumgartner for sharing and communicating the methodological approaches within the Punctuated Equilibrium Theory. The efforts of Jones and Baumgartner offer new and interested scholars the opportunity to communicate about how to analyze issue attention across countries and enable the sharing of data collection and analytical techniques among experienced scholars. Similar efforts are needed for the other theories.

For the typical researcher applying a theory, another way to help develop and communicate best practices is to be as transparent as possible in all aspects of the research. There is no better way to learn from mistakes, communicate methods, and offer convincing results.

THEORETICAL SILOS

The most successful theories of the policy process have been associated with an active research program supported by scholars who continuously develop and test a theory for years or even decades. This has resulted in tacit knowledge and shared understandings among scholars applying a particular theory. Naturally, from years of specialization, a silo effect emerges in which some scholars develop expertise in one theory and not others.

Theoretical specialization is an indicator of progress because it usually involves clearer conceptualizations, better specification of concept interactions, and improved methods of data collection and analysis. There are, however, several shortcomings. One is that theories are often misunderstood or even forgotten because they become difficult to understand, teach, and apply. One example is the Institutional Analysis and Development framework, which can be very difficult to learn and apply for scholars without direct access to those knowledgeable and experienced with the framework. Another is the Policy Sciences Framework (Lasswell 1971; Clark 2002), a complicated theory taught by only a few academic programs and applied by a relatively small number of scholars. Another shortcoming is that theories become understood only superficially, and many of their intricacies are overlooked. This becomes problematic when scholars attempt to apply a theory or to critique and compare theories in classes, textbooks, or journal articles. A final shortcoming is when scholars, seeking to solve a problem or answer a question, overlook theoretical or methodological insights previously gleaned but not communicated outside a theory-based research program. As a result, these scholars re-create solutions to problems already solved.

While embracing the necessity for theoretical specialization and recognizing the inevitability of theoretical silos, we need to consider the following questions:

How should new and experienced policy researchers approach established theories, given the specialization that occurs therein? The chapters in this volume provide good but still incomplete summaries of the policy process theories. Often missing from the chapters, or difficult to understand in reading them, is a depth associated with the theories that relates to the lessons learned from prior publications and the tacit knowledge and skills held by the people associated with the research programs supporting each theory. The point in drawing attention to this theoretical depth is not that scholars wanting to apply a theory must join a research program or spend years mastering the internal intricacies of a theory before an application. Rather, the point is that scholars new to a theory should approach it with an acknowledgment that depth exists and apply it accordingly. Similarly, scholars experienced with a theory should recognize and better communicate their tacit understanding and experience, maintain a healthy skepticism of their assumptions, and stay receptive to different ways of thinking about and applying the theory.

What are some of the strengths and weaknesses of the different roles scholars play in advancing theory? As the field progresses and as theories found in this volume and beyond emerge and develop, scholars play different roles in relation to the theories. Some scholars specialize in testing and developing one theory; others generalize by knowing multiple theories without specializing in a single theory. Scholars also generalize by borrowing bits and pieces of multiple theories to help solve practical problems, and sometimes scholars remain casual observers of theories and use them primarily in teaching and not in research.

Despite representing artificial caricatures, such simplifications provide some basic lessons.[6] Each of these roles contributes to advancing the study of policy processes but can effectively generate silos of interpretation. Specialists offer the necessary expertise in assessing the empirical or theoretical quality of the theory but can have difficulty placing a theoretical application within a broader literature, take for granted shared meanings of concepts, assume the importance and relevance of the theory, and presume standards of quality in applying the theory beyond their research program. Generalists offer a useful check on the potentially narrow perspective of specialists and assess theoretical work from the broader perspective of the literature. However, generalists often overlook the depth and evolution of theories in the field and frequently compare and contrast theories superficially. Scholars who specialize in substantive domains can provide commentary on the overall clarity and general quality of the theoretical argument but are often unskilled in assessing the strength of a theoretical application. The effects of silos can be minimized if scholars take the necessary steps to improve the strengths and mitigate the weaknesses of their respective roles.

How can scholars develop expertise in more than one theory? For new and experienced scholars, working within a field populated by multiple theories can be challenging (Cairney 2013). No single theory provides a comprehensive description and explanation of policy processes. Certainly, some theories are more compatible than others and more easily applied in tandem, especially if the goal is not a theoretical contribution but rather valid insight in describing and explaining a particular case study. Similarly, a general understanding of the theories usually suffices for teachers and for policy advocates. If the goal is to make a theoretical contribution by applying two or more theories at the same time, the task is usually very difficult. A realistic path forward for experienced scholars is to develop the knowledge and skills in learning and applying one theory and then, if desired, expanding to another theory, and so forth. Publishing should follow a similar sequential path, with initial publications for one theory, subsequent publications for another theory, and possibly attempts at publications using more than one theory.

NAVIGATING A FIELD OF
ESTABLISHED AND NEW THEORIES

In 2013, the *Policy Studies Journal* published a volume of new theories of the policy process (Schlager and Weible 2013). The purpose of the special issue was to provide intellectual space for scholars seeking to advance new and innovative approaches for studying policy processes and to counter the possibility that the established theories represented a collective, yet single, lens for perceiving the policy process, thereby stifling advancement. The new-theories special issue is a reminder that new theories have been, and are constantly being, created and developed. The special issue and the fourth edition of this volume also prompt several questions about advancing the field into the future:

Why have established theories been abandoned, and why should they continue to be developed? Theories have populated the field of policy process research from the beginning. Over time, some policy process theories have stopped being used and developed because of a combination of the following four reasons: (1) alternate approaches exist that better describe and explain the same phenomenon; (2) the theoretical insight and hypotheses are shown to be false, no longer valid, or no longer useful; (3) the theory is subsumed into a different theory; and (4) the concepts and theoretical logic become too convoluted and difficult to understand. One example of an abandoned theory is the funnel of causality (Hofferbert 1974), which is no longer applied or developed because the theoretical logic was overly simplified, the insights have been subsumed by other theories, and alternate theories exist for addressing similar phenomena. Additionally, one of the most important lessons from the past is that theories are usually not abandoned just because a hypothesis or two is falsified. Instead, the falsification of hypotheses has typically led to revisions of the theory. By reversing this logic, a similar list of reasons can be offered for continuing the development of a theory: the lack of an alternate and better theory, the theory still provides valid insight, the application of the theory occurs independently of existing theories, and the theory is reasonably clear and understandable.

When should new theories be created and developed? There is no right answer to this question because it comes down to individual prerogative, creativity, inspiration, and dedication. Still, some simple observations of past theory development can help inform possible answers. Consider two examples: the Advocacy Coalition Framework and the Institutional Analysis and Development framework. The Advocacy Coalition Framework was first written by Paul Sabatier in 1982, developed with Hank Jenkins-Smith over several years, and then published five years later by Sabatier (1987). The Institutional Analysis and Development framework took a team of scholars more than a decade to create, with one of the early versions written by Vincent Ostrom and Timothy Hennessey (1972) and the first publication by Larry Kiser and Elinor Ostrom (1982). Both frameworks' emergences were supported by empirical data and formulated by a group of seasoned scholars with an acute understanding of the current theoretical limitations as well as a good idea for a better theory. Similar observations hold for most of the theories in this volume: they have typically been created by experienced scholars who were willing to devote years to the effort, who had a deep awareness of the field and were dissatisfied with current approaches, and who used empirical data to inform the theoretical insight they promoted.

Although new theories will inevitably develop and better theories are always desired, a greater need is the development of best practices associated with applying theory. As suggested earlier, the field is held back not by a lack of good theories but rather by a lack of methodological approaches to conceptualize concepts clearly, measure concepts reliably and validly, and analyze the data soundly.[7] Inherently, theory and methods are entwined in research, but too much emphasis has been placed on the former and not enough on the latter.

BROAD IMPACTS

Broad impacts are defined generally as benefits from research for society. They are a fundamental criterion used by many granting agencies for assessing the quality of research, increasingly expected by universities and the public, often the primary interest of students studying public policy, and a concern of many public policy scholars. The topic of broad impacts has also been one of the most enduring themes in the study of public policy (Lasswell 1956; Ranney 1968; deLeon 1997). Scholars have debated whether public policy research should be conducted for practical or scientific reasons and whether scholars should become involved in politics or focus primarily on research.

Within the field of public policy, scholars have approached broad impacts differently. One way to begin to grasp the issue is to understand the partition of public policy studies into policy analysis and policy process research. Policy analysis is the science and craft of providing client-oriented advice, usually for a particular policy decision. Tools of the trade in policy analysis include cost-benefit analysis, multicriteria analysis, equity analysis, and logic models. The leading textbooks include Weimer and Vining (2010) and Bardach (2011). Although there are exceptions, policy analysis typically requires that the researcher become engaged, to some extent, in affairs outside academia and deal with a problem of societal importance. In contrast, policy process research has traditionally emphasized the theoretical, focused more on describing and explaining a policy issue rather than on making a recommendation about a particular policy decision, and has often been conducted without a client. Additionally, policy process scholars have been more likely to argue that policy process research can be valuable for science's sake.[8]

Given the demands on academia today, policy process research needs to be conducted, both for science's sake and with attention to broad impacts.[9] The challenge is to expand and develop the theory-based study of policy processes such that broad impacts become a part of scholarship, while scientific integrity continuously improves. This challenge is approached by considering three questions:

How can policy process theories be conducted to help achieve broad impacts? Policy process theories can be used to achieve broad impacts in multiple ways. I describe two of them. The first is to use policy process theories to portray the context of a policy issue by collecting the data and sharing the insight with people involved in the policy process, usually through a form of engaged scholarship (Van de Ven 2007). For example, policy process theory can be used to map both political and institutional landscapes. The Advocacy Coalition Framework, the Multiple Streams Framework, Policy Feedback Theory, and the Narrative Policy Framework can be informative in depicting politics surrounding a policy issue. The Institutional Analysis and Design framework can be useful in mapping institutional landscapes. Mapping both political and institutional contexts is not necessarily useful in making a recommendation for a single policy decision, but it is more useful in understanding the context in which many decisions are made.

The second way is to use policy process theories to inform the evaluation criteria used to assess policy alternatives or evaluate existing policies in informing a single policy decision. The practice of policy analysis involves the consideration of alternatives for dealing with a problem and a comparison of alternatives based on various evaluation criteria. One evaluation criterion frequently used in policy analysis is political feasibility. The theories used to map political landscapes can also be used to assess political feasibility. Another common criterion in policy analysis is distributional equity in relation to the potential impacts of alternatives, which could be informed by the Policy Feedback Theory. In addition to evaluating alternatives, the theories might also be used to evaluate previous policy decisions. Recent work inspired partly by Punctuated Equilibrium Theory has explored the long-term overinvestment of policy in the form of policy bubbles, which provides another possibility for assessing policy effectiveness (Jones, Thomas, and Wolf 2014). In using policy process theories in policy analysis, a crucial step is to articulate the methodological procedures for informing evaluation criteria in comparing alternatives.

To what extent can practical lessons be drawn from policy process theories? Broad impacts can also be gained by drawing lessons from the insights gleaned from policy process theory. Some recent examples include Shipan and Volden's (2012) practical lessons from innovation and diffusion models, Weible et al.'s (2012) lessons for influencing the policy process from multiple theories, and Schlager and Heikkila's (2011) summary of some practical insights from the study of common pool resource theory. Lesson drawing in this vein should continue.

What other steps can be taken to expand the broad impacts of policy process theories? The insights of policy process research are often less about a particular policy alternative or decision, as done in policy analysis, and more about the processes embedding public policy over extended periods. The task ahead is to develop assessment indicators informing the various degrees to which policy processes are detrimental or beneficial for society. To some extent, policy process theories already accomplish this task. The Policy Feedback Theory helps inform the extent to which a policy and processes of implementation might negatively affect civic engagement. The Advocacy Coalition Framework depicts intransigent conflicts in which opposing coalition members exaggerate the power and maliciousness of their opponents in the devil shift and fail to learn from useful information sources. The Narrative Policy Framework might indicate the degree to which framing contests demonize opponents through narratives. The Institutional Analysis and Development framework can inform aspects of the rules-in-use in supporting self-governance. Potential indicators for understanding the detrimental and beneficial aspects of the policy process exist, but they need to be formally explored and vetted as a collection.

To begin this exploration and vetting, a short and incomplete list to consider in assessing the extent to which processes are detrimental or beneficial for society includes the following:

1. Policy capacity and learning (Howlett 2009; Jenkins-Smith et al. 2017, see Chapter 4, this volume; Heikkila and Gerlak 2013)
2. Policy legitimacy, durability, and coherence (May and Jochim 2013)
3. Trust or the lack of demonization (Putnam, Leonardi, and Nanetti 1994; Jenkins-Smith et al. 2017, see Chapter 4, this volume; Shanahan et al. 2017, see Chapter 5, this volume)
4. Political equality and civic engagement (Dahl 2006; Mettler and SoRelle 2017, see Chapter 3, this volume; Schneider, Ingram, and deLeon 2014)
5. The quality of institutional designs of rules-in-use, rules-in-form, or both (Ostrom 2005; Mazmanian and Sabatier 1983)

The purpose of providing such a list is not to offer a definitive and final set of indicators for assessing policy processes but rather to begin a discussion about how theories in this volume and beyond can be used and perhaps further developed to assess what is beneficial and detrimental for society in various policy processes.

CONCLUSION

This volume is modest in its breadth, yet ambitious in its goals. It offers comprehensive summaries, as well as a critical comparison, of the most established and utilized theories of the policy process. As argued in this concluding chapter, the field has progressed, but challenges remain. If the global community of policy process scholars work together to resolve these challenges, then the localized and generalized knowledge embodied in our theories will increasingly represent the diverse contexts found around the world.

NOTES

1. As in the opening chapter, the term *theories* is defined generically to mean a range of approaches that specify the scope of inquiry, lay out assumptions, provide a shared vocabulary among members of a research team, and clearly define and relate concepts in the form of principles and testable hypotheses and propositions.

2. Similar lists can be found in McCool (1995), Theodoulou and Cahn (1995), and Shafritz, Layne, and Borick (2005).

3. I offer a few quotes to illustrate how some of the early scholars perceived that the field was messy, that theory was necessary, or both:

- "We must, therefore, proceed to simplify these complexities and that we attempt by breaking down complex issues and systems into component parts and processes" (Mitchell and Mitchell 1969, 11).
- "We are going to look at policy making as an extremely complex analytical and political process to which there is no beginning or end, and the boundaries of which are most uncertain. Somehow a complex set of forces that we call 'policy making,' all taken together, produces effects called 'policies.' We want to learn what we can about the network of causes of these effects" (Lindblom 1968, 4).
- "If political scientists were to say that all parts of the process and all aspects of public policies and policy issues are their meat, they would be adopting a field of inquiry without limits, and might soon find themselves shoulder to shoulder with professors and researchers of almost all other disciplines and trying to help solve all kinds of problems" (Van Dyke 1968, 35).
- "Clearly, we need guidance on what to think about or look for and on how to proceed" (Lasswell 1971, 15).
- "Our aim, however, is not to rewrite such manuals [of political action] but rather to elaborate a conceptual framework within which inquiry into the political process may fruitfully proceed" (Lasswell and Kaplan 1950, ix–x).
- "The major difficulties in forming a conceptualization of the policy process are to overcome the misleading notions that have prevailed because of confusion of what happens with what many people *wish* would happen, to distinguish what was intended from what occurred, and to reflect the complexity of the process in contrast to the simpler models that have been applied to it" (Bauer and Gergen 1968, 25).

4. The first edition of this volume was criticized for its American chauvinism in that the theories, with the exception of the Institutional Analysis and Development framework, were predominately applied in the United States with few, if any, applied outside (Dudley et al. 2000). The theories are now regularly applied outside the United States.

5. The spread and growth of empirical applications for many of the theories have also created a new challenge in lesson learning in developing a theory and for gaining insight into policy processes. Although there are many ways to learn lessons from these empirical applications, one of the simplest—and currently underutilized—ways is to conduct comprehensive reviews of the empirical applications. Examples of recent reviews include Sotirov and Memmler (2012), who conducted a comprehensive review of Advocacy Coalition Framework applications in natural resource and environmental issues; Graham, Shipan, and Volden (2013), who reviewed the literature on innovation and diffusion models; and Jones et al. (2016), who reviewed the literature on the Multiple Streams Framework.

6. I saw these roles when I was editor of the *Policy Studies Journal*. I valued them all, which I hope comes through clearly in the text.

7. This observation might not hold for the Punctuated Equilibrium Theory and innovation and diffusion models for which the methods and the models may have advanced at a faster rate than the theory.

8. Scholars working in policy processes, including Schneider and Ingram (1997) and deLeon (1997), have argued for the need for broad impacts for decades.

9. Obviously, some scholars should, and will, continue to focus on the science, others on broad impact, and still others on both. These different foci are legitimate and need to be encouraged; the point is that past efforts have emphasized more the science than the broad impacts and a broader emphasis including both is needed.

REFERENCES

Almond, Gabriel A., and James S. Coleman, eds. 1960. *The Politics of the Developing Areas.* Princeton, NJ: Princeton University Press.

Bardach, Eugene. 2011. *Practical Guide for Policy Analysis: The Eightfold Path to More Effective Problem Solving.* 4th ed. Washington, DC: CQ Press.

Bauer, Raymond A., and Kenneth Jay Gergen, eds. 1968. *The Study of Policy Formulation.* New York: Free Press.

Blomquist, William, and Peter deLeon. 2011. "The Design and Promise of the Institutional Analysis and Development Framework." *Policy Studies Journal* 39 (1): 1–6.

Buchanan, James M., and Gordon Tullock. 1962. *The Calculus of Consent.* Ann Arbor: University of Michigan Press.

Cairney, Paul. 2013. "Standing on the Shoulders of Giants: How Do We Combine the Insights of Multiple Theories in Public Policy Studies?" *Policy Studies Journal* 41 (1): 1–21.

Clark, Tim W. 2002. *The Policy Process: A Practical Guide for Natural Resources Professionals.* New Haven, CT: Yale University Press.

Cobb, Roger W., and Charles D. Elder. 1972. *Participation in American Politics: The Dynamics of Agenda-Building.* Boston: Allyn and Bacon.

Dahl, Robert A. 1961. *Who Governs? Power and Democracy in an American City.* New Haven, CT: Yale University Press.

———. 2006. *On Political Equality.* New Haven, CT: Yale University Press.

deLeon, Peter. 1997. *Democracy and the Policy Sciences.* Albany: State University of New York Press.

Dodds, Anneliese. 2013. *Comparative Public Policy.* New York: Palgrave Macmillan.

Downs, Anthony. 1972. "Up and Down with Ecology: The Issue Attention Cycle." *Public Interest* 28 (1): 38–50.

Dudley, Geoffrey, Wayne Parsons, Claudio M. Radaelli, and Paul Sabatier. 2000. "Symposium: Theories of the Policy Process." *Journal of European Public Policy* 7 (1): 122–140.

Easton, David. 1953. *The Political System: An Inquiry into the State of Political Science.* New York: Alfred A. Knopf.

Eller, Warren, and Glen Krutz. 2009. "Policy Process, Scholarship, and the Road Ahead: An Introduction to the 2008 Policy Shootout!" *Policy Studies Journal* 37 (1): 1–4.

Freeman, J. Leiper. 1955. *The Political Process.* New York: Random House.

Froman, Lewis A., Jr. 1968. "The Categorization of Policy Contents." In *Political Science and Public Policy,* edited by Austin Ranney, 41–54. Chicago: Markham Publishers.

Graham, Erin R., Charles R. Shipan, and Craig Volden. 2013. "The Diffusion of Policy Diffusion Research in Political Science." *British Journal of Political Science* 43 (3): 673–701.

Heclo, Hugh. 1978. "Issue Networks and the Executive Establishment." In *The New American Political System,* edited by Anthony King, 87–124. Washington, DC: American Enterprise Institute.

Heikkila, Tanya, and Paul Cairney. 2017. "Comparison of Theories of the Policy Process." In *Theories of the Policy Process,* 4th ed., edited by Christopher M. Weible and Paul A. Sabatier, 301–327. Boulder, CO: Westview Press.

Heikkila, Tanya, and Andrea K. Gerlak. 2013. "Building a Conceptual Approach to Collective Learning: Lessons for Public Policy Scholars." *Policy Studies Journal* 41 (3): 484–512.

Hjern, Benny, and Chris Hull. 1982. "Implementation Research as Empirical Constitutionalism." *European Journal of Political Research* 10 (2): 105–115.

Hofferbert, Richard I. 1974. *The Study of Public Policy.* Indianapolis: Bobbs-Merrill.

Howlett, Michael. 2009. "Policy Analytical Capacity and Evidence-Based Policy-Making: Lessons from Canada." *Canadian Public Administration* 52 (2): 153–175.

Jenkins-Smith, Hank C., Daniel Nohrstedt, Christopher M. Weible, and Karin Ingold. 2017. "The Advocacy Coalition Framework: An Overview of the Research Program." In *Theories of the Policy Process,* 4th ed., edited by Christopher M. Weible and Paul A. Sabatier, 135–171. Boulder, CO: Westview Press.

Jones, Charles O. 1970. *An Introduction to the Study of Public Policy.* Belmont, CA: Wadsworth.

Jones, Bryan D., and Frank R. Baumgartner. 2012. "From There to Here: Punctuated Equilibrium to the General Punctuation Thesis to a Theory of Government Information Processing." *Policy Studies Journal* 40 (1): 1–20.

Jones, Michael D., Holly L. Peterson, Jonathan J. Pierce, Nicole Herweg, Amiel Bernal, Holly Lamberta Raney, and Nikolaos Zahariadis. 2016. "A River Runs Through It: A Multiple Streams Meta-Review." *Policy Studies Journal* 44 (1): 13–36.

Jones, Bryan D., Herschel F. Thomas III, and Michelle Wolf. 2014. "Policy Bubbles." *Policy Studies Journal* 42 (1): 145–169.

Kiser, Larry L., and Elinor Ostrom. 1982. "The Three Worlds of Action: A Metatheoretical Synthesis of Institutional Approaches." In *Strategies of Political Inquiry,* edited by Elinor Ostrom, 179–222. Beverly Hills, CA: Sage Publications.

Lasswell, Harold D. 1951. "The Policy Orientation." In *The Policy Sciences,* edited by Daniel Lerner and Harold D. Lasswell. Palo Alto, CA: Stanford University Press.

———. 1956. *The Decision Process.* College Park: University of Maryland Press.

———. 1971. *A Pre-View of Policy Sciences.* New York: American Elsevier.

Lasswell, Harold D., and Abraham Kaplan. 1950. *Power and Society: A Framework for Political Inquiry.* Vol. 2, 3–15. New Haven, CT: Yale University Press.

Lindblom, Charles E. 1959. "The Science of Muddling Through." *Public Administration Review* 19:79–88.

———. 1968. *The Policy-Making Process.* Englewood Cliffs, NJ: Prentice Hall.

Lowi, Theodore, J. 1964. "American Business, Public Policy, Case-Studies, and Political Theory." *World Politics* 16 (4): 677–715.

———. 1972. "Four Systems of Policy, Politics, and Choice." *Public Administration Review* 32 (4): 298–310.

May, Peter J., and Ashley E. Jochim. 2013. "Policy Regime Perspective: Policies, Politics, and Governing." *Policy Studies Journal* 41 (3): 426–452.

Mazmanian, Daniel A., and Paul A. Sabatier. 1983. *Implementation and Public Policy.* Glenview, IL: Scott Foresman.

McCool, Daniel. 1995. *Public Policy Theories, Models, and Concepts: An Anthology.* Englewood Cliffs, NJ: Prentice Hall.

Mettler, Suzanne, and Mallory SoRelle. 2017. "Policy Feedback Theory." In *Theories of the Policy Process,* 4th ed., edited by Christopher M. Weible and Paul A. Sabatier, 103–134. Boulder, CO: Westview Press.

Mills, C. Wright. 1957. *The Power Elite.* New York: Oxford University Press.

Mitchell, Joyce M., and William C. Mitchell. 1969. *Political Analysis and Public Policy: An Introduction to Political Science.* Chicago: Rand McNally.

Ostrom, Elinor. 2005. *Understanding Institutional Diversity.* Princeton, NJ: Princeton University Press.

Ostrom, Vincent, and Timothy Hennessey. 1972. *Institutional Analysis and Design.* Bloomington: Indiana University, Workshop in Political Theory and Policy Analysis.

Putnam, Robert D., Robert Leonardi, and Raffaella Y. Nanetti. 1994. *Making Democracy Work: Civic Traditions in Modern Italy.* Princeton, NJ: Princeton University Press.

Ranney, Austin. 1968. "The Study of Policy Content: A Framework for Choice." In *Political Science and Public Policy,* edited by Austin Ranney, 3–21. Chicago: Markham Publishers.

Sabatier, Paul A. 1987. "Knowledge, Policy-Oriented Learning, and Policy Change: An Advocacy Coalition Framework." *Knowledge: Creation, Diffusion, Utilization* 8 (4): 649–692.

———. 1991. "Toward Better Theories of the Policy Process." *PS: Political Science and Politics* 24 (2): 147–156.

Schlager, Edella, and Tanya Heikkila. 2011. "Left High and Dry? Climate Change, Common-Pool Resource Theory, and the Adaptability of Western Water Compacts." *Public Administration Review* 71 (3): 461–470.

Schlager, Edella, and Christopher M. Weible. 2013. "New Theories of the Policy Process." *Policy Studies Journal* 41 (3): 389–396.

Schneider, Anne L., and Helen M. Ingram. 1997. *Policy Design for Democracy*. Lawrence: University Press of Kansas.

Schneider, Anne L., Helen Ingram, and Peter deLeon. 2014. "Democratic Policy Design: Social Construction of Target Populations." In *Theories of the Policy Process*, 3rd ed., edited by Paul A. Sabatier and Christopher M. Weible, 105–150. Boulder, CO: Westview Press.

Shafritz, Jay, Karen Layne, and Christopher Borick. 2005. *Classics of Public Policy*. New York: Pearson Longman.

Shanahan, Elizabeth A., Michael D. Jones, Mark K. McBeth, and Claudio M. Radaelli. 2017. "The Narrative Policy Framework." In *Theories of the Policy Process*, 4th ed., edited by Christopher M. Weible and Paul A. Sabatier, 173–213. Boulder, CO: Westview Press.

Shipan, Charles R., and Craig Volden. 2012. "Policy Diffusion: Seven Lessons for Scholars and Practitioners." *Public Administration Review* 72 (6): 788–796.

Simon, Herbert. 1996. *The Sciences of the Artificial*. 3rd ed. Cambridge, MA: MIT Press.

Sotirov, Metodi, and Michael Memmler. 2012. "The Advocacy Coalition Framework in Natural Resource Policy Studies—Recent Experiences and Further Prospects." *Forest Policy and Economics* 16:51–64.

Theodoulou, Stella Z., and Matthew Alan Cahn, eds. 1995. *Public Policy: The Essential Readings*. Upper Saddle River, NJ: Prentice Hall.

Truman, David B. 1951. *The Governmental Process*. New York: Alfred A. Knopf.

Van de Ven, Andrew H. 2007. *Engaged Scholarship: A Guide for Organizational and Social Research*. New York: Oxford University Press.

Van Dyke, Vernon. 1968. "Process and Policy as Focal Concepts in Political Research." In *Political Science and Public Policy*, edited by Austin Ranney, 23–40. Chicago: Markham Publishers.

Weible, Christopher M., Tanya Heikkila, Peter deLeon, and Paul Sabatier. 2012. "Understanding and Influencing the Policy Process" *Policy Sciences* 45 (1): 1–21.

Weible, Christopher M., Paul A. Sabatier, Hank C. Jenkins-Smith, Daniel Nohrstedt, Adam Douglas Henry, and Peter deLeon. 2011. "A Quarter Century of the Advocacy Coalition Framework: An Introduction to the Special Issue." *Policy Studies Journal* 39 (3): 349–360.

Weible, Christopher M., and Edella Schlager. 2016. "The Multiple Streams Approach at the Theoretical and Empirical Crossroads: An Introduction to a Special Issue." *Policy Studies Journal* 44 (1): 5–12.

Weimer, David L., and Aidan R. Vining. 2010. *Policy Analysis: Concepts and Practice*. 5th ed. Upper Saddle River, NJ: Prentice Hall.

About the Contributors

Frank R. Baumgartner is Richard J. Richardson Distinguished Professor of Political Science at UNC–Chapel Hill. His work has focused on agenda setting, lobbying, and issue framing in the contexts of US politics as well as in comparative perspective. With Bryan Jones, Dr. Baumgartner created the Policy Agendas Project, and with many collaborators he has worked to create a comparative network of agendas scholars. His books (many of which are coauthored) include *The Politics of Information* (2015), *The Politics of Attention* (2005), *Agendas and Instability in American Politics,* all with Bryan D. Jones. Other books include *Deadly Justice: A Statistical Portrait of the Death Penalty* (2017), *Agenda Dynamics in Spain* (2015), *Lobbying and Policy Change* (2009), *Basic Interests* (1998), and *The Decline of the Death Penalty and the Discovery of Innocence* (2008). Dr. Baumgartner has received numerous awards and recognitions, including a lifetime achievement award from the Political Organizations and Parties section of the American Political Science Association.

Frances Stokes Berry is Reubin O'D. Askew Eminent Scholar and Frank Sherwood Professor of Public Administration and past director of the Askew School of Public Administration and Policy at Florida State University. She is a fellow in the National Academy of Public Administration and was a Fulbright Scholar in Taiwan in 2009. Dr. Berry won the ASPA/NASPPAA Distinguished Research Award for 2013–2014. She currently serves as president of the Public Management Research Association (2015–2017) and has served as president of the Network of Schools of Public Policy, Affairs, and Administration (NASPPAA). Dr. Berry's research on public policy, strategic and performance management, and innovation and diffusion has been published in the *Journal of Public Administration Research and Theory, Public Administration Review, American Political Science Review, American Review of Public Administration,* and other public management and political science journals.

William D. Berry is Marian D. Irish Professor and Syde P. Deeb Eminent Scholar in Political Science at Florida State University. Dr. Berry's research interests include public policy, American state politics, and research methodology. He is a frequent contributor to *American Political Science Review, American Journal of Political Science, Journal of Politics,* and other political science journals. He has written (or coauthored) five books and has been awarded four National Science Foundation grants. Dr. Berry has received the Policy Studies Organization's Harold Laswell Award for outstanding career contributions to the study of the policymaking process.

Paul Cairney is professor of politics and public policy at University of Stirling. Dr. Cairney's research interests are in comparative public policy, including comparisons of policy theories (*Understanding Public Policy,* 2012), policy outcomes in different countries (*Global Tobacco Control,* 2012, with Donley Studlar and Hadii Mamudu), Scottish politics and policy (*The Scottish Political System Since Devolution,* 2011), comparisons of UK and devolved government policymaking and policy outcomes ("Policy Convergence, Transfer and Learning in the UK under Devolution," *Regional and Federal Studies* 22 [3]: 289–307, with Michael Keating and Eve Hepburn), and the revival of debates on policymaker "rationality" (*The Politics of Evidence Based Policy Making,* 2016). His blog is https://paulcairney.wordpress.com/cv/ and Twitter handle is @Cairneypaul.

Michael Cox is an environmental social scientist who studies community-based natural resource management, environmental governance, and the evolutionary determinants of cooperation in natural resource management settings. He has conducted empirical fieldwork-based analyses of irrigation systems in the southwest United States, Peru, and Kenya. His current empirical work is focused on community-based fisheries and rice irrigation systems in the Dominican Republic. For the past several years he has led a synthetic project on social-ecological governance, the details of which can be found at http://sesmad.dartmouth.edu/. Before coming to Dartmouth, he worked under Lin Ostrom at Indiana University's Workshop in Political Theory and Policy Analysis.

Tanya Heikkila is professor and codirector of the Workshop on Policy Process Research at the School of Public Affairs at the University of Colorado, Denver. Dr. Heikkila's research focuses on collaboration and conflict in environmental policy and governance. She has explored institutions for resolving water resource conflicts, the politics of hydraulic fracturing, and the organization of collaborative ecosystem restoration programs. Her research has been funded by the National Science Foundation, the Alfred P. Sloan Foundation, and the PepsiCo Foundation. Dr. Heikkila has coauthored three books and has published numerous articles in the fields of public policy and administration and environmental governance.

Nicole Herweg is a postdoctoral researcher in the Department of Political Science at the University of Heidelberg, Germany, from where she received her

PhD in political science in 2015. Dr. Herweg's research interests are in comparative public policy. Her research focuses in particular on policy processes, energy policy, and European Union politics. She is the author of *European Union Policy-Making: The Regulatory Shift in Natural Gas Market Policy* (2017) and has published in academic journals, including *the European Journal of Political Research, Journal of Comparative Policy Analysis, Policy Sciences,* and *Policy Studies Journal.*

Karin Ingold is associate professor and director of the Institute of Political Science at the University of Bern, Switzerland. Dr. Ingold leads a research group on "Policy Analysis and Environmental Governance" affiliated with the Institute of Political Science and the Oeschger Centre for Climate Change Research at the University of Bern as well as with the Social Science Department at the Aquatic Research Institute (Eawag) in Zürich. Her research focuses on climate, energy, water, and natural resources management and policy. She is particularly interested in policy processes and policy design in her studies as well as in the application of social network analysis. She is an associate editor of *Policy&Politics* and is on the editorial board of the *Policy Studies Journal,* the *Swiss Political Science Review,* the *European Policy Analysis Journal,* and *Connections.*

Hank C. Jenkins-Smith is George Lynn Cross Research Professor in the Political Science Department at the University of Oklahoma and serves as codirector of the National Institute for Risk and Resilience. He earned his PhD in political science and public policy from the University of Rochester (1985). He has been a policy analyst for the US Department of Energy and held faculty positions at Southern Methodist University, the University of New Mexico, and Texas A&M University and is currently at the University of Oklahoma. Dr. Jenkins-Smith has published books, articles, and reports on public policy processes, risk perception, national security, weather, and energy and environmental policy. He has served on National Research Council committees focused on policies to transport spent nuclear fuel and dispose of chemical weapons and as an elected member of the National Council on Radiation Protection and Measurement.

Bryan D. Jones is J. J. "Jake" Pickle Regent's Chair in Congressional Studies in the Department of Government at the University of Texas at Austin and director of the US Policy Agendas Project there. He is the director of the US Policy Agendas Project and sponsors the web presence of the Comparative Policy Agendas Projects (http://www.comparativeagendas.net/). His primary work is in the area of policy processes and how they interact with American governing institutions. Dr. Jones has published articles in the *American Political Science Review, American Journal of Political Science, Journal of Politics, Journal of Public Administration Research and Theory,* and the *Policy Studies Journal.* His book with Frank Baumgartner, *Agendas and Instability in American Politics,* launched the study of punctuated equilibrium in policy studies.

Michael D. Jones is assistant professor of political science at Oregon State's School of Public Policy. He received his PhD in political science in 2010 from the University of Oklahoma and holds a bachelor's and master's in political science, both granted from Idaho State University. Dr. Jones's research focuses on the role and influence of narrative in public policy processes, outcomes, and science communication. His work has appeared in academic journals, such as the *Policy Studies Journal, Social Science Quarterly, Political Psychology,* and *PS: Political Science and Politics.*

Mark K. McBeth is professor of political science at Idaho State University, where he teaches courses in public administration and public policy. Dr. McBeth's research interests include public policy process theory, environmental policy, and the role of policy narratives in the public policy process. Dr. McBeth is the coauthor (with Randy S. Clemons) of *Public Policy Praxis: A Case Approach to Policy and Analysis,* now in its third edition. He has published in many academic journals, including *Policy Studies Journal, Review of Policy Research, Policy Sciences, Journal of Borderland Studies,* and *Public Policy and Administration.* Dr. McBeth has completed a variety of research grant and contract work with entities such as the US Environmental Protection Agency, the US Forest Service, and the Northwest Area Foundation.

Suzanne Mettler is the Clinton Rossiter Professor of American Institutions in the Government Department at Cornell University. She is the author of *Degrees of Inequality: How Higher Education Politics Sabotaged the American Dream* (2014); *The Submerged State: How Invisible Government Programs Undermine American Democracy* (2011); *Dividing Citizens: Gender and Federalism in New Deal Public Policy* (1998), which was awarded the Kammerer Award and the Martha Derthick Award from the American Political Science Association (APSA); and *Soldiers to Citizens: The G.I. Bill and the Making of the Greatest Generation* (2005), which was also awarded the Kammerer Award as well as the J. David Greenstone Award. Dr. Mettler has published numerous articles in the *American Political Science Review, Perspectives on Politics, Studies in American Political Development,* and *Journal of Health Policy, Politics, and Law,* among other scholarly journals and edited volumes. She has also published op-eds in the *New York Times* and *Los Angeles Times* and contributed to the *Washington Monthly* and *Salon.*

Peter B. Mortensen is professor of political science at Aarhus University, Denmark. Dr. Mortensen's research interests include agenda setting, public policy, public spending, and public administration. Since the completion of his PhD in 2007, he has published three books and more than thirty articles in international peer-reviewed journals, including articles in *American Journal of Political Science, Comparative Political Studies, European Journal of Political Research,*

Journal of Public Administration Research and Theory, Governance, and *Policy Studies Journal.*

Daniel Nohrstedt is associate professor of political science in the Department of Government at Uppsala University, Sweden, where he is also co–research director in the Center for Natural Disaster Science (CNDS). Dr. Nohrstedt's research interests include policy process theory, crisis and disaster management, collaborative governance, policy network research, and environmental policy. Dr. Nohrstedt is the author of several book chapters and journal articles focusing on processes of collaboration, learning, and policy change in the context of resilience, crises, and disasters. His published work appears in, for instance, *Global Environmental Change, Policy Studies Journal, Public Administration, Journal of Public Administration Research and Theory, American Review of Public Administration,* and *Journal of European Public Policy.*

Claudio M. Radaelli is Professor of Political Science, Jean Monnet Chair in Political Economy, and Director of the Centre for European Governance at the University of Exeter, in the United Kingdom. He has published eight articles and written or edited seventeen books and special issues of academic journals. His main fields of specialization include the theory of policy learning, Europeanization, the Narrative Policy Framework, and regulatory reform. He was awarded two European Research Council's advanced grants, one in 2009 on *Analysis of Learning in Regulatory Governance* (ALREG) and one in 2016 on *Procedural Tools for Effective Governance* (Protego).

Edella Schlager is a professor in the School of Government and Public Policy at the University of Arizona. Her research focuses on comparative institutional analyses of water laws, policies, and property rights. In particular, she is interested in the design and performance of polycentric systems of water governance and how well such systems of water governance adapt to changing environmental, legal, and social circumstances. She has published articles in a variety of journals, including the *Policy Studies Journal* and the *American Journal of Political Science.* Dr. Schlager is coauthor of two books on western water governance, *Common Waters, Diverging Streams: Linking Institutions and Water Management in Arizona, California, and Colorado* (with William Blomquist and Tanya Heikkila); and *Embracing Watershed Politics* (with William Blomquist). She is also the lead editor of *Navigating Climate Change Policy: The Opportunities of Federalism* (with Kirsten Engel and Sally Rider).

Elizabeth A. Shanahan is associate professor of political science at Montana State University. Dr. Shanahan's research interests include the development and application of the Narrative Policy Framework, other theories of the policy process, and social-ecological system dynamics. She is coeditor (with Michael D. Jones and Mark K. McBeth) of *The Science of Storytelling: Applications of Narrative Policy Framework in Public Policy Analysis*. Dr. Shanahan has also published in many academic journals, is active as a social science liaison with a National Science Foundation EPSCoR grant, and has received funding from the National Science Foundation, Inland Northwest Research Alliance, and US Geological Survey.

Mallory E. SoRelle is an assistant professor in the Government and Law Department at Lafayette College. Her research explores how the development and design of public policies and political institutions in the United States influence the political behavior of both elite and ordinary Americans. Dr. SoRelle's current project examines how the development of a US political economy of credit influences policymakers', public interest groups', and citizens' engagement in the politics of consumer financial protection and the consequences of that engagement for both political and economic inequality. She earned her PhD in government from Cornell University, and she holds a master's degree in public policy from the Harvard University Kennedy School of Government and a bachelor's degree from Smith College.

Jale Tosun is professor of political science at the Institute of Political Science at Heidelberg University. She received her doctoral degree from the University of Konstanz; the corresponding research was published as the monograph *Environmental Policy Change in Emerging Market Democracies—Central and Eastern Europe and Latin America Compared* (University of Toronto Press). Together with Christoph Knill, she has coauthored the textbook *Public Policy: A New Introduction* (Palgrave Macmillan) and is currently coauthoring with Ross Gillard the monograph *Contested Energy Policies: European Climate Change Leadership and Policy Resilience* (Rowman & Littlefield). Her research interests encompass various topics in comparative public policy and political economy as well as public administration. She is associate editor for the journal *Policy Sciences*.

Christopher M. Weible is professor at the School of Public Affairs at the University of Colorado–Denver. He received his PhD in ecology with an emphasis in environmental policy analysis from the University of California, Davis, and earned a master of public administration and a bachelor of science in mathematics and statistics from the University of Washington. He codirects the Workshop on Policy Process Research (WOPPR). His research focuses on policy conflicts and policy processes.

Samuel Workman is associate professor of political science in the Department of Political Science at the University of Oklahoma. He is also a research faculty member at the Center for Risk and Crisis Management, a fellow of the Center for Intelligence and National Security, and an affiliate of the Comparative Agendas Project. His research and teaching interests lie in the fields of American politics, public policy, and research methodology. He is the author of *The Dynamics of Bureaucracy in the U.S. Government: How Congress and Federal Agencies Process Information and Solve Problems* (2015). His work has also appeared in the *Policy Studies Journal*, the *Journal of Public Administration Research and Theory*, and *Cognitive Systems Research*.

Nikolaos Zahariadis is Mertie Buckman Professor of International Studies at Rhodes College. A native of Greece, he has published extensively on issues of comparative public policy and European political economy. His latest edited *Handbook on Public Policy Agenda Setting* was published in 2016. He has been a Fulbright Scholar, an ESRC-SSRC Visiting Fellow, a Policy Studies Organization Fellow, an Adjunct Scholar at the Woodrow Wilson International Center for Scholars, and a National Bank of Greece Senior Research Fellow.

Reimut Zohlnhöfer is a professor at the Institute of Political Science at Heidelberg University, Germany. Previously, he worked at Bremen University's Center for Social Policy Research, the Center for European Studies at Harvard University, and the University of Bamberg. He has published articles in various academic journals, including the *British Journal of Political Science, Comparative Political Studies*, the *European Journal of Political Research*, the *Journal of European Public Policy*, and the *Policy Studies Journal*, and has recently coedited a book on the state of the art of the Multiple Streams Framework, *Decision-Making under Ambiguity and Time Constraints: Assessing the Multiple-Streams Framework* (with Friedbert W. Rüb).

Index